Ethnonationalism in the Contemporary World

Since the appearance of his seminal article 'Self Determination: The New Phase', Walker Connor has exerted a profound influence upon scholarship dealing with nationalism.

In *Ethnonationalism in the Contemporary World*, world-renowned scholars employ various aspects of Connor's work to explicate the recent upsurge of nationalism on a global scale. In keeping with the growing awareness that the study of ethnonationalism requires an interdisciplinary approach, the contributors represent a number of academic disciplines, including anthropology, geography, history, linguistics, social psychology, sociology, and world politics. The book discusses issues such as identity, ethnicity and nationalism, primordialism, social constructionism, ethnic conflict, separatism, and federalism. It also features case studies on the Basque country, South Africa, and Canada.

This volume, now available in paperback, should prove essential reading for anyone interested in problems associated with ethnicity and nationalism. At a time when many states are drastically reshaping their foreign and military policies in response to what is termed 'the terrorist threat', it offers a guide to understanding the ethnonational forces that underpin much of the terrorist activity.

Daniele Conversi is Senior Lecturer in Politics at the University of Lincoln, UK. He has taught at the Government and History departments at Cornell and Syracuse Universities, as well as at the Central European University, Budapest.

Ethnonationalism in the Contemporary World

Walker Connor and the study of nationalism

Edited by
Daniele Conversi

Routledge
Taylor & Francis Group

LONDON AND NEW YORK

First published 2004
by Routledge
11 New Fetter Lane, London EC4P 4EE

Simultaneously published in the USA and Canada
by Routledge
29 West 35th Street, New York, NY 10001

Routledge is an imprint of the Taylor & Francis Group

Typeset in Baskerville by M Rules
Printed and bound in Great Britain by
Antony Rowe Ltd, Chippenham, Wiltshire

British Library Cataloguing in Publication Data
A catalogue record for this book is available from the British Library

Library of Congress Cataloging in Publication Data
Ethnonationalism in the contemporary world: Walker Connor and
the study of nationalism / edited by Daniele Conversi.
    p.   cm.
  Includes bibliographical references and index.
      1. Nationalism. 2. Ethnic relations – Political aspects.
  3. Ethnicity – Political aspects. 4. Ethnic groups – Political activity.
  5. National characteristics – Political aspects. 6. World politics.
  7. Connor, Walker, 1926– I. Conversi, Daniele.
  JC311.E885 2002
  320.54′09′045–dc21   2002069899

ISBN 0–415–26373–5 (hbk)
ISBN 0–415–33273–7 (pbk)

Contents

Contributors

John Coakley is a lecturer in politics at University College Dublin, Director of the Institute for British-Irish Studies there, and former Secretary General of the International Political Science Association (1994–2000). He is the author of many articles and chapters in books on comparative and Irish politics and on problems relating to nationalism and ethnicity. His publications include *The Social Origins of Nationalist Movements* (Sage, 1992); *The Territorial Management of Ethnic Conflict* (Frank Cass, 1993; 2nd edn forthcoming 2002) and *Politics in the Republic of Ireland* (3rd edn, Routledge, 1999). He is co-author of a forthcoming book entitled *The Rise of the Irish Presidency* (Four Courts Press, 2002).

Walker Connor is currently Distinguished Visiting Professor of Political Science at Middlebury College. He has held resident appointments at, *inter alia*, Harvard, Dartmouth, Trinity (Hartford), Pomona, Rensselaer Polytechnic Institute, the London School of Economics, the Woodrow Wilson International Center for Scholars, Oxford, Cambridge, Bellagio, Warsaw, Singapore, and Budapest. The University of Nevada named him Distinguished American Humanist of 1991/1992 and the University of Vermont named him Distinguished American Political Scientist of 1997. His books include *The National Question in Marxist-Leninist Theory and Strategy* and *Ethnonationalism: The Quest for Understanding*. He is currently completing a criticism of the recent literature on nationalism and a monograph on the psychological wellsprings of national identity and behavior.

Daniele Conversi received his PhD at the London School of Economics. He taught at the Government and History Departments at Cornell and Syracuse Universities, as well as at the Central European University, Budapest. While at the LSE, in 1990 he co-founded the Association for the Study of Ethnicity and Nationalism (ASEN). His book, *The Basques, the Catalans, and Spain*, now available in a new US paperback edition (2000), has been acclaimed by political scientists, historians, anthropologists and sociologists alike, and has been positively reviewed in nearly forty international journals. He is currently working on a larger volume on 'theories of nationalism', as well as writing on resistance movements to cultural globalization.

William A. Douglass is Professor Emeritus in social anthropology at the Center for Basque Studies of the University of Nevada, Reno, which he founded in 1967 and directed until 2000. He has authored and edited fourteen books and more than 100 articles. Of greatest relevance to the present volume, Douglass co-authored (with Joseba Zulaika) *Terror and Taboo: The Follies, Fables, and Faces of Terrorism* (1996), edited *Basque Politics: A Case Study in Ethnic Nationalism* (1985), and co-edited *Basque Politics and Nationalism on the Eve of the Millennium* (1999).

John Edwards received a PhD (in psychology) from McGill University in 1974. He is now Professor of Psychology at St Francis Xavier University in Nova Scotia. His research interests are in language, identity and the many ramifications of their relationship. He has lectured and presented papers on this topic in some thirty countries. Professor Edwards' own books include *Language in Canada* (Cambridge, 1998), *Multilingualism* (Penguin, 1995) and *Language, Society and Identity* (Blackwell, 1985). He is also the author of about 200 articles, chapters and reviews. Professor Edwards is a member of several psychological and linguistic societies, as well as scholarly organizations for the study of ethnicity and nationalism. He is a fellow of the British Psychological Society, the Canadian Psychological Association, and the Royal Society of Canada. Professor Edwards is on the editorial boards of ten language journals, and is the editor of the *Journal of Multilingual and Multicultural Development*; he also edits a companion series of books.

Joshua A. Fishman is Distinguished University Research Professor of Social Sciences, Emeritus, at Yeshiva University, New York, and Visiting Professor of Education at Stanford University. Fishman is acknowledged as the founder of sociology of language, a spirited advocate of bilingual education in the USA, and a sympathetic friend of all groups who strive to maintain their ancestral languages. His first major study of the sociology of language, *Language Loyalty in the United States* (1964) was followed, a year later, by *Yiddish in America*. In 1968, he published three major books: *Bilingualism in the Barrio* (a pioneering study of a multilingual community), *Language Problems of Developing Nations* (the earliest major collection in language planning), and *Readings in the Sociology of Language* (a first attempt to define the new field). His prolific publication continued, amounting by now to over 900 items which have shaped and defined modern scholarly study of bilingualism and multilingualism, bilingual and minority education, the relation of language and thought, the sociology and the social history of Yiddish, language planning, language spread, language shift, language and nationalism, language and ethnicity, and (most recently) ethnic and national efforts to reverse language shift. Among his most recent books is *In Praise of the Beloved Language* (1997). Since its founding in 1973, he has been the editor of the *International Journal of the Sociology of Language*.

Donald L. Horowitz is the James B. Duke Professor of Law and Political Science at Duke University, North Carolina. In 2001, he was Centennial Professor of Government at the London School of Economics. Professor Horowitz is the author of, among other books, *Ethnic Groups in Conflict* (1985; reissued 2000); *A Democratic South Africa? Constitutional Engineering in a Divided Society* (1991); and *The Deadly Ethnic Riot* (2001). His current research focuses on constitutional design for severely divided societies. Professor Horowitz is a member of the American Academy of Arts and Sciences.

Robert J. Kaiser is Associate Professor of Geography and Director of the Center for Russia, East Europe and Central Asia (CREECA) at the University of Wisconsin-Madison. He is the author of *The Geography of Nationalism in Russia and the USSR* (1994), co-author of *Russians as the New Minority in the Soviet Successor States* (1996), and numerous scholarly articles and chapters in multi-authored volumes.

Brendan O'Leary is Head of Department and Professor of Political Science at the London School of Economics. Since September 2001, he has been Visiting Professor of Political Science at the University of Pennsylvania. He is the author, co-author and co-editor of numerous books and a long-time admirer of Walker Connor.

William Safran is Professor of Political Science at the University of Colorado at Boulder. He is the author of *Veto-Group Politics* (1967), *Ideology and Politics: The Socialist Party of France* (1979) and *The French Polity* (5th edn 1998); and co-author of *Comparative Politics* (1983) and *Politics in Europe* (3rd edn 2001). He has contributed chapters to more than 30 books and numerous articles on French and comparative politics, as well as on nationalism, ethnicity, diaspora, and the politics of language. He has taught at City University of New York and the universities of Grenoble and Bordeaux. He served as President of the Research Committee on Politics and Ethnicity, the International Political Science Association, and is the founder editor and the current editor-in-chief of the international journal *Nationalism and Ethnic Politics*.

Anthony D. Smith is Professor of Ethnicity and Nationalism at the London School of Economics. His most recent books include *Nationalism and Modernism* (1998) and *National Identity* (1991). He is the founding editor and editor-in-chief of the international journal *Nations and Nationalism*.

Thomas Spira is Professor Emeritus of History at the University of Prince Edward Island, Charlottetown, Canada. He has authored numerous articles and books on varied topics involving nationalism from varied national, ethnic and chronological perspectives. He was the founder editor of the journal, *Canadian Review of Studies in Nationalism*.

John Stone is Professor and Chairman of the Department of Sociology at Boston University. His previous appointments have included positions at Columbia University, St Antony's College, Oxford, Goldsmiths' College, University of London, and George Mason University. He has written extensively on race and ethnic relations and sociological theory and he was the founding editor of the international journal *Ethnic and Racial Studies*.

Preface

Initially conceived as a *Festschrift*, this book has become much more than that. It remains *au fond* a tribute to Walker Connor's pioneering work, but from this premise it also expands into new directions.

The tribute is owed both to the scholar and the man. Those who have had the good fortune to cross Walker's path will have recognized in him a great humanity and interest in human affairs. His versatility, sincere wisdom, deep knowledge of and affection for other cultures make Walker a unique kind of cosmopolitan – without the frills normally associated with this term.

Walker, the lover of fine arts, historical heritage and natural beauty, as well as the gifted communicator, will remain imprinted upon us and all those who have encountered him. Having met him in Vermont, Galicia, England, Tuscany, Hungary and Belgium, I have come to cherish his humanity and sincere interest in a great variety of human cultural endeavours. In his natural habitat, a remote mountain home in the woods of Vermont, we saw him driving a huge tractor, snow-shoeing on the hills, and trekking with his family and many friends. Vermont, this most liberal of US states, remains a natural haven for scholars and artists escaping the clutches of big-mall America and small-town mediocrity. There, the pace of life lingers on a fully human scale.

Commencing with the 1967 appearance in World Politics of his landmark essay, 'Self-Determination: The New Phase', Walker Connor has exerted a profound influence upon scholarship dealing with nationalism. Connor's academic output is not characterized by overproduction, but by a commitment to true scholarship. Each of the two outside referees for this volume – neither of whom know Walker personally – lauded his *oeuvre*. Wrote the first:

> Walker Connor is indeed a seminal, lucid, influential and contentious writer in the field . . . There are . . . those who know and have been inspired by Walker Connor's work, and those interested in ethnicity and nationalism who by some failure of education have not yet read Walker Connor. The star quality of Walker Connor is the clarity and accessibility of his writing.

Added the second:

Connor, throughout his long and prolific career, has written seminal works on the area of nationalism and ethnicity and certainly deserves such homage. In a clear and penetrating style, Connor developed ideas that went against the established paradigms of the period when the study of nationalism was not a fashionable discipline. As an iconoclast of misleading dogmas, Walker Connor did not hesitate to take issue with some of the fashionable intellectual trends of the 1960s, such as entrenched paradigms of Development Studies that saw nationalism as an epiphenomenon of some developmental economic logic or as the unavoidable result of the process of modernization. The titles of some of his most important works, 'Nation-Building or Nation-Destroying?' and 'A Nation is a Nation, is a State, is an Ethnic Group, is a . . .' reveal the flavour of an author who is both an iconoclast of dogmas and a builder of seminal literature.

With a distinguished team of established experts writing authoritatively on their fields, this book has the privilege of including representatives from a wide spectrum of disciplines, from history to geography, from law to political science, from international relations to sociolinguistics. The essays collected here are by no means comprehensive; nor could they be, given the vast scope of the book's theme. They represent an attempt to explore from a variety of perspectives a question that Walker Connor has never tired of asking: What are the sources, varieties and meaning of ethnonational mobilization? The essays are presented to Walker Connor by grateful colleagues and friends in the hope that he will find them interesting.

Acknowledgements

I wish to thank warmly Crawford Young from Madison, Wisconsin, for his very helpful initial feedback, despite being unable to participate in the project. I would have liked to contact other scholars to join us in this project, but the response has been more enthusiastic than originally expected. I hope that none will feel excluded for this reason. Initially, I contacted the late Myron Weiner, who very much regretted he could not participate. Among the contributors, I wish to thank Anthony D. Smith for his invaluable help at different stages of the process, as well as for some perceptive general comments. I have also received helpful feedback from John Coakley, Thomas Spira, and Charlie Cooper, especially for the Introduction. Thanks for assistance is also due to Jocelyn Maclure and the two anonymous referees. Most of all, thanks to all the contributors who have chosen to devote their effort and offer their talents to bring such a marvellous volume to completion. But I know that a special thanks is due to one person, and with particular affection, Mary Connor. Finally, most of our warmest thanks go to Walker for having provided many of us with wonderful company, guidance and insight over the years.

The authors and publishers would like to thank the *Canadian Review of Studies in Nationalism* for granting permission to reproduce the article 'Nationalism and Political Illegitimacy' by Walker Connor (VII: Fall, 1980).

1 Conceptualizing nationalism

An introduction to Walker Connor's work

Daniele Conversi

Vastly neglected until around twenty years ago, nationalism has become the pivotal theme in a number of scholarly, as well as popular, publications. In the wake of the Communist order's dissolution, the number of published works on various aspects of nationalism has been steadily rising, turning into a sweeping tide and a fashionable industry. Walker Connor is one of the scholars of nationalism and ethnic conflict who has contributed most towards establishing a conceptual grounding for this emerging discipline. His pioneering work has tackled systematically the most relevant problems in the field, while identifying its primary fault lines and clarifying its key concepts. Connor's prescience in forecasting current international developments is now widely acknowledged, making him one of the most quoted authors in the field over the past thirty years. In the 1970s and 1980s, when few dared to contemplate the underlying strength of nationalism and secession, he advanced some of the most challenging arguments in this direction. When fewer than a handful of savants indulged in writing on the resilience of ethnic roots, Connor was producing a set of seminal essays. Indicative of the continuing relevance of Connor's contribution is the considerable output of new thinking on the subject that has recently emerged.

This volume brings together a number of specialists who are investigating this area in new ways, adding to the debate pioneered by Connor. Here, a group of the most prominent American and European scholars of nationalism join together to offer a new perspective on themes and issues that have been focal points in Connor's approach and which remain critical to our understanding of nationalism. The contributions reflect approaches drawn from a wide range of disciplines. Before briefly introducing each chapter, we shall first highlight Connor's contribution to the socio-political literature by describing some of the key themes he has addressed.

Key concepts in the study of nationalism

Walker Connor was one of the first scholars to address systematically the lack of an appropriate terminology in the study of nationalism, particularly in political science.[1] This was a crucial issue, given also that nationalists themselves thrive on such ambiguities.[2] The need for a clear and unequivocal definition of key concepts in the field has been essential. The opening chapter of this volume offers one of Connor's most significant achievements in conceptual clarification.

Political philosophers have pointed to the existence of 'essentially contested concepts'.[3] In the philosophers' view, such an 'essentially contested' character has more to do with the neutrality of these concepts, than with their clarity. Clarity, however, encompasses neutrality: those rare concepts whose definition is universally and univocally accepted are less prone to be misused and tied to the ideological convenience of each scholar and practitioner.

The term preferred by Connor, and since then incorporated in most of the nationalism literature, is '*ethnonationalism*'. This denotes both the loyalty to a nation deprived of its own state and the loyalty to an ethnic group embodied in a specific state, particularly where the latter is conceived as a 'nation-state'. In other words, ethnonationalism is conceived in a very broad sense and may be used interchangeably with nationalism. For instance, Connor subsumes within the same spectrum anti-EC feelings in Denmark, Britain or Norway (Connor 1994a: 168, 1994b), as well as anti-immigrant feelings such as emerged, say, in Switzerland in the 1970s (Connor 1994a: 35, 154 and 177) and, generally, racism and xenophobia. As nationalism refers simultaneously to state and non-state nationalisms, the distinction between the two forms of nationalism is blurred: the emotional attachment to lineage, ancestry and continuity is shared by both those who have power and those who are deprived of it.

However, since such a broad usage of the term lends itself to criticism, further clarification is needed. What all the phenomena described above have in common is a deep emotional thrust and, most importantly, the effect of privileging co-ethnics versus outsiders. This involves a strict form of favoritism or, in van den Berghe's (1987) words, ethnic 'nepotism'. Such favoritism (and accompanying exclusionary practices) derive from the irrational belief that, descending from common ancestors, we all are related and form part of the same 'extended family'. Both Horowitz and Smith have explored this powerful link in depth, and both their contributions to this volume highlight this dimension by relating it to Connor's approach. Ethnicity, then, remains the most central and powerful element in the development of nationalism. But what is 'ethnicity'?

Ethnicity normally refers to a belief in putative descent: that is, a belief in something which may or may not be real. It is a perception of commonality and belonging supported by a myth of common ancestry. Therefore, it does not necessarily suggest tangible elements of culture. It is somehow immaterial. Connor (1993) has stressed the *subjective* and psychological quality of this perception, rather than its objective 'substance'. More generally, 'identity does not draw its sustenance from facts but from perceptions, perceptions are as important or more than reality when it comes to ethnic issues' (Connor 1997: 33). The term ethnicity is a relatively recent acquisition in the English language. According to Glazer and Moynihan, its first sociological use dates back to David Riesman's work in 1953.[4]

In line with coeval mainstream politicians, modernization theorists tended to confusingly substitute the word nation for the very different concept of *state*. For example, at least up to the 1970s, the concept of *nation-building* was meant to define a top-down élites-led project of 'national' construction almost totally detached from any pre-existing popular feeling or socio-anthropological reality. Connor stripped such an undue appropriation of its ambiguous meaning (1972, 1978), revealing that the term provided an ideological disguise for state-building – often in its most authoritarian form. Any process of nation-building insensitive to ethnic nuances and local subjectivities implies a parallel process of *nation-destroying* among minority groups.

The tendency to conflate nation and state also led to a confusion between (1) ethnic (national) consciousness/loyalty and (2) civic (state) consciousness/loyalty. For a long time, political scientists avoided the use of the word 'nationalism' in reference to either separatist or autonomist movements developing outside, or against, the existing state. The nationalism of stateless nations was therefore labelled in several ways, for instance, sub-nationalism, micro-nationalism, ethnic nationalism, ethnism, ethnicism, ethno-regionalism, parochialism, regionalism, or linguistic nativism.[5] By contrast, state nationalism was treated as a given, whereas daily practices of 'banal nationalism' were blatantly ignored (Billig 1995). Most often, state nationalism was assumed to be intrinsically 'civic' (Brown 2000), especially when opposed to the nationalism of stateless nations, which was seen as quintessentially 'ethnic', hence 'primordial'.[6] Connor has very effectively revealed and denounced this blunder. All the chapters in this volume share an awareness of this terminological conundrum.

Connor (1994a: 42) defines the nation as a self-differentiating ethnic group.[7] Two main consequences stem from this definition. First, it postulates a continuity between the ethnic and the national dimensions. Second, the emphasis on self-awareness implies a stress on perception and, hence, on the psychological realm. Given this subjectivity, the *nation* is a self-defining category, that is, it is often not definable externally.[8] In other words, it is the subjective experience of self-awareness that brings the nation into being. And given the connection between ethnicity and nationalism, it also follows that the most quintessentially modernist construction, the true nation-state, is *au fond* an ethnic state.[9]

As stressed by Smith in this volume (Chapter 3), most forms of nationalism have been, and are, ethnic. Connor goes further, maintaining that all nationalism is ethnically predicated, and those who employ the term nationalism to refer to a civic identity or civic loyalty are confusing *patriotism* with nationalism. *Ethnos* and *nation* are equivalents: the former derived from ancient Greek, the latter from Latin. It follows that the term *ethnonationalism* is largely tautological, since ethnicity permeates nationalism anyway.[10]

Is hence the nation the modern garb through which previously existing *ethnies* 'modernized' themselves into a world of nation-states?[11] If this is the case, we can then subsume within nationalism all possible trends aimed at the survival and self-preservation of an ethnic group. However, as Connor has pointed out, it is impossible to define nationalism in terms of its own goals, in part because the latter are often shifting. If we do that, we end up with endless and imprecise definitions of nationalism.

Challenging the dogma of economism

During much of the Cold War, econo-centric theories permeated socio-political accounts of past and present events. Conflicts were customarily explained as a consequence of backwardness, economic crisis, uneven development or relative deprivation. The prescriptive coda was hence that conflicts could be cured by addressing economic grievances. In the apogee of welfare state politics, economic development became the panacea. This was obviously the flip side of the Marxist dogma reigning in the Eastern bloc. In a classical twist of the human psyche, alleged arch-enemies (liberals and Marxists) ended up resembling each other in their diagnoses and prescriptions. But their titanic clash transformed all other struggles into irrelevant distractions or epiphenomenal appendages.

The powerful direct or indirect influence of Marxism in the social sciences until the 1980s can account for much of the intellectual débâcle. In the 1970s, Connor began what would eventually become an eight-year research undertaking into the relationship between Marxist-Leninism and nationalism. The result was the seminal *The National Question in Marxist-Leninist Theory and Strategy* (Connor 1984a). As a student of comparative nationalism, Connor felt compelled to undertake this project because, as he stated in the book's Introduction, 'The experiences of sixteen states, most of them ethnonationally heterogeneous and accounting *in toto* for approximately one-third of the world's population, are simply too significant to be ignored, particularly when these states claim to have the formula for harnessing and dissolving nationalism.' The formula was called 'Leninist National Policy' and, as analyzed by Connor (1984a: 38), consisted of three injunctions:

(1) Prior to the assumption of power, promise to all national groups the right of self-determination (expressly including the right of secession) while proffering national equality to those who wish to remain within the state.
(2) Following the assumption of power, terminate the fact – though not necessarily the fiction – of a right to secession, and begin the lengthy process of assimilation via the dialectical route of territorial autonomy for all compact national groups.
(3) Keep the Party free of all nationalist proclivities.

Connor documented that the Leninists' first injunction paid handsome dividends. This stratagem was a key element in the assumption and consolidation of power by Lenin, an essential element in the rise to power of Mao-Zedong, and probably the single most important factor in the success of Ho Chi Minh and Tito. By contrast, Connor documented the failure of injunctions 2 and 3. Rather than dissipating within Marxist-Leninist societies, nationalism was growing at both the mass level and within the confines of the parties.[12] It would be difficult to exaggerate the gap between Connor's analysis and the prevalent opinion at the time. At least until the late 1980s, the overwhelming number of scholars, as well as Western governments and their intelligence agencies, in effect accepted the contention that the Leninist states had solved their national question. Those few who, along with Connor, maintained the contrary were treated patronizingly at best.

In the Soviet Union, particularly during the Stalinist years, the entire territory seemed to be firmly under central *apparatchiky* control. George Orwell's novel, *Nineteen-Eighty-Four*, clearly described 'Oceania' as a highly centralized bureaucracy, not a federation of semi-sovereign republics. Indeed, federalism in the Soviet camp was largely fictitious and nominal, as control remained firmly in the hands of the Communist Party. The original Marxist postulate had to be adapted to reality: Lenin's answer to the national question was skilfully devised to keep the empire together. The 'solution' was to give a high degree of formal autonomy to the empire's constituent nations, including a nominal right to *self-determination*. Local élites were either coopted or eliminated. The centre of everything became the Party with its pyramidal disposition of power down to the 'federal' level. But this was supposed to provide a mere provisional framework: in the long run, national loyalties were to be overcome by the creation of a new, allegedly a-national, Soviet man. The granting of autonomous status to most ethnic groups was to be a prelude to the fusion of all nations and races into a mythical *homo sovieticus*. With the advantage of hindsight, it is easy to say that Connor's diagnosis (that national appeals were to prove more irresistible than socio-economic class and ideology) has been fully vindicated by history.[13]

Connor had underlined the sharp distinction in position between Marxists and nationalists. Most socialist regimes subsumed two conflicting flanks within themselves: a Marxist and a nationalist one. This cleavage corresponded to the familiar one present in most Marxist movements: 'The nationalists would therefore contend that, in a test of loyalties, national consciousness would prove more powerful than all *intra national* divisions, including that of class. Marxists, on the other hand, would maintain that class consciousness would prove the more powerful' (Connor 1984a: 5). As Connor anticipated, the contrary did indeed occur: nationalism triumphed over socialism virtually everywhere. Indeed, this triumph of nationalism was particularly pervasive in the Socialist camp, that is, among socialist or post-socialist intellectual and political élites.

However, Marxist political praxis also emblazoned the right to self-determination, notably in the works of Lenin and Stalin. Such incongruity between proletarian internationalism and the right to self-determination originated in the specific historical circumstances (post-Wilsonian Europe) and geographical area (crumbling Russian empire) in which Marxist political strategists were simultaneously compelled to operate. 'Thus, Marxist-Leninist movements have learned to cloak their pre-revolutionary appeals in ethnonational garb' (Connor 1984a: 357). As Fishman shrewdly pointed out, 'classist Marxists joined these movements only when they triumphed and then only to capture them from within, since Marxism failed to destroy them from without' (1980: 80). But nationalist movements have been quick to seize on this ambiguity, by either denying (if already possessing a state) or exalting (if deprived of it) the right of self-determination.

Despite developments in Eastern Europe, economism still represents a conspicuous element within the literature on nationalism, notably among instrumentalists and constructivists (see Chapter 5 by Fishman). As such, it runs counter to a sharp – and so far as this author is aware, publicly unchallenged – criticism of the explanatory power of economic forces set forth in an article by Connor (1984b). The article substantiates that ethnonationalism appears to operate independently from economic variables and that perceived economic discrimination can merely work as a reinforcing variable, as a 'catalytic agent, exacerbator, or choice of battleground' (ibid.: 356). To put economic issues at the centre of the analysis means to miss the primary point, namely that ethnic movements are indeed ethnic and not economic.

Modernity and legitimacy: a contrast with Ernest Gellner

In Max Weber's classical aphorism, the state is that institution which exercises 'the monopoly of the *legitimate* use of physical force within a given territory':[14] the emphasis should rightly be on the adjective 'legitimate'. Nationalism is indeed a movement aimed at challenging or capturing the existing political order's legitimacy; moreover, its goal is the state's 'de-' and 're-legitimation'. Connor's own contribution in this volume is a seminal analysis of the centrality of the principle of legitimacy in the study of nationalism. Here he shows how political legitimacy is indeed central to the sustenance of any nation. By their very existence secessionist movements reflect a lack of legitimacy on the part of the central state. The state is no longer seen as representing one's own nation (or nations), hence it is challenged on its own ground.

To take a significant example, the legitimacy of the Francoist state in Spain (1939–75) lasted only insofar as it could guarantee the monopoly of legitimate violence, through a mixture of coercion and consensus. The consensus partly stemmed from the Civil War trauma, which had caused nearly a million deaths, placing Spain on the verge of self-annihilation. The memory of war horrors, including those perpetrated by intra-Republican factionalism, had led most Spaniards to accept Francoism as a lesser evil.[15] Its main justification resided in its 'order and peace' programme, in spite of ruthless repression.[16] Yet, control through both coercion and consensus was shattered by the rise of Basque nationalism in its most radical form to date. As the regime opened up to the West, the state's monopoly of violence was challenged on its own 'terrain', while the emergence of terrorism revealed in turn the regime's widespread lack of consensual legitimacy (Conversi 1997).[17]

But how does state legitimacy relate to the rise of ethnic conflict and competing nationalisms? When the state is unable to reform itself, it is often tempted to use coercion. However, by enacting repressive policies to deal with ethnic dissent, the state further loses credibility, hence legitimacy. The adoption of drastic measures reveals the state's critical weakness. In other words, violence itself may delegitimize the state. In self-perpetuating dictatorships, there are fewer open clues to any underlying lack of legitimacy. But the authoritarian system's illusory façade normally collapses as soon as coercion loosens its grip. Coercion and repression figured prominently in pre-democratic Europe. Nation-formation was preceded by long sanguinary wars, which sapped the living strength of ordinary people and their capacity to counter-mobilize.

Like most of the contributors to this volume, Connor grounds his definition of nationalism on Weberian postulates.[18] This orientation is shared by Ernest Gellner, who has produced what is probably the most commented upon theory of nationalism.[19] Both Connor and Gellner regard nationalism as an organizing and a legitimizing principle. For both, *legitimacy* lies at the core of nations and nationalism. Gellner defines nationalism as the principle that 'the rulers should belong to the same ethnic (i.e., national) group as the ruled' (1983: 1). Note that the inverse formula gives *ipso facto* legitimacy to ethnic cleansing: to claim that the inhabitant of a specific constituency must share the same ethnic lineage of its leaders is to give *carte blanche* to mass expulsion and the drastic re-drawing of boundaries to suit the group's pedigree. Moreover, this political precept holds that 'nation and political power should be congruent' (ibid.: 1). This longing for congruence is the historical hallmark of all national–totalitarian attempts to erase ethnic opposition by homogenizing entire areas of the globe.

Gellner, like Connor, envisages the nation as a product of modernity. Yet, there is a difference in the timing and the quality of their assessment. Gellner sees industrialization as the catalyst of nation-formation, whereas for Connor the nation – as a mass, in contrast to an élite phenomenon – materializes as a tangible social formation only with late modernity, notably with the diffusion of compulsory education and conscript armies.[20] Challenging perennialist accounts of the antiquity of nations, Connor's approach is more 'modernist' than Gellner's. In this way, Connor can be identified as a 'late modernist', an interpretation clearly stated in Smith's contribution in this volume (see Chapter 3).

The methodological quality is also dissimilar. Connor and Gellner share much more than is normally acknowledged, but what is implicit in Gellner is made explicit in Connor: Gellner's overarching theory moves in a conceptual vacuum. Nation, ethnicity, language and culture are often blurred in his otherwise crystalline and fascinating explanation of the rise of nations and nationalism. Despite some clear-cut and memorable definitions, a careful reading of Gellner's work reveals that the core of his explanations is *culture* as an organizing principle: a highly formalized standardized culture needs, and is needed, by a state, which in turn becomes its political roof and ultimate protector. Despite the fact that it underlies much of Gellner's definition of the nation, ethnicity is only vaguely addressed as such. The nation is rather the end product of epochal forces of social change. Culture is central to it, but culture is defined mainly in terms of language: thus Gellner's vision can also be said to be 'glotto-centric'. Connor's chapter on nationalism and legitimacy in this volume takes care of some of this confusion by offering a much more parsimonious and trenchant set of definitions.

Modernization and modernism

Various assumptions about the diffusion of nationalism underlie scholarly research. Throughout the 1960s, 1970s and, to a certain extent, during the 1980s, the modernization paradigm dominated political science.[21] Modernization theorists, epitomized by Karl Deutsch and other post-war political scientists,[22] emphasized that increased communications would erase ethnic cleavages and result in the successful achievement of 'nation-building'.[23] As mentioned earlier, this model was analogous to the one blazed abroad by its Soviet 'anti-thesis': both mirrored each other. According to Deutsch (1966), modernization is characterized by the presence of 'social mobilization', that is, the process through which the ancestral bonds within the individual's value system are eroded, and by which these individuals become freely available to new forms of socialization. Such theory remained the unchallenged dogma in social science for nearly thirty years following World War II.

In his own adaptation of modernization theory, Connor (1972, 1973, 1987) perceived a very different consequence for nationalism flowing from increasing contacts and communications: nationalism spreads as communications spread.[24] In particular, this is the foreseeable reaction by peoples who undergo the steam-rolling action of nation-building:

> The rapid spread of literacy, the greater mobility of man, made possible by revolutionary strides in the form of transportation and communications, have rapidly dissipated the possibility of cultural isolation . . . These developments not only cause the individual to become more aware of alien ethnic groups, but also of those who share his ethnicity.[25]

Connor's approach has hence been identified as belonging to *conflictual modernization theories*, which replaced the previous *melting pot modernization theories* of Deutsch and others (Newman 1991).[26] The former stresses that modernization leads to the reinforcement of current ethnic identities, the latter that it leads to amalgamation, fusion (in Marxist-Leninist jargon), assimilation, or the merging of identities. Most classical modernization theory generalizes and extrapolates such conclusions from the experience of immigrants into the American context. It is an entirely different matter to apply the same concepts to territorially-based, indigenous minorities. For this purpose Connor has distinguished 'homeland' from immigrant societies (Connor 1994a: 81–82 and 154–155; and 2001: 53–57).[27] As policy-makers can no longer ignore, assimilation, especially forced assimilation, of homeland-based minorities is not a harbinger of integration. On the contrary, it has often a boomerang effect. More often than not, conflict and assimilation are consummate bed-fellows (Conversi 1999). Even in immigrant societies there is now a debate whether assimilation is feasible or even desirable, although it is still expected to occur.

The importance of modernity for the rise of nationalism is accepted almost universally by scholars of nationalism, with a few partial exceptions (for instance, Hastings 1997). Even ethno-symbolists, notably Anthony D. Smith, agree that nationalism is an intrinsic characteristic of the modern world (Smith 1981: 37).[28] Other scholars, such as Tom Nairn (1977), go as far as seeing modernization as the foremost cause of international conflicts. By dismantling local boundaries, economic development and market forces provoke 'atavistic urges' leading to conflict, hatred and wars. Contrary to the vision of Kant and other philosophers, the global spread of trade and commerce did not lead the world on a highway to universal peace. The century of trade expansion and unmitigated Western supremacy has also been the century of total war, genocide and unequaled miseries, often under the double banner of rapid modernization and the defence of the homeland. Thus, there is a direct link between modernization, animosity and nationalism (Nairn, cited by Smith 1981: 39). My own research suggests that the impact produced by industrialization and modernization was perhaps the most relevant factor in the rise of anti-state nationalism in Spain (Conversi 1997).

Anthropologists, since at least Frederick Barth (1969), also envision ethnic identity as the outcome of intense interaction and transactions between groups.[29] Indeed, both modernists and perennialists (in particular, Armstrong 1982) concur that ethnic boundaries are strengthened in response to intense interaction. However, the ultimate price may be at the expense of culture, and cultural erosion is apt to lead to further and deeper conflict.[30]

Nationalism as an emotional bond

Perhaps the most commonly attacked of Connor's viewpoints is his focus on the non-rational, emotional and unaccountable nature of nationalism. The three chapters of this volume by Smith, Horowitz, and Fishman deal specifically with this dimension. Academic criticism has often targeted any alleged 'psychologist' emphasis on the 'need to belong'. Therefore, this need remains largely disregarded, neglected or at least unexplored, in spite of its universality. At the same time, many studies assume it as a background, supplementary or even underlying theme. Waking up in amazement to the 'revival' of ethnic feelings, scholars were belatedly compelled to address the unexpected endurance of ethnic attachments. But any such academic bewilderment had to confront the issue of the *persistence* of the 'need to belong'.[31]

Nationalist movements are often thought to manifest a solipsist attitude. Connor rightly points out the 'general insensitivity that one national group and its leadership customarily exemplify towards the rights of other groups' (1973: 15–16). This clearly points to the deep non-rational character of even the most rationally-looking nationalist movement: 'irrationality' resides precisely in the incapacity to coordinate one's efforts with those of potential allies, simply because the latter do not belong to the same ethno-biological pool.[32] His anti-universalist bent is incompatible with rational thought. On the one hand there may be a sensible motive in many people's historical aversion against universalism and cosmopolitanism. On the other hand the incapacity to coordinate efforts with other groups is often self-defeating, as most twentieth-century wars have demonstrated. However, there have been instances in which 'inter-nationalist' cooperation has worked well, at least for some time.[33]

But Connor's crucial point on the unreasonable, illogical, unsound character of most nationalisms must be underscored:

The peculiar emotional depth of the 'us'-'them' syndrome which is an intrinsic part of national consciousness, by bifurcating as it does all mankind into 'members of the nation' versus 'all others' appears thereby to pose a particularly severe impediment to coordinated action with any of the 'others'.[34]

It seems that one group, as soon as it has grasped the levers of state power, is unable to recognize any legitimacy or validity in the anti-state sentiments of other groups. This has indeed happened in post-Soviet Eastern Europe: Azeri versus Armenians in Nagorno-Karabagh, pan-Romanian nationalists fighting Russian separatists in Moldova, Georgians suppressing Ossetian autonomy immediately after achieving independence. It has occurred during the early stages of de-colonization (as in Sri Lanka, Indonesia, Israel and many other states). The phenomenon dates back to the very inception of nationalism as *the* legitimizing political principle (whenever one wishes to identify its birth). In his London exile, Giuseppe Mazzini had discovered how the supra- or inter-national project of a Young Europe had ineluctably foundered in the face of the instinctive solipsism of all the various 'Young' movements (Young Italy, Young Ireland and the like), eventually leading several decades later to its most xenophobic and bloodthirsty avatar, the Young Turks. This irrationality leads ultimately to a widespread sense of *sacro egoismo* and an all-pervasive moral relativism: 'Though very sensitive to real or imagined threats to the survival and aspirations of one's own group, appreciation of this same sensitivity among other groups is apparently very difficult to project'.[35] As Zygmunt Bauman rightly reminds us:

> few known nations enthusiastically endorsed the right of the others to the same treatment they claimed for themselves . . . The national game has been a zero-sum game: sovereignty of the other has been an assault against one's own. One nation's rights were another nation's aggression, intransigence or arrogance.
>
> (1989: 54)

In this extreme form of Hobbesian individualism, nationalism reveals its non-rational, often self-defeating, character. The abdication of universal reason is, however, shared by nationalism with many other forms of group behaviour. But, as Connor puts it, it is the particular link between groupness (and hence exclusion) and ethnicity (hence, putative descent and kinship) which makes it particularly impermeable to rational reasoning.

The European Community is supposed to provide one of the first contemporary historical alternatives to the irrationality and mutual exclusiveness of nation-states. But, shortly after the time of the Maastricht Treaty signing (7 February 1992), when 'European Union' was the incontrovertible shibboleth, Connor (1994b) anticipated that the project was failing to achieve a popular mandate, while ethnic sentiments were stirring below the surface in the form of both state and stateless nationalism.

A critique of intellectual elitism

One of Connor's most intriguing themes is his critique of Western intellectual elitism (Connor 1994b). This refers to two aspects: first, the prevalent attitude of post-war scholars dismissing ethnonationalism as a quaint phenomenon whose days were numbered – and irremediably so; and second, and most importantly, the almost exclusive focus on élites as key, indeed unique, protagonists of mass political processes.[36] As for the first, the issue of scholarly estrangement from reality and ivory towers is touched upon by John Stone (Chapter 7). A cavalier tradition of superciliousness has percolated through most post-war studies of nationalism in Western, particularly British, academia. One obvious reason has been the reaction to the extreme horrors brought about by nationalist excesses associated with the two World Wars. But much of the patronizing top-down language is often derived from several overlapping traditions: part of mainstream Liberal thought, as in the case of Kenneth Minogue (1967) and Elie Kedourie (1960);[37] or of the competing Marxist viewpoint, as in the case of Eric Hobsbawm (1983).[38] Or it may be a question of blasé inflection: even Benedict Anderson's (1983) wonderfully evocative portrayal of the rise of vernacular nationalisms betrays an occasional condescending tone in his choice of words (especially, the all-famous and oft-misquoted title of his book, *Imagined Communities*) from Britain's Liberal-Marxist tradition – though without a hint of imperial arrogance. But, despite the technological stress on 'print' and the materialist emphasis on 'capitalism', the idea of an 'imagined' community remains the pinnacle of subjectivism.

As for the second issue, the analytical focus on élites as the only significant factor is a widespread practice: Gellner' s approach is elitist insofar as he considers urbanized masses as a vacuum needing to be filled from above with cultural content. Gellner was also unable to resist the use of elitist jargon, although this often involved a recourse to witty irony, as in his famous representation of 'Ruritania'.

An author who followed precisely the opposite trend was Liah Greenfeld (1992), who can be usefully compared to both Gellner and Connor. Greenfeld's work can be seen as vindicating the prominent place of ideas in human development, hence as representing an implicit, but cogent, critique of Gellner's structuralism.[39] Yet, in doing so, she adopted an even more élite-focused approach: Gellner may have been an elitist in virtue of his Oxbridge academic upbringing, but he was not theoretically nor methodologically so. Indeed, nationalism in his view is the product of epochal wide-ranging social changes permeating the whole social spectrum, not just the whimsical outcome of elitist dreams. Moreover, whereas modernization for Gellner inevitably led to nationalism, for Greenfeld the opposite holds true: nationalism is the causal factor leading to modernity. In other words, it is the nationalist idea which creates the basis for the advent of modernity. But, in order to determine that ideology prevails over material conditions, the focus must be on the spread of ideas rather than on social structure. In turn, this inevitably implies a focus on *élites*, particularly the intellectuals as creators and producers of those ideas.

In contrast, Connor (1990) argues that a nation is not brought into being when its élites decide it to be so, but when the 'subjective' experience of nationhood pervades the larger social body. In order to be called such, a nation has to exist in the feelings and daily experience of ordinary people. A nation does not rise in the mind of intellectuals alone, but is realized when there is a widespread belief in belonging to a nation.[40] A certain resemblance to Ernest Renan's (1823–1892) view of subjectivism (the nation as a 'daily plebiscite') can be recalled here. However, Connor's *analytical* subjectivism can be opposed to Renan's *political* subjectivism, as Renan simply identifies popular human experience as the central feature of 'nation-ness'. In Connor, subjectivism is the upshot of common political experiences and shared feelings, not merely of an élite's vision. Such a subjective feeling can be brought about by *longue durée* processes in which institutions such as the state, the army, the Church and mass education are involved, but it cannot be treated as the invention of arbitrary attempts by nation-builders, especially if the latter clash with a deeply established sense of ethnic continuity.

Outline of the book

This book is divided into four parts. Part I deals with Connor's central emphasis on emotions (which is often mis-branded as 'primordialism') and, at the same time, his conception of the modern character of nationalism. Part II is concerned with three case studies, the Basque Country, South Africa and Quebec, where Connor's theoretical framework is tested against historical and contemporary developments. Part III relates to the broader applied political dimensions of Connorian analysis, such as the case of federalism, third-party intervention and political religion. Part IV explores the wider implications of Connor's approach in the realms of geography and terminological tools, followed by an epilogue on theories of nationalism.

We have already discussed Connor's own opening Chapter 2. The book's first section analyses Connor's vision of the continuity and the emotional character of ethnonational feelings. The first issue to be tackled then is whether nationalism is the expression of something recent or historically deeper and more continuous. From an *ethno-symbolic* perspective, Anthony D. Smith (Chapter 3) disputes Connor's assertion that nations were absent before late modernity. He discerns instead that the major attributes of nationhood had been established before the modern age. Yet, in doing so, he deploys the same critical arsenal utilized in this book by Connor himself in Chapter 2: both would agree that one cannot simply infer the absence of ethnic feelings from the 'silence' of the peasant 'masses', considering that their 'silence' (possibly related to their lack of access to written communication and cognate media) might have extended to other forms of allegiance, notably religion and place. In other words, there is no way of ascertaining that the majority of the population in pre-industrial societies had no notion of ethnic self-awareness or kinship. This remains a critique of Connor's modernist approach, by emphasizing the continuity between pre-modern ethnic institutions and modern nations. Some groups persisted, other disappeared or melted away, such as various barbarous hordes. For instance, the latter's cohesion, continuity and persistence despite moving across vast continents can be explained by the existence of a belief in collective descent and election: being long deprived of a defined territory of their own, they had to stress ancestry myths even more in order to maintain that group's cohesion and social order that only can derive from a sense of collective kinship. Finally, kinship ties are emotionally binding to a far greater degree than other forms of allegiances. Scholars are therefore right in focussing on their emotional impact.

This is the main task adopted by Joshua A. Fishman's in Chapter 5 with his 'insider's view'. He reinstates the importance of the affective, non-rational bond in the study of ethnicity, arguing that *primordialism* tends to become a self-view, whereas *constructivism* is normally a 'view of the other'. Each view is found to be situationally advantageous to each protagonist at different times. His is also a plea for the rediscovery of the emotive component of human relations in place of the uncharitable, narrow, hidebound, one-sided limits of cold reason and rationalist analysis. Therefore, this chapter represents a useful distillation of the 'primordialist' approach, whereas the unaccountable, mysterious force of ethnicity is considered paramount. The language–ethnicity link is deemed to be central to this primordial perception. Fishman argues that the perceived importance of language has a long tradition predating modernity. However, the modernist view can be easily encapsulated by saying that the old European principle *cuius regio, eius religio* has turned into the more modern *cuius regio, eius lingua*. In some way, this chapter is unique in advocating openly and uncompromisingly the scholarly legitimacy of primordialism. But what has the primordialist approach brought to theories of nationalism? Is there a 'primordialist school'?

In Chapter 4, Donald Horowitz attempts to identify an underlying primordialist stream in some of the founding theories of ethnicity and nationalism. The main contention with 'the primordialists' is not their assumption of an uninterrupted essence and continuous endurance of ethnic identities, but a series of confusions stemming from the unwillingness to analyse ethnonationalism as a relevant phenomenon in its own right. Among other things, this leads to the lack of an appropriate distinction between mobilization in defense of one own's culture and the political use of ethnicity for boundary-rising purposes. Scholars must distinguish between (*in-group*) solidarity and (*out-group*) conflict, on the one hand, and between ordinary maintenance of social cohesion and the creation of new (hence non-primordial) enmities, on the other hand. Group identity should be conceptually distinguished from antipathy toward outgroups, because groups can live side by side without the need of particular animosities. Ethnic boundaries can be socially constructed only over relatively long periods of time. Therefore, the contribution of rational actors and their decisions remains limited. Horowitz finally proposes a theory of 'evolutionary primordialism', according to which the ability to cooperate in groups would provide an evolutionary advantage likely to be associated with cooperation in kinship-based communities. Self-homogenization and conformism will be related to the propensity of individuals to assume a high degree of homogeneity within groups.

Part II consists of three distinctive case studies. In the first one (Chapter 6), William Douglass explores the depth of the emotional bond in the making of Basque ethnonational identity. Following Connor's depiction of the nation as a self-aware ethnic group, he enquires whether the racial component makes up an intrinsic part of the ethnicist discourse and whether race and ethnicity could really be separable. But if ethnicism (the celebration of one's own ethnic identity, in either a pluralist/tolerant way or an hierarchical/intolerant way) can be conceived as a positive phenomenon, the same cannot be said of exclusionary practices: forms of exclusion may be extremely variable, from acceptance of those who share the same cultural markers and symbols, to rejection of foreigners. The exacerbated racist overtones of Sabino de Arana (1865–1903), the founder of Basque nationalism, are put into the wider picture of a clash between immigrants and natives following the advent of modernity and industrialization. A focus on the historical legacy of the Spanish state brings Douglass' analysis to the quest for purity of blood (*limpieza de sangre*) inherited by Spain's early attempts of 'nation-building'. But the idea of a Basque 'race' was not simply the offshoot of increasing self-awareness (itself a consequence of increasing contacts and encroachment by the state): it was simultaneously the product of the outer imaginary and external categorization by non-Basques in an epoch, the late nineteenth century, when racialist 'scientific' discourse was fully legitimate and largely undisputed.

John Stone's Chapter 7 on the end of apartheid in South Africa is also deeply informed by a Connorian perspective. He concurs with Connor's anti-elitist approach and his sobering warnings about the difficulty of predicting outcomes in ethnic conflicts with traditional social/political science tools. As with Fishman's piece, he also attacks the persisting 'ivory towers' attitudes of elitist academics who failed to anticipate the end product of the anti-apartheid struggle. The major underplayed factors were: the end of Cold War bipolarism with its all-pervasive impact, the opposition élites' ability to negotiate, the capacity of accommodation of the existing regime, and the relative absence of widespread personal animosities between black and white peoples despite the official doctrine of racial segregation. Stone explores two central themes found in Connor's writings. The first considers the power of ethnonationalism as a source of group identity in a racially divided society. The second assesses the ability of sociologists, political scientists and historians to understand and predict the dynamics of social change in a society characterized by such deep racial and ethnic divisions. South Africa has become a textbook case and role model: ethnic conflict resolution has rarely been so smooth and relatively harmonious, at least in periods of democratic transition. Would it hence be advisable to extend the analysis beyond the unusual case of apartheid South Africa to a few instances bearing some resemblance with it? For instance, in Milosevic's Serbia, apartheid was applied *de facto* (rather than by law) against Albanians and other minorities. But here apartheid was preceded, accompanied, and followed by a mixed bag of policies, from centralization to genocide, from anti-Constitutionalism to 'secession by the centre'.[41] However, by examining the case of South Africa during the apartheid era (1948–90), the importance of Connor's scholarship can be appreciated and the value of his insights demonstrated.

In Chapter 8, John Edwards offers a robust critique of the idea of 'civic' nationalism, by drawing on the case of Quebec within the Canadian federation. Like

Connor, Edwards argues that all nationalisms are *au fond* ethnic, but that they tend to present themselves more fashionably in 'civic' disguise. The reality is that nationalism can rarely (if ever) be civic.[42] He therefore joins Connor in questioning the possibility of a 'civic' form of nationalism, and of a purely 'patriotic' (non-ethnic) attachment to state institutions.[43] Edwards also points to the dangers of questioning the legitimacy of multi-national polities *per se*. He argues that 'civic' nationalism is a misnomer, as it remains at heart a matter of preference for co-ethnics: despite nationalist pronouncements of providing an inclusive arena and sharable platform for the entire society, ethnicity stays implicitly in the background. Of course, to have a universal validity this argument needs to be applied to other cases, especially those usually quoted as prototypes of civic nationalism. The recent upsurge of vindictive, revengeful 'nationalism' in the United States has shown to the world the non-inclusive nature of American patriotism, a phenomenon that has been systematically studied by only a few scholars (Marvin and Ingle 1999; see also Billig 1995: 154–173). In several ways, such a purportedly 'civic' identity can hardly exist without an external enemy or without externalizing internal strife: according to scholars like David Campbell, US identity is founded on the identification of an external enemy (Campbell 1998), while others consider of paramount importance the internal outsider (Zulaika and Douglass 1996). However, Edwards' important critique is limited to Quebecois nationalist discourse, where the emphasis is shifted from the negative terms 'secession' or 'separation' to a more positively marked one: 'sovereignty'. This is again in tune with Connor's critique of the use and misuse of nationalism-related terminology: it is this confusion which benefits nationalists and populists, while it obfuscates political analysis.[44]

In the first chapter of Part III, Brendan O' Leary (Chapter 9) addresses another aspect of Connor's problematics: whether federal arrangements can re-legitimate existing multi-national policies at a time of ethnonational turmoil. O'Leary pays tribute to Connor's pioneering work on how federations were deployed as systems of control in multi-national and multi-ethnic Marxist-Leninist regimes, and then asks whether the same might be suggested of federations in liberal democracies. Reformulating Connor's and Gellner's emphasis on the homogenizing repercussions of nationalism, O'Leary then addresses whether federations conform to an 'iron law', requiring a dominant people or *Staatsvolk* if they are to remain democratic, majoritarian and stable. He finds provisional evidence that they do. However, federations lacking a dominant people may be democratic and stable only if they adopt non-majoritarian devices and procedures. Consociationalism is hence needed to redress possible imbalances in federations without a hegemonic core. He finally speculates on whether this limited optimism has any significance for the future of the European Union. But O'Leary's focus on the *Staatsvolk* is *not* a throwback to Deutsch's school of social communication, which postulated the need of an assimilationist or hegemonic core in order to run cohesive political communities.

In Chapter 10, William Safran addresses the issue of third-party interventions as tools of conflict resolutions, on the ground that there are discrete and cohesive entities such as 'the French', 'the Germans', and other ethnic groups. Accordingly, the latter's sense of groupness has its bearing on international relations and must be taken into account in any attempt to mediate. The mandate of third-party interventions should therefore be merely to terminate violent conflict, rather than to establish more comprehensive long-term solutions. Safran seems to argue that third-party interventions could only be successful if they become more genuine, real, sincere, detached, disinterested, honorable and just. But, if this is the case, can there be any agreed criterion of inter-ethnic fairness and impartiality? There are legitimate fears that once one abdicates to 'cultural' or 'historical determinism' (on these, see Chapter 14), no conflict resolution seems possible except by Divine Intervention. If one assumes that third-party arbitration is bound to fail because of its intrinsic flaws (rather than because of the choices of incumbent politicians and the features of exiting ethnic conflicts), then we come up with a drastic primordialist view of international relations. If no universal, non-partisan behavior is conceivable, groupness simply renders groups resilient to any single political engineering solution.[45] Safran also highlights the gloomy side of international relations, namely that political élites are bound to turn a blind eye on, and even support, other states' oppression of their minorities – unless they oppress 'kin' minorities. Following a Jacobin archetype, the state and its organic intellectuals tend intrinsically, nearly unthinkingly, to uphold state centralism, abroad as well as at home: that may perhaps explain, say, Western support for Milosevic's regime until around 1999.

John Coakley (Chapter 11) draws upon Connor's warning that ethnic strife cannot be shallowly discerned as being predicated upon tangible elements. Among a few possible 'core values' of nationhood, language is conceivably the predominant one, but other markers can be chosen by proto-nationalist élites.[46] Whereas in Chapter 6 Douglass focused on 'race', here Coakley focuses on an even more contentious core value of nationalist mobilization, religion. Three sets of questions are addressed: (1) Do religious belief systems have particular political implications such that religious communities may form a basis for ethnic mobilization – analogously with linguistic communities? (2) Are there particular structural conditions that have the potential to encourage the manipulation of religious forms and symbols as mechanisms for enhancing ethnic solidarity? and (3) To what extent does reliance on religious criteria promote inter-ethnic contact or shape the character of ethnic conflict? Pointing to the need to distinguish between *ethnic* and *religious* conflict, Coakley argues that in twentieth-century Europe most religious conflicts were *not* ethnic in nature, whereas most ethnic conflicts did *not* have a significant religious dimension. Europe's most bitter 'religious' wars took part in an age that would conventionally be seen as pre-national, although their echoes are allowed to continue into the contemporary period. The empirical evidence relies mainly on the Catholic–Protestant, Protestant–Orthodox, Catholic–Orthodox and Catholic–Orthodox–Muslim interfaces in Europe, with the Balkans and Northern Ireland providing most of the illustrative evidence.

In Part IV, Robert Kaiser (Chapter 12) focuses on the geopolitical dimension of Connor's work and, in particular, on the importance of national homelands and geographical space for ethnic groups. He examines the ways in which homeland images, myths and symbols have been used to nationalize space and territorialize national identity. In doing so, Kaiser picks up on a number of themes raised by

Connor about perceptions of homelands in ethnonationalism and inter-ethnic relations. After a brief review of the reasons for the centrality of homeland making in nationalization projects, the chapter focuses on the instruments through which national homeland images are constructed, maintained, and communicated to populations undergoing nationalization. Among the tools of nation-making which nationalists have at their disposal is the drawing of maps. In the final section, the chapter assesses the impact of globalization, transnationalism and the rising numbers of people living in diaspora on national homelands and territorialized nations. Although accentuated by modernity, territoriality is not its offspring.[47] Against modernization theory, territoriality is unlikely to disappear at a time of global secularization and individualism. The chapter concludes that national homeland images continue to exert a powerful influence on popular perceptions of identity, and remain among the most effective instruments that nationalists have at their disposal to mobilize their national communities. Transnationalism and the rising number of people living in diaspora have not undermined the ability of national homeland myths and symbols to territorialize identity and call the nation to action, and may actually have enhanced their potency in these regards, not least among those members living in diaspora themselves.

In Chapter 13, Thomas Spira returns to the terminological conundrum. He argues that the twin-concepts of ethnicity and nationality are inextricably linked in both research and practice. In an ideal world, the two expressions would be neatly segregated, each with its own meaning and definition clearly enunciated by members of the scholarly community. Unfortunately, such is not the case. These terminologies have evolved over the past few decades, subject to the varied interpretations of numerous social science specialists, their viewpoints sharpened by their own disciplinary, ideological, national, and other, affiliations and inclinations. Noting the conspicuous resemblances between ethnicity and nationality (most of their features intertwine and overlap, whereas few characteristics diverge), Spira points to the need for scholars to identify at which point ethnicity and nationality diverge – a task in which they have not so far succeeded. Further to Connor's terminological breakthroughs, such research is necessary in order to lend precision and accuracy to investigations in the etiology of nationalism. It should be possible to distinguish nationality from ethnicity by invoking a more rigorous 'dimensionalistic' approach to the problem, wherein the items measured are given values according to the intensity of the standard against which they are judged.

The Conclusion (Chapter 14) provides a general assessment of the status of the discipline, as well as a critique of some underlying trends, including some emerging in this book. Three stumbling blocks are identified in the form of underlying approaches: *essentialism, cultural determinism*, and *historical determinism*. Further directions of research are pinpointed in the intersection between studies of nationalism and the gray, undefined, and chaotic area of globalization studies – where the very word 'globalization' still lacks a minimum standard of clarity and definition.

Chapter 15 provides an exhaustive bibliography of Connor's works, ordered according to type of publication (books, journal articles, contributions to anthologies, and occasional papers).

Notes

1 See, in particular, Connor (1978).
2 For instance, for most Catalan nationalists Catalan nationhood long predates modernity, so they question the usefulness of the terms 'ethnie' or 'ethno-nation'? Wouldn't that downplay or detract from our claims? Why should we adopt the term 'ethnie' if the more conventional and clear term 'nation' is readily available? (Conversi 1997: 6–7). See also Keating (2000), McRoberts (2001) and Payne (2000).
3 John Gray (1978: 394) argues that 'a concept moves into an area of essential contestability when any use of it involves taking up a partisan non-neutral standpoint with respect to rival forms of life and their associated patterns of thought'.
4 See Glazer and Moynihan (1975: 1), also quoted in Connor (1994a: 101).
5 For a criticism of many of these terms, see Connor (1972, reprinted in Connor 1994a).
6 Critics of this position include Agnew (1997: 317–24) and Guibernau (1999).
7 See, in particular, Connor (1994a: 102–103), as well as Chapter 2. Elsewhere Connor (1994a: 202) offers a compatible and empirically testable definition of the nation as the largest group of people who feel that they are ancestrally related, the largest group that can be aroused or energized by appeals to a common blood-link.
8 As the nation is itself a tool of definition, it cannot be defined in universal terms, that is, abstractly and extra-contextually (Conversi 1995). Sami Zubaida (1978) claims that 'from the point of view of the . . . social theorist, there cannot be any systematic way of designating a "nation". Any attempt to do so can only be a purely arbitrary definition'.
9 See also van den Berghe (1996).
10 Connor (1972, 1973, 1978, 1987, 1990). See also Gellner (1983).
11 See Smith (1998); Conversi (1995).
12 In August 1979 Connor presented his findings at a tension-filled meeting of the International Political Science Association held in Moscow.
13 Scholars of different persuasions, such as Ernest Gellner, anticipated the same 'manifest destiny' for mankind.
14 Weber (1991: 78, my emphasis).
15 Aguilar (1998) has argued that this had an effect which reverberated through the transition to democracy as well.
16 This bears considerable similarities with former Yugoslavia. After the Partisan victory following World War II, people were fed up with violence and longed for a strong state which could protect them. Thus, all ethnic groups supported Tito.
17 This is a widely recognized phenomenon: for instance, George Schöpflin (2000) has argued that not merely nationalism, but ethnicity itself is the crucible of consent for the modern rationalizing state.
18 Weber placed 'ethnic group' and 'nation' on the same level, while arguing that 'the sentiment of ethnic solidarity does not by itself make a nation' (1991: 173).
19 Gellner and Connor belong to two very different academic traditions. Gellner initially knew about Connor's work through Anthony D. Smith (and as Smith's supervisor at the LSE). Mutual contacts between Gellner and Connor date to the 1980s when they attended numerous conferences together, culminating in Connor's visiting position at Cambridge (1990).
20 The sub-text is that culture and violence are the two alternative ways of moulding the nation (Conversi 1999).
21 The modernization paradigm is not to be confused with *modernism*. On the latter, see Smith (1998).
22 For a critique of the modernization paradigm, see Ferrarotti (1985) and Gusfield (1967). Moreover, after the Iranian revolution in 1979, the conventional view that modernization automatically leads to secularism has also been questioned. This of course may overlook the fact that 'political religion', as Gellner would argue, is merely a form of nationalism and modernization, rather than a return to tradition. The collapse of the

Soviet Union has dealt a *coup de grâce* to the 'social mobilization' paradigm still held by Deutsch's imitators and epigones.

23 Deutsch is the principal source of the modernization theory as applied to the studies of nationalism. For a devastating critique of Deutsch's view, see Connor (1972).

24 See Connor (1972, 1973).

25 Connor (1973: 3–4).

26 Conflictual modernization theorists eventually include Anthony D. Smith (1998) and Tom Nairn (1977). Eric Hobsbawm (1994) has also reckoned the spread of nationalism as a reaction to several aspects of modernization, particularly secularism.

27 From a political philosophy viewpoint, Will Kymlicka (1995, 2000) has also stressed the conceptual difference between the immigrant experience and that of indigenous, ethnonational or homeland people. For the 'border case' of the Mexican-Americans, see Connor (1985).

28 This thesis is shared by most historians (Kohn 1955: 10–15; Hobsbawm 1994; Seton-Watson 1977) and anthropologists (Gellner 1983).

29 In Barth's words, 'though the naïve assumption that each tribe and people has maintained its culture through a bellicose ignorance of its neighbours is no longer entertained, the simplistic view that geographical and social isolation have been the critical factors in sustaining cultural diversity persists' (1969: 9).

30 On the relationship between cultural erosion, assimilation and the spread of ethnic violence, see Conversi (1999).

31 It should be noted that Connor has never employed the phrase 'need to belong'. A 'need to belong' can relate to all sorts of groups – social, professional, peer, class, civic, etc. Connor avoids the phrase because, standing alone, it does not explain why the ethnic group should exert a particularly emotional magnetic attraction.

32 In discussing the nature of the ethnonational bond, Connor insisted on the adjective '*non-rational*' rather than 'irrational'. In doing so, he hoped to convey that the bond was not opposed to reason, it was simply outside the sphere of reason or, to quote the title of one of his articles, it was 'Beyond Reason' (Connor 1993).

33 On the solidarian relationship between different nationalist movements (Basque, Catalan, Quebecois, Irish, etc.), see Conversi (1993). Note the wave of sympathy for the Baltic peoples and the rush for recognition of their self-determination as independent nation-states in Central Europe (Hungary, Poland, etc.) and Northern Europe (Iceland and other Scandinavian countries). A common feature was the ideal that small nations should support each other (George Schöpflin, personal observation).

34 Connor (1973: 17).

35 Connor (1973: 16).

36 In contrast to Walker Connor, my own approach is more centered on the role of culture and institutions and, consequently, on the role of *élites* who have been shaping both of them. Particularly crucial is the binding role of a distinctive culture or, in its absence, more confrontational forms of political mobilization (Conversi 1997, 1999). In this respect, my position explicitly departs from Connor's emphasis on mass emotions.

37 For a critique of the limits of mainstream liberal thought in this respect, see Kymlicka (1995).

38 For a critique of Hobsbawm, see Hastings (1997) and Smith (1998).

39 Yet, Gellner is mentioned only briefly in a footnote as representative, with Ben Anderson, of 'the conventional view' (Greenfield 1992: 496).

40 This contrasts with Liah Greenfeld's argument that a nation is when the intellectuals begin to conceive it. See Greenfeld (1992,1997).

41 On the idea of 'secession by the centre', see Conversi (2000).

42 For Connor's approach to this, see Chapter 2.

43 This view is also expressed by A.D. Smith, while it is rejected, among others, by the Canadian Charles Taylor, whereas Michael Billig has identified the pervasive presence of ethnic symbolism in daily rituals of civic patriotism. See also Marvin and Ingle (1999).

44 One may wonder whether the concept of civic nationalism might share some of the chimera-like semblances of another imperfect concept, democracy. Like democracy, civic nationalism is always imperfect because in the name of representation it inevitably involves the rule of the few. In the case of all forms of nationalism, it is the rule and culture of the few which are imposed in both cases, ethnic and civic nationalism – even though a 'perfect' civic nationalism, like a 'perfect' democracy would involve a two-ways, even and fair distribution of information with a parallel process of bottom-up diffusion of culture.

45 In this view, behind any mediation there may well be a conspiracy. If one were to follow this logic *à la lettre* and to its conclusions, the first casualty would be US foreign policy: should one interpret US successive failures to deal with various post-Cold War conflicts emerging in and around Europe as a deliberate attempt to weaken the inter-European fabric? Wouldn't the US primeval instinct be of weakening European stability in order to warn off any steps towards the establishment of an improbable competing superpower – however remote this prospect may really be?

46 On the concept of 'core value', particularly language, see Conversi (1997: 164ff.).

47 Similarly, Grosby (1995) and Smith (1998) argue that territorially-bound identities are not a modern phenomenon, but an ancient and long-lasting, as well as universal, human characteristic.

References

Agnew, John (ed.) 1997. *Political Geography: A Reader*. London: Edward Arnold.

Aguilar, Paloma 1998. 'The Memory of the Civil War in the Transition to Democracy: The Peculiarity of the Basque Case'. *West European Politics*. 21(4): 5–25.

Armstrong, John A. 1982. *Nations before Nationalism*. Chapel Hill, NC: University of North Carolina Press.

Anderson, Benedict 1983. *Imagined Communities: Reflections on the Origin and Spread of Nationalism*. London: Verso.

Barber, Benjamin R. 1996. *Jihad vs. McWorld*. New York: Ballantine Books.

Barth, Frederick (ed.) 1969. *Ethnic Groups and Boundaries: The Social Organization of Culture Difference*. London: Allen & Unwin.

Bauman, Zygmunt 1989. *Modernity and the Holocaust*. Ithaca, NY: Cornell University Press/Polity Press.

Billig, Michael 1995. *Banal Nationalism*. London: Sage.

Brown, David 2000. *Contemporary Nationalism: Civic, Ethnocultural, and Multicultural Politics*. London: Routledge.

Campbell, David 1998. *Writing Security: United States Foreign Policy and the Politics of Identity*. Minneapolis: University of Minnesota Press.

Connor, Walker 1972. 'Nation-Building or Nation-Destroying?' *World Politics*. XXIV: 319–355.

—— 1973. 'The Politics of Ethnonationalism'. *Journal of International Affairs*. 27(1): 1–21.

—— 1978. 'A Nation is a Nation, is a State, is an Ethnic Group is a . . .'. *Ethnic and Racial Studies*. 1(4): 377–397.

—— 1984a. *The National Question in Marxist-Leninist Theory and Strategy*. Princeton, NJ: Princeton University Press.

—— 1984b. 'Eco- or Ethno-Nationalism.' *Ethnic and Racial Studies*. 7 (October): 342–359.

—— 1985. (ed.) *Mexican Americans in Comparative Perspective*. Washington, DC: Urban Institute Press.

—— 1987. 'Ethnonationalism'. In Samuel Huntington and Myron Weiner (eds) *Understanding Political Development*. Boston: Little, Brown & Company: 196–220.

—— 1990. 'When is a Nation?' *Ethnic and Racial Studies.* 13(1): 92–103.

—— 1993. 'Beyond Reason: The Nature of the Ethnonational Bond'. *Ethnic and Racial Studies.* 16(3): 374–389.

—— 1994a. *Ethnonationalism: The Quest for Understanding.* Princeton: Princeton University Press.

—— 1994b. 'Elites and Ethnonationalism: The Case of Western Europe'. In Justo Beramendi, Ramón Máiz, and Xosé M. Núñez (eds) *Nationalism in Europe: Past and Present.* Santiago de Compostela, Spain: Universidade de Santiago de Compostela Press: 349–361.

—— 1997. 'Ethnic Identity: Primordial or Modern?' In Trude Andersen, Beate Bull, and Kjetil Duvold (eds) *Separatism.* Bergen, Norway: University of Bergen Press: 27–40.

—— 2001. 'Homelands in a World of States'. In Montserrat Guibernau and John Hutchinson (eds) *Understanding Nationalism.* Oxford: Blackwell.

Conversi, Daniele 1993. 'Domino Effect or Internal Developments? The Influences of International Events and Political Ideologies on Catalan and Basque nationalism'. *West European Politics.* 16(3): July 1993: 245–270.

—— 1995. 'Reassessing Theories of Nationalism: Nationalism as Boundary Maintenance and Creation'. *Nationalism and Ethnic Politics.* 1(1): 73–85.

—— 1997. *The Basques, the Catalans, and Spain: Alternative Routes to Nationalist Mobilization.* London: Hurst/Reno: University of Nevada Press.

—— 1999. 'Nationalism, Boundaries and Violence'. *Millennium: Journal of International Studies.* 28(3): 553–584.

—— 2000. 'Central Secession: Towards a New Analytical Concept? The Case of Former Yugoslavia'. *Journal of Ethnic and Migration Studies.* 26(2) April: 333–356.

—— 2001. 'Ernest Gellner i el multiculturalisme'. *L'Espill.* 7: 37–63.

Deutsch, Karl W. 1953. *Nationalism and Social Communication: An Inquiry into the Foundations of Nationality.* Cambridge, MA: MIT Press.

Ferrarotti, Franco 1985. *The Myth of Inevitable Progress.* Westview, CT: Greenwood Press.

Fishman, Joshua A. 1980. 'Social Theory and Ethnography: Language and Ethnicity in Eastern Europe'. In Peter Sugar (ed.) *Ethnic Conflict and Diversity in Eastern Europe.* Santa Barbara, CA: ABC-Clio.

—— 1997. *In Praise of the Beloved Language: A Comparative View of Positive Ethnolinguistic Consciousness.* Berlin and New York: Mouton de Gruyter.

Gellner, Ernest 1983. *Nations and Nationalism.* Oxford: Basil Blackwell/Ithaca: Cornell University Press.

Ghai, Yash (ed.) 2000. *Autonomy and Ethnicity: Negotiating Competing Claims in Multi-Ethnic States.* Cambridge: Cambridge University Press.

Glazer, Nathan and Moynihan, Daniel P. (eds) 1975. *Ethnicity: Theory and Experience.* Cambridge, MA: Harvard University Press.

Gray, John 1978. 'On Liberty, Liberalism and Essential Contestability'. *British Journal of Political Science.* 8: 394.

Greenfeld, Liah 1992. *Nationalism: Five Roads to Modernity.* Cambridge, MA: Harvard University Press.

Grosby, Steven 1995. 'Territoriality: the Transcendental Primordial Feature of Modern Societies'. *Nations and Nationalism.* 1(2): 143–162.

Guibernau, Montserrat 1999. *Nations Without States: Political Communities in a Global Age.* Oxford: Blackwell Publishers.

Gusfield, Joseph R. 1967. 'Tradition and Modernity: Misplaced Polarities in the Study of Social Change'. *American Journal of Sociology.* 72(4): 351–362 .

Hastings, Adrian 1997. *The Construction of Nationhood: Ethnicity, Religion and Nationalism.* Cambridge: Cambridge University Press.

Hobsbawm, Eric J. 1983. 'Introduction: Inventing Traditions; Mass Producing Traditions: Europe, 1870–1914'. In Eric J. Hobsbawm and Terence Ranger (eds) *The Invention of Tradition.* Cambridge: Cambridge University Press.

—— 1994. 'Nation, State, Ethnicity, Religion: Transformations of Identity'. In Justo G. Beramendi, Ramón Máiz, and Xosé M. Núñez (eds) *Nationalism in Europe: Past and Present.* Santiago de Compostela: Santiago de Compostela University Press, 1: 33–45.

Horowitz, Donald L. 1985. *Ethnic Groups in Conflict.* Berkeley: University of California Press (ch. 2: 'A family resemblance': 55–92).

Keating, Michael 2000. 'The Minority Nations of Spain and European Integration: A New Framework for Autonomy?' *Journal of Spanish Cultural Studies.* 1(1): 29–42.

Kedourie, Elie 1960. *Nationalism.* London: Hutchinson.

Kohn, Hans 1955. *Nationalism: Its Meaning and History.* Princeton, NJ: Van Nostrand.

Kymlicka, Will 1995. *Multicultural Citizenship: A Liberal Theory of Minority Rights.* Oxford: Oxford University Press.

—— 2000. *Politics in the Vernacular.* Oxford: Oxford University Press.

Loughlin, John 2000. 'The Transformation of the State and the New Territorial Politics'. *'L'intégration européenne entre émergence institutionnelle et recomposition de l'Etat.* Paris: CEVIPOF–CERI.

McRoberts, Kenneth 2001. *Catalonia.* Oxford: Oxford University Press.

Marvin, Carolyn and Ingle, David W. 1999. *Blood Sacrifice and the Nation.* Cambridge: Cambridge University Press.

Minogue, Kenneth R. 1967. *Nationalism.* London: Batsford.

Nairn, Tom 1977. *The Break-up of Britain.* London: New Left Books.

Newman, Saul 1991. 'Does Modernization Breed Ethnic Political Conflict?' *World Politics.* 43(3): 451–477.

Payne, Stanley G. 2000. 'Catalan and Basque Nationalism: Contrasting Patterns'. In Shlomo Ben-Ami, Yoav Peled, and Alberto Spektorowski (eds) *Ethnic Challenges to the Modern Nation State.* New York: St. Martin's Press.

Petrosino, Daniele (1994) 'Presentazione' (Introduction to the Italian translation). In Walker Connor *Etnonazionalismo: Quando e perché emergono le nazioni.* Rome/Bari: Edizioni Dedalo, 1995. Italian edition of *Ethnonationalism.*

Schöpflin, George 2000. *Nations, Identity, Powers.* London: Hurst.

Seton-Watson, Hugh 1977. *Nations and States: An Enquiry into the Origins of Nations and the Policies of Nationalism.* London: Methuen.

Smith, Anthony D. 1981. *The Ethnic Revival.* Cambridge: Cambridge University Press.

—— 1998. *Nationalism and Modernism: A Critical Survey of Recent Theories of Nations and Nationalism.* London: Routledge.

van den Berghe, Pierre L. 1987. *The Ethnic Phenomenon.* New York: Praeger.

—— 1992. 'The Modern State: Nation Builder or Nation Killer?' *International Journal of Group Tensions.* 22(3): 191–208.

—— 1996 'Denationalizing the State'. *Society.* January/February: 64–68.

Watts, Ron 2000. 'Federalism and Diversity in Canada'. In Yash Ghai (ed.) *Autonomy and Ethnicity: Negotiating Competing Claims in Multi-Ethnic States.* Cambridge: Cambridge University Press.

Weber, Max 1991. 'Class, Status and Party'. In H.H. Gerth and C. Wright Mills (eds) *From Max Weber: Essays in Sociology.* London: Routledge.

Yan, Ma Shu 1990. 'Ethnonationalism, Ethnic Nationalism, and Mini-Nationalism: A Comparison of Connor, Smith and Snyder'. *Ethnic and Racial Studies.* 13(4): 527–541.

Zubaida, Sami 1978. 'Theories of Nationalism'. In Garry Littlejohn (ed.) *Power and the State*. London: Croom Helm.

Zulaika, Joseba and Douglass, William A. 1996. *Terror and Taboo: The Follies, Fables, and Faces of Terrorism*. London: Routledge.

2 Nationalism and political illegitimacy*

Walker Connor

> The question, then, can only be put in the following terms: When, in what way, and for what reasons did state and nation come to be so closely linked together as to turn the principle of nationality into the ultimate principle of legitimacy in the modern State?
>
> (Alexander D'Entreves, *The Notion of the State*)

A prefatory note on terminology

The analysis of nationalism has long been hampered by slipshod terminology. If anything, the situation has further deteriorated since 1939, when the Royal Institute of International Affairs prefaced a major study of nationalism with a warning 'Note on the Use of Words', whose opening sentence read: 'Among other difficulties which impede the study of "nationalism", that of language holds a leading place'.[1] English-speaking societies are particularly prone to the careless interutilization of terms which in their pristine usage convey vastly different connotations. Thus, *nation* and *state* are commonly interutilized, and the term *nation-state* is regularly employed indiscriminately to refer both to uninational and multinational entities. As a result of this confusing interutilization of key terms, *nationalism* is used to connote two different concepts which are often in conflict with one another. At times it connotes identification with and loyalty to the nation in the sense of a human grouping which may or may not be essentially coterminous with a state (e.g., Croatian, Fleming, Scottish, or Ukrainian nationalism). More often it is used to connote identification with and loyalty to the 'nation' when the latter is used to indicate the state structure regardless of the national composition of the state's population (e.g., American, Argentinian, Indian, or Filipino nationalism).[2]

In order to avoid the confusion surrounding two vitally different and often antagonistic loyalties, this writer has found it useful elsewhere to employ the term *patriotism* to refer to state loyalty, and *ethnonationalism* to refer to loyalty to the nation. While this vocabulary serves to distinguish between the two loyalties, it tells us little about the latter. It implies general agreement concerning the meaning of *ethnic* which, unfortunately, is not the case. As used today by most American sociologists,

* Originally published in *Canadian Review of Studies in Nationalism*. VII (Fall 1980): 201–228.

ethnic group is used to connote 'a group with a common cultural tradition and a sense of identity which exists as a subgroup of a larger society'.[3] Such a definition makes ethnic group and minority synonymous, and could not therefore apply to the dominant peoples within a state (e.g., the English or German people), or within several states (e.g., the Arabs).

Originally, both *nation* and *ethnic* group referred to a group characterized by common descent. (*Ethnic* derives from the Greek *Ethnos* and *nation* from the past participle of the Latin verb *nasci*, meaning 'to be born'.) Max Weber, however, has pointed out that the key element is not the reality but the *myth* of common descent.

> The belief in group affinity, regardless of whether it has any objective foun-
> dation, can have important consequences, especially for the formation of a
> political community. We shall call 'ethnic groups' those human groups that
> entertain a subjective belief in their common descent . . . this belief must be
> important for the propagation of group formation; conversely, it does not
> matter whether or not an objective blood relationship exists. Ethnic member-
> ship (*Gemeinsamkeit*) differs from the kinship group precisely by being a
> presumed identity . . .[4]

Elsewhere, Weber notes that 'the concept of "nationality" [or 'nation'] shares with that of the "people" (*Volk*) – in the "ethnic" sense – the vague connotation that whatever is felt to be distinctively common must derive from common descent.'[5] In a similar vein, Tomotshu Shibutani and Kian Kwan define an ethnic group as composed of 'those who conceive of themselves as being alike by virtue of their common ancestry, real or fictitious, and who are so regarded by others.'[6] An old European definition of a nation, which was intended to be humorous and derisive and which Karl Deutsch cites as such, hit almost the same mark: 'A nation is a group of people united by a common error about their ancestry and a common dislike of their neighbors.'[7]

Although all of the preceding definitions are acceptable to this writer, they leave the student of nation-formation still in need of a term to describe a group of people who have not achieved group-consciousness, but who, in the opinion of out-side observers, are most apt ultimately to form a nation. Throughout large sections of the globe, meaningful identity is still restricted to the clan, village, or region.[8] It is therefore convenient to use ethnic group to refer to groups of people, such as the Quechuan-speaking people of South America or the Pushtu-speaking people of the Afghan-Pakistani border-region, who, though not as yet, are each apt someday to coalesce into a self-aware, self-differentiating national group. *Nation* is thus reserved for ethnic groups who have in fact achieved group self-awareness. As used herein, then, a *nation* is a self-differentiating ethnic group. *State* refers to one of the *major* political divisions of the globe. It does not, however, refer to a further sub-division, such as Bihar, California, Mato Grosso, or Saxony, even though such subdivisions are called states within their particular political structure. *Nationalism* and *ethnonationalism* both connote identity with and loyalty to the *nation*. *Patriotism* connotes identity with and loyalty to the state.

Self-determination

The doctrine that a people ought not to be ruled by those deemed aliens has rapidly gained converts during the past two centuries. At first untitled, then referred to as 'the principle of nationalities', and more recently as 'national self-determination', the doctrine postulates that any people, simply because it considers itself to be a separate people, has the right, if it so desires, to form its own state.[9] As such, it presumes that nationhood (national consciousness) constitutes the ultimate standard for gauging political legitimacy. By definition, no justification advanced for exercising political rule over a multinational unit can stand against it. Thus, when the government of a multinational state advances the argument that the minority has in fact enjoyed educational, economic, security-related, or other tangible advantages as a consequence of living within the state, advantages that would be lost with secession, the government thereby only presents an argument as to why a minority should rationally elect not to secede, but it does not thereby deny the fundamental right of the national minority to make the decision. On the contrary, it thereby implies that the right of decision rests with the group. Indeed, though in practice governments have been most reluctant to permit a valid measurement of a national group's sentiment with regard to secession, they have rarely denied *in abstracto* the right of a national group to secede. Governments have been more prone to conduct patently spurious plebiscites[10] or, even more commonly, to assert that the overwhelming majority of the group favor continued union and that whatever agitation the outsider can perceive is merely the handiwork of a few malcontents or *agents provocateurs*.[11] But by such studied efforts to avoid any public disavowal of the right which in practice they go to great lengths to deny, such governments in fact manifest a profound appreciation for the legitimizing power of the self-determination principle.[12] Phrased differently, though the political leaders of a multinational state do not themselves accept the proposition that the right to answer the question of whether or not a polity has a *legitimate* claim to the allegiance of a national group is the exclusive prerogative of the group itself, those same leaders do, by their indirection, indicate a belief that the proposition is a broadly held matter of conviction both within and without their country.[13]

Levels of legitimacy

By genus, then, national self-determination is an assertion of political legitimacy. But while it might therefore be anticipated that the literature on political legitimacy would prove of substantial benefit to the student of nationalism and nationalist movements, such expectations result in disappointment. More than a decade ago, a prominent political scientist compiled a listing of what he termed 'common but ambiguous political concepts'.[14] He warned that each of the itemized concepts could vary in meaning (a) depending upon the context within which the term was used, and (b) from user to user even with regard to the same context. Quite appropriately, legitimacy was included on the list.

The deficiency is both quantitative and qualitative. Considering its centrality to the discipline of political science, remarkably few attempts to subject the notion of political legitimacy to rigorous and comprehensive analysis have been under-taken.[15] Most authors who touch upon the subject of legitimacy do so only implicitly and often unwittingly. Moreover, though the issue of why any group of people ought to submit to being ruled is one of the vital, pervasive, and enduring questions of political philosophy, scholarly histories of political thought fail to syn-thesize thinking on the topic. Such works are peppered with separate commentaries on the notion of legitimacy as found in the writings of one or another philosopher, but offer no focussed discussion of legitimacy *per se*.[16]

The tendency to ignore or slight the concept of legitimacy is underscored when one searches for a definition. Dictionaries of political science customarily contain no such entry.[17] Nor do similar works in philosophy.[18] Though by no means per-fect, the record of sociological dictionaries is much better, probably because (a) sociologists claim Max Weber as one of their own, and (b) the notion of legitimacy was a major element in Weber's writings.[19] But though he often used the term, Weber apparently also neglected to offer a definition.[20]

It may well be that those authorities who have neglected to offer a definition of political legitimacy have done so because they consider the concept to be self-explanatory and unambiguous.[21] If so, they are mistaken. Particularly injurious to scholarship has been the failure to distinguish between levels of legitimacy, for proper analysis requires an awareness of at least three distinct categories:

(1) *regime-legitimacy* refers to the propriety or rightfulness of the rule of a particu-lar individual, clique, or administration.
(2) *government-legitimacy* is associated with a particular form of government and with its corresponding ideology and institutions, regardless of the individuals who momentarily occupy its key positions.
(3) *state-legitimacy*, the broadest of these categories, is concerned with the justifi-cation of the political unit itself, rather than with either individuals or governments.

As is customarily true with social classifications, these three categories in practice often blur into one another. The case for legitimacy of the German Third Reich, for example, rested upon an indissoluble intertwining of (1) the Leader, (2) gov-ernment by a party-élite with its own ideology (Nazism), and (3) the racial (read national) state and its destiny. Nevertheless, an awareness of the distinctions among the three levels of legitimacy is vital, because forces challenging legitimacy at one political level need not pose a threat to another.[22] What is essential for this discus-sion, however, is the fact that the relationship of state-legitimacy to the other two classifications is that of the whole to the parts. To deny legitimacy to a regime is not to deny it to a government. To deny legitimacy to either a regime or a government is not to deny it to a state. To deny it to a state is to deny it to all three levels.

In most but not all cases, the type of activity engaged in as a means of remedy-ing a matter of political illegitimacy will identify the level of legitimacy being attacked. A pairing of some common political activities with the level of legitimacy that they challenge would appear as follows:

Level of legitimacy under challenge	Form assumed by the challenge
Regime-legitimacy	Recall, vote of no confidence, impeachment, assassination, 'palace revolution', coup d'état
Government-legitimacy	Political revolution
State-legitimacy	Secessionist movement

The schematic does not include all common types of political activity. To name but three omissions, politically motivated riots and revolts have been excluded because they may serve as a vehicle for challenging legitimacy at the regime-, government-, or state-level, and autonomist movements have been excluded because they can represent a challenge to either government- or state-legitimacy.[23]

The literature on legitimacy ignores this triadic classification. Moreover, while failing to make these distinctions, the writings of the leading contemporary authorities on legitimacy make manifest that their authors have been concerned with *only* regime- and/or government-legitimacy.[24] And, since national self-determination is an assertion concerning state-legitimacy, this literature seldom, if ever, mentions it.

The neglect of national self-determination by contemporary authorities on legitimacy may therefore be viewed as a consequence of their general inattention to state-legitimacy. But if we turn from contemporary writing to the history of political thought, how are we to explain the fact that none of the renowned political philosophers anticipated, much less attempted to legitimize, the notion of national self-determination prior to its actual surfacing in the late eighteenth century?[25]

As noted, the issue of why people should submit to *any* authority is a central question to philosophy, and, over the centuries, several political philosophers had addressed themselves to the ostensible purpose and justification of the state.[26] However, in part precisely because they did contemplate the *state*, their discourses also bear little pertinence to the notion of national self-determination. Treating, as they did, the state *in abstracto*, they reveal little concerning the rightful jurisdiction of such a polity. To Plato, the end-purpose and justification of the state may have been justice; to Aristotle, that purpose was 'the highest good, i.e . . . to produce a certain moral character in citizens, namely a disposition to virtue and the performance of virtuous actions';[27] to Hobbes, it was peace and order. But such goals are in fact related more to regime- and government-legitimacy than to state-legitimacy. They disclose nothing about the citizenry to be incorporated. If a regime or government promotes justice, virtue, or domestic tranquility, it is owed legitimacy; if it does not, then it is not. Such models could conceivably pertain to a village-size community or to a universal political structure. The envisaged state could be coterminous with a single religion or be multireligious. It could be monoracial or multiracial, monolingual or multilingual, national or multinational.

Popular popular sovereignty

The idea of national self-determination therefore arrived on stage without the benefit of intellectual heralds. Those writers most intimately associated with it (such as

Johann Fichte, Ernst Arndt, Friedrich Jahn, Frantisek Palacky, and Giuseppe Mazzini) are its disciples rather than its prophets.[28] How can one explain the emergence of an idea without prophesiers? This seemingly enigmatic feature of the history of national self-determination may quite paradoxically serve as a signpost to the nature of national self-determination, including its claim of legitimacy. It suggests that the idea of national self-determination did not in and by itself represent a totally new, self-contained principle of politics but was merely a variant of some other concept. A study of the intellectual and political milieu at the time of its emergence suggests that popular sovereignty is that concept, and that national self-determination is best understood as a natural outgrowth or special interpretation of the notion of popular sovereignty.

Two preconditions were indispensable for the gestation of the self-determination idea: (1) the national consciousness of peoples and (2) the doctrine of popular sovereignty. The necessity for the former need not long detain us. A people must be aware that they constitute a national group before they insist on rights – political or otherwise – in the name of the nation. Even today, many people have not achieved national awareness. To them, the meaningful world still ends with the village, region, clan, or tribe. However, many, though certainly not all, peoples of Europe had achieved a large measure of national consciousness before the French Revolution ushered in the Age of Nationalism, so we can conclude that national consciousness was a *necessary* but not a *sufficient* condition for the advent of national self-determination. Popular sovereignty – the notion that ultimate political authority rests with the people – was the other necessary part of the equation.

With senses grown numb from too repetitious encounters with the expression *popular sovereignty*, and with the nearly uncontested status of the doctrine today, it is difficult to appreciate the truly revolutionary implications of this concept as recently as two-hundred years ago. Previously, the right to rule might have been defended as a gift from the gods (divine right), as a prerogative of royal blood, as the spoils of conquest, as a hereditary legacy, as a fidelity owed because of protection and/or other services rendered (feudalism), as flowing from the possession of the title to the property inhabited by the subjects, or as a combination of any of these. All such theories of politics shared the negative presumption that legitimacy had nothing to do with those who were ruled. The masses were solely the object, not the source of political authority. And if the people are not germane to the issue of legitimacy, then it follows that their ethnicity is not, either. Divine ordination, royal (in contradistinction to national) blood, inheritance, right of conquest, and the like, make no allowance for ethnonational considerations. And thus, prior to the French Revolution, the borders of empires, city-states, princely states, and even the post-1648, so-called 'modern states', were drawn with little or no regard for ethnic considerations. Ethnic distributional patterns were safely ignored without thereby risking a challenge to the state's legitimacy. But in a single sweep, the notion of popular sovereignty undermined all such claims to legitimacy, and thereby infused ethnicity with a combustible political potential.

The notion of popular sovereignty did not just burst upon the scene. Unlike national self-determination, it had had its proponents among political philosophers dating back to ancient times. Within such circles, it appeared to grow progressively more popular, and the late Charles Merriam, one of its more august chroniclers, informs us that well before the close of the Middle Ages, it had become almost *the theory* of legitimacy among scholars.

So universally prevalent was the idea of original popular sovereignty that 'from the end of the 13th century it was an axiom of political theory that the justification of all government lay in the voluntary submission of the community ruled.' Government based on the consent of the governed was the ruling theory in the Middle Ages.[29]

But if popular sovereignty had become a favorite of philosophers by the 1300s, it continued to lack for practitioners for hundreds of years thereafter. Why were there no fifteenth-, sixteenth-, or seventeenth-century Bismarcks, Cavours, O'Connells, or Sun Yat-sens? The philosophers' concept of *the people* in whom sovereignty was said to be vested appears to have been too abstractly intellectual, too remote from human experiences and sensations, to have ignited crusades in its name. Who was this otherwise undifferentiated and unidentified *people*? What Joseph de Maistre in 1796 would deprecatingly say of the notion of *man* (as embodied in the Declaration of Rights of Man and Citizen) would apply, with at least equal validity, to the notion of *the people*.

> During my life, I have seen Frenchmen, Italians, Russians, and so on; thanks to Montesquieu, I even know that one can be Persian; but I must say, as for *man* [read: *the people*], I have never come across him anywhere; if he exists, he is completely unknown to me.[30]

History would record that it was indeed primarily through 'Frenchmen, Italians, Russians, and so on' that popular sovereignty was to be carried throughout the globe. Article 2 of the very Declaration against which de Maistre inveighed first illustrated what a short, almost imperceptible and unconscious transition it was from the notion of *the people* to *my people*, that is to say, *my nation*: 'The source of all sovereignty resides essentially in the nation; no group, no individual, may exercise authority not emanating expressly therefrom.' Similarly, note how a reviewer of a book on the French Revolution made this same unconscious linkage of popular sovereignty with the nation:

> Popular sovereignty is an awesome idea precisely because it means nothing less than the existential freedom of a people to be responsible for its own fate, without recourse to any 'father'. The regicides created this terrible and magnificent freedom, the only one commensurate with the fullness of human potential. With the execution of Louis, they could solemnly declare to the nation: 'From this moment, one will no longer write the history of France, but rather the history of the French.'[31]

In short, *l'état c'est moi* had become *l'état c'est nous*, and the *nous* was identified with the nation.[32]

From the vantage point of abstract logic, some such further refinement of *the people* was necessary if popular sovereignty were to serve as an adequate theory of state legitimation. Otherwise, the extent of a state's proper jurisdiction could not be ascertained. It is, in effect, the manner in which one definitionally draws the human borders of a state that defines the state's claim to legitimacy. For example, Ernest Renan's 'plebiscite of every day' recommends itself as an apt description of the legitimizing principle which infuses popular sovereignty. [33] But as in the case of the philosophy of Plato, Aristotle, and Hobbes, the phrase tells us nothing about the limits of such a state. Certainly Renan did not mean that any individual or group whose plebiscitary inclination was negative had the right of secession. But without such an option, his state, just as those of the earlier theorists, could be racially, ethnically, and culturally homogeneous *or* heterogeneous.[34]

There were, to be sure, alternative ways of defining *the people* in addition to making it coincidental with an ethnonation. Particularly where great distance intervened between two human segments of a single polity and where a clear ethnic division was absent, geography might become the principal criterion for defining a people who were said to possess a right to secede under the doctrine of popular sovereignty.[35] Thus, the eighteenth- and nineteenth-century secessions of the North and South American colonies were manifestations of secession conducted in the name of popular sovereignty, but not of secession in its national form. Similarly, in a situation where a state has been constructed without the emotional mortar of an ethnic bond, geographic or regional secession (in contradistinction to national secession) is always a possibility.[36] Immigrant states – such as Argentina, Australia, Canada, and the United States – whose mythical, 'typical' citizen is a polygenetic figure, are particularly susceptible to such challenges.[37] Moreover, as we are reminded by the successful movement to create Pakistan as one of two successor states to what had been a single British India, a decision to define the people in religious terms cannot be totally ruled out.

Nevertheless, as evidenced by the comparative scarcity of regional secessions since the late eighteenth century, as well as by one already successful and several other current ethnonationally inspired secessionist challenges against Pakistan, incontestably the most common variant of popular sovereignty has been the national one. Nearly everywhere, it proved to be the equating of *the people* with *my people*, that is to say, with *my nation*, that was to breathe life into the otherwise sterile concept of popular sovereignty. It would, therefore, not be too amiss to define national self-determination as *popular* popular sovereignty. Once the nation has been substituted for *the people*, it is the national group that becomes the final arbiter in determining whether the state or states in which it resides is to be perceived as legitimate or illegitimate. 'Let my people go!' therefore became an increasingly common ejaculation of nationally conscious minorities.

The changes in political borders wrought by this new standard of legitimacy in its as yet relatively short history are astonishing. In the one hundred and thirty year period separating the Napoleonic Wars from the end of World War II, all but three of Europe's states had either lost extensive territory and population because of ethnonational movements or were themselves newly created 'self-determined' states.[38] The impact upon non-European areas during this period was far less pronounced.[39]

However, one increasingly detected the message of national popular sovereignty in the growing demands – heard both in the local colonies and in their mother countries – for decolonization.

Since the newly emancipated colonies were themselves almost uniformly ethnically heterogeneous, it might be argued that decolonialism should be treated as equivalent to geographic rather than to national secession. However, it was under the banner which proclaimed that a people ought not to be ruled by those deemed aliens that the decolonial campaigns were waged. The liberation movements were indeed multiethnic in their composition, but there was agreement among the ruled (or, more accurately, among their élites) on the need to rid the system of the *most alien* element. And *most alien* was a judgment predicated more upon skin pigmentation than upon geography.[40] Indeed, one of the many whimsical aspects of the history of national movements conducted by minorities has been the frequency with which the new state that they seek to create will also, in turn, contain minorities. The recent proliferation of national movements within the former colonies, as well as within the older states of Europe, illustrates, however, that self-determined states which contain minorities can expect internal movements demanding that the principle of ethnonational legitimacy be carried further toward fulfillment. Approximately half of all contemporary states have recently experienced ethnonationally inspired dissonance, and the list can be expected to grow.[41] Most significantly, the list of afflicted states suggests that no categorization of multinational states is immune. The contagion of ethnonationalism has exhibited an unusual level of immunity from all of the customary variables, such as median income, degree of urbanization, level of industrialization, literacy rate, geographic location, form of government, socioeconomic philosophy, and even the length of time that the state has been in existence.[42]

The irregular trajectory of self-determination

Once underway, then, the idea of national self-determination has rapidly gained converts. However, this trend toward universalization of the idea has not been one of uniform progress, but one which has proceeded with troughs (e.g., the seeming serenity of most of the national minorities of Western Europe from 1945 to 1965) and with swells (e.g., the widespread national unrest within Europe in 1848, again in the 1890s, and still again in the early 1970s).[43] The irregularity of the pattern may be attributed in part to the fact that the world's ethnic groups have achieved national awareness at different points in history, that a great many groups had not achieved it at the time of the French Revolution, and that, though several have subsequently done so, many others have yet to achieve it. Since national consciousness is one of the two necessary preconditions of the linkage of ethnicity and legitimacy, it follows that group appreciation of that linkage has also emerged somewhat sporadically.[44]

Catalysts and soporifics have also been at work.[45] Among the former might be mentioned (1) the demonstration effect which caused each national movement to give rise in other minds to the question, 'If they have that right, why do not my people also?'; (2) increases in the intensity of contacts among national groups due to quantitative and qualitative improvements in communications and transportation (and often given a special impetus by an alien invasion or occupation of the ethnic homeland); (3) the increasing evidence that small as well as 'great' nations could operate a viable state; (4) changes in the world power scene and in the prevailing attitudes of influential élites which made it decreasingly likely that a weak people might achieve independence, only to be swallowed up by another; and (5) the fame and prestige sporadically accorded to the doctrine of a natural linkage between ethnicity and legitimacy because of its public espousal by such luminaries as Napoleon Bonaparte, Louis Napoleon, Karl Marx, Friedrich Engels, Lenin, and Woodrow Wilson. Somnolence, on the other hand, has often been encouraged by a periodic decimation of potential leadership,[46] or by the reaction that follows immediately in the wake of a war or insurrection involving militant nationalism.[47]

Beyond all of these considerations, however, it is in the very nature of ideas to evolve in irregular fits and starts. The idea of popular sovereignty permeated the world of intellect long before it elicited popular support in the world of action. Its subsequent history further illustrates the paradoxes that one is apt to encounter when reviewing the history of an idea. It also sheds additional light on the interaction between the idea of popular sovereignty *per se* and its particular form of national self-determination.

A major reason why the close interrelationship between self-determination and popular sovereignty has not been readily recognized is that we confront national self-determination movements where we do not see democratic forms, and popular sovereignty would appear to demand democracy. In theory this might be correct, but in practice it certainly has not been. Democracy requires popular sovereignty, but the reverse is not true. Authoritarianism proved sufficiently elastic to thrive in a world in which popular sovereignty appeared destined to become the universal principle of politics. Earlier we examined popular sovereignty from the viewpoint of its mass converts, and noted that national groups were the principal key to its propagation. But as an illusionary fiction rather than as a reality, its propagation has been materially assisted by authoritarian regimes and individuals who were its opportunistic manipulators rather than its devotees. Modern authoritarians, in substance not different from their pre-eighteenth-century counterparts, learned to mask their own notions of the font of political power behind formal lip service to the notion that the source of all legitimate authority is *the people*.

Authoritarianism, as well as democracy, may, of course, exist in either ethnically homogeneous or heterogeneous states. With an eye to events in Germany and Japan during the 1930s and 1940s, it also appears evident that the ethnically homogeneous (or near homogeneous) environment affords the best opportunity for an extreme aggrandizement of power through the manipulation of ethnonational proclivities in a manner to induce the *voluntary*, unrestrained submission of the masses to the will of the leadership. If leaders are able to convince the masses that theirs is the legitimate voice of the nation – the expression of the nation's will – the subsequent sense of fidelity and blind faith reposed in their person by the masses will be far more unrepressed and unconditional than would be the case were the leader a mere political figure, no matter how respected or charismatic (e.g., a Hitler versus an Eisenhower or Kennedy). If such ethnonational leaders arise not just within a nation but within a true nation-state, they will be further aided in the quest for supreme power by having at their disposal the state's multi-faceted capacity for persuasion and coercion. Napoleon was the first major figure to grasp the significance of joining ethnonational and state-legitimacy. A Corsican of Genovese descent who fought for Corsican independence as a youth, Napoleon later realized that his personal ambitions could be better fulfilled by the harnessing of the masses' ethnonational zeal to an established state structure. This in turn required an overt transformation of his ethnic heritage, a deception accomplished by the simple expedient of frenchifying the spelling and pronunciation of his family name. He would justify his subsequent, highly autocratic tenure of office as follows: 'We have been guided at all times by this great truth: that the sovereignty resides in the French people in the sense that everything, everything without exception, must be done for its best interests, for its well being, and for its glory.'[48] And later imitators who would similarly countenance no resistance to their will, would nonetheless eschew titles such as emperor in lieu of the leader of the national group that is, *der Führer* or *il Duce*.

The authoritarian figure in an ethnically homogeneous state therefore has been able to exploit the coincidence of *the people* with *the nation*. But such states are exceptions. Authoritarian figures in the ethnically complex state, who wish to strengthen their legitimacy by paying lip-service to the masses as the font of legitimacy, will find it convenient to address their remarks to *the people* or *the citizenry*, while glossing over ethnic considerations. But this compulsion to pay lip-service to the masses as the repository from which all political legitimacy flows has become a nearly universal concomitant of modern authoritarianism, and, as a result, the notion of popular sovereignty (though not *popular* popular sovereignty) has nearly completed its global sweep. Rare indeed is the state leader who fails to pay formal homage to the people and their destiny as the source of his power and his *raison d'être*.[49] Systems claiming to be old-styled monarchies, sheikdoms, or empires are now in danger of extinction.[50] Recent events in Ethiopia represented a major milepost in the demise of such *ancien régimes*. Therein, Haile Selassie, purportedly the 225th successor to a hereditary title dating back 3,000 years to the Queen of Sheba, was overthrown. The military junta which engineered the coup against the world's oldest claim to legitimacy was certainly at least as authoritarian as had been the Emperor, but their right to take such action was justified by their self-depiction 'as representatives and guardians of the interests of the people.'[51]

Marxist-Leninist states were a part of this sweeping nominal victory of popular sovereignty. Though Marxists define the state in which they have come to power as 'the dictatorship of the proletariat', the proletariat is in its essence the people, minus a remnant of bourgeois, anti-state counterrevolutionaries. And after a sufficient lapse of time to permit such elements to wither or reform, *the proletariat* and *the people* should become synonymous. For all practical purpose, therefore, the Soviet Union's 1936 constitutional assertion that 'all power is vested in the working people' could be construed as an unequivocal commitment to popular sovereignty.[52] And Premier Khrushchev's reference to the 'state of all the people',[53] later incorporated into the 1977 constitution, did not represent a radical departure from Marxist-Leninist political thinking.[54]

By and large, then, state leaders have been preachers but not practitioners of popular sovereignty. But as Georges Sorel reminded us, myths have a way of providing their own reality.[55] In acknowledging and publicizing the principle that all legitimate power derives from *the people*, governments have been preparing the scene for that mental metamorphosis which changes *the people* into *my people*. And among minorities this substitution presages increased sentiment for national self-determination. It bears repeating that once it is popularly assumed that sovereignty resides in the people, then any people who conceive themselves as constituting a separate people is apt to view a right to create its own state as self-evident and therefore incontestable. As a result, even decidedly non-democratic governments, in paying lip-service to popular sovereignty, have helped to spawn that doctrine's national variety.[56]

This does not imply that each state must formally adopt the principle of popular sovereignty before it is apt to face internal challenges to its legitimacy predicated upon national aspirations. Just as the notion of popular sovereignty often became activated within an *ancien régime* as a response to foreign precedent, so too can its national variety. And as the number of such precedents has increased, the likelihood of one or several of them serving as catalysts has also increased. Any state is therefore vulnerable. But leaders who, regardless of their sincerity, repeatedly refer to *the people* in reverential terms as the source of legitimacy, thereby fertilize the local soil for the implanting of the idea of national self-determination.

Multinational states all along the democratic–authoritarian spectrum have therefore proven vulnerable to national movements. But do not such movements constitute a more natural foe of those multinational states tending toward the democratic pole of that spectrum? If a system is to remain *truly* (not just ostensibly) committed to the legitimizing principle of popular sovereignty, can it logically deny that doctrine's national variant? John Stuart Mill thought not:

> Where the sentiment of nationality exists in any force, there is a *prima facie* case for uniting all the members of the nationality under the same government, and a government to themselves apart. This is merely saying that the question of government ought to be decided by the governed. One hardly knows what any division of the human race would be free to do if not to determine with which of the various collective bodies of human beings they would choose to associate themselves.[57]

To Ernest Barker, who agreed with Mill, the result was predictable: unassimilated democratic states will tend to dissolve into as many democracies as there are nations within them.[58] Recent events within Canada and the democracies of Western Europe support such a prognostication. On the other hand, the significant fact may be that many old democracies, despite ethnically predicated fissures, have managed to hang together. How is one to account for their preservation throughout two-hundred years of the national epoch?

The matter may perhaps be best approached by considering all states, democratic and non-democratic alike. If national self-determination is such a generally compelling force, a natural inclination of people, why are there so few nation-states? How can one account for the poor record of self-determination to date? Elsewhere, this writer has attempted to analyze the reasons for the unenviable record of militant self-determination movements and suggested several reasons, the most important of which was the inherently negative view that governments take of such movements and the disproportionate advantages that governments have at their disposal in such a confrontation.[59] But while such explanations may aid in understanding the lack of success of active movements which clearly have enjoyed broadscale support throughout their respective nation, movements such as those among the Kurds and the Ibos, they do not explain why most nations have not exemplified a similar, grass roots devotion to national independence, regardless of the odds. And they certainly do not explain why people in a democratic society have not voted overwhelmingly for separatist parties. The survival of the multinational state as the principal form of polity, some two hundred years into the national era, raises the ultimate question concerning state legitimacy. Is legitimacy necessary for a state to survive in relative peace? Will people often passively accept the fact of existence within a state to which they do not extend a sense of legitimacy?

The non-essentiality of state legitimacy

The literature has assumed that legitimacy is necessary for a modern state to function.[60] Beginning with the observation that coercion, by itself, is counterproductive and therefore an insufficient foundation upon which to construct a durable, functioning system, authorities have considered a lack of extensive, overt coercion, when combined with a low level of visible resistance to the system, as evidence that the system enjoys legitimacy. As a syllogism, this reasoning would proceed as follows:

(1)   Coercion cannot constitute a sufficient foundation for the maintenance of a viable political system.
(2)   Political System X is (a) not characterized by coercion and (b) has been maintained over an extended period of time.
(3)   Therefore, Political System X must be viewed as legitimate by all major segments of the population.

This syllogism is defective, because a wealth of evidence indicates that systems (regimes, governments, and states) can enjoy a calm atmosphere in the absence of legitimacy.

Most multinational states are not characterized by an excessive level of discernible coercion. Yet, the foreign policies of states demonstrate a broadly held conviction among political leaders that national minorities within other states do not perceive the system under which they are ruled as legitimate. Foreign governments commonly perceive minorities as discontented Trojan horses. Lenin, for example, assigned the technique of appealing to the congenital discontent of national minorities a major role in ushering a communist party into power. And, indeed, the promise of self-determination, explicitly including the right of secession, made to their country's respective minorities played a vital role in the assumption of power by the communist parties of the Soviet Union, China, Yugoslavia, and Vietnam (that is to say, the four major parties which could claim to have come to power essentially on their own devices). Somewhat similarly, fascist Germany, Italy, and Japan also exploited the dissatisfaction of national minorities and succeeded with such peoples as the Bretons, Croatians, Flemings, Manchus, Mongols, Sardinians, and Slovaks. Today, appeals to one another's minorities are a major element in the relations among numerous sets of states including China and the Soviet Union, Libya and Chad, Bulgaria and Yugoslavia, Romania and Hungary, Angola and Zaire, Afghanistan and Pakistan, Cambodia and Vietnam, Ethiopia and Somalia, Czechoslovakia and Hungary, and Yugoslavia and Albania. The list could be multiplied. We have here, then, a time-tested stratagem of foreign policy, geared to the well-founded presumption that significant segments of a national minority do not perceive their current political status as legitimate.

What is particularly significant is that in many cases where a minority has in fact proven to be a Trojan horse, there has been no appreciable prewarning that the minority did not perceive its state as politically legitimate. The Ukrainians offered a striking example at the time of the Nazi invasion of the Soviet Union. That people's initial positive reception showered upon the invaders stunned Soviet leaders, who, given their reporting apparatus, would have been expected to be amongst the best informed of state-regimes.

In general, people can pursue their daily business, obey the laws, go to work, and the like, while living in a state to which they do not accord legitimacy. Consider, for example, the case of the Franco-Canadians whose general demeanor over the generations could be generally characterized as peaceful. But, during both World Wars, attempts to introduce compulsory military conscription precipitated large-scale draft riots and a stout resistance to fighting what Franco-Canadian leaders termed 'English wars.' Being, in their eyes, a non-legitimate political expression of the Québécois, the state of Canada could not elicit any real sacrifice in its name.

Or consider the following historical sketch of Northern Ireland, which illustrates that the Irish minority has never attached legitimacy to the Stormont government. And yet, until quite recently, this negative attitude toward the system did not take the form of violence.

> From the mid-1920s when the fighting over partition ended until the late 1960s when the conflict was renewed, Ulster was relatively peaceful, with 18 deaths traced to ethnic conflict. During this interlude, London was relatively indifferent to Northern Ireland's affairs, and Ulster's politics and government were dominated by the Ulster Unionist Party, representing the Protestant majority. Conservative in their politics and economics, the Unionists encountered little opposition from class-based parties like the Northern Ireland Labour party, a stable minority party. Catholics voted for parties dedicated to ending partition, and their elected leaders, rejecting the legitimacy of the Northern Ireland government, often boycotted their seats in the Ulster Parliament and refused to accept the title of loyal opposition when they did take their seats.[61]

.

Numerous other cases abound, as well, where minorities have undergone long periods of seeming acquiescence while withholding legitimacy from the state. The Spanish Basques, after exploiting the chaos of the 1930s to vote themselves independence, were almost immediately reunited by Franco in what superficially appeared to be a harmonious relationship with the Spanish state. Over the next forty years, the area became Spain's leading industrial and most prosperous region, free of overt manifestations of ethnonational dissatisfaction. The illusionary nature of this surface calm became increasingly apparent in the late 1960s, as priests and members of the militant, separatist organization, ETA, spearheaded an anti-Madrid movement. By 1978, more than two-thirds of all Basques demonstrated their lack of identification with the Spanish state by either abstaining or voting negatively with regard to a new democratic constitution that would accord the Basques far more autonomy than they had at any time other than their short-lived period of independence during the 1930s.[62]

The history of the Croats is similar. After docilely accepting union in a state dominated by Serbs at the end of World War I, the Croats subsequently found this relationship so intolerable that they accepted Hitler's offer of a puppet state, and took advantage of this period to wreak genocidal vengeance upon the Serbian community within Croatia. Following the war, an outwardly serene reunion with the Yugoslav state was interrupted in the 1970s by an outburst of anti-Belgrade nationalist fervor. Though the conventional prediction of the time was that this most recent demonstration of Croatian nationalism could only be quenched with political independence, the agitation was silenced by a purge of the leaders, and the streets of Zagreb became once more as peaceful and serene as those of Belgrade. But Croatian history warns against mistaking this most recent period of overt passivity as evidence that Yugoslavia has gained legitimacy in Croatian eyes.

The point, then, is that legitimacy cannot be inferred from a peaceful situation. There are several overlapping factors that may explain docility in the absence of a feeling that one's state is legitimate. The following is at best a rough outline of some of these factors:

(1) *Fear*: Granted that violent coercion cannot be used too frequently or too long or in too heavy doses, its periodic, small-scale application to 'examples' may prove a very effective means of persuading a population that overt resistance to an unpopular political system is not worth the entailed risk. How fear of reprisal can dampen a population's will has been eloquently captured by the former editor of a Czechoslovak journal:

> Where government stands for a long time, the citizen falls. Where does he fall? I will not try to please the non-Marxist enemy and say that he falls on the gallows. Only a few tens or hundreds of citizens do that. Our friends know that it is sufficient because it is followed by the fall of, perhaps, the whole nation into fear, into political indifference and resignation, into petty daily cares and little desires, into dependence on gradually tinier and tinier overlords, into a serfdom of a new and unusual type, impossible to explain to a visitor from abroad.[63]

Fears of physical coercion or incarceration fail to explain why people in a democratic society do not vote for nationalist parties. But fears can be wide-ranging, and the prospect of secession can raise fear of the unknown, the untraveled road. It can also raise fears, particularly among the elderly, of unemployment or of no governmental old-age assistance. It is probably not just coincidence that professional people, those with a sense of security and independence because of their training and vocation, have been disproportionately represented in separatist movements, and that, as one moves from the middle-aged to the post-middle-aged element, support for such movements sharply decreases.

(2) *Habit*: Aristotle was among the very earliest of philosophers to indicate the link between habit and political behavior. In emphasizing the consensual rather than the coercive side of law enforcement, he noted that 'the law has no power to command obedience except that of habit, which can only be given by time.'[64] Some two thousand years later, Max Weber, while substituting the word *custom* for *habit*, would substantively agree. Though noting that our knowledge as yet 'does not allow us to determine very clearly the point of transition from the stage of mere custom to the, at first vaguely and dimly experienced, "consensual" character of social action', Weber nonetheless insisted that habit is a principal reason why people obey the laws of the society in which they reside. Tradition, in the active form of habit, exerts an *oughtness* of its own. Most significantly, it is a force militating against change: 'The inner orientation toward such regularities contains in itself very tangible inhibitions against "innovations."'[65] Particularly when combined with fear of the unknown, the comfortableness of that with which one is familiar would explain a timidity concerning such an all-encompassing 'innovation' as a new state.[66]

(3) *Apathy and/or Inertia*: Apathy can, of course, be further broken down into a number of explanations ranging from a psychological state of mind such as fatalism ('If Allah wills . . . ') to the prevalence of energy-sapping parasites. In any case, it is one thing to grumble about the illegitimacy of rule by the Castilians, Han Chinese, or French, and something else to become actively engaged in terminating that rule. Even powerful mass movements may be divided into activists and sympathizers. Thus, the number of people actually willing to serve as guerrillas in a national war of liberation may be meager, while the number who demonstrate their agreement with the guerrillas concerning the illegitimacy of the political system by the passive act of refusing to give information on the guerrillas' whereabouts, despite governmental threats and offers of rewards, is necessarily impressive, or the guerrillas could not survive. But again, such a conviction concerning political legitimacy is for many not sufficient to motivate positive activity.

(4) *Apoliticalness*: If economists tend to place too much emphasis upon economic motivation, political scientists are prone to exaggerate the degree to which the typical person is emotionally involved in political matters. So-called highly authoritarian states often offer bewildering experiences to the visitor, who finds people pursuing their life-ways with apparent good cheer and outwardness. Such people have learned to accommodate themselves comfortably within limits prescribed by the authorities. The injunction not to speak or act in any way that

could be construed as 'antistate activity' does not weigh heavily on some shoulders. What the earlier cited Czech dissenter termed the 'petty daily cares and little desires' can be preoccupying. In democracies, the lack of interest in political matters is illustrated by low participation in elections, and by surveys indicating extremely meager knowledge of political issues and public figures. Even if they are convinced that alien rule is illegitimate, therefore, the issue may not generate enough enthusiasm by the apolitical segment of a minority to motivate it to join the national movement's ranks.

(5) *Political and Cultural Isolation*: The intensity of the urge to cast off a foreign yoke is influenced by the degree to which the yoke is felt. For the notion that alien rule is illegitimate rule to trigger action, it is necessary that the alien rule be perceived. Multinational, non-integrated states (such as pre-World War II Ethiopia, Iran, and Thailand) were able to survive for generations without ethnonationally inspired separatist movements because political and social control by the centre was a fiction. In effect, such units were comprised of a series of ethnocracies, as each group (or subgroup) ruled itself. But as communications and transportation networks made the presence of (a) the central government and (b) the dominant ethnic group felt in the periphery, ethnonational discord rose precipitously. So too, Basque, Breton, and Scottish nationalist movements gained strength as improved communication- and transportation-networks made the central government an increasingly pervasive force, and also led to an increase in the quality and quantity of contacts between the dominant group and the national minorities. A particular irritant to minority sensibilities (and, therefore, a catalyst for separatist sentiment) proved to be the increased presence of non-members of the minority within the homeland. In general, separatism has risen with in-migration. However, perception of the alien presence will vary among individuals. With a larger homeland, such as Quebec (or Scotland), some, because of their occupation, neighborhood, and/or reading and listening interests, will necessarily be more sensitized to the alien yoke than others. To these others, Ottawa and the Anglophones (or London and the English) will be too remote to their experience to ignite the fires of separatism.

(6) *Disorganization*: A resistance movement requires poles or foci about which to form and develop. A state which can atomize its population decreases the likelihood of effective antistate activity. Some states, through secret informers and infiltrators of social organizations (unions, churches, organized sports, and even the family) have proven adroit at isolating the individual. A leading Chinese composer and musician rendered this account concerning controls in the People's Republic during the Cultural Revolution:

> I was cautious about discussing such matters. Everybody and anybody could be attacked. I know many others felt as I did . . . but it was increasingly dangerous to admit it. There were party members who kept their membership secret. Even within one's own family it was necessary to be circumspect. I trusted my wife and children, but I knew individuals whose children reported on them; Youth League members were required to do this. It happened to the father of one of my daughter's schoolmates. Therefore, in some families,

especially if the children were 'progressive' and were trying to 'draw a line' (as the expression goes) between their parents and themselves, the adults stopped talking or changed the subject whenever the children entered. It was not uncommon for families to eat meals in silence for weeks at a time.[67]

In such societies, the odds of mounting a challenge to the state are slight indeed. But even in a democracy, a peaceful national movement may encounter problems. For example, the incarceration and expulsion of Breton leaders for purported collaboration with the Nazi occupiers impeded the Breton national movement for some years after the war. The state's control of the communications media may also inhibit a movement's ability to present its side of the issue. In early 1977, Canadian political leaders accused a number of CBC announcers on the French network of favoring the *Parti Québécois*. Apparently the former did not believe that secession merited 'equal time.'

A mélange of fear, habit, inertia, apoliticalness, political and cultural isolation, disorganization, and other overlooked factors may therefore help to account for a people's passive willingness to abide within a political system to which they do not ascribe legitimacy. And, from the perspective of the state apparatus, perhaps passivity is enough. Thus, for decades the British pursued a policy of buying the passivity but not the allegiance of the Pushtun tribes within northwestern British India, and Pakistan has continued the policy. Authorities in the Federal Republic of Germany, Switzerland, and other Western European states have wanted no more than passivity from their large guestworker communities; policies have been pursued that purposefully dissuade the guestworkers from developing an emotional attachment to the state. Only passivity, not legitimacy, is essential to the everyday, humdrum functioning of a society. But if the state requires more than passivity, if it hopes to invoke the symbols of the state as a means of gaining positive cooperation and sacrifice, legitimacy will be sorely missed. Simply because one person will not raise a hand against another does not mean that he would raise a hand to aid him.

By way of summary

Three major themes emerge from this discussion of nationalism:

(1) It is necessary to distinguish three levels of legitimacy: regime-, government-, and state-. The relationship of state-legitimacy to the other two classifications is that of the whole to its parts. To deny legitimacy to a regime is not necessarily to deny it to the government nor to the state. To deny legitimacy to a government is to deny it to the regime currently in power, but not necessarily to the state. To deny legitimacy to a state is to deny it to its government and to its present incumbents as well.

(2) National self-determination, as a variant of popular sovereignty and its most infectious form, represents an assertive theory of state-legitimacy.

(3) Legitimacy is not needed for a state to function, which helps to account for the durability of the multinational state well into the national era. However, as

attested by the rapid growth in the number of challenges launched against multinational states by nationally inspired forces, the revolutionary potential of the notion that alien rule is illegitimate rule is far from spent.

Notes

1 *Nationalism: A Report by a Study Group of Members of the Royal Institute of International Affairs* (1939: xvi–xx).
2 For additional comments on the imprecision surrounding *nation, state, nation-state,* and *nationalism,* see Walker Connor (1978: 376–400).
3 George Theodorson and Achilles Theodorson (1969: 135).
4 Max Weber, *Economy and Society* I (1968: 389).
5 Weber (1968: 395).
6 Shibutani and Kwan (1965: 47).
7 Deutsch (1969: 3).
8 For numerous illustrations of people at various levels of emerging awareness, particularly within southwest Asia, see Connor (1976: 9–25).
9 Popularization of the 'principle of nationalities' was assured when Napoleon III publicly embraced it as an official aspect of his foreign policy. See, for example, Redslob (1930), particularly pp. 28 *et seq.* See also Johannet (1923), particularly chapter 9, 'Le principe des nationalités au pouvoir.' It is generally believed that Marx and/or Engels coined the expression 'national self-determination'. For details, see Connor (forthcoming). However, popularity of the expression awaited its embrace by Woodrow Wilson during World War I.
10 After justifying its annexation of West Irian by conducting a questionable testing of popular sentiment in that region in 1969, the Indonesian government did not go even that far in justifying its annexation of Eastern Timor during 1976. Rather, having assured this new annexation by sending units of 'volunteers' from the Indonesian army, it justified this military intrusion as a means of guaranteeing 'the proper, orderly and peaceful exercise of the right of self-determination of the Portuguese Timor people.' See *Keesing's Contemporary Archives,* p. 27535.
11 A classical illustration is offered by the Pakistani authorities who, throughout the secessionist struggle in East Pakistan during 1971, regularly referred to the Bengali guerrillas as a few 'miscreants' or 'Indian agents'. See, for example, *Keesing's Contemporary Archives,* p. 24989.
12 Admittedly, the constitutions of many multinational states do implicitly deny the right of secession by references to an enduring union of peoples, by references to the entire territory as inalienable or inseparable, and by proscribing treason or other anti-state activities. But none explicitly deny the right of national self-determination. Indeed, some constitutions (for example, those of Czechoslovakia and Yugoslavia) contain references both to the right of national self-determination and to the unquestionable, permanent nature of the present political structure.
13 The early response of the Canadian federal government to the victory of the separatist-minded Parti Québécois in the provincial election of 1976 offers an interesting case study. Though explicitly neither denying nor admitting the right of Québécers to secede, the Canadian Prime Minister insisted that 'Québéc does not believe in separatism.' (Television address, 24 November 1976.) Federal government spokesmen suggested that, even if an affirmative referendum on secession were held in Québéc, it would require federal endorsement and United Kingdom approval. All such statements constitute an *implicit* rejection of the primacy of the self-determination principle.
14 John Wahlke, 'The Language and Methods of Political Science', in Wahlke and Dragnich (eds) (1966).

15 The surprising lack of academic effort engendered by political legitimacy is evidenced by the absence of any such entry in the *Encyclopedia of the Social Sciences* (1933), which was an attempt to set forth, *inter alia*, all of the important topics of social science research. The updated version of this attempt (*The International Encyclopedia of the Social Sciences* 1968), contains only an abbreviated discussion of the issue, and its sparse bibliography further attests to the paucity of literature. The bibliography contains not a single book written in English, with the word legitimacy in its title. The only two titles referring specifically to legitimacy are both in German, were published in 1866 and 1932 respectively, and were each addressed to a narrow application of the concept. The clear implication is that no contemporary scholarship on the topic exists.

16 To the reader who wishes to confirm this statement by consulting tables of contents and subject indices of the leading analysts of political philosophy, pertinent entries may include *authority* (often used in contradistinction to naked coercion), *consent*, *legitimacy*, *dynastic legitimacy*, *political legitimacy*, *obligation*, and *political obligation*. One explanation for the failure of contemporary theorists to address the matter of legitimacy is suggested by Anthony de Crespigny (in de Crespigny and Alan Wertheimer (1972: 7). He notes that political theory has come under attack from modern political scientists who maintain the 'spuriousness' of such 'central questions of classical political philosophy'as 'Why ought a subject obey his ruler?' or 'Why should I support *any* government?' The critics of classical political theory contend that such questions are too 'general to be answerable'.

17 One can consult without success Plano and Greenberg (1967); Plano and Olton (1969); Elliott and Summerskill (1966); Laqueur (ed.) (1973); A. M. Hymason (1974); Hermanson (1967); and Cranston and Lakoff (n.d.).

18 Those consulted included James Baldwin (ed.) (1957), 3 vols; Burger and Baker (1974); and Grooter and Seenberger (1967), 8 vols, which carried thirty-one sub-entries under *Political Philosophy, Nature of*, including such legitimacy-related items as *contract theory, sovereignty, state*, and *nationalism*.

19 An entry under legitimacy was found in *Encyclopedia of Sociology* (1974); in Hoult (1969); and in Gould and Kolb (1964). A pertinent entry under authority was found in Theodorson and Theodorson (1969). Pertinent entries were not located in John Zodrozny (1959); in Mitchell (1968): nor in Fairchild (1944).

20 Max Weber (1968), 3 vols. See particularly the sections entitled 'Legitimate Order', 'Types of Legitimate Order: Convention and Law', and 'Bases of Legitimacy: Tradition, Faith, Enactment', 1, 31–38.

21 Such a possibility is lent credence by the fact that many of the professional dictionaries and encyclopedias, though not deigning to define the expression, make use of it when explaining related phenomena. For example, Zodrozny (1959) defined *popular sovereignty* as 'the idea that the people who are governed are the only legitimate source of political power and authority'. Theodorson (1969) defines *authority* as 'power that is *legitimized* and institutionalized in a society or other social system'. *The Encyclopedia of Philosophy* notes that one view of nationalism holds 'that states are *legitimate* only if constituted in accordance with this principle'. We have also noted that scholars (including Weber) employ the term without feeling compelled to define it.

22 For example, although post-Salazar Portugal became the scene of bitter and often violent struggle between factions representing nearly every shade of political opinion from radical left to radical right, and although the struggle concerned not just who should rule but also the ideology and form of government to be introduced, the right of the state of Portugal to exist was not challenged by any of the forces operating within continental Portugal. In light of the following discussion, it is worth observing that Portugal is one of the world's few ethnically homogeneous states. By contrast with Portugal, the militant movements in Iran during 1978–79, that culminated in the downfall of the Pahlavi dynasty, represented a challenge to governmental legitimacy so far as Persian participants were concerned (regardless of whether the Persians were Islamic rightists

or radical leftists), but a challenge to state-legitimacy by Arab, Azerbaidzhani, Baluchi, Kurdish, and Turkmen militants.

23 The schematic is also unconcerned with the degree of violence involved in the political activity. Palace revolutions, coups d'état, political revolutions, and secessionist movements have all been known to be conducted by peaceful means.

24 Four of the more deservedly influential treatises on legitimacy have been those by Max Weber, David Easton, Leslie Lipson, and Seymour Lipset. Though Weber raised the important state-legitimacy issue of communal (*Vergemeinschaftung*) versus associative (*Vergesellschaftung*) relationships (Weber 1968: 40–43), as well as offering an insightful section on ethnic groups and nations (pp. 385–398), he does not link these discussions to his extended discourse on regime- and governmental-legitimacy. Thus, though he differentiates among what he terms charismatic, traditional, and legal legitimacy, all of these clearly pertain to regimes and governments, but not to states. Though Easton's notion of authority (by which he means legitimacy) is potentially applicable to state-legitimacy, his total discussion makes evident that he also has regime- and governmental-legitimacy in mind. See Easton (1971), particularly pp. 129 et seq. Similar comments pertain to Leslie Lipson's notion of authority. See Lipson (1970): 75 *et seq.* Similarly, although Lipset's definition of legitimacy as 'the capacity of the system to engender and maintain the belief that the existing political institutions are the most appropriate ones for the society' could quite evidently pertain to the notion of state-legitimacy, his subsequent discourse reveals that he was thinking solely of regime- and/or governmental-legitimacy. See Lipset (1960), particularly Chapter 3. Robert Dahl's treatment of political legitimacy is also confined to regime- or, at best, governmental-legitimacy. See Dahl (1976), particular pp. 61 *et seq.*

25 Machiavelli's final chapter of *The Prince*, written in 1513, might be viewed as a harbinger of the notion of national self-determination. There are, however, several elements which caution against too affirmative a judgment: (1) the chapter's theme of national liberation does not accord with the previous twenty-five chapters; (2) the case for the liberation of Italy is made more upon oppression and misrule by foreigners than upon a positive right of self-determination, and it therefore harmonizes with the medieval notion of the right to overthrow a tyrannical government (a right devoid of national considerations); (3) Italy then was even more truly 'only a geographic expression' than it would be three hundred years later, when so described by Metternich. With regard to the last point, it is questionable even today whether the sense of a single Italian national consciousness permeates the population of Italy. For further discussion, see this writer's 'The Political Significance of Ethnonationalism within Western Europe', in Connor (1976), particularly pp. 126 *et seq.* In any event, Machiavelli's comments on Italian liberation constituted at most an early suggestion of the idea of national self-determination rather than a developed discourse. As such, it held no discernible significance for the subsequent growth of the national idea, despite the great impact that other facets of *The Prince* have exerted upon political thought and practice. In the decades immediately prior to the French Revolution, Johann von Herder wrote extensively concerning the importance of the nation. However, his ruminations were restricted to the cultural sphere, and he did not anticipate any need for nation-states.

26 Here, the term state means the primary political unit of its day, a unit which has, of course, undergone significant alterations over the ages. To the Greek philosophers the unit was the *polis*; to Roman philosophers, the empire; and to modern writers, the *state*.

27 *The Nicomachean Ethics*, transl. J. A. K. Thomson (1955: 44). Though the *raison d'être* assigned by Aristotle to the *polis* was unrelated to the ethnic composition of its citizenry, he was not without ethnocentric impulses, nor unaware of possible problems arising from ethnic heterogeneity. In Book VII of his *Politics*, he boasted about the virtues of 'the Hellenic race', and opined that 'if it could be formed into one state, it would be able to rule the world'. In Book V of the same work, he noted that the presence of unassimilated peoples within a single polity tends to produce revolution. See *Politics* (1943: 216 and 291).

28　For an intellectual debate concerning whether Georg Hegel should be included on this list, see Walter Kaufmann (1970). The debate is put into particularly sharp focus by the contributions of Sidney Hook and Shlomo Avinieri.

29　Merriam (1900: 12). The inner quotation is by the German scholar, Otto Gierke.

30　de Maistre 'Considerations on France', in *The Works of Joseph de Maistre* (n.d.: 80).

31　Richard Andrews, in a review of Michael Walzer, *Regicide and Revolution: Speeches at the Trial of Louis XVI*, in *The New York Times Book Review*, 9 June 1974.

32　The notion of *l'état c'est moi* points up a major reason why earlier theories of state legitimacy were indistinguishable from theories of regime- and government-legitimacy, and are, as a result, of little relevance to the issue of state-legitimacy in the era of popular sovereignty. When the state is identified with a single person (a monarch or a traditional, pre-Napoleonic emperor) or with a royal élite (an aristocracy), regime-, government-, and state-legitimacy blur into a single whole. But with sovereignty vested in the people, state-legitimacy stands aloof.

33　See 'Qu'est-ce qu'une Nation?'. In Renan (1887: 276–310).

34　Renan ostensibly discoursed on his notion of *the nation*, not *the state*. But, in fact, his speech, which aimed at convincing German-speaking Alsatians to remain loyal to France, was a defense of the legitimacy of the multinational state.

35　Geographic distance, as used here, refers to communications-distance and psychological distance. Such concepts of distance are influenced by the level of communications technology, and are not to be equated with physical distance. For further discussion of types of distance, see Connor 'Myths of Hemispheric, Continental, Regional and State Unity', *Political Science Quarterly*, 84 (1969: 555–582).

36　But contrast the emotional content of the public utterances voiced in the name of a nationalist movement with the more reasoned arguments of a regional movement. While both customarily utilize such rational devices as the economic advantages which will accompany secession, the former will add such emotion-laden expressions as 'preservation of our chasteness from perverting, outside influences', 'the need to be masters in our own house' (or 'of the nation's destiny'), and the like.

37　Canada is only partly an immigrant society, being partly a multinational state. It faced both regional secession and, in the case of the Québécois, ethnonational secession. The problem confronting Ottawa in establishing its identity vis-à-vis the *popular* popular sovereignty of the Québécois has been nicely captured by Alan Cairns (1979: 23): 'The capacity of the federal government to maintain its legitimacy was weakened by the relatively underdeveloped sense of Canadian patriotism in the country as a whole. In conflict with a strong sense of nationality based on a living historically based primordial sense of nationalism, the potential of the centre rests on the inherently weaker sense of civic identity and the abstract conception of citizenship on which it can base its legitimacy.'

38　As to the three exceptions: one (Portugal) had accidentally entered the post-Napoleonic era as an ethnically homogeneous state, and the other two (Spain and Switzerland) had not been immune to ethnonational stirrings during the period.

39　Its growing impact was apparent, however, even before World War I, among the Japanese, Chinese, Armenians, and Levantine Arabs.

40　Otherwise, the same demands would not have surfaced both in the Rhodesias (ruled as overseas colonies) and in the Republic of South Africa (ruled from within).

41　For details, see Connor 'Self-Determination: The New Phase', *World Politics*, 20 (1967: 30–35); 'Nation-Building or Nation-Destroying', *World Politics*, 24 (1972: 319–355).

42　A list of troubled states as of 1972 may be found in Connor 'The Politics of Ethnonationalism', *Journal of International Affairs*, 27 (No. 1 1973: 21).

43　For a tracing of this historical unraveling, see *ibid*, 5–11.

44　At the end of World War I, for example, many Slovak leaders believed themselves to be Czechs, and the 1918 Constitution of the newly 'self-determined' state declared the existence of a single 'Czechoslovak nation.' Similarly, doubts arose concerning the national identity of the Serbs, Croats, and Slovenes. The official position of the new Yugoslav state was that they were merely tribal segments of a single Yugoslav nation. Needless to say, national consciousness has subsequently definitely emerged among all four of these peoples.

45 For a detailed discussion of a number of such catalysts and soporifics, with particular regard to the experience of Western Europe, Connor 'Ethnonationalism in the First World: The Present in Historical Perspective', in Milton Esman (ed.) *Ethnic Pluralism and Conflict in the Western World* (Ithaca: 1977): 19–45.

46 The very slow pace of the emergence of the Byelorussians is a case in point. Poles, Germans, and Russians have taken turns over the decades at decimating their leaders. For details, see Lubachko (1972). Despite the title, this history goes well back beyond 1917.

47 A desire for a period of quiet and a general coolness toward nationalism may be detected immediately after the Napoleonic Wars and the struggles of 1848. The most striking case, however, is that of Europe in the post-World War II period following the defeat of a fanatical movement whose major impulse was German ethnonationalism.

48 *Message to the Senate (1804)*, reprinted in Herold (1955: 72).

49 A rule-proving exception to this trend occurred in 1976, when the former Central African Republic was declared to be the Central African Empire by its leader who changed his title of 'President-for-life' to 'Emperor Bokassa I'. However, some lip-service to popular sovereignty was maintained when the new state was described as a constitutional monarchy. Bokassa was overthrown and the Republic restored in 1979. See *Keesing's Contemporary Archives*, p. 28172.

50 The overthrow of the Shah of Iran in 1979 was another milepost in this process. The remaining exceptions are Nepal and a number of dynastic houses within the Arab world. The latters' claims to legitimacy rest in part on purported descent from the Prophet.

51 *Declaration of the Armed Forces Committee*, July 18,1974. See *Keesing's Contemporary Archives*, p. 26733.

52 Article 3 of the Soviet Constitution of 1936. The fact that this constitution is popularly referred to as 'the Stalin Constitution' underlines the immense discrepancy between form and substance.

53 See Brinkley (1973: 387–401).

54 However, this did not prevent the leadership of the Chinese Communist Party, searching for issues in their polemics with Moscow, from criticizing Khrushchev's terminology on narrow, doctrinaire, though technically correct grounds:

> In the view of Marxists–Leninists, there is no such thing as a non-class or supra-class state. So long as the state remains a state, it must bear a class character: so long as the state exists, it cannot be a state of the 'whole people'. As soon as society becomes classless, there will no longer be a state. Then what sort of thing would a 'state of the whole people' be? Anyone with an elementary knowledge of Marxism–Leninism can understand that the so-called state of the whole people is nothing new. Representative bourgeois figures have always called the bourgeois state a 'state of all the people', or a 'state in which power belongs to all the people.' Certain persons may say that their society is already one without classes. We answer: No, there are classes and class struggles in all Socialist countries without exception.
>
> (*Open Letter of the Central Committee of the Chinese Communist Party July 1963*, reprinted in Henry Christman (ed.), *Communism in Action: A Documentary History* (New York, 1969): 260–261.

55 'Experience shows that the *framing of a future, in some indeterminate time*, may when it is done in a certain way, be very effective, and have very few inconveniences: this happens when the anticipations of the future take the form of those myths which enclose within them all the strongest inclinations of a people. . .' Sorel (1950: 134).

56 Some of the more tangible forms that this lip-service takes include one-party or other-wise farcical elections; office titles borrowed from democracies, such as *president* or *premier*; and extremely democratic-sounding constitutions.

57 *Considerations on Representative Government*, originally published in 1861. The citation may be found in the 1973 edition by Henry Holt and Company, p. 310.

58 Barker (1927: 17).

59 'The Politics of Ethnonationalism', *op. cit.*, particularly Part IV: 11–18.

60 See, for example, Dahl (1976: 61). A few authorities have cogently noted that, in pre-modern societies, the matter of legitimacy among remote segments of the populace may not arise, because the state is not a pervasive reality in their lives. In extreme cases, ostensible subjects of a state may be unaware of the existence of the state to which mapmakers have assigned them.

61 Terchek (1977: 49).

62 *The New York Times*, 8 December 1978. Slightly more than 70 percent of the electorate in the Basque provinces either abstained (as requested by the Basque Nationalist Party), or voted negatively. Given the large number of non-Basques who, in recent decades, have immigrated to this region in search of employment, it may be safely assumed that the percentage of abstentions and no votes among the Basques was substantially higher than the 70 percent figure.

63 The speaker was Ludvik Vaculik. His speech is excerpted in Steiner (1973: 147). Parenthetical material has been added. Though Vaculik refers specifically to govern-mental legitimacy, his comments would be equally applicable to state-legitimacy.

64 Aristotle *Politics* (11: 107).

65 Weber I (1968: 319–321). Dahl (1976: 44–50) uses the phrase 'trained control' in refer-ring to habit. Rose (1978: 29) has noted: 'Ordinary people do not require a rationale for political allegiance: what Bagehot called the "cake of custom" can suffice.'

66 *Comfortableness* need not imply contentedness. *The familiar*, as contrasted with the new, may simply be judged the lesser gamble.

67 'Interview with Ma Sitson', *Life* (4 July 1967).

References

Andrews, Richard 1974. 'Review of Michael Walzer, *Regicide and Revolution. Speeches at the Trial of Louis XVI*'. In *The New York Times Book Review*. 9 June.

Baldwin, James (ed.) 1957. *Dictionary of Philosophy and Psychology*. Gloucester. 3 vols.

Barker, E. 1927. *National Character and the Factors in its Formation*. London.

Brinkley, George 1973. 'Khruschev Remembered: On the Theory of Soviet Statehood'. *Soviet Studies*. 24 (January): 387–401.

Burger, Walter and Baker, Kenneth 1974. *Philosophical Dictionary*. Spokane.

Cairns, Alan 1979. 'French–English Conflict in Canada: The Ambiguous Role of Institutions'. Working paper prepared for the IPSA Round Table on Politics and Ethnicity. St Antony's College, Oxford, 26–28 March.

Connor, Walker 1967. 'Self-Determination: The New Phase'. *World Politics*. 20 (October).

—— 1969. 'Myths of Hemispheric, Continental, Regional, and State Unity'. *Political Science Quarterly*. 84 (December).

—— 1973. 'The Politics of Nationalism'. *Journal of International Affairs*. 27 (No. 1).

—— 1976. *Ethnicity in an International Context*. New Brunswick, NJ.

—— 1976. 'An Overview of the Ethnic Composition and Problems of Non-Arab Asia'. *Journal of Asian Affairs*. (Spring).

—— 1977. *Ethnic Conflict in the Western World*. Ithaca.

Cranston, Maurice and Lakoff, Sanford. *A Glossary of Political Ideas*. New York, n.d.

Dahl, Robert 1976. *Modern Political Analysis*. Englewood Cliffs, NJ.

de Crespigny, A. and Wertheimer, Alan 1972. *Political Theory*. Chicago.

d'Entreves, Alexander 1967. *The Notion of the State*. Oxford.

de Maistre, Joseph. 'Considerations on France'. In *The Works of Joseph de Maistre*. New York, n.d.

Deutsch, Karl 1969. *Nationalism and Its Alternatives*. New York.

Easton, David 1971. *The Political System: An Inquiry into the State of Political Science*. 2nd edn. New York.

Elliott, Florence and Summerskill, Michael 1966. *A Dictionary of Politics*. 5th edn. Baltimore.

Encyclopedia of the Social Sciences 1933. New York.

Encyclopedia of Sociology 1974. Guilford, CT.

Fairchild, Henry 1944. *Dictionary of Sociology*. Westport.

Gould, Julius and Kolb, William 1964. *A Dictionary of the Social Sciences*. New York.

Grooter, J. and Seenberger, G.J. 1967. *New Encyclopedia of Philosophy*. New York. 8 vols.

Hermanson, Rudolph 1967. *Dictionary of Political Science and Law*. Dobbs Ferry.

Hoult, Thomas 1969. *Dictionary of Modern Sociology*. Totown, NJ.

Hymason, A.M. 1974. *A Dictionary of International Affairs*. Washington, DC.

The International Encyclopedia of the Social Sciences 1968. New York.

Johannet, René 1923. *Le principe des nationalités*. Paris: Nouvelle Edition.

Kaufmann, Walter (ed.) 1970. *Hegel's Political Philosophy*. New York.

Laqueur, Walter (ed.) 1973. *A Dictionary of Politics*. rev. edn. New York.

Lipset, Seymour 1960. *Political Man: The Social Bases of Politics*. Garden City.

Lipson, Leslie 1970. *The Great Issues of Politics*. Englewood Cliffs, NJ.

Lubachko, Ivan 1972. *Belorussia under Soviet Rule, 1917–1957*. Lexington, KY.

Merriam, C.E. 1900. *History of the Theory of Sovereignty since Rousseau*. New York.

Mill, J.S. 1861. *Considerations on Representative Government*. 1973 edn. Henry Holt and Company.

Mitchell, G. Duncan 1968. *A Dictionary of Sociology*. Chicago.

Napoleon 1804. *Message to the Senate*, reprinted in *The Mind of Napoleon: A Selection from his Writings and Spoken Words*, ed. and trans. J. Christopher Herold. New York, 1955: 72.

Open Letter of the Central Committee of the Chinese Communist Party July 1963, reprinted in Henry Christman (ed.) 1969. *Communism in Action: A Documentary History*. New York: 260–261.

Plano, Jack and Greenberg, Milton 1967. *The American Political Dictionary*. 2nd edn. New York.

—— and Olton, Roy 1969. *The International Relations Dictionary*. New York.

Plato 1943. *Politics*. New York.

—— 1955. *The Nicomachean Ethics*. transl. J.A.K. Thomson. Baltimore.

Redslob, Robert 1930. *Le principe des nationalités*. Paris.

Renan, Ernest 1887. 'Qu'est-ce qu'une Nation?' In E. Renan *Discours et Conferences*. Paris: 277–310.

Rose, Richard 1978. *From Steady State to Fluid State: The Unity of the United Kingdom Today*. University of Strathclyde Studies in Public Policy: 26. Glasgow.

Shibutani, T. and Kwan, Kian 1965. *Ethnic Stratification: A Comparative Approach*. New York.

Sorel, Georges 1950. *Reflections on Violence*. New York.

Steiner, Eugen 1973. *The Slovak Dilemma*. Cambridge.

Terchek, Ronald 1977. 'Conflict and Cleavage in Northern Ireland'. *The Annals of the American Academy*. 443 (September): 49.

Theodorson, George and Theodorson, Achilles 1969. *A Modern Dictionary of Sociology*. New York.

Wahlke, John 1966. 'The Language and Methods of Political Science'. In John Wahlke and Alex Dragnich (eds) *Government and Politics*. New York.

Weber, Max 1968. *Economy and Society*. New York. 3 vols.

Zodrozny, John 1959. *Dictionary of Social Science*. Washington, DC.

Part I

Modernity and emotions

3   Dating the nation

Anthony D. Smith

To what period, if any, should we properly assign the origins and reproduction of nations? This is the subject of one of the most searching debates in the study of ethnicity and nationalism. The importance of this question is twofold. In the first place, the answer is likely to determine whether nations are phenomena specific to a particular historical period; and in the second place, it will reveal how deeply embedded nations are and to what extent they are likely to persist or give way to new kinds of human association. In the current debates about 'post-modernity', 'globalisation' and 'cultural imperialism', the problem of 'dating the nation' becomes a matter of fundamental significance.

Modernism and 'nation-building'

There was a time when such issues hardly troubled scholars. It was generally assumed that most nations were 'old', that is to say, they could be traced back to antiquity or the early Middle Ages, and that the modern epoch was witnessing their renewal after centuries of passivity and invisibility. This is a perspective which we can term 'continuous perennialism'. In this view, the nation is perennial and immemorial, in the sense that its modern expressions and manifestations are continuous with its early forms and expressions some centuries ago. Thus, it was held that, despite considerable changes, the modern Greeks and Egyptians could trace their origins *as nations* back to classical Greece and ancient Egypt; even though both countries had over the centuries suffered invasions, migrations and large-scale cultural transformations, their national identities were largely intact, and recognisably so.[1] This perspective was, of course, heavily influenced by an organic nationalism which posited the 'rebirth' of nations after centuries of somnolence, amnesia and silent invisibility.

Somehow, despite the forgetfulness of their members, the nation persisted in its state of 'slumber', to use Gellner's term, and like the Sleeping Beauty was at length awoken by the kiss of so many nationalist Prince Charmings. Nationalist imagery of renewal, reawakening and regeneration, soon found its way into the sober accounts of many pre-War historians, and helped to organise the historical discipline itself, as well as world history, along preordained national lines (Pearson 1993).

All this changed after 1945. The horrors of the Second World War, the evils wrought by racism and anti-Semitism, and the ways in which the dictators had used, and perverted, nationalism for their own ends, helped to undermine the hold of the accepted 'perennialist' paradigm of nations and nationalism. Moreover, the ongoing process of decolonisation in Asia and Africa turned the attention of scholars to the mass-mobilising, active and creative processes in the formation of nations, which came to be known as 'nation-building'. But, if it was possible to create nations 'under our very eyes', then perhaps even the nations of Europe, whose antiquity had for so long been assumed, were not really as old and venerable as had been supposed. Perhaps, after all, every nation was socially 'constructed', and should therefore be understood as a modern cultural artefact of relatively recent provenance? (see Hobsbawm and Ranger 1983).

Today, such 'modernism' is the dominant orthodoxy in the field. For the modernists, the nation, as well as nationalism, is both recent and novel. Theirs is a sociological, as well as a chronological, modernism. The nation is an innovation, a creation of the modern epoch, a response to, as well as a product of the equally novel historical processes of 'modernisation' – capitalism and industrialism, rapid urbanisation, the bureaucratic state, mass democracy, public education and secularisation. From the eighteenth century onwards, these processes came to dominate the life of Western societies, mobilising the middle classes and inspiring an activist and participant ethos of 'nation-building' and a desire to seize control of the state in the name of the nation. It therefore comes as no surprise that the first mass nations and nationalist ideologies and movements appeared at the end of that century.[2] To which the critics of modernism retort: it comes as no surprise, because the nation has been defined in modernist terms, as a 'mass' nation and as a modern social 'creation'.

The argument is circular. It presumes the modernity of a phenomenon which it then declares to be the product of modernisation, and hence to fit the modernist thesis of its modernity, both temporally and sociologically. But, suppose that we define the concept of the nation in terms of sentiments and ideas unrelated to any concept of modernity or to any particular historical period or process. The thesis that nations are modern and the product of 'modernisation' would then have to be established independently of its modernist definition, and especially of its presumed 'mass' and 'created' nature. If, for example, we defined the nation as a named group of human beings who occupy an historic territory and share common myths, memories and culture, and we could demonstrate that such groups could only be found in the 'modern world', only then could the modernist thesis be upheld.[3]

The difficulty, of course, with this procedure is that, to date, no such neutral definition has secured wide scholarly agreement, and that even if it could, it would hardly lend itself to modernist ends. It would be unlikely to support the thesis that nations were temporally and sociologically modern, and were the product of nationalist 'nation-building'. A wider, more neutral type of definition would most probably suggest that nations were to be found in all historical epochs, forming in response to a variety of social processes, and hence that the concept of the nation was neither historically recent nor sociologically novel.

Ethnonationalism

One of the first, and most acute, critics to point to this weakness at the heart of modernism was Walker Connor. In a series of seminal and penetrating articles, he addressed the major problems that had vexed scholars in this baffling field with compelling logic and vigour. In particular, Connor focussed on the then fashionable, but problematic ideas of 'nation-building' and cultural assimilation, as these had been developed by Karl Deutsch and the communications theorists. Deutsch had argued that the growth of nations could be charted through the clustering in given populations of various socio-demographic factors such as social and geographical mobility, trade, education, mass media and voting patterns. And he went on to claim that the processes of social mobilisation and mass communications tended to absorb different linguistic groups into co-cultural participant communities or nations, with the culture of the dominant group assimilating those of smaller ethnic groups (Deutsch 1966).

For Connor, this model of 'nation-building' was both misleading and erroneous. It was misleading because, despite Deutsch's own caveats in particular cases, it omitted the growing evidence of widespread ethnic separatism and the failure of cultural assimilation to keep pace with social mobilisation. It was erroneous because its definition of the nation omitted the crucial psychological element of ethnicity, and saw the development of nations and nationalism in terms of the trajectories of the dominant Western 'nation-states'. Now these national states appeared to conform (albeit imperfectly) to Deutsch's idea of a dominant cultural nationality assimilating smaller, peripheral ethnic groups and their languages through the agencies of the modern state. Moreover, the level of economic and cultural development of Western national states suggested that theirs was the universal trajectory of nation-building, one in which the dominant nationality used the power of the state to back its claims to pre-eminence, and thereby become a 'nation'. For Connor, such 'nation-building' inevitably implied a large measure of correlative 'nation-destroying'. For, to create and build up the great dominant nations, it was necessary to assimilate, more or less violently, a great many other smaller ethnic groups and nationalities, quash their aspirations to become nations in their own right, and destroy the ethnic bases of their nationhood.[4]

Theoretically, the upshot of this critique was the need to return to the root of nations, which for Connor is a psychological bond that unites their members. This can only be found by making a clear distinction between state and nation, and between patriotism, the love of the territorial state, and nationalism, the love of the ethnic nation. Thus, we may speak of British patriotism, but only of English (or Scottish or Welsh or Irish) nationalism. The nation in its pristine sense, Connor defines as 'a group of people who *believe* they are ancestrally related. It is the largest grouping that shares such a belief' (Connor 1994: 212, italics in original). For Connor, the 'essence of a nation is intangible. This essence is a psychological bond that joins a people and differentiates it, in the subconscious conviction of its members, from all other people in a most vital way' (ibid.: 92).

Connor went on to argue that, unlike many scholars, most nationalist leaders 'have understood that at the core of ethnopsychology is the sense of shared blood, and they have not hesitated to appeal to it' (ibid.: 197). The nation is, therefore, 'the largest group that can command a person's loyalty because of felt kinship ties; it is, from this perspective, the fully extended family' (ibid.: 202).

On the other hand, this *sense* or conviction of kinship ties and unique descent on the part of the individual members need not, and usually does not, accord with the factual history of the designated nation. For Connor, the myth of ethnic descent should not be confused with real biological descent. Most nations are the product of many ethnic strains.[5]

> It is not chronological or factual history that is the key to the nation, but sentient or felt history. All that is irreducibly required for the existence of a nation is that the members share an intuitive conviction of the group's separate origin and evolution. To aver that one is a member of the Japanese, German or Thai nation is not merely to identify oneself with the Japanese, German, or Thai people of today, but with that people throughout time. Or rather – given the intuitive conviction that one's nation is unique in its origin – perhaps we should not say *throughout time* but *beyond time*.
>
> (ibid.: 202, italics in original)

This conviction, says Connor, is based on a powerful and non-rational (but not *ir*rational) feeling of the members. It can be analysed by studying its appeals and stimuli; but it cannot be rationally explained. To attempt to do so, is inevitably to miss the depth and power of national conviction, and its ability to override even a strong loyalty to the state and its institutions.

It is this crucial distinction between state and nation, and between patriotism and nationalism, that leads Connor to coin a term for the original, pristine sense of nationalism, namely, *ethnonationalism*. The use of this term cuts across the fashionable contemporary dichotomy of 'civic' and 'ethnic' nationalism. Connor is claiming that there is only one kind of nationalism, ethnic nationalism; and this is what reanimated the minority ethnic groups of Western Europe and Canada, and would later do the same in the former Soviet Union. What is called 'civic' nationalism is really only patriotism; this is indeed a 'rational' kind of loyalty and, unlike ethnonationalism, it can be rationally explained (Connor 1994: Chapter 8).

From ethnic group to nation

But, why 'ethnonationalism'? For Connor, the use of this term underlines the ethnic, and kinship, basis of the nation. In fact, nations are really only self-aware ethnic groups. An ethnic group, on the other hand, though its members 'must know ethnically what they *are not* before they know what they *are*', need not be self-aware:

> An ethnic group may be readily discerned by an anthropologist or other outside observer, but until the members are themselves aware of the group's

uniqueness, it is merely an ethnic group and not a nation. While an ethnic group *may*, therefore, be other-defined, a nation *must* be self-defined.

(ibid.: 103, italics in original)

For Connor, members of ethnic groups constitute 'peoples not yet cognisant of belonging to a larger ethnic element' (ibid.: 102). 'In such cases, meaningful identity of a positive nature remains limited to locale, region, clan, or tribe. Thus, members need not be conscious of belonging to the ethnic group' (ibid.: 103). These are essentially 'pre-national peoples'' or 'potential nations', peoples for whom nationhood and national identity lie in the future (ibid.: 79–80 and 102).

When, then, is a nation? This is a subject of considerable contention among historians, and Connor cites a number of opinions that tend to place the origins of nations in the earlier or later Middle Ages. Now, it might be thought from the preceding discussion that Connor would share their view, since the nation is simply a self-aware ethnic group, and ethnic groups have abounded in all periods and places. Instead, he opts for the formulations of Carlton Hayes and Hans Kohn to the effect that people's loyalties before the epoch of modernity were religious and dynastic rather than national. Indeed, Connor's own version of modernism is even more radical. Citing the great study of Eugene Weber which dates the transformation of peasants in rural France into a nation of Frenchmen and women to a period as late as the Third Republic, and making use of census data that reveal how little national feeling European immigrants to the United States possessed at the turn of the twentieth century, Connor concludes that 'claims that a nation existed prior to the late nineteenth century should be treated with caution' (ibid.: 224; cf. Weber 1979).[6]

Theoretically, Connor's argument is based on the assertion that nations and nationalism are mass phenomena and that therefore only when the great majority of a designated population has become nationally aware, can we legitimately speak of it as a nation. In authoritarian states like Nazi Germany and fascist Japan, we can ascertain their nation-formation after the event, because the population could clearly be mobilised along national lines. But in democracies, mass participation as measured in elections provides the best indicator of nation-formation, because in a democracy, 'the refusal to permit large sections of the populace to participate in the political process may be viewed as tantamount to declaring that those who are disenfranchised are not members of the nation' (Connor 1990: 99). Thus, the English could hardly begin to be described as a nation before the 1867 Reform Act, which gave the vote to some 80 per cent of the adult male population, and certainly not a fully-fledged nation until 1918, when the remaining 20 per cent of men and all women over thirty years of age secured the vote. This raises the question, 'At what point did a sufficient number/percentage of a given people acquire national consciousness so that the group merited the title of nation?' When can we say that 'a quantitative addition in the number sharing a sense of common nationhood has triggered the qualitative transformation into a nation'? (ibid.: 99).

When indeed? For Connor, there is no simple answer, no single formula. The formation of nations is a process, not an event. 'Events are easily dated; stages in a process are not' (ibid.: 99). There is a further problem. Nationalism is a mass phenomenon, and the masses have, for the most part, been mute about their group identities throughout recorded history. Connor's view of the pre-modern masses is similar to Gellner's. Till recently, they have lived in isolated rural pockets, usually in a state of dependance (if not serfdom) to the gentry and other élites; Connor cites the case of the Polish serfs siding against their Polish landlords when the latter rose up and fought for their national (élite) liberation. Moreover, the masses tended to be illiterate; so, our records of group identity are confined to members of the élite. How misleading these can be is demonstrated by the case of Arab nationalism. While a large proportion of Arab intellectuals have believed in a pan-Arab nation and have sought to inculcate their conviction in the Arab masses, 'after more than a half-century of such efforts, Arab nationalism remains anomalistically weak' (Connor 1994: 79–80; cf. Gellner 1983: Chapter 2).

Nevertheless, in state after state, ethnonationalism has triumphed in the modern epoch; and this is because 'Since 1789, the dogma that "alien rule is illegitimate rule" has been infecting ethnically aware peoples in an ever-broadening pattern' (Connor 1994: 169). The marriage of popular sovereignty with ethnicity, which produced the doctrine of national self-determination from 1789 onwards, was catalysed (but not caused) by modernisation, and specifically by the instruments of mass communications, which have increasingly brought peoples into contact, especially after the Second World War. Whereas in a pre-nationalist epoch, contact and empire often led to the cultural assimilation of the less self-conscious and developed peoples, in the era of nationalism modernisation has paradoxically separated peoples by bringing them into contact and amplifying their demands for self-government and independence. Hence the rise of ethnic autonomy movements in the West, and of ethnonationalisms in the East, with the result that over twenty new states have been added to the existing number. In each case, modernisation and communications have increased the intensity of ethnic group contacts and the perception thereof, to the point where such contacts were seen as a threat to group identity, and an ethnonationalist response ensued (ibid.: 170–74; and Connor 1973).

Nations and modernity

Here, perhaps, lies the answer to Connor's question: when is a nation? When a sufficient number of people feel threatened by intergroup contact and become aware of their ethnic identity, and when they seek to participate in national politics to redress the situation. If modernisation cannot explain *why* the nation came into being, it can certainly tell us when it did so (ibid.: 170–171).

This conclusion is puzzling, for it is at one and the same time logical and paradoxical. Logically, it flows from Connor's premises that (a) the nation is a self-aware ethnic group and (b) nationalism is a mass phenomenon. 'Self-awareness' is an attribute of the individuals who compose the nation, and the quality of being a nation, or 'nation-ness', is one that attaches, not to groups as such, but to individuals – the members of the group. It is the members of a nation who are aware that they belong to a nation; and only when a sufficient number feel they belong, can we say that an aggregate of individual members constitutes a nation.

But there is also something paradoxical in combining a perennial ethnicity with a radical national modernism. Connor, after all, insists on the ethnic nature of nations, thereby linking nationhood closely to an ubiquitous and perennial ethnicity. But, if the nation is simply a self-aware ethnic group, and ethnic groups (or 'pre-national peoples') can be found throughout history, why must we wait for the modern epoch for nations to form? On Connor's premises, we would expect them to appear whenever large numbers of the members of ethnic groups felt they constituted a nation, that is, whenever they came to feel that their group was unique and to believe that they were ancestrally related; and such feelings, according to Connor, are likely to emerge whenever groups come into contact and their members feel a threat to their identity.

Now, while the modern epoch has certainly helped to bring different peoples into frequent contact, it is by no means unique in this respect. We may cite such well-known cases as the Roman empire, or the late medieval period, when large numbers of members of different peoples came into regular contact through travel, trade, warfare, colonisation and religious movements; and when empires and states extended their sway, posing threats to the identities of many peoples. The historical record of these encounters is full of ethnic rivalry and conflict, as well as of ethnic self-awareness. It is quite clear from such accounts as Doron Mendels' of the Hellenistic and Roman worlds, and Adrian Hastings' of the later medieval world, that ethnicity and the politics of self-aware cultural identity were widespread and fundamental, not just for élites, but for the mobilisation of large numbers of people, usually in wars or through religious rituals. Why, then, if nations are simply self-aware ethnic groups, insist on the modernity, indeed the very recent date, of nations? (Mendels 1992; Hastings 1997).

One answer might be that nationalism, as an ideology and movement, is modern; and nationalism has been important in providing a blueprint of the nation-to-be and of a world of nations. But this would not account for Connor's insistence on a twentieth-century dating for most nations, since nationalism was a doctrine that became politically dominant in the early nineteenth century, at least in Europe and the Americas. Nor would it address the argument, advanced by Hastings and Armstrong, that several nations have antedated the ideology of nationalism by some centuries and have displayed strong national sentiments well before the advent of a formal theory of nationalism (Armstrong 1982; Hastings 1997: Chapters 1–2).

The 'mass nation'

I think this insistence on the radical modernity of nations comes from deeper sources in Connor's work, namely, from the excessive importance he gives to psychological variables, as well as to the individual, and hence to quantitative methods of research.

To take the latter issue first. Throughout, Connor insists on the primacy of the individual, and sees the nation as the sum of its individual members. We can really only grasp the 'essence' of the nation through an understanding of the beliefs and sentiments of its members. Not just of some of its (privileged) members, but of all of its members. Hence the quest for sources of evidence that will throw light on the attitudes of the common people (the masses) towards the idea of the nation. Hence, too, the insistence on the mass nature of nations and nationalism.

There is, of course, a long and fruitful tradition of applying quantitative and survey methods to social and political issues, both historical and contemporary. In one sense, Connor's work fits well into this tradition, with its empirical orientation and its assumption of methodological individualism. At the same time, Connor is aware of the limitations of such methods. He reminds us of the paucity of hard data in pre-modern epochs relating to the beliefs and feelings of non-élites; even in the modern period, we know very little about how peasants and artisans felt and thought about wider loyalties than the family and neighbourhood. This suggests that quantitative surveys (or 'head-counting') in this field should be treated with caution.

It also makes Connor's assertion of the absence of nations before late modernity all the more puzzling. How can we assume that the silence of the peasant masses is evidence of their lack of ethnic awareness, and hence of their nationhood? After all, pre-modern peasants were often equally silent about their religion or locality; but historians tend to argue that they were usually quite conscious of these ties. Perhaps the problem is not their silence, but their localism, which may impede a wider ethnic awareness? But this conventional picture of peasant households separated from each other and lacking wider links (Marx's 'sack of potatoes') needs to be qualified in view of the evidence of regional trade, of involvement in religious ceremonies and movements, of mobilisation for war, and of the influence of central ('Great') traditions. *How much* such wider ties meant to the peasant masses, we shall probably never know; but it is not unreasonable to suppose at least some measure of ethnic and religious awareness on their part.[7]

But there is a wider issue here. Must our understanding, indeed our definition, of the concept of the nation be so closely tied to 'the masses'? Is it really that helpful to research and understanding to assume that the nation is a 'mass phenomenon'? Is this not to link our concept of the nation too closely to the ideals and rhetoric of nationalism?

In many ways, this is the crux of the matter, the boundary that divides the basic paradigms of understanding in this field. For modernists, and on this issue we must include Walker Connor (albeit with some qualification), national*ism*, the ideology, defines the meaning of the concept of 'nation', as well as being largely responsible for bringing historical nations into being. For their opponents, the perennialists (and the primordialists), nations antedated nationalism, and the concept of the nation provided the basis for the ideology of nationalism.

Now, the ideology of nationalism includes the modern belief in popular sovereignty, the political primacy of *all* the people. It is the marriage of popular sovereignty with ethnicity that, for Connor, forms the doctrine of national self-determination which is the very heart of nationalism. This appeal to all the people as the sole legitimate source of power has been the basic and recurrent political motif since 1789, and the implication is that this idea was unknown, or at least of no account, before the French Revolution. This is why there were no nationalisms prior to modernity, and hence no nations. For, only when all the people become aware of, and are involved in, the community, as the ideology of nationalism prescribes, can we speak of them as truly constituting a 'nation' (see Kedourie 1960).

There are a number of questions here. While it is true that the ideology of nationalism proclaims the sovereignty of 'the people' and preaches their brotherhood (and latterly their sisterhood), in practice the nation has often been deemed to be constituted well in advance of the realisation of such *fraternité* and *sororité*. Massimo d'Azeglio's celebrated statement, that 'We have made Italy, now we must make Italians', actually attests to the (physical) existence of the nation (and not just as an élite idea) prior to the nationalisation of all of its members. In other words, it is not really necessary in practice for a nation to be a 'mass' nation at the point of its inception. In this sense, might not the nation constitute a duality – both an existing reality of cultural geography and a future project of social inclusion? Conversely, is it useful to declare a population a nation, only at the conclusion of an often long process of 'nation-formation'? The classical picture of the growth of nations from tiny élite nuclei in the early modern (or late medieval) period to the mass nation of late modernity may not, after all, prove a universal model. Perhaps we should rather see in this model an important part of the ideology of nationalism and its self-presentation, and hence its case for forming the nation? (see Hroch 1985).

In fact, it may be more useful for research and understanding to view the 'process' of nation-formation in more fluid and less evolutionary (and teleological) terms. After all, several 'processes' go into the making of nations, including the selection and codification of myths, symbols and traditions; the standardisation of language and culture; the rediscovery of ethno-history and the crystallisation of collective memories; the establishment of rites and ceremonies of the nation as a sacred communion of the faithful; the territorialisation of ethnic memories and of their political expressions; and the public inculcation of values, sentiments and traditions of the community. These processes may progress *pari passu*; alternatively, some may form and become widespread, while others hardly appear; and each process may be subject to 'reversals' and 'diversions'. Nor can we discern any determinate order, sequence or timing among these processes. There are many ways to make a nation, or for a nation to form. Hence the complexity and difficulty of 'dating the nation'.

Moreover, even if we could provide rough periods for each process, this still leaves open the question of 'dating', since the choice of the point in the process when it suffices to constitute a nation, is entirely arbitrary. Was 'Italy', for example, created in 1800 or 1870, or is it still being created? Or is it a recreation of Roman *Italia*?[8]

My point is that popular identification 'doth not a nation make'. At least, not alone. Connor is right to highlight the inadequacy of defining nations solely in terms of the attitudes and activities of élites, as many modernists continue to do;

and he has performed an invaluable service in reminding us of the need to give the majority of the designated population a much more central definitional and explanatory role. But, it does not advance matters to tie the definition of the concept of the nation so intimately to the number or proportion of individuals identifying with it, especially if this is something which, for pre-modern periods, we shall never be able to establish with any degree of certainty.

Moreover, to attempt to do so, is to rule out some historians' usage of the term 'nation' to fit their period of study, or to invite historians of different periods to use the same term in different ways, ones not necessarily in tune with modern nationalism's ideal of the 'mass nation'. Thus, medievalists like Adrian Hastings and John Gillingham are quite happy to use the term 'nation' (and, indeed, 'nationalism') in the absence of mass participation. Hastings, indeed, is quite explicit:

> one cannot say that for a nation to exist it is necessary that everyone within it should want it to exist or have full consciousness that it does exist, only that many people beyond government circles or a small ruling class should consistently believe in it.
>
> (Hastings 1997: 26; see also Gillingham 1992)

Hastings adds that, unless a society was composed exclusively of nobles and peasants, the fact that many of the peasantry had little sense of being part of it, does not of itself invalidate the existence of nations in early modern Europe. And he makes the crucial point that, in a France which was originally centred around the Paris region long before most of the peasants of what later became 'France' spoke French or felt themselves to be 'French', the early French nation must not be judged in terms of its later or present-day population and boundaries.[9]

The result of applying this quantitative methodology and its individualist underpinning would rule out, in advance, any relationship between, say, ancient and modern 'Armenia', or ancient and modern 'Israel'; the same proper name would be designating quite different referents, because the majority of the population of ancient Armenia and Israel *may* have felt little or no identification with the concept of an Armenian or Israelite 'nation'. Perhaps; but, again, perhaps not. We cannot know. Steven Grosby has argued, for example, that on a number of criteria – attachment to an historic translocal but bounded territory, common language, belief in a single deity and law with territorial jurisdiction, a belief on the part of many in the existence of the whole named people – we are entitled to term ancient Israel and Armenia 'nations', without incurring the guilt of a 'retrospective nationalism' (though this does not tell us whether there is any continuity between ancient and modern Armenia or Israel); after all, the fit between the sociological category of 'nationality' (as he terms it) and the modern national state is as problematic as it was in antiquity. In other words, in defining the concept of the nation we need to consider a number of different criteria and weigh the balance of probabilities in this elusive field, rather than rely on a largely quantitative approach (Grosby 1991 and 1997).

Psychology and structure

The other main problem with Connor's approach is its heavy reliance on psychological variables, and its psychological definition of the nation. For Connor, the essence of the nation is a psychological bond, based on kinship ties. Connor defines the nation in subjective terms, in terms of the beliefs and sentiments of individuals about their ancestry. The nation is, as we saw, the largest group of people 'who *believe* they are ancestrally related' (Connor 1994: 212, italics in original), 'the largest group of people that can command a person's loyalty through felt kinship ties' (ibid.: 202). Connor is not interested in real kinship ties or genuine ancestry; indeed, he makes the vital point that it is not what is, but what people *feel* is, that is significant for ethnicity and nationhood, and that, for the most part, what is felt to be ancestral and kin related does not correspond to any historical ancestry or actual kinship.

But does this mean that we are debarred from attempting to explain the intangible feelings and intuitive convictions of the members of nations? Does it follow that, because the nation may be defined in psychological terms, it cannot be *explained* in rational terms? On the contrary: we regularly attempt to explain social psychological phenomena in cultural and structural terms. Nor need we claim that ethno-psychological phenomena are inherently 'non-rational'; one could equally well argue that, in many circumstances, the drive for independence and national identity are quite rational (see Hechter 1992 and 2000). Nevertheless, Connor has a point. Modernist explanations (in terms of rational choice, relative deprivation, the modern state, industrial culture or invented tradition) generally pay little attention to psychological factors, and are often blind to the powerful sentiments and beliefs that constitute a sense of ethnicity and an ideal of nationhood. But that does not mean that we have to embrace a largely psychological position in seeking to define and explain nations and nationalism.

Let us agree with Connor that there are powerful subjective components of both ethnic groups and nations; and that our definition of the concept of the nation should reflect them. Thus, myths of origin will figure in any useful definition, as will shared memories and an attachment to an historic territory, or 'homeland'. But, while these subjective components may define the sense of common *ethnicity*, they cannot suffice for the more complex concept of nationhood. Here, we need to add other elements like a single public culture and common rights and duties for members; both are often taken to be components of the ideal-type of a nation, and figure prominently in nationalist ideology (see Smith 1986: Chapter 2 and 1991: Chapter 1).

In other words, the undoubted subjective components of the concept of nationhood need to be supplemented by more 'objective' components. This is true for both modernist definitions which delineate the concept of the nation in terms of the ideologies of nationalism; and for perennialist definitions which seek to establish the concept of the nation, independently of and prior to the ideas of the nationalists. As we saw, Connor's own definition is strictly psychological, and though he seeks to tie it to the ideology of nationalism and hence to modernity, it would more plausibly lend itself to a transhistorical perspective, given the ubiquity of kinship ties and sentiments. In this connection, it is an interesting thought that, contrary to the assertions of most classical historians, Connor's approach and definition would almost certainly imply the existence of not only ancient Armenian and Israelite nations, but also of an ancient Greek nation. In all three, we find evidence of considerable collective awareness on the part of a large portion of, at least, the male population (again, we have hardly any evidence of the feelings of women in the ancient world). In the Greek case, this is in spite of the lack of Greek political unity, the fierce loyalty of citizens to their *polis*, and the deep ethnic subdivisions of Ionian, Dorian, Aeolian and Boeotian tribes and dialects. Notwithstanding, most ancient Greeks possessed a clear sense of the distinction between 'Greek' and 'non-Greek' or 'barbarian', at least since the Persian Wars. This intense Greek belief in their cultural superiority was, in turn, based on a sense of ancestral relatedness, recounted in their genealogical myths; hence, on Connor's psychological definition, the ancient Greeks constituted a 'nation' *par excellence*, long before the advent of nationalism (Hall 1992; but cf. Alty 1982; Finley 1986: Chapter 7).

National symbols and institutions

These contradictions in the dating of nations flow from the problems of an overly psychological approach to nations and nationalism, and from an insistence that nationalism and nations are necessarily mass phenomena. But, if purely subjective elements – attitudes, sentiments and beliefs – are insufficient to define a nation, what other types of component need to be included? There are, I think, two kinds of component, the symbolic and the institutional. I shall treat each briefly.

The first refers, not just to specific symbols (anthems, flags, coinage, etc.), but to the gamut of symbolic elements, including memories, traditions, codes, myths and values. These 'ethno-symbolic' elements, and especially codes, memories and myths, form vital components in the definition of *ethnies* and nations. Without them, a national community would lose its distinctive character and *raison d'être*. This has become once again an issue in an age of cultural imperialism and the 'flooding' of indigenous symbolism by standardised Western mass communications. In pre-modern epochs, the existence of distinctive symbolic repertoires in different populations indicated the presence of separate *ethnies*, whose members might be more or less self-aware. Even if our records are the product of specialist élites, they often reflect a much wider constituency. More important, the longer a symbolic heritage persists, the greater the likelihood that we are in the presence of a vibrant and distinctive ethnic tradition and community. Moreover, a focus on symbolism allows one to trace, through extant documents, codes and artefacts, the durability of ethnic cultural heritages, and their relationship with the modern nations that claim them, rather than having to rely on more or less informed guesses about the numbers who, in any period, may be aware of their ethnic or national identity (see Smith 1999: Introduction).

Equally important for the definition, but even more for the explanation of nations, are the institutional elements. I have in mind such institutions as codes of law, educational practices, customs, rituals and liturgies (particularly of churches), artistic styles, specialist lore, and centres and institutions of prestige (especially dynastic). Some of these institutions overlap with those of the polity, where one is present, but their purpose is different. Where the institutions of the polity are directed towards the maximisation of power and physical resources, those of nations are concerned with the prestige and the distinctive culture of the community. Unlike John Breuilly, who discerns only churches and dynasties as possible institutional carriers of ethnicity in pre-modern epochs, I would argue that, along with the language code, each of the institutions listed above may serve as long-term vehicles for the reproduction of the distinctive heritage and character of ethnic communities and nations in each generation. Given the centrality of a public culture and common membership in the concept of the nation, the definition of the latter needs to include institutional, as well as symbolic and psychological, components.[10]

None of this should be understood as gainsaying the significance of the psychological elements that Walker Connor has so aptly highlighted and elucidated in his definition of the concept of the nation, nor its basis in ethnic, and ultimately kinship, sentiments, however fictive their actual historical origins. But, vital as they are, psychological elements do not exhaust the range of components that compose the ideal-type of the nation. A fuller, more rounded definition of the concept requires the mingling of 'subjective' and 'objective' components, and this suggests a definition of the nation as *a named human population occupying an historic territory, and sharing myths, memories, a single public culture and common right and duties for all members* – a definition flexible enough to fit various historical periods, from those where membership of the nation was fairly restricted and the public culture and rights and duties did not extend to everyone within the boundaries designated *at that time*, to the modern 'mass nation' where practically everyone within the designated boundaries partakes of membership, the public culture and common rights and duties (see Smith 1991: Chapter 1).

'Ancient' nations?

What are the implications of this analysis for the problem of the 'dating of nations'? We have already seen how arbitrary it must be to assign a date or even period for particular nations, or indeed to choose between the 'inception' and the 'completion' of the process of forming the nation. Besides being evolutionist and teleological, such a view assumes what is to be demonstrated, namely, that nation-formation is a 'process' with a recognisable beginning and end, one that accords with the self-image of nationalism. Since the ideology of nationalism is undoubtedly a modern phenomenon, and nationalism so often designates nations, should we not expect to find that the process of nation-formation is modern and that most nations are therefore modern?

Most nations, perhaps, but certainly not all. There is enough evidence to demonstrate that, on most of the criteria used to define the concept of the nation, nations can be found in various periods of history, if only intermittently and temporarily. Of course, this concept of the nation is not identical with that of the 'mass nation' which Connor and the modernists embrace; but nor is it so different as to require another type-name. Thus, we might distinguish 'ancient' from 'modern' nations, not just in chronological terms, but also sociologically – the main difference being the extent to which the members are deemed to be equal citizens (if not always treated as such). In the ancient world, 'citizenship' was often understood in religious terms, as membership of and participation in the congregation, and 'culture' was often segmented by class, rather than being a standardised, public attribute of the community (see Breuilly 1993; cf. Grosby 1997).

Nevertheless, with these provisos, I think we can demonstrate the existence and vitality of nations in ancient Judea and Armenia, and possibly Sassanid Persia, as well as in medieval Japan, Korea and England. In all these examples, we find a named human population occupying an historic territory, or 'homeland', sharing myths, symbols and memories, possessing a distinctive public culture (albeit unstandardised), and common rights and duties for many, if not all, of the (usually male) members, though this is often understood in religious terms. These examples, I would contend, suffice to undermine the more radical forms of 'modernism'.

On Connor's own assumptions, this is hardly an unexpected conclusion. If we drop the assertion that nations (not nationalism) must be 'mass phenomena', then we would expect that a phenomenon rooted in ethnicity (and ultimately in presumed kinship ties) would not be confined to any particular period of history.[11] We would expect to find the type of community and identity which we term 'nation', wherever ethnic communities were strongly rooted and their members became aware of their cultural distinctiveness. That is often the case with 'chosen peoples', *ethnies* who possess powerful myths of origin and divine election. Such myths have been much more widespread and influential than is commonly supposed; and we should not be surprised if the strength of this conviction (along with other ethnosymbolic resources), contributed to the creation of nations out of often heterogeneous elements. Even in the ancient world, this was an active, purposive enterprise; it required a Moses, a St. Gregory, a Muhammad, and their followers, or some powerful rulers and their ministers, to give it shape (see Smith 1999: Chapter 3).

The same is true of nations in later, medieval, periods. Particular rulers and nobles, or various missionaries and clerics, schooled in distinct religious traditions, helped to forge ethnic communities out of unself-aware 'ethnic categories', often by providing rituals and liturgies, scripts and written vernaculars for the transmission of ethnic memories, myths and symbols; the classic instance is that of the missionary saints Cyril and Methodius in the Balkans (Petrovich 1980).

Then, in a further development, other élites enabled these communities to become nations by claiming on their behalf an historic territory and creating a common public culture and equal rights and duties for their members; these were often nationalist intellectuals and professionals, though in some early cases like England, Scotland, France and Holland, various rulers, nobles and clerics took the lead. This suggests that we can infer the development of particular nations from evidence of common myths of ancestry and shared memories, claims to historic territories, and the creation of public cultures and law codes granting members of the community at that time equal rights and duties. Given the many processes involved, it would prove well nigh impossible to specify a period for the formation of the nation; all we could say is that, on the available evidence, several of these processes were converging to turn an ethnic community into a nation over several generations.

This progression, from an ethnic *category* to an ethnic *community* to a nation, follows the logic of the definition we have given, and it undoubtedly represents the most common pattern of historical development. But, and here I depart from Connor, we do find some instances of a different, even reversed pattern: from state to nation and ethnic community. For example, in Eritrea, the sense of a distinctive Eritrean identity was formed not only by a measure of geographical separation, but also by its separate colonial (Italian and British) administration, and by prolonged warfare. So the sense of common nationhood has been nurtured by the myths, symbols, memories and public culture of colonialism and a common struggle, and by claims to an historic territory, though, in the future, these political symbols of 'patriotism' (in Connor's terminology) may be combined with ethnic symbolic components, drawn from one or other of the ethnic communities that inhabit the Eritrean homeland (see Cliffe 1989).

Either way, dating the nation proves to be no simple matter. It cannot be ascertained simply by questioning the population of the designated nation as to the degree of their collective self-awareness. This is only one element in the ensemble of components of national identity, and an often uncertain one. Besides, this procedure assumes what needs to be shown; the population in question has been selected because it, and only it, comprises an already designated nation – a nation, in other words, named and differentiated on other and *prior* grounds, such as language or culture, history or territory, or a combination of these – grounds which are assumed by both members and outsiders.

This brings us to a final point: that nations exist in a world of nations, or at least, in a region of nations, and in relation to other nations. Even in antiquity and even among the most solipsist and chosen of peoples, it was assumed that the world consisted of analogous communities – inferior, no doubt, but still commensurable. The Hymn of Akhnaton specifically includes the nations of the world in the worship of the Sun-disk, the Aton; the sculptures on the staircase of the Apadana in Xerxes' palace in Persepolis portray the offerings of all the peoples of the ancient Near East; while the Old Testament is scathing in its denunciations of the idolatry of the heathen nations round about. The point is that nations are formed in relation to other nations, whether in alliance or enmity, through migration, conquest, trade, the flow of ideas and techniques, and so on. Their boundaries, as Fredrik Barth has shown, are crystallised and sustained through such contacts; and this has been the case, in varying degrees, across the centuries, not just in the modern world (see Barth 1969: Introduction; cf. Wiseman 1973).

This means that an additional factor in the dating of nations is some kind of 'recognition' by other nations and/or polities in the area, at least implicitly through relationships and interactions, from which we can infer the existence of particular nations in history. But here, again, we need to exercise caution; the presence of such relationships does not, of itself, tell us whether the community in question is a 'nation', only that this is one of several possibilities.

Conclusion

The problem of dating the nation has haunted the study of nationalism, and Walker Connor has performed an invaluable service both in bringing it into the open as an issue in its own right and in revealing its importance for an understanding of the place of the nation in history and in the contemporary world. But the question of when is a nation is bound up with the prior question of what is a nation, and this problem will not be solved by spiriting it out of existence and substituting concepts like 'nationness' and 'national practices', as Rogers Brubaker recommends (1996: Introduction). Connor himself has been quite clear on this point, and has provided a compact and incisive definition of the nation, which he has then applied with clarity and rigour to the historical processes of nation-formation. It is a definition that offers a powerful corrective to the fashionable 'constructionist' approaches and definitions of the last two decades. In differing from his psychological approach and quantitative methodology in this area of study, and arguing for the inclusion of symbolic and institutional components in the definition – and hence the 'dating' – of nations, I do not mean in any way to diminish the significance of Walker Connor's achievement. On the contrary: without his powerfully argued and thought-provoking articles, the study of nationalism would still be mired in the confusions of terminology and imprecision of concepts which characterised earlier generations of scholars in this field.

But there is more to Walker Connor's achievement. He has consistently addressed the deep passion and wide resonance that the ideal of the nation evokes across the world and this has led him to uncover the powerful psychological wellsprings of both its homely beauties and its volcanic terror. It is a measure of that achievement that, even where we may dissent from some of his conclusions, we can continue to draw inspiration and wisdom from his clear-sighted and penetrating analyses of nations and nationalism.

Notes

1 For advocacy of Greek continuity over the millennia, see Carras (1983); but cf. Kitromilides (1989). On the Pharaonic movement of the 1920s, see Gershoni and Jankowski (1987: chapters 6–8). For a general discussion of 'continuous perennialism', see Smith (2000: Chapter 2).

2 The main proponents of the classical modernist paradigm of nations and nationalism are Elie Kedourie (1960), Karl Deutsch (1966), Ernest Gellner (1983), Eric Hobsbawm (1990), Benedict Anderson (1991) and John Breuilly (1993). For an analysis of this paradigm, see Smith (1998: Chapters 1–6).

3 Besides being 'mass' and 'created', the modernists' nation is also 'territorial, 'legal-political', 'nationalist' and 'inter-nationalist'. That is to say, the modern nation is also a territorially bounded, self-governing political community whose members possess the

legal status of citizens, legitimated by the universal ideology of nationalism, and part of an inter-national order; on which, see Smith (1995, 53–57).

4 For studies of 'nation-building', see the essays in Deutsch and Foltz (1963); and for Connor's early and best-known onslaught on this position, see Connor (1972).

5 This emphasis on *myths* of origin, as opposed to actual biological descent, differentiates Connor's position sharply from Van den Berghe's (1979) sociobiological account.

6 See Carlton Hayes (1931) and Hans Kohn ([1944]1967). Connor's argument involves three assumptions: nations are necessarily mass phenomena; national awareness is tantamount to participation; and, in democracies, participation is measured by voting. Here I concentrate on the first assumption.

7 As Hobsbawm (1990: chapter 2) concedes. For the development of wider regional-local ethnicities in Europe during the Middle Ages, see Reynolds (1984: Chapter 8) and Lydon (1995).

8 Perhaps a survey of national feeling in Horace's and Virgil's Italy would have revealed a high level of *amor Italiae*. But would that make Roman Italy a 'nation' and modern Italy its 'Mark II' revival? On ancient Roman and Italian sentiment, and Roman attitudes to 'barbarian' *nationes*, see Balsdon (1979); for modern Italian sentiment, or *italianité*, see Hearder (1983: Chapters. 6–7, 11) and Riall (1994: 70–74).

9 This point is important in highlighting the 'blocking presentism' (Peel 1989) of modernism: if the nationalists (and some perennialists) are guilty of a 'retrospective nationalism', the modernists are equally culpable of applying a canon of the 'modern nation' (territorial, populous, culturally homogeneous, cross-class, created and nationalist) to pre-modern populations in the same area and bearing the same name and a cognate culture, in order to demonstrate that they cannot, and must not, be regarded as 'nations'. Such *a priori* reasoning leaves little scope for exceptions or for ethnic formations.

10 On this issue, see Breuilly's (1996) critique of my view, and my reply in Smith (1998: 196–198).

11 In fact, nationalism, whatever its rhetoric and aspirations, is very often a minority phenomenon (though not necessarily an élite one), as in some familiar Eastern European cases from the last century; see Argyle (1976) and Hroch (1985).

References

Alty, J.H.M. 1982. 'Dorians and Ionians'. *The Journal of Hellenic Studies*. 102: 1–14

Anderson, Benedict 1991. *Imagined Communities: Reflections on the Origin and Spread of Nationalism*. 2nd edn. London: Verso.

Argyle, W.J. 1976. 'Size and scale as factors in the development of nationalist movements'. In Anthony D. Smith (ed.) *Nationalist Movements*. London: Macmillan.

Armstrong, John A. 1982. *Nations before Nationalism*. Chapel Hill, NC: University of North Carolina Press.

Balsdon, J.V. 1979. *Romans and Aliens*. London: Duckworth.

Barth, Fredrik (ed.) 1969. *Ethnic Groups and Boundaries*. Boston: Little, Brown and Co.

Breuilly, John 1993. *Nationalism and the State*. 2nd edn. Manchester: Manchester University Press.

—— 1996. 'Approaches to nationalism'. In G. Balakrishnan (ed.) *Mapping the Nation*. London and New York: Verso: 146–174.

Brubaker, Rogers 1996. *Nationalism Reframed: Nationhood and the National Question in the New Europe*. Cambridge: Cambridge University Press.

Carras, C. 1983. *3,000 Years of Greek Identity – Myth or Reality?* Athens: Domus Books.

Cliffe, Lionel 1989. 'Forging a nation: the Eritrean experience'. *Third World Quarterly*. 11(4): 131–147.

Connor, Walker 1972. 'Nation-building or nation-destroying?' *World Politics*. 24: 319–355.

—— 1973. 'The politics of ethno-nationalism'. *Journal of International Affairs*. 27: 1–21.

—— 1990. 'When is a nation?' *Ethnic and Racial Studies*. 13(1): 92–103.

—— 1994. *Ethno-Nationalism: The Quest for Understanding*. Princeton, NJ: Princeton University Press.

Deutsch, Karl 1966. *Nationalism and Social Communication*. 2nd edn. New York: MIT Press.

Deutsch, Karl and Foltz, William (eds) 1963. *Nation-Building*. New York: Atherton Press.

Finley, Moses 1986. *The Use and Abuse of History*. London: Hogarth Press.

Gellner, Ernest 1983. *Nations and Nationalism*. Oxford: Blackwell.

Gershoni, Israel and Jankowski, Mark 1987. *Egypt, Islam and the Arabs: The Search for Egyptian Nationhood 1900–1930*. New York and Oxford: Oxford University Press.

Gillingham, John 1992. 'The beginnings of English imperialism'. *Journal of Historical Sociology*. 5: 392–409.

Grosby, Steven 1991. 'Religion and nationality in antiquity'. *European Journal of Sociology*. XXXII: 229–265.

—— 1997. 'Borders, territory and nationality in the ancient Near East and Armenia'. *Journal of the Economic and Social History of the Orient*. 40(1): 1–29.

Hall, Edith 1992. *Inventing the Barbarian: Greek Self-definition through Tragedy*. Oxford: Clarendon Press.

Hastings, Adrian 1997. *The Construction of Nationhood: Ethnicity, Religion and Nationalism*. Cambridge: Cambridge University Press.

Hayes, Carlton 1931. *The Historical Evolution of Modern Nationalism*. New York: Smith.

Hearder, Harry 1983. *Italy in the Age of the Risorgimento, 1790–1870*. London and New York: Longman.

Hechter, Michael 1992. 'The dynamics of secession'. *Acta Sociologica*. 35: 267–283.

—— 2000. *Containing Nationalism*. London and New York: Oxford University Press.

Hobsbawm, Eric 1990. *Nations and Nationalism since 1780*. Cambridge: Cambridge University Press.

Hobsbawm, Eric and Ranger, Terence (eds) 1983. *The Invention of Tradition*. Cambridge: Cambridge University Press.

Hroch, Miroslav 1985. *The Social Preconditions of National Revival in Europe*. Cambridge: Cambridge University Press.

Kedourie, Elie 1960. *Nationalism*. London: Hutchinson.

Kitromilides, Paschalis 1989. '"Imagined Communities" and the origins of the national question in the Balkans'. *European History Quarterly*. 19(2): 149–192.

Kohn, Hans [1944] 1967. *The Idea of Nationalism*. 2nd edn. New York: Collier-Macmillan.

Lydon, James 1995. 'Nation and race in medieval Ireland'. In Simon Forde, Lesley Johnson and Alan Murray (eds) *Concepts of National Identity in the Middle Ages*. Leeds: Leeds Studies in English, University of Leeds.

Mann, Michael 1993. *The Sources of Social Power*. Vol. II. Cambridge: Cambridge University Press.

Mendels, Doron 1992. *The Rise and Fall of Jewish Nationalism*. New York: Doubleday.

Pearson, Raymond 1993. 'Fact, fantasy, fraud: perceptions and projections of national revival'. *Ethnic Groups*. 10: 1–3, 43–64.

Peel, John 1989. 'The cultural work of Yoruba ethno-genesis'. In Elisabeth Tonkin, Maryon McDonald and Malcolm Chapman (eds) *History and Ethnicity*. London and New York: Routledge: 198–215.

Petrovich, Michael 1980. 'Religion and ethnicity in Eastern Europe'. In Peter Sugar (ed.) *Ethnic Diversity and Conflict in Eastern Europe*. Santa Barbara, ABC-Clio: 373–417.

Reynolds, Susan 1984. *Kingdoms and Communities in Western Europe 900–1300*. Oxford: Clarendon Press.

Riall, Lucy 1994. *The Italian Risorgimento*. London and New York: Routledge.

Smith, Anthony D. 1986. *The Ethnic Origins of Nations*. Oxford: Blackwell.

—— 1991. *National Identity*. Harmondsworth: Penguin.

—— 1995. *Nations and Nationalism in a Global Era*. Cambridge: Polity Press.

—— 1998. *Nationalism and Modernism*. London and New York: Routledge.

—— 1999. *Myths and Memories of the Nation*. London and New York: Oxford University Press.

—— 2000. *The Nation in History*. Hanover and London: University Press of New England and Cambridge: Polity Press.

Van den Berghe, Pierre 1979. *The Ethnic Phenomenon*. New York: Elsevier.

Weber, Eugene 1979. *Peasants into Frenchmen: The Modernisation of Rural France 1870–1914*. London: Chatto and Windus.

Wiseman, D.J. (ed.) 1973. *Peoples of the Old Testament*. Oxford: Clarendon Press.

4   The primordialists

Donald L. Horowitz

Anyone who has read Walker Connor's influential works knows that he is scrupulous about terminology (see Connor 1984: xiv; Connor 1987: 197; Connor 1994: 89). Connor understands that how one names a phenomenon affects how one thinks about it. I intend to be less scrupulous about terms than he is, but only in the interest of explicating a certain school of thought. The term I shall be careless with is *primordialism*. Walker Connor (1994: 106) does not embrace that term, on the ground that it connotes the primitivism of ethnic sentiments and a sense that so-called primordial attachments 'will wither away as modernization progresses'.

Although I thoroughly agree that *primordial* has just such a pejorative connotation and that it delegitimizes and archaizes ethnic sentiments, the term also has a different connotation, of fundamentality, which initially commended it to the attention of those who imported it into ethnic studies. Nevertheless, alternative terms that suggest themselves, such as *fundamentalist*, strike me as less satisfactory still, and so, even though all primordialists do not accept the label, I shall argue that it groups together usefully those who approach ethnic relations and ethnic conflict in a certain way. I shall use the term, even as those I stamp with the label, Walker Connor included, are free to abjure it, and I shall suggest that some recent lines of inquiry may well accord *primordial* a more positive valence than it has so far enjoyed.

In clustering several writers together under a common rubric, I am aware of the danger of creating an 'imagined community' of primordialists. But this community has already been created, often with quite a lot of imagination. Primordialism has become the straw man of ethnic studies. Primordialists deserve a more careful reading than they usually receive. What I mean to do here is to say what they say, say what it contributes to ethnic studies, and say something about the need to deal with many questions primordialists leave open. I shall argue that the contribution of primordialism is narrow but important and that, properly understood, primordialism raises major questions that still call out for answers, and I shall discuss some lines of inquiry that promise to provide answers to some of those questions.

What primordialists contribute

Undoubtedly, primordialists are the most caricatured and most maligned for their naïveté in supposing that ethnic affiliations are given rather than chosen,

immutable rather than malleable, and inevitably productive of conflict. The matter
has reached the point at which anyone wishing to make an argument about the flu-
idity of identities or the rationality of pursuing a conflict has half the argument
made by citing the allegedly contrary view of unnamed, benighted primordialists.
So evocative is the epithet, there is reason to suspect the primordialists are no
longer much read.

Before the upsurge of what has come to be called *ethnicity* (for a brief etymology,
see Glazer and Moynihan 1975), there was a serious historical literature on nationalism (e.g., Kohn 1967; Hayes 1950). Much of that literature deals with the origins
of nations, attempting to distinguish types of nationalism (organic and territorial,
for example) and to draw out the consequences of varying formative experiences
(see Smith 1991: 81–82). When much of this writing was being done, nationalism
was viewed as a *problem*, principally a European problem; and European nations,
whatever the vicissitudes of their formation, were mainly seen as having already
been formed. This view, moreover, was not wholly wrong: the boundaries of most
European ethnic groups proved to be remarkably stable during the twentieth century. In Asia and Africa, on the other hand, anthropologists and political scientists
were discovering, in the period following World War II, that group boundaries were
fluid, that many groups were relatively recently formed, and that the seemingly
hard-and-fast linguistic, cultural, and historical foundations of group identity so
obvious in Europe (although historically not fixed there either) were not indispensable to ethnogenesis elsewhere (see Vansina 1966; Young 1965; for synthesis
and examples, see Horowitz 1985: 64–70; Kasfir 1979: 372–374, 378–385;
Anderson *et al.* 1974: 28–38).

There seemed to be two kinds of European nationalism, one of them
founded on a more inclusive connection to territory and a watered-down view
of group membership by descent, the other more firmly rooted in ancestry and
surrounded by mystical ideas of community. France might stand for the former,
Germany for the latter. One had its origins in the Enlightenment, the other in
the Romantic tradition (Brubaker 1992). The latter nationalism seemed far
more virulent and productive of conflict, and it is not surprising that it should
have been viewed as paradigmatic, even where group boundaries were fluid, for
in Asia and Africa there was usually not an identifiable attachment to the whole
territory.[1] If *primordial* means preceding state organization (Smith 1986: 12),
then the ethnic attachments in the then-new states might have seemed to fit the
definition (as they also might in Eastern Europe), although such an observation
would have missed the part played by colonial rule in shaping and reshaping
ethnic boundaries.

There are, however, other meanings of *primordial*. For some critics, the vice of the
primordialists is their alleged association with the idea of inevitable ethnic hatred
and with a sense of ethnic identity as 'primeval, original, primitive, or fundamental' (Hardin 1995: 149). But those sometimes called primordialists seem to be
arguing for something rather different.

The point is that there are durable ethnic bonds, that ethnicity (or ethnonationalism) is a phenomenon rather than an epiphenomenon, that it cannot be

reduced to a 'pressure group that mobilizes in order to compete for scarce resources', or to the ambitions of a few leaders, or to a social class (Connor 1994: 73–74). Instead, 'a certain ineffable significance is attached to the tie of blood' (Shils 1957: 142). There is 'some unaccountable import attributable to the very tie itself' (Geertz 1963: 109); the matter goes to the need for belonging, to 'basic group identity' (Isaacs 1975: 42). The primordialists' point is that ethnic affiliations belong to the class of fundamental affiliations that reflect feelings of intense solidarity and are capable of inducing selfless behavior on the part of group members (Connor 1993: 377, 382, 387; Shils 1957: 133, 138; Shils 1995: 97, 100). Apart from the core function of belonging, these deep ties are not generally thought to perform any function (but cf. Isaacs 1975: 42, 215) – hence the effort to deprecate instrumental reconceptualizations – and most primordialists see ethnicity as a depressingly destructive force, all the more deplorable because of the depth of attachment they sense in it.

Of course, what is meant by 'ineffable significance', 'unaccountable import', and 'basic group identity' is left unexplained in these formulations. Furthermore, there is no effort at explaining how some affiliations become primordial, while other candidate-affiliations lose out, or why ethnic boundaries settle where they do, including some subgroups and excluding others. The neglect of the functions beyond belonging that such affiliations might perform is also unfortunate. There is little about ethnogenesis, or the causes of conflict, or its variations, or its amelioration. However significant it may be, the primordialists' message is, in the end, a narrow one pertaining to the intensity of ethnic affiliations. Still, that message raises a question familiar in other settings: the relationship of self-interest to altruism, conceived in terms of group loyalty.

Contrary to what has been said about them (e.g., Pieterse 1997: 367–368), primordialists do not fail to notice that ethnic group boundaries are not simply given or that group boundaries change over time. Geertz (1963: 109) speaks of the 'assumed' givens of social existence. Isaacs, who explicitly accepts the term *primordialist*, understands that identities change over time, that group cultures are not fixed, and that ethnic history is falsified to meet the needs of the present; and he acknowledges that the extent of the interethnic hostility on which he is focused is a variable, not a constant (Isaacs 1975: 115, 205–206, 217). Primordialists do not, however, choose to explain any such variation. Because primordialists are concerned to make a causal point in the large, theirs is a macro-perspective. One searches in vain for their taxonomies of conflict behavior and their identification of intervening variables. They propound no specific theories of ethnic secession, or ethnicity and party, or ethnic violence. They focus, above all, on the intensity of group identifications and the sentiments that frequently flow from them: affection, hatred, the willingness to sacrifice (e.g., Shils 1957: 138; Connor 1993: 385).

In emphasizing sentiment, some primordialists deny the role of calculation altogether (Connor 1993: 382; Shils 1995: 109), while the remainder play it down. Walker Connor, for instance, speaks of the 'non-rational', but still explicable, nature of ethnic and national bonds. There is, he says, a 'sense of kinship', a 'feeling of consanguinity' that often does not accord with historical fact but still produces the willingness to make great sacrifices (Connor 1993: 377, 382, 387). Edward Shils, who brought the term *primordial* into current usage, stresses affiliations that reflect a 'state of intense and common solidarity', often demanding far-reaching individual sacrifice for the group (1957: 133, 138). For Shils, ethnic and national ties are both primordial in the sense that they are 'connected to vitality', to the things without which people cannot live (Shils 1995: 97). One of these is traditionality, the persistence of the past into the present; another is a 'collective self-consciousness focused on boundary-generating referents' (Shils 1995: 100). These constitute the essence of community that ethnic and national affiliations are called upon to provide. For Shils and for Harold Isaacs (1975: 217), a sense of community necessarily generates awareness and comparative evaluation of other communities, and these can turn to conflict over material and non-material goods.

What primordialists leave open

What the primordialists provide is an account of the thick nature of ethnic affiliations, based as they are on community, even communion, at a level that can only be justified by myths of common ancestry and analogies of ethnicity to the family. Shils (1957) traces sociological theories of intensely solidaristic groups to Ferdinand Tönnies' (1940) conception of *Gemeinschaft*. Primordialists would say that attempts to account for ethnic-conflict behavior instrumentally amount to explaining *Gemeinschaft* conduct on the basis of *Gesellschaft* assumptions (see Connor 1994: 205–206). The narrowness of their message is precisely its advantage. It is a message of inestimable importance, unattended or discarded to the enduring disadvantage of ethnic-conflict studies. One can take from primordialists their well-developed understanding of the thick nature of ethnic attachments and utilize other perspectives to investigate the many questions they leave open.

Some of the most interesting aspects of ethnicity and conflict lurk in precisely what primordialists neglect or deny: the way in which ethnic identities arise out of interactions with other groups rather than out of a merely inward focus, the determinants of group boundary change and of variable conflict intensity, the role of élites in altering ethnic consciousness, the interplay of passion and calculation, and the use of political institutions to exacerbate or reduce conflict. The primordialist account fails to acknowledge that, once it identifies a need for group identity, it has not proved that the emotional foundations of ethnicity are altogether incompatible with rational action on the part of group members.

If one accepts Shils' statement that primordial ties are connected to a sense of origins and a sense of community, both of which people find indispensable, the very next question ought to be why these are such urgent and arguably universal needs. Ethnicity surely has something to do with more general tendencies of human beings to sociality (Horowitz 1999), but beyond that the functions of groupness remain subject to speculation. Some theorists have speculated that the ability to cooperate in groups would provide an evolutionary advantage (Brewer and Miller 1996). Since the benefits of cooperation would decline beyond a certain group size, many environments will have multiple groups. The ready-made character of kinship and ethnicity might be particularly advantageous in group formation and maintenance. The advantages of ingroup cooperation might then, over long periods of time, feed back into passionately positive sentiments about group affiliations. But all of this constitutes only one line of speculation about the connections of ethnicity to more general needs for community. Other lines might also be compatible with the primordialist insight. And, as of now, this line of speculation is developed only in a skeletal way. I shall return to some other lines of approach shortly.

Economists have been developing a view of ethnic groups as service-producing clubs that operate because they engender the trust that facilitates transactions (Congleton 1995; Wintrobe 1995). This view is more compatible with primordialist premises than it might seem at first, because it rests on the nature of ethnicity as an affiliation, with high barriers to entry and exit. Those barriers can only be so high because the affiliation is based mainly on birth and because it engenders such intense loyalty. This, of course, suggests that the loyalty precedes any service that is provided.

The general point of this discussion is to indicate that primordialist thinkers, by stressing the thick nature of ethnic bonds, have paved the way for theories of community that, as of now, are in their incipient stages. Read sympathetically, the primordialists open a variety of fruitful lines of inquiry.

As I said, most primordialists understand that even relatively durable affiliations are mutable; they do not propound any doctrine of the inevitability of conflict. Yet primordialists do tend to emphasize the conflict-proneness of ethnic groups and the destructive effects of intensely held identities. It seems to me that they are not sufficiently explicit about the distinction between affirming an identity and pursuing a conflict, between maintaining ingroup solidarity and cultivating outgroup antipathy. These distinctions are important. Ethnic groups commonly favor ingroup members against all comers. I use the term *favor* in two senses: they hold the ingroup and its members in generally higher esteem (though not necessarily in all respects), and they discriminate in favor of ingroup members. That favoritism, however, does not, by itself, imply hostility toward those who are disfavored. Toward many outsiders, there is simply indifference. And so the determinants of hostility cannot be identical to the determinants of group identity: they are additional (see Brewer 2001).

The persistence of group identity, then, no matter how deeply felt, is not synonymous with antipathy, even well established antipathy, toward particular outgroups. In recent years, a great deal of attention has been devoted to the regulation or control of intergroup antipathy and its political manifestations (see, e.g., Lijphart 1977; Horowitz 1991). Much less attention has been paid – none at all by primordialists – to longer-term declines in patterns of interethnic hostility. Indeed, because they are longer term, such declines often escape notice altogether. Three brief examples will make the point.

In the nineteenth century, violent ethnic conflict was common in the United States. New immigrants met with hostility from older immigrants. The Germans, who had met with resentment in Pennsylvania in the eighteenth century, fared no better in other locations in the nineteenth. In Louisville, for example, there was anti-German violence in 1855. By then, in Pennsylvania itself, earlier German immigrants were well accepted. Irish immigrants, however, were rejected. In 1844, serious anti-Irish violence occurred in Philadelphia. Within a matter of decades, these antipathies faded and were overtaken by others, particularly the antipathy between blacks and whites. Later still, among many American whites, consciousness of ethnic origins was largely forgotten (Alba 1990).

Fading is the right term to describe antipathy between Mainlanders and Taiwanese in Taiwan and between Thais and Chinese in Thailand. In both cases, there was serious intergroup violence after World War II. In Taiwan, the process of conciliation was facilitated by the existence of a hostile China and the need for the Kuomintang regime to prove its legitimacy by a successful democratization, which could only be accomplished by incorporating Taiwanese into the party and the regime. Social integration and political integration have proceeded in tandem. They have in Thailand as well, but by a different route. Chinese cultivated ties with Thai military and civilian officials and then with the democratization movement of the 1980s. In both countries, intermarriage rates rose dramatically, undermining the firmness of intergroup boundaries.

Although I have hinted at the direction of explanations for the reduced intensity of ethnic hostility in the three cases, my point is not to pin down an explanation but merely to mark the sharpness of the change over the course of the decades. The mutability of sentiments does not prove the primordialists wrong. Ethnic attachments are powerful, fundamental, and related to the strong need for community and kinship. Undoubtedly, ethnic affiliations were experienced in these ways by all the groups just mentioned. Nonetheless, the hostile sentiments associated with these affiliations underwent considerable change.

Primordialism is inimical, as Connor has argued repeatedly, to explanations based on ephemeral economic competition. For Connor, the ethnic tie is based on 'a sense of sameness or oneness of kind' that derives from a myth of common descent (Connor 1994: 145). But it is not at odds with an array of causal explanations that see the development of such a sense of sameness and such a myth of descent in terms of recurrent human needs for cooperation and sociality, and it does not condemn the human species to perpetual conflict and violence. It is a point of view about a certain kind of community that still allows for the development of theories of community, and it is assuredly not a full theory of ethnic conflict.

Evolutionary primordialism

In emphasizing the intense solidarity generated by ethnic ties, those who see group identity in terms of the ineffable significance of blood have inadvertently opened the way to new lines of inquiry by scholars who wish to link ethnicity to evolution. If group sentiment performs the important functions enumerated by primordialists, why are those functions so important? I mentioned earlier the evolutionary advantages likely to be associated with cooperation in groups and the convenience of constituting such groups on a kinship basis. Other theorists have regarded ethnicity as kinship writ large and ingroup favoritism as merely a particular instance of genetic favoritism (van den Berghe 1981).

A different approach to the same issues begins with the simple observation that, in spite of constructivist theories of ethnicity – and in spite of changes in group boundaries over time – ethnicity is experienced primordially by participants. That is, there is evidence that group members believe ethnic-group membership may only be acquired biologically (Gil-White 1999). Many group members also appear to believe that ethnic groups have innate natures, in rather the same way that different species do. To explain this, Francisco Gil-White argues that human beings are programmed to think in terms of natural living kinds and that ethnic groups elicit this tendency because they appear in relevant ways to be similar to species (Gil-White 1999; 2001). In particular, ethnic groups practice category-based endogamy and define membership by descent.

Earlier writers had spoken of the competitive tendency to think of groups as if they were species as a tragic misperception that they called 'pseudospeciation' (Leach 1973; Erikson 1974: 28). Gil-White concedes that the analogy of ethnic groups to species is mistaken: 'An ethnic so-called "nature," after all, is nothing if not a set of culturally transmitted norms and behaviors, and therefore believing these literally to result from biological descent is an ontological error' (Gil-White 2001: 518 [emphasis omitted]). In spite of this, he contends, bad ontology 'may be good epistemology' (ibid.). If more-or-less endogamous groups do have different sets of norms from each other, and these are transmitted intergenerationally, then treating ethnic groups as separate living kinds will actually be helpful in anticipating their behavior. From here, the link to evolutionary theory is straightforward: interacting with members of groups who do not share norms about social exchange may entail fitness costs; and, if so, a cognitive framework that sharply demarcates ethnic groups as if they were natural kinds has survival value.

For Gil-White, then, the essentialist reasoning about ethnicity so deplored by constructivists is or historically has been adaptive. If true, this has large implications for debates about ethnic-group behavior. Ethnic-group boundaries may still be – inevitably are – socially constructed and reconstructed, but only over relatively long periods of time and with, at best, limited input from the individual decisions of rational actors: it is the *processing* of information, rather than conscious choice, that is involved (cf. Horowitz 1985: 67–70; Horowitz 2001: 50).

This version of evolutionary primordialism is consistent with the propensity of individuals to assume a high degree of homogeneity within outgroups, to speak in terms of group character or group nature, in rather the same way as they speak of human nature, and indeed explicitly to speak in terms of species analogies (see Horowitz 2001: 543–544 and 461–462, respectively). It also squares with experimental evidence that interpersonal similarity in tastes, attitudes, and values engenders empathy; genetic (or putatively genetic) origins are potent sources of similarity and of cues that signal similarity (Horowitz 2001: 48–49).

Indeed, it is possible to go further. Although Gil-White denominates the analogy of ethnic groups to species as an ontological error, in one respect even this may not be completely so. Although ethnic traits are acquired by cultural transmission, so are certain species traits.[2] Moreover, among animals, subspecies differentiation is common and is often based on insubstantial differences, yet has strong effects in social interaction and in virulent niche competition (see Horowitz 2001: 462–463 for references).

A theory of evolutionary primordialism would, of course, still need considerable elaboration and verification. For example, although group affinities are often founded on presumed similarity of norms, intergroup conflict is by no means a straightforward function of normative distance. (In ecological terms, of course, there would be reason to expect greater conflict among groups that are normatively closer, rather than more distant.) There is also the need to specify exactly what the fitness costs of interacting across group lines might be. Those who emphasize the evolutionary advantages of interpersonal cooperation argue that, historically, relatively small group size would have been optimal (Brewer 1999). Since distributive costs would have set in rapidly as group size increased, avoidance of such costs would be a good reason for establishing sharp boundaries.

Here, however, another line of research becomes pertinent. It takes little imagination to recognize how dangerous encounters with strangers might be in the anarchic conditions of prehistory and how important it would therefore be for individuals to be able to classify collectivities of strangers. If the likelihood of harm increased when people encountered groups of strangers, then it would be advantageous to avoid such encounters. From this, Mark Schaller (1999) hypothesizes that categorical representations about groups emerged in order to facilitate avoidance of dangerous interactions. Negative evaluations of outgroup members foster wariness of them. This wariness would have been advantageous for survival. But wariness alone would have been insufficient, for not all intergroup encounters would have been harmful. It would also be useful to be able to link distinguishing characteristics of individual outgroup members with their behavioral tendencies. From these beginnings, Schaller speculates, an apparatus of cues would have grown up to allow people to construct categorical representations of groups and individuating representations of group members. This is a theory with considerable bearing on issues of group identity, homogeneity, stereotypes, and discriminatory behavior (see also Schaller and Mueller 2000).

As always with evolutionary hypotheses, there is a danger of constructing just-so stories, teleological tales of what must have been. Yet, whatever the connections ultimately turn out to be, it can scarcely be possible that the emergence of group loyalties would have nothing to do with needs for cooperation or that ethnocentrism would have nothing to do with the evolutionary utility of assessing danger.

For such needs, of course, *primordial* would be, ironically enough, exactly the right term, and primordialists and those who have sneered at them for emphasizing the irrational, deep-seated quality of group sentiments will both have to reconsider. In evolutionary theory, deep-seating may be a sign of rationality, albeit perhaps yesterday's rationality.

Political entrepreneurs and primordialism

There is one further matter in the conventional critique of the primordialists that requires attention. That is the role of 'political entrepreneurs' who are said to be ubiquitously at work stirring up ethnic sentiments and whose activities are thought to provide the *coup de grâce* to primordialist delusions (see, e.g., Crawford and Lipschutz 1998). It is not possible to deny that politicians have some causal connections with ethnic conflict (as they must also have connections with its amelioration), but the assumptions commonly embedded in the tale of political entrepreneurs who stir up hitherto quiescent followers are both numerous and debatable. Here I want to raise the sole objection that is pertinent to this essay.

The objection is simply stated. The tacit assumption is usually that political entrepreneurs are cynical manipulators whose activities are governed by self-interest alone. But what if political entrepreneurs are themselves primordialists? When I first did an extended period of fieldwork in Malaysia, I recall being startled upon discovering that, in candid moments, well educated, sophisticated politicians expressed ethnic hostility, often based on views of outgroup members that considered behavioral traits to be more or less immutable. There is no necessary contradiction between the pursuit of individual self-interest and the utilization of a primordial cognitive frame. One unusually talented aspiring Malaysian politician published a well-known book on the subject of group traits, and it featured some lively genetic speculation (Mahathir 1970).

If ethnicity is commonly experienced primordially, it is, at the very least, an important empirical question whether political entrepreneurs depart in significant ways from prevailing patterns of cognition. Some may do so: there is, for example, no gainsaying the effects of education on views of ethnic and racial traits in much of the Western world since 1945. But the blanket assertion that political entrepreneurs are merely self-interested, cynical manipulators is just that: an assertion. Walker Connor (1984: 540–543) was able to show that, even within the Kremlin during the Soviet period, top leaders were not immune to ethnic or nationalist sentiment. Is it not plausible, then, that – whatever their other motives – political entrepreneurs who foment ethnic conflict are also, as Connor (1987: 205), echoing Bismarck, would say, 'thinking with their blood'? If this turns out to be true, those who would like to write off the contribution of the primordialists altogether will need to find another trump card.

Notes

1 Unlike some other primordialists, however, Shils (1995: 97) takes the position that territorial affinities are 'no less primordial' than birth affinities.
2 See Bonner (1980) and de Waal and Johanowicz (1993) for a fascinating experiment concerning interspecies learning.

References

Alba, Richard 1990. *Ethnic Identity: The Transformation of White America*. New Haven: Yale University Press.

Anderson, Charles W., von der Mehden, Fred and Young, Crawford 1974. *Issues of Political Development*. Englewood Cliffs, NJ: Prentice-Hall.

Bonner, John Tyler 1980. *The Evolution of Culture in Animals*. Princeton, NJ: Princeton University Press.

Brewer, Marilynn 1999. 'Social Identity, Group Loyalty, and Intergroup Conflict.' In Charles Hermann *et al.* (eds) *Violent Conflict in the 21st Century: Causes, Instruments and Mitigation*. Chicago: American Academy of Arts and Sciences.

—— 2001. 'Ingroup Identification and Intergroup Conflict: When Does Ingroup Love Become Outgroup Hate?' In R. Ashmore, L. Jussim, and D. Wilder (eds) *Social Identity, Intergroup Conflict, and Conflict Reduction*. New York: Oxford University Press: 17–41.

Brewer, Marilynn B. and Miller, Norman 1996. *Intergroup Relations*. Milton Keynes: Open University Press.

Brubaker, Rogers 1992. *Citizenship and Nationhood in France and Germany*. Cambridge, MA: Harvard University Press.

Congleton, Roger D. 1995. 'Ethnic Clubs, Ethnic Conflict, and the Rise of Ethnic Nationalism'. In A. Breton *et al.* (eds) *Nationalism and Rationality*. Cambridge: Cambridge University Press: 71–97.

Connor, Walker 1984. *The National Question in Marxist-Leninist Theory and Strategy*. Princeton, NJ: Princeton University Press.

—— 1987. 'Ethnonationalism'. In Myron Weiner and Samuel P. Huntington (eds) *Understanding Political Development*. Boston: Little, Brown: 196–220.

—— 1993. 'Beyond Reason: The Nature of the Ethnonational Bond'. *Ethnic and Racial Studies*. 16(3): 373–389.

—— 1994. *Ethnonationalism: The Quest for Understanding*. Princeton, NJ: Princeton University Press.

Crawford, Beverly and Lipschutz, Ronnie D. (eds) 1998. *The Myth of 'Ethnic Conflict': Politics, Economics and 'Cultural' Violence*. Berkeley, CA: University of California Press.

de Waal, Frans B.M. and Johanowicz, Denise L. 1993. 'Modification of Reconciliation Behavior Through Social Experience: An Experiment with Two Macaque Species'. *Child Development*. 64(3): 897–908.

Erikson, Erik H. 1974. *Dimensions of a New Identity*. New York: W.W. Norton.

Geertz, Clifford 1963. 'The Integrative Revolution: Primordial Sentiments and Civil Politics in the New States'. In C. Geertz (ed.) *Old Societies and New States*. New York: Free Press.

Gil-White, Francisco J. 1999. 'How Thick Is Blood? The Plot Thickens . . .: If Ethnic Actors Are Primordialists, What Remains of the Circumstantialist/Primordialist Controversy?' *Ethnic and Racial Studies*. 22(5): 789–820.

—— 2001. 'Are Ethnic Groups Biological Species to the Human Brain? Essentialism in Our Cognition of Some Social Categories'. *Current Anthropology*. 42(4): 515–554.

Glazer, Nathan and Moynihan, Daniel P. (eds) 1975. *Ethnicity: Theory and Experience*. Cambridge, MA: Harvard University Press.

Hardin, Russell 1995. *One for All: The Logic of Group Conflict*. Princeton, NJ: Princeton University Press.

Hayes, Carleton 1950. *The Historical Evolution of Modern Nationalism*. New York: Macmillan Co.

Horowitz, Donald 1985. *Ethnic Groups in Conflict*. Berkeley, CA: University of California Press.

—— 1991. *A Democratic South Africa? Constitutional Engineering in a Divided Society*. Berkeley, CA: University of California Press.

—— 1999. 'Structure and Strategy in Ethnic Conflict: A Few Steps Toward Synthesis'. In B. Pleskovic and J. Stiglitz (eds) *Annual World Bank Conference on Development Economics, 1998*. Washington, DC: World Bank: 345–370.

—— 2001. *The Deadly Ethnic Riot*. Berkeley, CA: University of California Press.

Isaacs, Harold R. 1975. *Idols of the Tribe*. New York: Harper & Row.

Kasfir, Nelson 1979. 'Explaining Ethnic Political Participation'. *World Politics*. 31(3): 365–388.

Kohn, Hans 1967. *The Idea of Nationalism*. 2nd edn. New York: Collier-Macmillan.

Leach, Edmund 1973. 'The Integration of Minorities'. Second Annual Minority Rights Group Lecture. London: mimeographed.

Lijphart, Arend 1977. *Democracy in Plural Societies*. New Haven, CT: Yale University Press.

Mahathir bin Mohamad 1970. *The Malay Dilemma*. Singapore: Donald Moore.

Pieterse, Jan Nederveen 1997. 'Deconstructing/Reconstructing Ethnicity'. *Nations and Nationalism*. 3(3): 365–395.

Schaller, Mark 1999. 'Intergroup Vigilance Theory'. Unpublished manuscript. University of British Columbia, Department of Psychology.

Schaller, Mark and Mueller, Annette 2000. 'The Dangers in the Dark: Effects of Ambient Darkness and Beliefs in a Dangerous World on Stereotypes and Prejudice'. University of British Columbia Department of Psychology.

Shils, Edward 1957. 'Primordial, Personal, Sacred and Civil Ties'. *British Journal of Sociology*. 8(1): 130–145.

—— 1995. 'Nation, Nationality, Nationalism and Civil Society'. *Nations and Nationalism*. 1(1): 93–118.

Smith, Anthony D. 1986. *The Ethnic Origins of Nations*. Oxford: Basil Blackwell.

—— 1991. *National Identity*. Reno: University of Nevada Press.

Tönnies, Ferdinand 1940 (1887). *Fundamental Concepts of Sociology*. Trans. C.P. Loomis. New York: American Book Co.

van den Berghe, Pierre 1981. *The Ethnic Phenomenon*. New York: Elsevier.

Vansina, Jan 1966. *Introduction à l'ethnographie du Congo*. Brussels: Centre de Recherche et d'Information Sociopolitiques.

Wintrobe, Ronald 1995. 'Some Economics of Ethnic Capital Formation and Conflict'. In A. Breton *et al.* (eds) *Nationalism and Rationality*. Cambridge: Cambridge University Press: 43–70.

Young, Crawford 1965. *Politics in the Congo*. Princeton, NJ: Princeton University Press.

5 The primordialist–constructivist debate today[1]

The language–ethnicity link in academic and in everyday-life perspective

Joshua A. Fishman

A real primordialist–constructivist debate has not yet emerged in Western social science. At least it has not materialized in most places during most of the twentieth century.[2] Indeed, even in the nineteenth century, only relatively minor or second-level theorists with a primarily ethnically restricted appeal were avowed primordialists: the Comte Joseph Arthur de Gobineau (1843–1859) in France, Ludwig Gumplowitz (1838–1909) in Germany, Houston Stewart Chamberlain (1855–1927) in Great Britain.[3] Their usually accompanying racism left them increasingly isolated intellectually even then, although the term 'race' certainly did not mean the same for all of them.

The *constructivist* approach views societal, political, economic and historical processes and circumstances as determinant in 'constructing' nations and ethnic groups. These processes and circumstances fashioned, influenced, and determined the nature and importance of ethnicity. In turn, *ethnicity* was variously defined, roughly denoting distinctive and local cultural identity. Needless to say, constructivism gained relatively unchallenged control of the academic sociological imagination. This control was evidenced by, and resulted from, an unusual degree of underlying agreement between Marx, Weber and Durkheim. Nearly all mainstream social theorists assumed that the growing rational and integrative nature of modern society would leave precious little need or room for social identities based on 'myths' of cultural uniqueness and authenticity.

This mainstream control was challenged only on two fronts: that of the *humanities* and that of popular political and cultural '*daily life*' (Fishman 1999). The latter areas subsume philosophy, religion, literature, art, music, folklore, folk-life, history and their respective reflections in most of the mass media, journalism and in much of popular culture and public education. This is a huge orbit incorporating much of high and low culture. To this very day, these areas have commonly remained staunchly and positively primordialist in their orientations. Their conviction is that local sociocultural reality was, and should remain, marked by perspectively primordialist authenticity, uniqueness, mission and greatness. This wide range of views has remained unabated, both as a formative influence and as a reflection of public opinion. It may even have increased in response to the standardization, globalization and massification of worldwide econotechnical and political arrangements.

What follows is a discussion of two types of 'proof' and drifts of argumentation along seven different 'fronts'. Each of the proofs is separately experienced as internally satisfying. And each of them is generally uninfluenced by, and even normally unaware of, the evidence or convictions of the other to the contrary. The 'Western' academic reader may well consider primordialist convictions and intuitions as repugnant, uninformed or self-centered. Yet, the advancement of social science would be enhanced by pondering both the substantive content and the sociocultural functions of these views. An open approach to these views would contribute to our understanding, more than dismissing them summarily as heretofore. Scholars must first understand these views in order to take them seriously, if only in order to fathom their power and dynamics.[4]

The basic nature of the language–ethnicity link

In primordialist circles,[5] the language–ethnicity link is frequently regarded as legitimated by sanctity, as *materia sancta* per se, God, angels, miraculous events, or the works, prophets and teachings associated with the foregoing. It is thus seen as morally binding and eternally valid, while being validated via hallowed inter-generational linkages and obligations. The persistence of authentic ethnic identity without its traditionally associated language is considered impossible. From the mighty Romans and Sumerians to the tiny Manxmen and Australian Aborigines, copious 'evidence' of the past co-extinction of language-and-ethnicity linkages is widely known and cited.

The constructivist view counters with as much 'evidence' in which loss of the traditionally associated language has not resulted in loss of the corresponding ethnic identity. A commonly cited case is that of post-independence Ireland: many Irish speak only English and yet still consider themselves to be Irish. The same occurs among various diaspora: many Jews who speak neither Yiddish nor Hebrew still consider themselves Jews; in the USA, many anglified hispanics (e.g., nuyorkinos) still identify themselves as hispanics. And in Spain many Castilian-speaking Basques still consider themselves to be thoroughly Basques (yet the same cannot be said about Catalan speakers). Obviously, each side can and does find such 'evidence' in accord with its own basic tenets, while persevering with them. What is an eternal and essential link for one camp is no more than a fortuitous and replaceable feature for the other.

Herderian notions of linguistic centrality are in no way of any lesser appeal to contemporary late modernizing aggregates (Macedonians, for example), than they were to earlier modernizers in the late sixteenth and seventeenth centuries (the French, the English, for example). In the Herderian view, the traditionally associated *Volksprache* is considered to be the spark that sets the *Volksgeist* in motion. Language then nourishes it along authentic channels for the purposes of contemporary problem-solving.

The causal consequences of the authentic language–ethnicity link

In primordialist accounts worldwide, the protection and furtherance of the language–ethnicity link are seen as having definite and desirable consequences. The foregoing are often *globally* characterized in terms of authenticity, moral responsibility, the cultivation of traditional greatness, and fidelity to an ethnocultural or ethnoreligious mission. On the other hand, they are *narrowly* pinpointed in connection with specific problem-solving efforts pertaining to immediate concerns. Language is expected to foster, if not to guarantee, the greatness and ingenuity of those glorious historic moments and periods when it was employed. There is dependence on the unique kind of inspiration which may derive from fidelity to the old beloved languages and identities, no matter how revered they may actually have been in former times, or may retrospectively be interpreted as having been.

For the constructivists, however, the lack of empirical proof of any of the above claims is taken to indicate that linguistic determinism along unique ethnocultural lines is contrafactual. This constructivist pretension is advanced regardless, among other things, of the strong hypothesis developed by the linguist Benjamin Lee Whorf (1897–1941) with its experimental transformation.[6] Nevertheless, the constructivist conviction that new challenges require new resources, ideas, ideals and inspiration is also well beyond empirical confirmation. In short, primordialists claim to derive the new *desiderata* (resources, ideas, ideals, inspirations) from the old sanctities, whereas constructivists claim to derive them by leaving the old ones behind.

The challenge of empiricism

Is empirical proof needed for the above claims? If so, is such proof the final and determining arbiter of social conviction, identity and action? Constructivists never tire of finding historical and archaeological holes in primordialist claims *vis-à-vis* authenticity. Rather than being based on *bona fide* findings, 'authenticity models' are easily demonstrated to be no more than subjective preferences for artificial and ideologically motivated reconstructions of some unauthentic 'never-never' world.

Primordialists, on the other hand, are often unabashed about admitting that their convictions are based upon postulates that are above and beyond mere factual proof – and, correspondingly, above bare empirical truth. They are quick to point out that science too has its 'primitives' in the form of first principles and convictions: physicians are convinced that life is worth saving, while jurists are personally invested in the view that law-abidingness is the basis of civilized society. Primordialists argue that their own preference for an 'authenticity'-anchored model of language and ethnicity is no different, nor worse than similar value-based models in the realms of constructivist-controlled research.

A particularly damning shortcoming in the eyes of constructivists is the ungenuineness of 'authenticity'. Precisely because the primordialists' ideal models are supra-rational, they are deemed to be vastly preferable to the direction of change that typifies modern empirical life. Love, loyalty and self-denying altruism, they argue, should not be repudiated or disowned in the social arena any more than in the sphere of individual interaction.

The Secret Life of Walter Mitty vs Ibsen's *Wild Duck*: ideal worlds that are worlds apart

Constructivists accuse primordialists of fostering a wildly improbable, self-congratulatory and ethnocentric *Secret Life of Walter Mitty* world. Here an eternal and exaggeratedly substantial moral universe of fidelity and creativity hangs in the balance of particularistic implementations based on language and ethnicity. However, primordialists are equally dismissive of the constructivist's coolly rational, confirmable truths. They see in them only an avenue to postmodernist alienation from integrative social and cultural values.

Typically, primordialists ask: of what value is 'liberation from superstition'? What can humanity gain from such liberation, if it leads to standardization of lifestyles, to the destruction of pride in the uniqueness of history, culture and identity? Constructivists believe that small languages and peoples are of no real importance in 'the greater scheme of things'.[7] But does this have any saving grace in comparison to the cultivation of local dignity and identity? A small people may be only a speck, a blip on the world-market screen, but it can still be 100 per cent of itself. And it will be most likely bilingual and bicultural as well. Primordialists accuse constructivists of simplifying and impoverishing human life via their advocacy of large-market solutions to all human problems

The tragedy of language loss vs the travesty of fixating on 'useless languages'

Anthropology and sociology have come to recognize the substantial validity of the primordialist's nightmare: peoples that have lost their historically related language and its traditionally associated and intertwined ethnoculture pass through a cruel 'neither life nor death' experience. They lose their established sense of a moral universe, of an image of the good life, of the attainability of intergenerational continuity, of a meaningful past, present and future, of a rightful place in the grander design. This loss occurs much before newer self-defining behaviors and normative expectations in all of these respects are articulated, internalized, established and realized. But the above sad scenario does not move the constructivists from prophesying or anticipating the brave new world of unified markets and closely attuned mega-values, mega-cultures and mega-languages. 'How many peoples and languages does the modern world need?', they never tire of asking. 'How many can it afford?' Their concern is for the number of languages and cultures the world 'really' needs or can 'really' support. They thereby imply and predict successively lower estimates than were ever entertained before. The above 'market-based outcomes' are estimated entirely on the bases of self-interest and purported economies of scale. Both are bases which have been rationally apparent to, and admired by, Western intellectuals – at least since the Roman times (Fishman 1977). Nonetheless, the worlds of religion, art, music, literature and philosophy have consistently rejected these estimates as impoverished and impoverishing.

The price of an ethnolinguistically diverse and pluralistic world

For nearly half a century the Parliament of the European Union has followed the principle of 'full linguistic equality' at the polity level for its member states. Denmark has been as entitled to send and to receive all communications in its state language at the Parliamentary meetings in Strasbourg, as are the many-times-larger France or Germany. This convention has lasted for a very considerable period of time in the communications between the first twelve member states, with nine languages being recognized for all parliamentary purposes. But with the admission of states 13, 14 and 15 (Austria, Sweden and Finland) this very costly arrangement has 'temporarily' been set aside. As even more member states are considered,[8] no newer permissible parliamentary languages are likely to be added to the roll. Such a halt appears even more likely in connection with the following six countries now already headed toward EU membership: Bulgaria, Latvia, Lithuania, Rumania, Slovakia and Turkey. Even then, the full roster of European states will not yet have been completed: another dozen are still waiting (or sulking) in the wings: Iceland, Albania, Switzerland and additional components of the former Soviet Union (Belarus, Moldova, Armenia, Georgia, etc.) and the Former Yugoslavia (Macedonia, Croatia, Bosnia, Serbia – with or without Kosovo and Montenegro).

The constructivists have little doubt but that the EU will finally and inevitably have to head in a more parsimonious direction of a smaller number of operational languages. Indeed, the current nine languages already require the ability to handle seventy-two types of translation. The EU may then proceed in a more selective direction – perhaps not quite as selectively as that previously taken by the Council of Europe, the United Nations and the League of Nations. What better testimony can there be, that even the most affluent segment of the society of nations cannot afford the full ethnolinguistic diversity which still marks its own ranks? This is not just in terms of the organizational costs of the translation service. It is even more so in terms of the costs of possibly heightened civil strife that ethnolinguistic diversity purportedly engenders. And finally there is the more materialistic consideration of lowered per capita gross national product attributed to linguistic heterogenesty.

If this is true in more modernized and less heterogeneous Europe, how much truer must it be in the many times more heterogeneous Africa, Asia, Latin America and Pacific Oceania? The primordialists respond that no such costs have ever been incontrovertibly demonstrated: indeed, they have been strongly and empirically questioned (Fishman 1991). But such response remains either unknown or, if known, ignored. Imperviousness to rational empirical data is thereby shown to be very far from being the primordialist monopoly that has often been claimed.

Indeed, states have a propensity to make primordialist claims upward in the power-scale (i.e., when appealing to higher and stronger states and multi-state bodies) and to make constructivist claims downward (when laying down the law to smaller and weaker political entities). Thus, France appeals to the conscience of the civilized world on behalf of its own language of culture as a bulwark against the monolith of English, but it has no patience when Bretons, Occitans and Alsatians stake out claims for their own survival when faced by the monolith of French. What better evidence can there be that the constructivist vs primordialist debate is anchored, not so much in basic analytical or philosophical positions (e.g., empiricism vs. romanticism), as much as in fluctuating self-interest?

What kind of help do 'latecomers' need and want?

Out of a probable universe of some 5,000 or more languages surviving in the world, only a few hundred are today utilized for literacy-related functions. But most of these few hundred have arrived at literacy only within the past century. Primordialists advocate helping these 'latecomers to literacy' to find a place in the sun on the already crowded literacy beach. It is hoped that such a place may help these smaller and weaker languages to ward off the extinction which has been predicted for thousands of them during the twenty-first century. Sociolinguistic sophistication is particularly needed, in order to help the 'latecomers' attain the diglossic bilingual and biliterate arrangements upon which their own longevity might very well depend.

However, the above direction of problem-solving leaves the constructivists unconvinced. If latecomers are to be assisted, so the argument goes, such assistance should proceed along economic, industrial and commercial lines, rather than along *linguacentric* lines. The latter are indeed viewed as being far more counterproductive than productive in terms of the realistic needs of latecomers. Once again we must note the tendency of constructivism to underestimate the enriching potential of multilingual cultural arrangements. Multilingual societies, with two, three, four and even more languages – for various functions (secular and religious, modern and traditional) are scattered all over the globe and have functioned admirably for centuries and even millennia. It is the small and weak who have generally learned how to arrive at, and to maintain, such arrangements. They have done so nevertheless while viewing the world through primordialist prisms when it comes to the cores of their own identities.

Two differing *Weltanschauungen*

The primordialist–constructivist disagreement is often portrayed as a struggle between emotion and reason, between ideology and information. At times it is seen as a contest between past- and future-orientedness, or between conservatism and modernity. Yet, it can be better envisaged as a disagreement between pluralist and monistic ideologies – to which one could attach a divergence between separatist and unificationist credos. Both sides (rather than one side or the other, as is usually charged) are motivated in terms of a particular moral imperative, by an image of the good world yet to be attained (Fishman 1972). At the scientific level, they correspond to another opposition: on the one hand, the supra-scientific values placed upon terralingual and human cultural diversity; on the other hand, productive efficiency and the economy. Both points of view have their activists and their analysts. They are not in themselves an activist versus an analytic camp, as is sometimes alleged.

To assuage the travails of stateless peoples and languages without institutional protection, the constructivists advocate new identities along the lines of absorption by larger, better established economic entities. The use of international auxiliary languages, eventually including World English, will come to the aid of this goal. They point out that this has ever been the lot of competitively disadvantaged peoples/ethnicities and languages.

Primordialists do not necessarily disregard market economy or the global community but they put their ameliorative faith into reversing language shift locally, with a rational use of language planning efforts (Fishman 1991). As known in sociolinguistics, language planning comes in two forms: status planning (normalization) and corpus planning (elaboration and standardization).[9] It is status planning which receives the lion's share of recognition, by means of which corpus planning can be functionally modernized and advanced (Fishman 2000). Steps that appear to be monopolistic, power-playing and authoritarian internal colonialism to primordialists appear as disruptive, uncivilized and hopelessly cantankerous to constructionists, as well as outrageously centrifugal when resisted.

Interestingly enough, the modern world is heir to both of the above traditions: mainstream self-aggrandizement and sidestream insistence on self-determination. They are both very much alive, the one eliciting and confronting the other, as the several ethnonationalist conflicts and imbroglios reveal. The constructivist view is much more university based, at least in the West, whereas the primordialist view is much more disadvantaged-community based. But there are notable regions of the Western world where the latter view has found university recognition, particularly in tumultuous times. Their quite separate and very disparate motivational bases and rhetorical traditions have too long delayed their joint analysis and recognition, an enterprise the importance of which Walker Connor (1994) has long advocated.

Both views have too long been differently studied, constructivism via 'outside objectivism' and primordialism via 'inside subjectivism'. The view from within has had a long and fruitful history both in anthropology and in phenomenological psychology. It requires investigators to cultivate an 'emic' stress, so that peoples can come to be seen, known and appreciated in accord with their own self-images. The views of writers, poets, pastors, folklorists, journalists and philosophers provide invaluable evidence along these lines. Ethnocultures need to know much more about how others see them, but they all also need to know how they see themselves and how they see others. As Walker Connor well knows, the humanities and ethnosciences (ethno-cognition in particular) have a major unrecognized contribution to make in this connection. This is so not because they have greater perspectival or truth-value relevance. It is so because they provide a greatly different perspective, a more 'soulful' claim to the truth as popularly 'experienced'. Therefore, they must not be overlooked or laughed out of court. The more this contribution is recognized, the more primordialism and constructivism will be recognized as alternative strategies available to, and utilized by, all cultures in arriving at, and in making use of, their own fluctuating views of all of the factors and circumstances that surround them and that have created them.

The primordialism–constructivism debate may no longer seem to be a live issue in the western academy, like the value of religion or the existence of God, but it is a topic which is very real in the lives, hopes and dreams of ordinary men, women and children all over the world. As Walker Connor has said on more than one occasion, the academy ignores the ongoing relevance of this debate and its outcomes 'on the ground' at its own peril.

Notes

1 Dedicated, with sincere thanks, to the members of my Winter 1999 Seminar in 'Language and Ethnicity' at Stanford University, where this chapter was first presented as a lecture, roughly along its current lines.
2 I have been called a 'primordialist' once or twice. I distinctly remember Ernest Gellner doing so in 1976, at a meeting at which Walker Connor was also present. After the meeting, he called me aside and, referring to the above, asked me 'What's new in the world of Yiddish?' I believe the label was used mostly because of my being too successful at conveying the primordialist viewpoint, rather than for espousing it.
3 On the influence of Count de Gobineau, see Douglass' chapter.
4 Some of the other chapters will certainly help in this direction.
5 These are copiously cited throughout (Fishman 1997).
6 See Fishman (1960).
7 Viz. the Puerto Rican pop lament '*A nadie le importa, pues no habla ingles*'.
8 The next ones with which admission negotiations are already well underway are Cyprus, the Czech Republic, Estonia, Hungary, Malta, Poland and Slovenia.
9 *Status planning* refers to efforts to change the functions of a language (for use in government, the courts, education); *corpus planning* refers to efforts to change the structure of a language (orthography, nomenclatures, punctuation systems). They are linked to each other, indeed, two sides of the same coin.

References

Connor, Walker 1994. *Ethnonationalism: The Quest for Understanding*. Princeton, NJ: Princeton University Press.

Fishman, Joshua A. 1960. 'A Systematization of the Whorfian hypothesis'. *Behavioral Science*. 5: 323–339.

——— 1972. *Language and Nationalism: Two Integrative Essays*. Rowley: Newbury House. Reprinted in its entirety as part of *Language and Ethnicity in Minority Sociolinguistic Perspective*. Clevedon: Multilingual Matters. 1989: 105–177 and 269–367.

——— 1977. 'Language, Ethnicity and Racism'. *Georgetown University Roundtable on Languages and Linguistics*. 297–309. Reprinted in *Language and Ethnicity in Minority Sociolinguistic Perspective*. Clevedon: Multilingual Matters. 1989: 9–23.

——— 1991a. *Reversing Language Shift: Applied and Theoretical Foundations of Assistance to Threatened Languages*. Clevedon: Multilingual Matters.

——— 1991b. 'Inter-polity Perspective on the Relationships between Linguistic Heterogeneity, Civil Strife and Per Capita Gross National Product'. *Journal of Applied Linguistics*. 1: 5–18.

—— 1997. *In Praise of the Beloved Language: A Comparative Exploration of Positive Ethnolinguistic Consciousness*. Berlin: Mouton de Gruyter.

——(ed.) 1999. *Handbook of Language and Ethnicity*. New York: Oxford University Press.

—— 2000. 'The Status Agenda in Corpus Planning'. In Richard Lambert and Elana Shohamy (eds) *Language Policy and Pedagogy: Essays in Honor of A. Ronald Walton*. Amsterdam: Benjamins: 43–51.

Part II
Case studies

6   Sabino's sin

Racism and the founding of Basque nationalism

William A. Douglass

Walker Connor is the consummate comparativist and synthesizer. Above all, he is an intellectual adventurer, always disposed to run the risks inherent in juxtaposing sweeping *longue durée* historical patterns to yesterday's and today's news items. In this way, he is able to discern patterns in the seemingly chaotic and idiosyncratic nation-building process of different periods and places. He has thereby provided us with frameworks within which to situate our particular interests and case studies.

This chapter seeks to employ Walker's eclectic and adventuresome approach in an attempt to understand the controversial racialist discourse associated with Basque nationalism, and particularly during its foundational phase in the late nineteenth century. The movement's founder, Sabino de Arana y Goiri (1865–1903),[1] has indeed been customarily accused by his adversaries of being a racist. While, as we shall see, there is more than enough evidence to support the charge, many critics simply used it as a sufficient criterion to invalidate the Basque nationalist project as flawed and, ultimately, pathological.[2]

Like Connor (1994), I believe that nationalism is more an emotional sentiment, grounded in psychological commitment to ethnic particularism, than a rational economic and political choice (though, to be sure, rationality is at play as well). I would further argue that for most of the past century, with the globe divided up entirely into 'recognized' states and their colonial empires, no new ethnonationalist movement could emerge *ex nihilo*. Rather, the challenge from below (or within) contests the historical cultural and political claims of an existing, i.e. triumphant, state configuration(s) with *alternative* interpretations of the ascendant superordinate nationalist power's versions of ostensibly *shared* history, culture and politics.

In the Basque case, when Arana launched his ethnonationalist movement in the 1890s, the foes were Spanish and French nationalism (although to date more the former than the latter). The cornerstone of Arana's argument was that, although racially superior to their neighbors (particularly Spaniards), the Basques were in grave danger of being denatured politically and exploited economically by the centrist Spanish and French states, as well as diluted demographically (assimilated) within their far larger populations. In the process all that was particularly Basque, and most notably the language, would be lost forever. Arana ultimately sought to carve an independent Basque state, which he called Euzkadi, out of the existing

Spanish and French ones. He coined the expression *zazpiak bat* ('the seven are one'), reference being to France's three traditional Basque territories and Spain's four. It is scarcely surprising that Spanish and French nationalists were (and remain) anxious to dismiss (when not actively opposing) Basque nationalism. The nub (and rub) of the matter was (is) that in most concrete historical cases the creation of someone's state has been at the expense of another's (others') nation – a point that recurs throughout the extensive corpus of Connor's work.

The European racialist discourse

In situating Arana within fin-de-siècle Europe the issue was not who was racist, the rarity was the non-racialist.[3] The scientific and industrial revolutions resulting from Enlightenment thought, combined with four centuries of successful European imperial expansion, had removed doubt from all but the most skeptical European mind that Caucasians were superb racial stock, a view supported totally by nineteenth-century physical anthropological investigation.

At a minimum,[4] humankind could be divided into three great races: superior Caucasoids, intermediate Mongoloids and inferior Negroids. The most influential synthesis of this viewpoint, as well as its canonical text,[5] is Count Gobineau's *The Inequality of Human Races* (1967: 205–212), written in 1853.

At the same time, there was an internal European intellectual debate regarding the superiority or inferiority of certain 'races', 'peoples', 'stocks' or 'nationalities' within the Caucasian category. The main venues of European scientific racial discourse were France, England and Germany. Not surprisingly, the notion emerged of a Nordic, Teutonic, Germanic and, ultimately, Aryan racial stock common to this corner of Western Europe, that was clearly superior to that of southern and central Europeans (Biddiss 1979: 28).

Poliakov (1974) surveys five centuries of European racialist thought in order to understand the origins of the anti-Semitism that produced the Holocaust. He argues that discovery of the New World, which brought Europeans into contact with previously unknown (to them) peoples, cast the first doubts upon monogenism, i.e. the Adam-as-original-ancestor-of-humankind view of human history. It was the French Enlightenment, and particularly Voltaire, that argued for polygenism as the proper scientific, as opposed to theological, doctrine for the study of obvious human variation (Poliakov 1974: 131–133).

Polygenism admitted two new possibilities (among many others). The first (in anticipation of subsequent primate and human paleontological studies) was that there might be a continuum rather than clear division between bestiality and humanity (with the obvious implications and potential for the ranking of human races in terms of their determined inferiority or superiority).

The second possibility was that all of humanity need no longer be viewed as descended from the Garden of Eden and passed through a Jewish (Old Testament) filter. Drawing heavily upon the studies of Sanskritists that demonstrated linguistic correlation within an Indo-European language family, the Aryan alternative posited an original Aryan homeland somewhere in Central Asia (in or near Tibet), from which colonists of the great race fanned out and created the Old World's major civilizations (Poliakov 1974: 188–199). For Gobineau, these even included the Chinese and Egyptian, as well as the Greek and Roman (1967: 212). The 'Germanic races' provided both the epicenter and greatest expression of European Aryanism (Poliakov 1974: 198–214). It was the dispersion of Germanic races throughout Western Europe 'which in the fifth century transformed the Western mind' (Gobineau 1967: 212).

By the first half of the nineteenth century the discipline of physical anthropology, based upon the measurement[6] of human phenotypes for classificatory purposes (e.g. stature, cranial capacity and shape, hair, skin and eye color, etc.), provided the empirical evidence for scientific racism. While this proved to be a fairly straightforward (if erroneous) exercise in distinguishing among Gobineau's 'great races', when applied to Caucasians in their European homeland, and during its nationalist era, the discourse was immediately framed by historians in territorial (nation-state) and 'national character' terms. Thus, Jules Michelet, in the 'Introduction' to his *History of France* (1831) states:

> Germany gave her Swabians to Switzerland and to Sweden; her Goths to Spain, her Lombards to Lombardy, her Anglo-Saxons to England, her Franks to France. She gave both a name and renewal to all the peoples of Europe.
>
> (cited in Poliakov 1974: 33)

In discussing Germanic (i.e. Frankish) hegemony in France as well as Germanic successes in central Europe, Poliakov notes:

> the Frank, a Germanic man and a free man, may equally be contrasted with the serf (= *servus*) as with the slave (= Slav). Thus the key words in French political history slyly hint at the superiority of the German stock over the Latins and over the Slavs. This was a superiority both of race and of class, because the two notions of upper and lower classes and of superior and inferior races, which are quite distinct today, were not so easy to disentangle when it was a question of contrasting conquering peoples with those they had conquered.
>
> (ibid.: 17)

In effect, there was confounding of ostensible biological and linguistic evidence within a presentist historical framework in order to derive an understanding of the continent's contemporary political divisions, as well as the internal make-up and rank ordering of racial stocks within each of Europe's states. Furthermore, if biology mattered,[7] then there was the challenge of explaining the rise and fall in the fortunes of ancient, medieval and modern civilizations, states and empires – particularly in light of the fact that no national territory, including Germany, seemed to be populated by a single racial stock. It was in this regard that the tautological circle was closed and the triumphs of Western Europe's ascendant nineteenth-century powers (France, Germany and England) became the *prima facie* evidence of their Nordic racial superiority,[8] just as Spain's exhaustion and Italian impotence were the results of a predominantly Latin inferiority.[9]

In sum, nineteenth- and early twentieth-century European racialist discourse produced an enormous muddle, an intellectual morass perhaps unprecedented in the history of Western 'science', while demonstrating the near impossibility of applying true objectivity to self-scrutiny in human affairs. The consequences were far from academic or benign, since the discourse was directly responsible for two colossal human tragedies – the eugenics movement and the Holocaust. Regarding the latter, polygenism provided Europeans with an alternative interpretation to that of direct, common descent from and with Jews, thereby opening the door to rampant anti-Semitism (as well as proscription of other inferior races such as Gypsies, Slavs, etc.) in the defense of Aryan racial integrity (Poliakov 1974: 255–325).

Basque racialist discourse

Poliakov begins his analysis with Spain,[10] and specifically the early efforts of Archbishop Isidore of Seville (560–634 AD) to reconcile the vanquished, thoroughly Latinized, Iberians with their Visigothic (Germanic) conquerors (1974: 11), while celebrating the recent (589 AD) conversion of the latter's monarchy to Christianity. In his *History of the Goths, Vandals and Suevi* (1970), Isidore argued that, while the Visigoths were descended from Magog, the Iberians were the heirs of Tubal, both sons of Japhet and grandsons of Noah. Iberians and Goths were therefore blood brothers, irrespective of the existing uneven power relationship.

In 711 the Iberian peninsula experienced the first of a long series of invasions that culminated in Muslim control of all but a restricted northern region running along the Cantabrian shoreline from the Kingdom of Asturias in the west to the Catalan counties bordering the Mediterranean in the east (including Bizkaia and Gipuzkoa, as well as parts of Araba and Navarra in the Basque homeland). These Christian forces initiated a centuries-long Reconquest which, in the late fifteenth century (1492), during the reign of Fernando and Isabel, triumphed over the last Muslim stronghold of Granada. According to Poliakov:

> After the Christian *Reconquista*, the baptized descendants of Moslems and Jews found themselves branded with dishonour, and laws for maintaining purity of blood divided Spaniards into two castes, the pure-blooded Old Christians and New Christians whose blood was tarnished. The dividing line was not the Germanic or Iberian stock of the remote ancestor but his orthodoxy or heterodoxy. Spanish theologians worked out a doctrine according to which the false beliefs of both the Moors and Jews had soiled their blood, and this stain or '*nota*' had been transmitted by heredity to their furthest descendants, who were set apart in the almost untouchable caste of the New Christians or *conversos*. Thus, in defiance of the dogma proclaiming the regenerative virtue of baptism, an institutional form of racism made its first appearance in European history. The theologians who invented this doctrine did not dispute that both

categories of Christians were descended from the common father, Adam, but they did maintain that the rejection of Christ had corrupted the *conversos* biologically.

(1974: 12–13)[11]

In sixteenth-century Spain there was a regular obsession with the purity of one's blood. The country was entering its Golden Age of imperial expansion within both Europe and the world, and access to key posts within the civil and ecclesiastical administrations required noble status. While Poliakov is correct in asserting the importance of religious orthodoxy in affirming Old Christian claims, he is wrong in dismissing the racial criterion. In point of fact, the purity-of-blood discourse was framed in terms of Gothic descent which established not only the claimant's Old Christian but also noble status (i.e. descent from Isidore of Seville's conquerors rather than conquered).

In 1526 Bizkaia promulgated its 'New Fuero',[12] proclaiming Bizkaian collective nobility and precluding persons of non-noble (i.e. New Christian) blood from settling therein. The following year Gipuzkoa followed suit (*Nueva recopilación* 1976: 326). When, in 1696, Miguel de Aramburu was commissioned by the provincial government (*Diputación*) of Gipuzkoa to compile Gipuzkoa's foral tradition, he summed up two centuries of Basque historiography in a preamble which states:

> There is no specific mention in the sacred scriptures regarding the place in which descendants of the Patriarch Noah founded, for the first time, their settlement and domicile in the initial populating of Spain after the universal flood: however, there is very specific information, grandly founded in tradition [*autoridad común*] that Tubal, fifth son of Japhet, and grandson of the second father of humankind, was the first to come to this region from Armenia with his family and companions after the confusion of tongues in Babylon, and that his first stop and settlement was in the lands situated between the Ebro River and the Cantabrian Ocean. Thus state the ancients and the moderns . . .

After noting Armenian etymologies in Gipuzkoan place names as the first proof of the foregoing, Aramburu states:

> the second witness to Tubal's presence is the Basque language itself, legacy of the resulting confusion when God created seventy-two languages at the destruction of the Tower of Babel. Basque was the language of Tubal and his followers, and they were the ones to introduce it into Spain, where it became the original tongue of this kingdom.

The Basque language is the *prima facie* evidence that Basques were the original settlers of Iberia since it was conserved many years, until its inhabitants were, at different times, oppressed by diverse nations, and they forgot their primitive tongue and received those used by their conquerors, as subjects of their violations.

But this never transpired in the Province of Gipuzkoa, and its surrounding [Basque] areas, because in these places foreigners have never triumphed as they have in the other regions of Spain, and the natural language of the primitive settlers has been conserved gloriously, their descendants continuing the possession of their estates, which have come down to them until the present through inheritance, without the arrivals of the Egyptians, Caldeans, Hebrews, Greeks, Carthaginians, Romans, Alans, Svevs, Vandals, Goths and Arabs, who dominated absolutely in almost all of the rest of the kingdom, and who introduced their national languages, erasing that of the Gipuzkoans in their land, defended and maintained always with valor by the true descendants of the Patriarch Tubal, against all the power of the foreigners, who never managed to deprive Gipuzkoans of their most ancient and free heritage; which, in truth may not be denied through any assertion of discourses whether the most scrupulous or incredulous.

(Nueva recopilación 1976: 5–8)

Thus, more than a millennium after Isidore of Seville invoked it regarding Spanish origins, Tubalism was alive and well but in the service of Basque particularism. However, as Monreal notes, it was not particularism for the purpose of confrontation or separatism. Basques were loyal to Spain and willing collaborators in both the Spanish national and imperial projects (1985: 31–32). Indeed, Aramburu's late seventeenth-century dissertation on Basque uniqueness was offered, 'for the greater honor of the Spanish nation, service of its Kings and Lords, and grand estimation of their country' (*Nueva recopilación* 1976: 7–8).

Greenwood argues, erroneously,[13] that a mid-eighteenth-century text by the Gipuzkoan priest Manuel de Larramendi represents a watershed. He developed extremely virulent ethnic slurs against the Castilians, singling them out as the worst of all Spaniards. Larramendi viewed Spanishness and Basqueness as mutually exclusive and conflicting (1977: 97–98).

Greenwood follows Caro Baroja's lead in branding Larramendi as a 'precursor of the modern racists' (Caro Baroja 1958: 89). I would, however, disagree with the Greenwood/Caro Baroja reading of Larramendi. Tejada and Percopo note that, far from being a 'virulent' or 'vituperative' text, its anti-Castilian 'darts' can be 'counted on the fingers of one hand' (1965: 166). Instead of being anti-Spanish, Larramendi, as a confirmed Tubalist, regarded the Basques to be the original, unsullied Spaniards. His real targets are the frenchified Castilian toadies of the Bourbon rulers in Madrid who were undermining Basque privileges. And while he does launch a few pejorative statements against Castilians in general, he is mainly on the defensive against the Castilian anti-Basque barbs of his day – notably that the language was sheer gibberish[14] and that Basque claims to universal noble status were pretentious. That is, by virtue of the Tubalist we-are-the-original-Spaniards argument, combined with the we-were-never-subsequently-sullied-by-the-blood-of-foreign-invaders one, the claim was for universal noble status of all Basques, including humble peasants and artisans. From at least the time of Cervantes, the rustic Bizkaian 'nobility' was an object of Castilian scorn and satire (cf. Chapter 8 of Book One in the *Quixote*). Larramendi was reacting directly against the barbs of his contemporary, Don Carlos Osorio, who ridiculed Gipuzkoa's 'noble' shoemakers, 'noble' tailors, 'noble' peasants, 'noble' charcoal burners, etc. Larramendi denounced Don Carlos and his ilk as, 'idle nobles, lazy nobles, useless nobles, uncultured, self-evidently unsuitable, who, just to look at them provokes vomit and indignation' (1985: 147–148). He added:

> Even supposing that these *hidalgos* and nobles of Castile are descended directly from the Goths, a supposition that I make gratuitously, I ask: were these Goths from which they come, and which provide their family lines, *hidalgos* and nobles? None of them were villeins or had a manual trade? All were soldiers? Give us a break. Were they not barbarians, thieves who in the name of genteel and Arian [not to be confused with Aryan] conquerors, came from distant lands? And were there not among their thousands many sons of tailors, shoemakers, and other tradesmen of those lands from which they left?
>
> (1985: 166)

Larramendi saves his greatest spite for his fellow Gipuzkoans who were accepting the notion of Castilian superiority – and particularly women who displayed the immodest dress styles dictated by Madrid fashion and his fellow priests who insisted upon preaching in the more prestigious Castilian language to monoglot rural Basque congregations (1985: 223, 304–305).

Finally, rather than implacably anti-Spanish, Larramendi concludes:

> I see that you will always call Gipuzkoa a corner of Spain, and you do well; but you will be obliged to call it a precious, rational, cultivated corner; a tidy and clean corner like silver and gold; a corner of a noble, honorable and generous people, which has earned a thousand laurels through its deeds and service to the Crown, for the honor and the triumphs of Spain.
>
> (1985: 322)

Creating a Basque race

Throughout this chapter we have relied heavily upon Poliakov to lead us through the maze of European racialist discourse. However, in the second paragraph of his first chapter, he introduces a (from our viewpoint) key caveat: 'we will not . . . tarry to expound the exceptional case of Basque language and culture' (1974: 11). Poliakov clearly recognized that such digression accesses a whole other set of issues, a discourse within the discourse, as it were, that would further complicate his already exceedingly complex and daunting mission.

The 'exceptional' Basque case regards the early recognition within the scientific challenge to theological interpretations of human origins that the Basques could not be accommodated within the emerging view that historical Europe was the legacy of prehistorical invasions of the continent from the east by related speakers of the Indo-European family of languages.[15] As we have seen, during the first half of the nineteenth century, thanks to the Sanskritists, language reigned supreme as the evidence that defined the parameters of the scientific racialist research agenda and discourse. In 1821 German philologist Wilhelm von Humboldt published his treatise on the uniqueness of Basque and its 'Ancient Iberian' (rather than Indo-European) credentials (1821).[16]

If the Basques were not Indo-Europeans, who were they?[17] Could they perhaps be the living remnants of a proto-European population that antedated, but was then overwhelmed and largely displaced by, the successive waves of Indo-European invaders of the continent? Such questions fired the imaginations of major figures in the emerging discipline of physical anthropology. By mid-century, Anders Retzius, the Swedish anatomist who systematized craniometry, and Paul Broca, the founding father of French anthropology,[18] were debating Basque anthropometry. Broca published an article entitled 'Sur les caractères du crâne des Basques' ('On the Characteristics of Basque Skulls') and six years later he stated:

> You know that the Basques are the only people in Western Europe that still speak a language unrelated to the Indo-European stock. It is therefore natural that they are considered to be the last and pure representatives of the so-called autochthonous races that occupied the soil of this part of Europe before the era of the Asiatic invasions. This conclusion is without a doubt far from being rigorous, because it may easily be shown that the Basques, through mixture with the Indo-Europeans, have lost all or part of the primitive characteristics of their race, but without abandoning for that reason their primitive language. It is nevertheless probable that, if their language is the only one to have survived, while those of the prehistoric peoples around them were extinguished, leaving barely a few geographic names here and there as testimony to their ancient existence, it is because this small mountainous region that the Basques still occupy today was never completely subjugated by the invaders, and that they yet conserve if not political sovereignty at least a numerical preponderance. It is therefore permissible to believe that their physical features have been less modified by their cross-breeding than that of other peoples of Western Europe.
>
> (1868: 1–2)

There was the notion, then, that Basques, if not a 'pure' proto-European race, were at the least the continent's 'purest' contemporary representatives of it. Investigations of the implications of such a viewpoint continue to the present day, but are beyond the scope of the present study.[19] For our purposes, suffice it to say that by Sabino's time European scientific racism largely accepted the conclusion that there was a 'Basque race', a creation more of the intellectual circles of Paris and Stockholm than Basque (or Spanish) ones (Sánchez-Prieto 1993: 388–393).

Sabino's political agenda and racialist views

Arana's Basque ethnonationalism was directed primarily against Spain for reasons other than simply his putative Spanish citizenship. By this time there were clear differences in the dynamics of the respective playing fields afforded by the Spanish and French Basque Countries, as well as the vulnerability of Spain and France to an internal ethnonationalist challenge. These included:

1   A geographic and demographic preponderance of the Spanish Basque Country (over its French Basque counterpart) which contained approximately six-sevenths of the Basque homeland and, in Arana's day, about nine-elevenths of its total population.

2   Marked economic disparity manifested particularly in the industrial development of Bizkaia and parts of Gipuzkoa, versus the bucolic economy of the French Basque area, dominated by fishing and peasant agriculture. Spanish Basque industry and attendant urbanization attracted workers from throughout Spain, a process which threatened to make Spanish Basques a minority in their home area while marginalizing their culture and language into rural enclaves.

3   Diametrically opposed nineteenth-century national histories. Despite the defeat of Napoleon and the humiliation of the Franco-Prussian War, for the French it was a period of national triumph in which France ascended as a major player on the European scene and as an imperial power on the global one (Doyle 1986: 306–318). For Spain the century opened with (brief) loss of national sovereignty (to the French) and the dissolution of much of its New World colonial empire through the American independence movements. From the 1830s through the mid-1870s Spain experienced civil strifes known collectively as the Carlist Wars. By the 1890s there were serious independence movements in Spain's few remaining colonies.

4   Significantly differing paradigms in their respective nation-building histories. Until brought into the orbit of French Bourbonism in the eighteenth century, the Spain of Fernando and Isabel experienced nearly two subsequent centuries of Hapsburg rule imbued with respect for regional cultural and linguistic differences (*las Españas*). Within this framework there was a Basque foral tradition whereby the Spanish monarchs respected Basque particularisms – including exemption from military conscription, freedom from direct taxation and sovereignty regarding trade and tariffs. It was only during the late nineteenth century (1876), indeed during Arana's childhood, that the Basque *fueros* were all but abolished by Madrid, unilaterally and seemingly definitively, in the aftermath of the foralists' defeat in the last Carlist conflict. In France, prior to the Revolution Basques also enjoyed a degree of foral autonomy *vis-à-vis* Paris (though never to the degree of their ethnic counterparts in Hapsburgian Spain). However, any such political particularism was abolished by the triumph of Jacobin centralism. Thenceforth France would be arguably the quintessential centralized state on the planet, as well as among the least sensitive to ethnic differences (let alone ethnonationalist claims) within its borders.

It is also necessary to situate Arana within the social, political and intellectual climate of his times. He was born into a devoutly religious, upper-middle-class Carlist family in the city of Bilbao. He therefore experienced the bitterness of the Carlists' débâcle in the intimacy of his home, including his family's period of political exile in France. He attended university in Barcelona at a time that a Catalan ethnonationalist movement was in its formative stages.[20] When Arana declared first a Bizkaian (Arana Goiri 1932) and then Basque right to independence, his rallying political slogan was *Jaungoikoa eta Lagizarra* – or 'God and Tradition'. The former was iteration of Carlist Catholic confessionalism in the face of secularism emanating both from a laical-liberal Madrid and the socialist politics of Bizkaia's rapidly growing industrial work force. The latter revindicated a centuries-long foral tradition that had become the faintest of echoes of its former self.

In short, in Arana's view, a new ethnonationalist political movement was required to fill the void caused by the prostration and incapacity of Carlism to serve as an effective counterweight to Spain's unilateral abolition of Basque political autonomy and a 'Spanish invasion' which threatened to minoritize and marginate Basques in their own homeland, while raising a very real spectre of ethnic and class conflict.

The truly 'revolutionary' part of his political agenda was its separatism, a sentiment that Arana promoted primarily through his writings in his own newspaper, the *Bizkaitarra*, begun in 1893. He also created its organizational expression by founding (in 1895) the forerunner of the Basque Nationalist Party in order to contest municipal and provincial elections.

As Watson remarks:

> It was an era of profound social and economic change which itself challenged traditionally-held identities, and its seems not inappropriate to speak in terms of an ontological struggle between Basque and Spanish nationalism. However, while the former had to depend on an initial minority following and the use of symbolic constructions in its ideology, the latter had at its disposal the full force of state power.
>
> (1996: 198–199)

In many respects Sabino is a tragic figure. For most of his contemporaries his campaign must have seemed downright comical. Initially, his newspaper had miniscule circulation and his party but a tiny following. Arana himself was fined, censored and imprisoned on several occasions.[21] He died prematurely of Addison's disease aged 38, providing the by then growing Basque nationalist movement with its first martyr.

Arana was not an intellectual in the scholarly sense (Conversi 1997: 59). Rather than an original thinker, he was more a polemicist, synthesizer and purveyor of ideas – he seldom, if ever, cited authority for his arguments, so we can only infer his 'sources'. There are, however, ways in which Sabino was a true visionary. In articulating his radical Basque nationalism (i.e. independentism), he underscored the Basques' shameful dilemma in being colonized by Spain, and thereby anticipated the subsequent internal colonialism arguments of Lenin, Gramsci, Preobrazhensky, Bukharin, and Hechter (as applied to regions within European states) (Hechter 1999: xiii–xiv). He empathized with the colonized peoples of the world, and would most certainly have sympathized with the views of Frantz Fanon (1963). In questioning the South African situation of his day, Arana denounced the aggression of the English against the Boers, as well as that of the Boers against the Kaffirs. He cited the evidence that whites in South Africa organized sporting campaigns of extermination against the blacks and concluded,

> Such is the unending history of humanity. It is how the Greeks comported themselves in Asia, the Romans in three parts of the [known] world, the followers of Mohammed everywhere, the Spaniards in the New World, the Anglo-Saxons in North America, and it is how all the powers are proceeding today in China.
>
> (*Partido Nacionalista Vasco* 1995: 206)

Unlike Larramendi, who fulminated against the superior airs of a Spain that, in the mid-eighteenth century, remained one of Europe's respectable national and imperial powers,[22] Arana's foil was an all but prostrate country whose imperial colonial legacy was in its death throes. Indeed, for him it was the Basques' shameful stain to be dominated by the central authority of such a pathetic state and colonized by what (as we have seen) the wider European racialist discourse regarded to be inferior 'Latin' racial stock.

Arana delighted in Spain's tribulations, showing sympathy for the Moroccans in Spain's North African conflict of his day and delighting in its humiliating defeat in the Spanish-American War (1898). Indeed, one of his imprisonments resulted in 1902, when his telegram congratulating President Roosevelt for having freed Cuba from slavery (i.e. Spanish colonial domination) was intercepted by Spanish authorities (Conversi 1997: 68).

Regarding Sabino's racialism, Conversi (perhaps too charitably) concludes,

> It is not certain how justly Arana can be accused of being a racist, as he is by many of his opponents. Indeed he never espoused a biological theory of racial superiority, nor did he believe in a universal hierarchy of races.
>
> (1997: 68)

Fair enough. However, he did coin the pejorative terms *Maketania* (derived from *La Mancha*) for non-Basque (particularly Castilian) Spain and *Maketo* for its inhabitants. In this regard, Arana was a Tubalist without Tubal,[23] as it were, stating his belief that the Basques were the pure remnants of the ancient Iberian original inhabitants of the peninsula, whereas the *Maketos* were an inferior mish-mash of racial stocks, the precipitate of non-Basque Spain's history of periodic invasions (Arana Goiri 1978: 52). He was particularly incensed by the *maketismo* or *españolismo* prevalent even in the Basque circles of his day. While he subscribed to the prevalent nineteenth-century view that the language was the most important diacritical feature of Basque uniqueness, he underscored his anti-assimilationist mind set by noting that should Spaniards learn Basque then Basques should simply abandon the language and learn Russian or Norwegian instead (Arana Goiri 1978: 188)! He was given to constant reminders of such thinking, for example:

> Many who are Basques do not know Basque.
> This is bad.
> There are several *Maketos* who know it.
> This is worse.
>
> (Arana Goiri 1995: 258)

Sabino's racialist treatises, while perhaps not constituting a clear biological theory of race, are myriad. In one article entitled 'The Law of Race' he revisited the notion of Basque universal nobility and the sixteenth-century restrictions in the *fuero* prohibiting non-Basques from residing in Bizkaia. Rejecting Poliakov's subsequent view that the purity of blood issue regarded orthodoxy alone, Arana contends that Bizkaia was protecting its racial purity against the possible invasion of Muslims and Jews who were being expelled from Spain at that time. He notes:

> while the words *Moors* and *Jews* that appear in [sixteenth-century] Spanish legislation should always be understood as expressions of religious profession, their presence in Bizkaian laws, to the contrary, may well flow from the racial spirit, and not a religious one.
>
> (Arana Goiri 1978: 200)

In his article 'What are we?' ('*Que Somos*') Sabino trots out a laundry list of invidious comparisons between Basques and *Maketos*: a sample includes:

> The physiognomy of the Bizkaian is intelligent and noble; that of the Spaniard inexpressive and gloomy. The Bizkaian walks upright and manly; the Spaniard . . . has a feminine air (example, the bullfighter).
> The Bizkaian is energetic and agile; the Spaniard lax and dull. The Bizkaian is intelligent and skillful in any type of task; the Spaniard lacks intelligence and ability for even the simplest of jobs. The Bizkaian is hardworking (witness his slopes cultivated to the hilltops); the Spaniard is lazy and slothful (witness his immense plains absolutely devoid of vegetation). The Bizkaian's character degenerates through contact with the outsider; the Spaniard needs from time to time a foreign invasion to civilize him
>
> (ibid.: 56)

And so forth.

Arana also anticipated the problem faced recently by the Baltic States in the aftermath of the collapse of the Soviet Union, namely that of dealing with a large 'foreign' (i.e. Russian) population in their midst. In an article entitled 'Purity of race'. Sabino proposed that in an independent Bizkaia foreigners in general would be allowed to reside only under consular privilege and would be precluded from naturalization. Regarding Spaniards in particular, given the gravity of the extant state of affairs, the Bizkaian parliament should consider expulsion during the first years of independence with the possibility of their controlled re-entry at some future time. Full citizenship in Bizkaia would be reserved for full-blooded Bizkaians, with recognition that the status of 'mestizo' families (i.e. those resulting from Basque/non-Basque unions) would have to be worked out juridically by Parliament (ibid.: 193).

Discussion

By now it should be evident that there was nothing inherently 'sinful' about being a racialist in *fin-de-siècle* Europe. What, then, was Sabino's sin in coopting for his Basque ethnonationalist purposes both a European racialist discourse that viewed Latins to be inferior and another which regarded Basques to be not just the oldest Iberians but also the proto-Europeans? The key lies in understanding the internal state dimension of an implicit superior-core versus inferior-periphery distinction that permeates the European racialist discourse that we have considered.

In Gobineau's general or planetary purview the core is the great white race (with its civilizing capacity and mission) while the peripherals are the yellow and black ones.[24] In the internal Caucasian debate the Nordic/Teutonic/Aryan superior core of northwestern Europe is contrasted to weaker/inferior Latins to the south and Slavs to the east. However, we may posit that the superior core was perceived as *entirely* surrounded by an inferior periphery – since, for at least some observers, to the north the Finns (as speakers of a Finno-Ugric, i.e. non-Indo-European tongue) were clearly inferior and the Laplanders [Saami] were possibly sub-human (as reindeer herders and hence Europe's closest equivalent to a truly primitive culture?) (Poliakov 1974: 261–267).

To the west there were the Celts, regarding whom British racialist discourse is particularly revealing. Indeed, the brutal treatment accorded to the highland Scots and the Irish was justified in part by their near sub-human status. According to some, Irish poverty and fecundity were the inevitable result of a barbarous nature and papist mentality (Curtis 1968; Lebow 1976). Irish were depicted as 'black' in their skin pigmentation, a means of relegating them to the world's inferior colored stocks (Curtis 1968: 72–73, 119). Some even discerned simian-like traits in the Irish (Curtis 1971).

It is in this last example that we discern the power of core–periphery racialist discourse as a feature of the self-definition of the individual state in late nineteenth-century Europe. The quintessential demonstration of each state's national culture was reflected in its capital city (Paris, London, Madrid, Moscow, etc.), i.e. the nerve center of the core. All else being equal, national pride demanded that the capital serve as the showplace of national accomplishment for the citizenry and foreigners alike. In the Spanish case, Sabino Arana was committing the unpardonable in asserting the racial superiority of the periphery *vis-à-vis* the core as justification for their total political estrangement, i.e. Basque independence. In this regard Arana's sin was indeed (a European) original!

Notes

1 Conversi notes that, unlike most nationalisms, that of the Basques was essentially shaped by one person. To wit, 'Arana single-handedly formulated its first political programme, coined its name, defined its geographical extent, founded its first political organisation, wrote its anthem and designed its flag' (1997: 53).

2 For example Aranzadi *et al.* (1994) and Aranzadi (2000: 60–62).

3 From our post-Holocaust, post-eugenics perspective it is particularly difficult to appreciate the intellectual climate of the times. In the words of one critic, reviewing Carlton Coon's controversial work *The Origin of Races* (published in 1962), 'It requires a degree of courage to write a book on Races of Man in this era of the New Prudery, when r_ce has replaced s_x as the great dirty word' (quoted in Shipman 1994: 215).
  In the introduction to his seminal work, *The Aryan Myth*, Léon Poliakov notes,

> There can be no doubt that if, at the beginning of this century, the West still entertained the flattering notion of its superior civilization, often thought of as an Aryan birthright, the Hitlerite catastrophe banished such ideas from political and public life so effectively that now a fresh confusion has arisen, between science and ethics. Anti-racism has been promoted to the rank of a dogmatic orthodoxy which the present state of anthropological knowledge is unable to corroborate, but which will brook no criticism, and which is an impediment to sober thinking. This has produced a self-censorship, to a great extent retroactive, by authors of all kinds, but particularly historians who, often without knowing it, try to reinterpret the history of modern thought under this influence. *It begins to look as if, through shame or fear of being racist, the West will not admit to having been so at any time*, and therefore assigns to minor characters only (like Gobineau, H.S. Chamberlain, etc.) the role of scapegoats.

> (1974: 5, his emphasis)

4 There were, of course, a plethora of classificatory systems positing considerable variety of sub-types within what Gobineau labeled 'the three great races' (1967: 205).

5 Biddiss regards Gobineau as the 'father of racist ideology' (1970).

6 Or 'mismeasurement' as the case may be (cf. Gould 1981).

7 Robert Knox summed up Disraeli's views as follows: 'race in human affairs is everything, is simply the fact, the most remarkable, the most comprehensive, which philosophy has ever announced. Race is everything: literature, science, art – in a word, civilization depends on it' (1862: 1).

8 Near the end of his life Gobineau experienced the bitterness of his country's defeat in the Franco-Prussian War (1870–71), which he translated into a kind of French self-loathing, prompting some of his co-national critics to brand him a germanophile (Biddiss 1970: 222).

9 It should be noted that not all scholars (and particularly those of denigrated peoples and states) accepted their racial 'fate' within the Aryanist framework. To be sure, modern Greeks and Italians were wont to emphasize their own superiority *vis-à-vis* other Europeans due to their (ancient) civilizational credentials and continuity of 'Hellenic' and 'Latin' racial stocks (Poliakov 1974: 68–69; Just 1989: 75–76).

10 Poliakov's work is essentially a history of European racism leading to the Holocaust. In his analysis, sixteenth-century Spanish anti-Semitism eventually culminates in the twentieth-century atrocity. Another major historian of the racist thought producing the Holocaust, George Mosse, concurs in discerning the baseline of European racism in Spain's sixteenth-century treatment of its Jews, but sees less subsequent historical continuity. Thus,

> Certainly in sixteenth-century Spain racism existed in its modern sense, for there the concept of 'purity of blood' was the justification for discrimination against anyone of Jewish descent. It could be argued that the Spanish *conversos* were the first

victims of racial persecution in Europe. Yet the Spanish policy toward 'Jewish Christians' faded with time and did not constitute a viable precedent for the rest of Europe.

(1978: xxix)

11 The issue of the Jewish *conversos* (their Muslim equivalents were known as *Moriscos*) was longer standing. As early as the eleventh century significant numbers of Jews were fleeing Muslim for Christian Spain in search of opportunity, as well as in the aftermath of persecution in the former. By the thirteenth century most Iberian Jews lived on Christian territory, where they were tolerated and privileged (Payne 1973: 78). At the same time, the successes of the Reconquest brought many Muslims under Christian rule. Over time there developed Christian discomfort with the infidels in their midst, who were first encouraged and then forced to convert to Catholicism.

In 1391 Castile experienced a major pogrom and the fifteenth century was punctuated with reprisals against the *conversos*, who were deemed to be too powerful and probably Crypto-Jews at heart. In 1478 the papacy approved Spain's request to establish its own inquisition under state control to combat the *conversos'* heresy.

At the time of Fernando and Isabel Castile's population of unconverted Jews (150,000) and *Conversos* (150,000) represented about 4 per cent of the population. In 1492, by royal decree, the unconverted were expelled from Spain. Payne estimates that more than 100,000 persons fled the country (1973: 211). Thousands of Muslims also abandoned Spain after their final defeat in Granada, while thousands more converted to Catholicism. Unlike the *conversos*, who constituted a financial élite, the *Moriscos* were, in the main, small holder agriculturalists with a much lower profile than Jews within Spanish society (ibid.: 214–215).

12 The *fueros* are the legal charters which accord Basques differential treatment in comparison with its other component regions within Spain. Interpretation of their genesis is at the core of historical disagreements between Spanish and Basque nationalists. For the former, the *fueros* were concessions of privilege to the Basques made by Castillian (and subsequently Spanish) monarchs. As concessions they could be (and, in the nineteenth-century, were) rescinded unilaterally by the Spanish government. Basque nationalists contend that the *fueros* are written codification of timeless Basque consuetudinary law, respect for which was a condition of (voluntary) Basque integration into a wider Iberian polity during the Middle Ages. Basque nationalists therefore reject Spain's claim to a right of unilateral action while reserving to the Basques a right of self-determination.

13 The Larramendi work, while written in the mid-eighteenth century, was first published in 1882 and could therefore not configure eighteenth-century, or even most of nineteenth-century, Basque/Spanish political discourse.

14 Larramendi also wrote the first Basque grammar which he entitled *The Impossible Overcome*, an exercise intended to demonstrate that Basque was, indeed, a true language!

15 By the mid-century the primacy of language as a diacritic of race was under severe criticism (Poliakov 1974: 255–261). However, initially it went largely unquestioned.

16 To this day, and despite nearly two centuries of efforts by philologists and linguists to discover affinities between Basque and other languages, so far as we know, Basque remains 'unrelated to any other language' (Katzner 1976: 36).

17 In commenting upon William G. Boyd's *Genetics and Races of Man: An Introduction to Modern Physical Anthropology* (1950), in which, based on their gene frequencies, Basques are distinguished as one of only six human races, a frustrated modern critic remarks,

the segregation of the Basques on the basis of their divergent blood groups did not seem to be sublimely wise. It was not as if they had green skins and square heads: they looked like ordinary Europeans, though speaking a strange language and having divergent blood group frequencies. The Basques could hardly be considered a category of living people equivalent to, say, the African, and they were certainly not phenotypically distinctive.

(Marks 1995: 131)

18 In 1859 Broca founded the *Société d'Antropologie de Paris* and was the prime mover of the *Revue d'Antropologie.*

19 Cf. Cavalli-Sforza, *et al.* (1991: 285–286) for statements that are entirely consonant with Broca's viewpoint. We might also note that for physical anthropologists like A.C. Haddon, father of British physical anthropology, the Basques were likely descended from an Upper Paleolithic Cro-Magnon population (MacClancy 1993: 111).

20 It is difficult to assess the importance of this. Shortly before Arana's stint in Barcelona Pi i Margall published (1877) his work *The Nationalities* calling for a federal Spain based upon regional cultural distinctions. In 1882 a young Philippine student, José Rizal, arrived in Barcelona, and we know that the future father of Philippine nationalism read Pi i Margall's work (Ortiz Armengol 1997: 14). That same year Sabino arrived in the Catalan capital to commence his studies and Larramendi's work *Corografía de Guipúzcoa* was first published in the city. Clearly, Arana was at least indirectly affected by Catalanism, and particularly the reverence accorded the language. In 1885, while still in Barcelona, he began to study Basque, and in 1888 published in that city the first part of his own Basque grammar (Conversi 1997: 57).

21 Possibly discouraged by the incapacity of radical independentism to attract popular support, as well as its demonstrated capacity to incur the wrath of Spanish authorities, by the end of his life Arana was moderating his views to advocate Basque regionalism within a united Spain. There is disagreement among Basque nationalists, as well as scholars, regarding the sincerity of this 'conversion.' For some, it was simply a tactical move on Arana's part to both garner political support and deflect political repression (Conversi 1997: 68–69).

If Arana's political radicalism seemed nothing short of quixotic when first announced, it obviously struck a certain chord. In 1898 Arana himself was elected to the provincial assembly of Bizkaia. The following year his supporters won five seats on the Bilbao city council. Indeed, shortly after Sabino's death the nationalists emerged as the second political force in Bizkaia. Ultimately, the Basque Nationalist Party would become the strongest single political party in Basque politics, a position that it enjoys at present.

22 Ringrose's recent (1996) revisionist work argues that not only was eighteenth-century Spain prosperous but the loss of the colonies in the nineteenth did not impede the country's economic growth to the extent that is commonly assumed.

23 Despite his ardent Catholicism, Arana never mentions Tubal and other biblical characters, a point which underscores the extent to which, by the late nineteenth century, scientific polygenism had triumphed over theological monogenism in European racialist discourse.

24 In this regard, nineteenth- and early twentieth-century physical anthropological research simply paralleled social anthropology's occidentalist bias – 'the Other', 'Here versus the Out There' – that has come under intense criticism over the last two decades (Lavie and Swedenburg 1996).

References

Arana Goiri, Sabino 1932. (first published in 1890) *Bizkaya por su independencia.* Bilbao: Verdez Achirica.

—— 1978. *Obras escogidas. Antología política.* San Sebastián: L. Haranburu.

—— 1995. *La patria de los vascos. Antología de escritos políticos* (compiled by Antonio Elorza). San Sebastián: R & B Ediciones.

Aranzadi, Juan 2000. 'Racismo y antirracismo en la antropología vasca'. *Cuadernos de Alzate.* 23: 43–46.

Aranzadi, Juan, Juaristi, Jon and Unzueta, Patxo 1994. *Auto de terminación.* Madrid: El País Aguilar.

Biddiss, Michael D. 1970. *Father of Racist Ideology: The Social and Political Thought of Count Gobineau.* New York: Weybright and Talley.

—— 1979. 'Introduction'. In Michael D. Biddiss (ed.) *Images of Race.* New York: Holmes and Meier.

Broca, Paul 1862. 'Sur les caractéres du crâne Basques'. *Bulletins de la Société d'Antropologie de Paris.* III: 579–591.

—— 1868. *Mémoire sur les crânes des Basques de Saint-Jean-de-Luz suivi de recherches sur la comparaison des indices céphaliques sur le vivant et sur le squelette.* Paris: Librairie Victor Masson et fils.

Caro Baroja, Julio 1958. *Los vascos.* Madrid: Ediciones Minotauro.

Cavalli-Sforza, L., Paolo Menozzi, Luca and Piazza, Alberto 1991. *The History and Geography of Human Genes.* Princeton, NJ: Princeton University Press.

Connor, Walker 1994. 'Beyond Reason: The Nature of the Ethnonational Bond'. In Walker Connor *Ethnonationalism. The Quest for Understanding.* Princeton, NJ: Princeton University Press, Chapter 8.

Conversi, Daniele 1997. *The Basques, the Catalans and Spain: Alternative Routes to Nationalist Mobilisation.* Reno: University of Nevada Press.

Curtis, Jr., L. Perry 1968. *Anglo-Saxons and Celts: A Study of Anti-Irish Prejudice in Victorian England.* New York: New York University Press.

—— 1971. *Apes and Angels: The Irishman in Victorian Caricature.* Washington, DC: Smithsonian Institution Press.

Doyle, Michael J. 1986. *Empires.* Ithaca, NY: Cornell University Press.

Fanon, Frantz 1963. *The Wretched of the Earth* (translated by Constance Farington). New York: Grove Press.

Gobineau, J.A. de 1967. *The Inequality of Human Races* (translated by Adrian Collins). New York: Howard Fertig.

Gould, Stephen Jay 1981. *The Mismeasure of Man.* New York and London: W.W. Norton.

Greenwood, Davydd 1977. 'Continuity in Change: Spanish Basque Ethnicity as a Historical Process'. In Milton J. Esman (ed.) *Ethnic Conflict in the Western World.* Ithaca, NY: Cornell University Press: 81–102.

Hechter, Michael 1999. *Internal Colonialism: The Celtic Fringe in British National Development.* Revised edn. New Brunswick/London: Transaction Publishers.

Humboldt, Wilhelm von 1821. *Prüfung der Untersuchungen über die urbewohnner Hispaniens vermittelts der Vaskischen Sprache.* Berlin: F. Dümmler.

Isidore of Seville 1970. (first published in 619 AD). *History of the Goths, Vandals and Suevi* (translated from the Latin by Guido Donini and Gordon B. Ford, Jr.). Leiden: E.J. Brill.

Just, Roger 1989. 'Triumph of the Ethnos'. In Elizabeth Tonkin, Maryon McDonald and Malcolm Chapman (eds) *History and Ethnicity.* London: Routledge.

Katzner, Kenneth 1976. *The Languages of the World.* New York: Funk and Wagnalls.

Knox, Robert 1862. *The Races of Men: A Philosophical Enquiry into the Influence of Race Over the Destinies of Nations.* 2nd edn. London: H. Renshaw.

Larramendi, Manuel de 1985. *Corografía de la Provincia de Guipúzcoa.* Bilbao: Editorial Amigos del Libro Vasco.

Lavie, Smadar and Swedenburg, Ted 1996. 'Introduction: Displacement, Diaspora, and Geographies of Identity'. In Smadar Lavie and Ted Swedenburg (eds) *Displacement, Diaspora, and Geographies of Identity.* Durham, NC: Duke University Press.

Lebow, Richard Ned 1976. *White Britain and Black Ireland: The Influence of Stereotypes on Colonial Policy*. Philadelphia: Institute for the Study of Human Issues.

MacClancy, Jeremy 1993. 'Biological Basques, Sociologically Speaking'. In Malcom Chapman (ed.) *Social and Biological Aspects of Ethnicity*. Oxford: Oxford University Press.

Marks, Jonathan 1994. *Human Biodiversity. Genes, Race and History*. New York: Aldine de Gruyter.

Monreal, Gregorio 1985. 'Annotations Regarding Basque Traditional Political Thought in the Sixteenth Century'. In William A. Douglass (ed.) *Basque Politics: A Case Study in Ethnic Nationalism*. Basque Studies Program Occasional Papers Series, No. 2. Reno, NV: Basque Studies Program: 19–49.

Mosse, George L. 1978. *Toward the Final Solution: A History of European Racism*. Madison, WI: University of Wisconsin Press.

Nueva recopilación de los fueros, privilegios, buenos usos y costumbres de la M.N.Y.N.L. Provincia de Guipúzcoa 1976. (Facsimile of 1867 edition of text first published in 1696.) Valladolid: Lex Nova.

Ortiz Armengol, Pedro 1997. 'Prólogo'. In José Rizal *Noli me tangere*. Barcelona: Galaxia Gutenberg.

Partido Nacionalista Vasco 1995. *El pensamiento de Sabino de Arana y Goiri a través de sus escritos*. Bilbao: Euzko Alderdi Jeltzalea.

Payne, Stanley G. 1973. *A History of Spain and Portugal*. Vol. 1. Madison, WI: University of Wisconsin Press.

Poliakov, Léon 1974. *The Aryan Myth: A History of Racist and Nationalist Ideas in Europe* (translated by Edmund Howard). New York: Basic Books.

Ringrose, David 1996. *Spain, Europe and the 'Spanish Miracle'. 1700–1900*. Cambridge: Cambridge University Press.

Sánchez-Prieto, Juan María 1993. *El imaginario vasco. Representaciones de una conciencia histórica, nacional y política en el escenario europeo 1833–1876*. Barcelona: Ediciones Internacionales Universitarias EIUNSA.

Shipman, Pat 1994. *The Evolution of Racism: Human Differences and the Use and Abuse of Science*. New York: Simon and Schuster.

Tejada, Elías and Percopo, Gabriella 1965. *La Provincia de Guipúzcoa*. Madrid: Ediciones Minotauro.

Watson, Cameron J. 1996. 'Sacred Earth, Symbolic Blood: A Cultural History of Basque Political Violence from Arana to ETA'. PhD dissertation, Basque Studies (History). University of Nevada, Reno.

7 Ethnonationalism in black and white

Scholars and the South African revolution

John Stone

In his perceptive exploration of the power and resilience of ethnonationalism, Walker Connor has stressed a number of recurring themes. One of these has been the 'divorce between intellectual theory and the real world' (Connor 1994: 28) that can explain part of the failure of many scholars to recognize the importance of nationalism in shaping some of the most fundamental conflicts of the past two centuries. Not all political and social scientists have ignored this central factor and some, singled out by Connor for their sound judgement, have been vindicated by the upsurge of nationalism many decades after their original predictions. Carlton Hayes' *Essays on Nationalism* (1926) is one such volume whose insights were to act as a source of inspiration for Connor in the 1960s, when he began to publish his influential articles on ethnonationalism.

Another theme of Connor's writings has been the critical psychological bond created by nationalism which makes it hard to analyse the phenomenon in terms of the rationalist models that pervade much of the scholarship in this field (Connor 1993). It is the aim of this chapter to explore two related issues. The first considers how South African society managed to resolve its problems of conflicting ethnonational loyalties within a racially polarized setting. The second assesses the degree of success that leading scholars of South Africa had in understanding and predicting its future throughout the period of *apartheid* (1948–90). Both questions explore central ideas in Connor's interpretation of nationalism: whether, 'when the chips are down', national identities will trump racial or class affiliations; and whether scholars of South Africa misunderstood the dynamics of nationalism which reduced their capacity to predict the negotiated transition towards non-racial democracy.

'Those who fail to learn the lessons of history, will be condemned to repeat them.' Santayana's aphorism is often quoted by social and political scientists,[1] but it is rare to find cases where his warning is applied to their own research. When events appear to challenge the expectations generated by the prevailing theories in the social sciences, the typical response is to declare the situation an exception to the general rule and focus attention on another problem. If it is an issue in which we have a strong intellectual investment, or if it is an anomaly that is too glaring to ignore, then there may be a temptation to indulge in a little revisionist history, massage the facts to fit in with a cherished theory, or stretch the theory to accommodate the recalcitrant facts.[2]

Of course, few would suggest that the 'lessons of history' are clear and unambiguous. Most important social and political turning points are the result of complex processes, the understanding of which requires long and patient analysis. Much of the evidence may not be readily available and the full impact of particular causal factors can rarely be appreciated until considerable time has elapsed. However, in the field of race and ethnic relations, few periods provide a better background against which to assess rival theories than South Africa under apartheid (1948–90),[3] and few events a superior testing ground for different predictions than the remarkable democratic transformation, or 'negotiated revolution', that signalled the demise of that system. The South African case is particularly interesting not only for the variety of different perspectives involved – combining social science models and ideological assumptions in varying proportions – but also for the failure of most of this scholarship to provide any more accurate prediction than that apartheid, in the long run, was doomed to failure.[4]

In the following sections, I will divide the era of apartheid into three major segments reflecting the evolution, consolidation and decline of the system. I will then consider the corresponding interpretations of selected scholars, whose writings represent important approaches to race relations, and contain explicit attempts to predict the social and political direction of the society. The period begins with the unexpected victory of D.F. Malan's National Party in the general election of 1948, and closes with F.W. de Klerk's speech rescinding the ban on the black liberation movements and the South African Communist Party. This last act of the apartheid state opened a negotiating process that resulted, four years later, in South Africa's first democratic elections and the final achievement of majority rule.

Anticipating apartheid: the early years, 1948–61

If 1948 represented a turning point in South African history, it was not so much because the years leading up to that fateful election were ones marked by racial tolerance and harmony. The significance of the date was that it represented a crossroads at which the political direction of the society would begin to diverge from the slowly evolving, global pattern of race relations in the post-war period. Britain's victory in the fight against the Axis powers had come at a heavy cost which had hastened its economic decline as a world power and weakened its ability to maintain control over a vast and scattered empire. Decolonization was an inevitable result of this diminished economic capacity, further undermined by huge war debts, and the eagerness of the United States to see the end of imperial tariffs against its own industrial exports in large parts of Africa and Asia. Furthermore, incipient nationalist forces had been encouraged by the democratic rhetoric of the Allied war effort – although much of it was not intended for colonial consumption – as well as the demonstration effect of early German and Japanese military victories over what had previously appeared to be invincible imperial armies. Ten years after Indian independence, Ghana led the decolonization of Africa, and the gradually escalating struggle for civil rights in America signalled the mainstream agenda of post-war race relations.

Against this background, the electoral victory of the National Party came as a surprise and ran in a direction contrary to these other powerful trends in global history. However, the prospect of a Nationalist political takeover was anticipated by some scholars, like the historian Arthur Keppel-Jones, who was one of the first to consider the consequences of this development in his book *When Smuts Goes* (1947). Although this work was written in a fictional style, like Orwell's *Nineteen Eighty-Four* published some two years later, it contained some remarkably shrewd insights into the character of the new, harshly autocratic regime bent on establishing a white supremacist state by whatever means necessary. Keppel-Jones correctly anticipated the techniques by which the Nationalist government, elected by a narrow majority of the white electorate, would systematically tinker with the constitution to make it virtually impossible for the party to be defeated in any future elections. The entrenchment of white rule and the relentless attack on all forms of potential opposition – liberal, nationalist or communist – broadly followed the path outlined in the book.

It was in discussing the decline and fall of the new Nationalist Republic that Keppel-Jones' predictions began to run into some unexpected developments. Inevitably, the further into the future we try to predict, the greater the tendency for complex, new factors to intervene in surprising and largely unanticipated ways.

In Keppel-Jones' fictional version of events the new Republic was soon enmeshed in a web of forces that would result in its own destruction. A major exodus of whites gathered pace, helping to undermine the industrial base of the society. While the magnates of the mining industry played along with the new regime believing, like the German industrialists of the 1930s, that they could ride the tiger of racial nationalism, a decision by the world financial community to demonetize gold added a crippling blow to an already weakened economy. Unemployment, poverty and repression stimulated the growth of the African resistance movement resulting in guerrilla warfare and an abortive uprising. The ensuing racial massacres and savage reprisals began the process of international intervention leading eventually to an Anglo-American invasion force which brought about the military downfall of the Nationalist republic. Given such an inauspicious legacy, it was only realistic to expect that the successor regime, now based on majority rule, would slowly decline into a quagmire of political assassination and economic corruption, leaving the country in the twenty-first century on the brink of total collapse. This tragic state of affairs was then viewed by white supremacists as the final vindication of their repeated assertions about the consequences of majority rule and foreign interference (Keppel-Jones 1947; Stone 1986: 414).

At least six major assumptions account for the failure of these predictions and they are associated with the following factors:

1   the speed and manner of decolonization
2   international migration
3   secondary industrialization
4   mineral reserves

5   African liberation movements
6   the impact of international pressures.

Although the book indicated the influence of an independent India on the development of events in South Africa, it totally failed to anticipate the tide of decolonization that was about to sweep the African continent. Thus the focus was on the xenophobic mentality of the Nationalist leadership rather than the significant transfer of power taking place throughout Sub-Saharan Africa which was to slowly increase the political, diplomatic and military pressure on the South African Republic.[5] The failure to foresee the correct African context in which the internal political struggles of the future republic would have to be resolved resulted in a series of related errors, one of which was in the predictions concerning patterns of black and white migration.

When Smuts Goes envisaged a major exodus of whites, drawn particularly from the English-speaking minority and the Jewish community, following closely on the heels of a Nationalist election victory. Neither of these trends occurred: white immigration exceeded emigration for much of the post-1948 period and the Nationalist leadership quickly discarded the virulent anti-Semitism which had been associated with its tactical flirting with Nazism. Only in the aftermath of heightened levels of racial conflict – following the Sharpeville massacre in 1960, the 1976 Soweto uprising and the township violence of the mid-1980s – was there a net loss in white population. During the 1970s, decolonization in Mozambique, Angola and Zimbabwe resulted in substantial increases in white immigrants from Africa, adding a strongly racist element to the non-Afrikaner, white population. It is true that a significant segment of younger, better-educated whites did leave the country and some, combining with increasing numbers of African political exiles, proved to be articulate and determined members of the anti-apartheid movement. Throughout the period, substantial flows of migrant workers from all over Sub-Saharan Africa were attracted to South Africa's mines and secondary industries, which remained a magnet for those seeking employment.

It was the strength of this industrial growth, building a diversified manufacturing and financial economy, that was largely unanticipated by the early analysts of a Nationalist victory. This massive industrialization in the post-war period simultaneously provided the means to consolidate white political supremacy but also unleashed forces that posed a threat to the ideological blueprint of apartheid theory. Just as the balance of numerical power was more crucially affected by black and white differential birth rates than by migratory movements, so, too, the flood of African workers into the major industrial conurbations offset all the attempts by the bureaucratic apparatus of the state to stem this process of social and economic integration. In the longer term, the integrated nature of the economy provided crucial new elements in the overthrow of white supremacy: the gathering strength of organized labour, the powerful tactics of consumer boycotts, and the expanding, politically-conscious, urban proletariat, so often associated with demands for social change.

A second factor in the anticipated collapse of the Nationalist republic was its 'precarious' reliance on gold and strategic minerals. In fact, for several decades these mineral reserves provided the apartheid government with a uniquely powerful shield against financial pressures and helped to cushion the costs of escalating military defence and the expensive task of developing a sanction-proof economy. Furthermore, substantial foreign investments for many years muted the criticism, and certainly the actions, of South Africa's major trading partners. While in the end international economic pressures provide a critical lever in forcing the Nationalists to the bargaining table, for more than three decades the impact of these factors worked in the opposite direction.

From the perspective of the 1940s, the prospects of a full-scale African uprising seemed a very remote possibility. As the oldest African liberation movement on the Continent, the ANC, since its inception in 1912, had been a non-violent organization devoted to the peaceful pursuit of social change and democracy. Almost half a century was to pass before uncompromising opponents were to force a change in tactics, although the armed struggle was never to be a crucial component bringing about a change in regime. Keppel-Jones looked to outside military intervention – an Anglo-American invasion force with African guerrilla action playing an essentially supporting role – as the most probable source of external change. In reality, foreign military intervention was not a serious proposition, Cuban military assistance to the MPLA in the devastating Angolan proxy war being the nearest example of direct 'outside' influence, but the fundamental imbalance of power between the SADF and the guerrilla fighters remained until the transition to democracy.[6]

While international intervention did not take place, international pressure was a totally different matter. The power games of the Cold War tended to work in favour of the apartheid regime, for as long as Pretoria mouthed an anti-Communist rhetoric, many Western governments were prepared to turn a blind eye to its racial policies, as they had to human rights abuses by right-wing dictatorships in both Central and South America, and other parts of Africa and Asia. By the middle of the 1980s, however, increasing pressure from a variety of sources – the United Nations, the Commonwealth and the Organization of African Unity – and anti-apartheid movements in Europe and the United States, combined with the diminishing threat from the Soviet Union, added an important impetus for change in the situation. All of this remained a distant prospect at the time of Smuts' surprise defeat.

Verwoerd's vision: the consolidation of apartheid, 1961–76

The period from the Nationalists' election victory until the Sharpeville massacre saw the steady erosion of most forms of legal opposition to white minority rule. A systematic strategy was pursued to harness the power of the state to crush anything more than a few tokens of democratic resistance while the internal and external factors that would eventually force a reversal of these trends had yet to be mobilized. Most scholarly analyses written during this period stressed the negative consequences of these policies, whether they were written by South Africans or by outsiders (e.g. Carter 1958; Hellmann 1949; Kuper 1956; Luthuli 1962; Marquard 1952; Ngubane 1963; Patterson 1957; Wilson and Mafeje 1963). A few books, written by scholars sympathetic to the regime attempted to provide a justification for the government policies (cf. Rhoodie and Venter 1960). In general, however, these works presented a critical review of the evolution of South Africa's increasingly oppressive pattern of race relations but left the future scenario full of disturbing, but vaguely defined, conflict.

It was not until the 1960s that serious speculation about the future of the society began to re-surface. The establishment of a Republic and the break from the Commonwealth; the beginnings of significant international isolation, as apartheid became a symbol of unacceptable racial oppression; and the start of the armed struggle by a nationalist leadership forced to recognize the futility of passive resistance, combined to suggest a possible threat to the status quo. Several influential studies written by Pierre van den Berghe (1964: 65; 67) contained an incisive account of the contending forces within South African society and a consistent prediction that the future prospects were extremely disturbing – 'A South Africa divided against itself awaits its impending doom' (1967: 110). Van den Berghe characterized the South African social system as one permeated by group conflict and exhibiting an almost complete lack of agreement on desirable goals. He argued that this situation combined with the twin forces of domestic industrialism and decolonization to the north were generating sufficient 'contradictions' to precipitate a violent overthrow of the ruling regime. Writing in 1965, he declared:

> the South African government cannot resist much longer the combination of mounting internal and external pressures, and the political change in South Africa cannot be peaceful. Indeed, all the symptoms of a pre-revolutionary situation are clearly present. The opposing forces of Afrikaner and African nationalism have become increasingly polarized ideologically, and both have shown an increasing readiness to use violence to achieve their aims. Lack of communication between the antagonists is complete; so are their unwillingness to compromise or negotiate, their disagreement about the 'rules of the game', and their reciprocal denial of legitimacy.
>
> (van den Berghe 1965: 182)

As a result of the situation:

> A South Africa divided against itself awaits the impending and inexorable catastrophe. The Whites claim a right to survival which hardly anyone denies them. But in claiming to assert that right, they have set themselves against the course of history, and have become an arrogant, oppressive *albinocracy*. Their pride and prejudice may well be their undoing. *Quos vult Jupiter perdere, dementat prius*.
>
> (ibid.: 262–263)

Van den Berghe's bold predictions were in accord with many of the social and political trends of the 1960s. There seemed to be an almost inevitable retreat of the colonial powers out of Africa; the Civil Rights movement was finally attacking the persistence of segregation in the United States, and there even appeared to be renewed democratic challenges to Soviet domination in Eastern Europe. However, some critics (including the author of this chapter) felt that van den Berghe's analysis was not fully convincing and found Lewin's much-quoted assessment, that there was 'no revolution round the corner', considerably more plausible (Lewin 1963; Stone 1973).

Van den Berghe had formulated his study of South Africa as an empirical challenge to the assumption of value-consensus in the theoretical writings of Talcott Parsons. In this respect he had correctly demonstrated the one-sidedness of conservative functionalism, but then seemed to slide into a over-determined model of structural integration whose 'contradictions' would necessarily precipitate a violent overturn of the ruling regime. Critics explained the failure of these predictions as a result, in part at least, of the misleading analogy drawn between South Africa and the crumbling colonial societies to the north. A more apt analogy, despite other major differences, seemed to be the ability of Israel to survive in the hostile environment of the Middle East:

> Each society contained minorities steeled by persecution, whether Nazi or British, believing that they fight for their very survival; both command a technology far more sophisticated than their adversaries; and both have powerful and wealthy sources of outside support. In the case of South Africa, the relative numbers of blacks and whites; the political control and independence of the Afrikaner élite; the relative wealth and self-sufficiency of the economy with its massive foreign investment; and the attitude of mind based on the realization that there is nowhere left to run – all these suggest differences from the ex-colonial countries in Africa which makes a direct comparison spurious. No one can accurately predict how far a ruthlessly determined and frightened élite, possessing the most modern sources of social control, can dominate a society by brute force and intelligence.
>
> (Stone 1973: 43)

While accepting the long-run growth in the strength of the African majority, the immediate effectiveness of the apartheid strategy to divide and rule suggested that the realities of white power would outweigh the potentiality of black power in the foreseeable future. Thus van den Berghe's model of South African society underestimated the importance of coercion in maintaining the political status quo, failed to see that technological forces would strengthen the white élite at the same time as the black masses, and ignored the unpalatable truth than technology is ethically neutral and its outcome on that score is indeterminate.

At about the same time, another American-based sociologist, Austin Turk, returned to the difficult task of trying explicitly to assess the 'futures of South Africa' (Turk 1967). He recognized that any attempt to predict was a question of probability involving a degree of chance that was constantly contaminated by political agendas. Turk specifically wished to avoid, as he put it, 'adding another item to the library of subtle polemic' (ibid: 402), and aimed to order possible out-comes from the most to the least probable. Like van den Berghe, an additional strength of his approach was a self-conscious effort to link his analysis of the South African situation to more general sociological propositions concerning conflict in multi-racial societies.

His basic model of the conflict rested on differences of power and authority channeled along the major societal division between 'whites' and 'non-whites'. The eight conceivable outcomes were as follows:

1   a reversal of power relations – black domination replacing white domination
2   conflict leading to white expulsion
3   genocide against the 'non-whites'
4   'assimilation'
5   non-racial re-alignment – a colour-blind, class society
6   secession of 'non-white' authorities
7   continued segregation
8   federal system of black and white areas.

The first two outcomes were dismissed as highly unlikely for a number of reasons. Twenty years after Keppel-Jones' predictions, Turk argued that external forces sent to intervene in a situation of severe racial conflict would be there principally to defend whites and protect Anglo-American investments. He noted the weakness of African opposition forces and the military power of the whites; stressed the integrative pressures binding Africans and whites both in the economy and at interpersonal levels; and observed that in the event of an African–white violent confrontation, Indians and Coloureds would probably side with the whites, and 'there is no doubt that the Afrikaners, especially, are fully prepared to resist to the death any revolutionary effort merely to substitute African rule for white' (Turk 1967: 405). Similarly, any attempt at a genocidal massacre of the African population by the whites would also trigger an external military intervention by Anglo-American forces.[7]

By dismissing the first three scenarios as highly unlikely, Turk focussed on the remaining options that were either 'integrative' or 'separatist'. He found neither of the integrative outcomes particularly plausible, whether the accommodation involved total group assimilation or the development of a non-racial, class society. For them to work would require a level of 'individualism' that appeared to be entirely lacking among 'the vast majority of South Africans in each of the conflicting parties' (ibid.: 407). The discussion of non-racialism revealed much the same assessment as van den Berghe, individualists remaining a tiny, ineffectual minority crushed between the monolithic forces of Afrikaner and African nationalism, with little prospect of a change of heart among significant proportions of either group. Far in the future, Turk mentioned the possible impact of economic and technological forces that might downplay the salience of racism; the chance that international economic pressures might become more effective; and that the sustained impact of urbanization could produce a gradual but significant shift in Afrikaner attitudes.

None of these developments appeared imminent in 1967, and Turk argued that some variant of a 'separatist' outcome was the most likely resolution of the conflict. While recognizing that the *Bantustans* were a sham, and that 'separate development' was 'really nothing more than verbal camouflage . . . for white domination', he still argued that the most plausible path to non-racial democracy lay in a 'racial federation'.

Although he fully appreciated the disrepute that federalist solutions had acquired during the apartheid era, Turk maintained that, what he termed, 'most real influentials' on both sides of the colour line would probably be willing to work within a few years for a 'transitory segregative accommodation guaranteeing significant improvements in the status of nonwhites' (ibid.: 410). In this manner, segregation would be maintained in a transitional period until power was devolved to a federation of states and thus the 'nearest thing to a final resolution of South Africa's political-racial conflict is most probably a federal system'.

In the fifteen-year period between Sharpeville and Soweto, a variety of different social science perspectives produced a range of possible scenarios: from outright race war, to a conflict-laden stalemate, to an unintended evolution of apartheid into a genuine federation of politically autonomous, ethnic states.

The racist republic: against the world, 1976–90

The uprising in Soweto in 1976 demonstrated the internal fragility of the apartheid system.[8] To the north, across the Limpopo, the illegal regime of Ian Smith was entering its last remaining years of defiance before the transfer of power to African majority rule in 1980 (Caute 1983). The election of Robert Mugabe to the leadership of an independent Zimbabwe coincided with a conservative political swing in both Britain and America, but little external threat appeared to face the Nationalist government, either in terms of military intervention or the prospect of serious and sustained economic sanctions. It was the slow internal transformation of the society, from the bottom to the top, that was beginning to sow the seeds of a political reconstruction of major proportions.

Social and political scientists at this time became increasingly polarized. On the one side, there were those influenced by the neo-Marxist school that interpreted apartheid as a higher form of capitalism, super-exploitation that would only be resolved by a liberation movement inextricably linked to a socialist economic strategy. On the other side, there were the neo-Conservative 'realists' who argued that there was little prospect of removing apartheid by force but that the same goal could be achieved by allowing capitalism to flourish so that colour-blind, market influences would gradually cause the end of racism. Both perspectives shared an economic determinism, but one that produced very different results and recommended diametrically opposed political strategies. It is true that such positions were not uncontested, with some critics objecting to the 'Stalinist orthodoxy' of 'middle class Marxists' (Leftwich 1974: 161 and 200), and others arguing that 'there is no invisible economic hand inevitably forcing a particular pattern of social change' (Barber, in ibid.; Leftwich 1974: 339).

Between the extremes were a number of scholars whose research suggested that a democratic settlement might just be possible, not only because of a gradual shift in the balance of power, but also as a result of incremental, but significant, changes in attitudes. In the aftermath of Soweto this was most definitely a minority viewpoint but it became rather more plausible in the years immediately prior to Mandela's release from prison. Some studies, like Howard Brotz's book on democracy and racial diversity, while claiming to break the 'ideological straitjacket' surrounding South African politics, amounted to little more than a plea for 'effective' and 'genuine' consultation between the government and the disenfranchised majority. Those who dismissed such proposals as 'exercises in futility' were themselves derided as 'coffee-house intellectuals' (Brotz 1977).

A more serious attempt to gather empirical data to shed light on these issues could be found in the studies of Theodor Hanf and his associates published initially in Germany in 1978, with an English edition appearing three years later. Hanf's guarded analysis of the prospects for peaceful change explored the possibilities of some form of consociationalism, seen against the findings of attitude surveys conducted among the élites and masses of both whites and urban blacks. It was criticized for exaggerating the support for Buthelezi and underestimating the popular enthusiasm for liberal unitary democracy, but nevertheless raised interesting questions about the possibility of a compromise between the extremes. The final sections of the book speculated about the future chances of establishing a consociational democracy in South Africa given the data from the surveys. The authors found that African leaders and the black urban population in general were still open to peaceful change, while the white power élite had the opportunity either to initiate change – since the majority of the electorate would not resist its leadership – or to obstruct it. This created an unusual situation giving the white élite 'its unique, and perhaps its last, privilege' (1981: 405). Hanf and his colleagues concluded that 'the present unilateral regulation of conflict in South Africa can persist for a long time; and . . ., like it or not, neither rapid peaceful change nor sudden revolutionary change is likely' (1981: xii). Writing a postscript to the English edition in August 1980, Lawrence Schlemmer also confirmed that the National Party leadership did not intend 'to devolve or share an iota of real power at this stage' (1981: 443).

The transition from UDI (Unilateral Declaration of Independence) in Rhodesia to a democratic Zimbabwe had taken fifteen years of armed struggle. At the beginning of the 1980s, it was, therefore, not unreasonable to expect that it would take a considerably longer time to dislodge the much more powerful white élite in South Africa. In fact, a comparable democratic revolution was accomplished in less than fifteen years by Zimbabwe's southern neighbour. Clearly the analogy drawn between the two societies was misleading and a very different mix of forces would be operating throughout the 1980s to bring about this surprising transformation.

The decade which began with the legalization of trade unions was to continue with the classic mix of concessions and repression that, since the seminal writings of Alexis de Tocqueville, has been noted as the usual swansong of an authoritarian regime. Most social and political scientists continued to hedge their bets, but some seasoned observers of the South African scene began to take the possibility of an evolutionary transition to democracy as a serious option. Adam and Moodley (1986) pointed to four distinct features of the South African conflict that might work as a counter-balance to the polarizing impact of apartheid. These included: (1) economic interdependence in a resource-rich society, where all groups had a vested interest in reaching an accommodation; (2) the fact that South Africa was a settler, rather than a colonial, society in which the conflict would not be resolved by 'the departure or defeat of an alien conqueror'; (3) that even though there was a formidable racial and ideological divide, all major groups shared common Christian values and were orientated towards 'Westernized consumerism'; and (4) that the ethnic élite had becoming increasingly pragmatic, recognizing the costs of apartheid domination and the potential benefits to be derived from reforms (1986: 248–263).

Despite these positive trends, they fully realized the possibility of an 'indefinite period of "violence without victory" if the two major antagonists continued to mis-judge their opponent's strengths (1986: 251), and a similar underestimation of white intransigence could be seen in the calculations of 'foreign liberals and the international left'. The implications of this last factor reflect the way in which an 'ethnically mobilized group clings to power at all costs' and can be explained in the following manner:

> At the core of this determination lie the perceptions that the Afrikaner can only survive as a group, or race; that this survival must be in South Africa . . . and that greater repression as well as concessions or negotiations, if necessary, but not total abdication of power, can best ensure this survival. Any collapse of the will to rule would presuppose a substantial dilution of Afrikaner group feelings into individual interest calculations. While this process of de-ethnicization has been underway ever since Afrikanerdom achieved power, the formidable legacy of mobilized ethnicity still blocks any individualistic, non-racial form of government and is likely to sabotage liberal, universalistic political incorporation for a long time to come.
>
> (ibid.: 252)

Writing at much the same time, Robin Cohen (1986) presented what he claimed was a 'more radical' scenario than the 'conservative' analyses that suggested either incremental reform or the capacity of the regime to maintain its control almost indefinitely. Arguing that the conservative bias emerged out of a 'top down blind-ness' that failed to give sufficient weight to pressures from 'the bottom of the social structure', rather than 'believing the regime's own statements about itself' (1986: 86–87), he suggested that continuing unrest, and its effects on foreign loans and investment, would have a significant impact on the status quo. Despite his radical claims, Cohen saw a major role for a black conservative party under Buthelezi's leadership and anticipated quite limited power sharing arrangements in urban areas to be negotiated by 'small opportunistic elements of the ANC' (ibid.: 89). Thus black majority rule would arrive 'after a period of prolonged and continuing political unrest and instability', but the achievement of state power would not guarantee the reversal of apartheid's heritage – deeply embedded social and economic inequalities. (ibid.: 94–95).

Two further contrasting interpretations illustrate the range of perspectives in the latter part of the decade, before the final unravelling of political apartheid in the fascinating developments of the early 1990s. Neither fully anticipated the speed with which the society would start towards a negotiated transition to democracy, and both stressed the difficulties facing any movement in this direction. In *Race, Class and the Apartheid State*, Harold Wolpe emphasized the regime's inability to 'offer an acceptable basis for a negotiated settlement' (1988: 103). He attributed this to the restrictions limiting the National Party leadership's options:

> even if the rather unlikely assumption is made that its *verligte* (enlightened) wing is prepared to agree to a non-racial democratic society – one person one vote – the regime itself is subject to extremely severe constraints from its social base . . . to secure its position against the inroads which extreme right-wing Afrikaner parties are making on its popular support, the National Party tends to adopt repression rather than reform and negotiation as its policy.
>
> (ibid.: 104)

Two additional difficulties faced any real chance of an agreement: first, the major redistribution of resources that would be demanded by 'the mass democratic opposition' – including the dismantling of the giant corporations, radical land reallocation, and huge investments in education, welfare, housing and health that 'even a reformed capitalism would be unable to undertake' (ibid.: 105); and second, the extreme imbalance of military power between the national liberation movement and the apartheid state. As a result, Wolpe saw little possibility of a solution to the political crisis without an escalation of the armed struggle coordinated with internal unrest and resistance.

From a very different political perspective, Berger and Godsell in *A Future South Africa* (1988) addressed the same fundamental issue of the manner in which ruling groups can be made, or induced, to give up power. Rejecting dire predictions, they posed the important comparative question, 'if democracy can come to Franco's Spain, why not to Botha's South Africa?' (1988: 292). However, they too rejected the prospect of a coerced change because of 'the realities of military power', thus leaving the search for a formula by which power-sharing could be 'made palatable' to the ruling group. Their solution rested on a non-racial capitalism and while 'neither paradise nor Armageddon awaits South Africa' the future was predicted to be a 'slow and often painful march towards modernity' (ibid.: 298).

The lessons of history: explaining 'Mandela's miracle'

From the beginning of the 1990s, the rapid transition towards democracy became readily apparent and attracted a flood of scholarly and journalistic attention. Understandably, much of this was focussed on the immediate problems of securing a relatively peaceful change, or simply describing the exciting developments towards a new social order.

It is possible to identify several major factors that were either misinterpreted, underemphasized or largely ignored, by scholars of diverse ideological persuasions. These included:

1   *The unpredictable shift in the geo-political context.* While most scholars were aware of the potential impact of external forces on South Africa, few anticipated the enormous repercussions that the end of the Cold War would have on the South African situation. As in other parts of the world, the collapse of a bi-polar, competitive international system completely altered the power structure, together with the perceptions and actions of most of the major parties, both inside and outside the country. This in turn helped to create the conditions for a negotiated settlement. It is inconceivable that the unbanning of the Communist Party would have been politically possible before the fall of the Berlin Wall and its inclusion in the package of proposals announced in de Klerk's 1990 speech was made despite the vigorous objections of powerful figures like Magnus Malan (Sparks 1995: 107). The transformation of Joe Slovo from Communist bogeyman to a crucial conciliator in the difficult transitional negotiations,[9] and subsequently to the position of Minister of Housing in the first Government of National Unity, would have been unimaginable against a background of Cold War ideological rivalry.

2   *A tendency to underestimate the remarkable political skills of Nelson Mandela.* While everyone acknowledges Mandela's symbolic role in leading the liberation struggle and the personal legitimacy that stems from his twenty-seven years in prison, the important factor of leadership in engineering a successful transition may well be his foremost contribution. South Africa has produced a long list of outstanding opponents of apartheid – Steve Biko, Chris Hani, Albert Luthuli, the Mbekis, Walter Sisulu, Joe Slovo, Robert Sobukwe, Oliver Tambo and Desmond Tutu, to mention the most prominent – but protestations of 'collective leadership' aside, it is doubtful if anyone could have managed the internal politics of a 'negotiated revolution' with greater skill and acumen. His ability to outmanoeuvre opponents like de Klerk and Buthelezi, while keeping the broad ANC coalition intact, and his success in building a climate of reconciliation despite bitter differences, is a unique achievement. In the never-ending debate between agency and structure, here is a case where the former appears to have played a decisive role (Sampson 1999).[10]

3   *An exaggeration of the intransigence of Afrikaner nationalism and a failure to appreciate important generational shifts in attitudes.* It is true that many sociologists noted these changes, but few felt that they would be sufficient to enable the élite to embark on a serious and rapid programme of pragmatic power-sharing. My own assessment, written around 1970 and based on the empirical finding that British immigrants to South Africa rapidly conformed to the racist norms of apartheid, is typical of the 'guarded pessimism' of many sociologists:

While some may find this a depressing omen for the future, it does contain at least one ray of hope: if attitudes are flexible in one direction, they may be equally flexible in the other. What is required is the 'right' social structure, though how to achieve it is an altogether different question.

(Stone 1973: 253)

It was difficult to imagine the immediate successors to Verwoerd, B.J. Vorster and P.W. Botha, having the vision and capacity to guide the country towards serious power sharing. F.W. de Klerk's role in starting this process was almost certainly based on a miscalculation about his capacity to control the outcome, but the fact that he was surrounded by several younger, pragmatic and flexible colleagues reflects an important transformation in the nature of Afrikaner nationalism (Giliomee 1997; Marx 1997).

4   *The surprising moderation of the majority of South Africa's population.* This suggests a need for caution in applying the theory of relative deprivation, and the related concept of the 'revolution of rising expectations', to contemporary South African society. Over the years, many observers of South Africa have noted the low levels of personal animosity between blacks and whites, despite the flagrant inequality, brutality and petty humiliations of the apartheid system (Waldmeir 1997). Some have ascribed this to the 'paternalistic' pattern of race relations under apartheid whose aim was to prevent the challenge to racial domination that would arise from increasingly competitive relationships in a non-racial society. Following Tocqueville's classic formulation of the dynamics of revolutions, most social and political theories would have predicted a heightened level of resentment and racial antagonism under these circumstances.[11] While it is true that such mechanisms may sustain opposition and resistance to oppression, the South African evidence suggests that they do not necessarily preclude evolutionary changes in regimes and rapid adjustments in inter-group attitudes.

South Africa's experiences during the period 1948–90 represent a fascinating background against which to re-evaluate influential theories of social and political science, and to develop a more sophisticated understanding of the vital and complex connections between democratisation and racial and ethnic diversity. If there is one 'lesson of history' that emerges from this exercise, it is that social scientists should be very cautious before they start to make predictions. For, as Walker Connor has noted:

The past need not be prologue. History – including the history of nationalism – does not operate independently of the whims and caprices of events and individuals. Even a proper regard for the historical development of nationalism does not, therefore, eliminate the hazards inherent in predicting future political developments.

(Connor 1994: 182)

Notes

1 I first encountered the quotation in the writings of the economist Robert Triffin whose ideas on international monetary reform in the 1960s had enormous potential significance for the South African economy with its heavy dependence on gold mining (Triffin 1960). Gold sanctions – moves to demonetize gold or to lower its price by getting Central Banks to sell off their reserves – were never used as a tactic against the apartheid regime. Ironically, it was the British government's sale of gold reserves at the end of the 1990s that was to compound the economic problems of a post-apartheid, democratic South Africa.

2 This is not to suggest that there is widespread deliberate fraud in the manipulation of data by social scientists. The process is much more subtle and pervasive, and includes the same types of influences, from intellectual inertia to the conservatism of research funding agencies, that Kuhn argued tended to support a particular scientific paradigm. (Kuhn 1962; Kincaid 1996).

3 I have chosen to end the era of apartheid in 1990 rather than 1994 because the focus of this analysis is on the predictive capacity of the social sciences. After de Klerk's speech it was clear to all observers that the fundamental political and social bases of apartheid were being dismantled, although the precise outcome of this process was still very much in doubt. As a result, certain important studies published between 1990 and 1994 are not included in the survey (e.g. Horowitz 1991; Adam and Moodley 1993).

4 Let me stress that it is *not* the purpose of this exercise to criticize other scholars' work, much of it undertaken several decades ago, from the vantage point of the late 1990s. My own research on South Africa, which began with fieldwork and interviews in the 1960s and consists of a number of subsequent publications, contains many of the errors common to the various social science interpretations of South African society.

5 This parallels the later error concerning the radical shift in the geo-political context following the collapse of Communism. However, in this case it enabled the nationalist leadership to move closer to international norms on race relations rather than increasing its isolation. Subsequent analyses have explored the similarities and differences between the two crucial transitions. (Adam 1995: 457–475; and on the Soviet transition, see Brown 1996; Dobbs 1997).

6 In the secret meetings between the Volksfront generals and the ANC, prior to the 1994 elections, Mandela is reported to have summed up the military situation as follows: 'If you want to go to war, I must be honest and admit that we cannot stand up to you on the battlefield, we don't have the resources.' However, he also pointed out: 'You cannot win because of our numbers; you cannot kill us all. And you cannot win because of the international community' (Sparks 1995: 204). It is doubtful whether Umkhonto we Sizwe was ever seen by the ANC leadership as much more than a tool of symbolic resistance (Mandela 1994).

7 The reluctance of American and European forces to intervene in Cambodia, Bosnia and Rwanda, despite widespread evidence of genocide, might suggest that such a conclusion was by no means likely. For the case in support of more pro-active policies in such situations see Goldstone (1997). Subsequent action in Kosovo, and inaction in Sierra Leone, reflect the ambiguous stance of Western powers towards intervention on humanitarian grounds.

8 Assessments of the significance of the Soweto uprising varied considerably. While John Brewer, writing in the mid-1980s, saw it as an important factor in galvanizing African opposition forces (1986: 407), other writers argued that it achieved very little. For different views on this matter, see Johnson (1977); Kane-Berman (1978); Carter (1980); Rotberg and Barrett (1980); Gann and Duigan (1981); Nolutshungu (1982).

9 Slovo is credited with supporting the 1992 proposals which mandated a coalition government for the first five years after democratic elections, and which guaranteed the job

security of existing civil servants and security forces personnel, thereby reducing the risk of a white backlash (Taylor 1995).

10 Another issue is the role of 'chance' as a factor in South African history. The so-called 'Battle of Bop' in March 1994, when heavily armed white extremists failed to prop up the regime of Lucas Mangope, and two were summarily executed in front of television cameras, certainly assisted the transition to democracy (Taylor 1994). Not only did it reduce the threat of TerreBlanche's Afrikaner Resistance Movement and other white vigilante groups, but its message also quelled any separatist leanings in KwaZulu.

In the longer sweep of South African history, speculation about the fate of certain key figures raises tantalizing questions: What if Hofmeyr had lived to succeed Smuts in 1948? What if Verwoerd had survived assassination in 1966. What if Mandela had suffered the same fate as Biko and Hani?

11 Although Tocqueville's seminal formulation of the theory of relative deprivation derives from his study of the French Revolution, he does apply the same insights to his earlier analysis of race relations in America (Stone and Mennell 1980: 215–250, 325–340).

References

Adam, H. 1995. 'The Politics of Ethnic Identity: Comparing South Africa'. *Ethnic and Racial Studies*. 18(3): 457–475.

Adam, H. and Moodley, K. 1986. *South Africa Without Apartheid*. Berkeley, CA: University of California Press.

—— 1993. *The Opening of the Apartheid Mind*. Berkeley, CA: University of California Press.

Berger, P. and Godsell, B. (eds) 1988. *A Future South Africa*. Boulder, CO: Westview Press.

Brewer, J. 1986. *After Soweto*. Oxford: The Clarendon Press.

Brotz, H. 1977. *The Politics of South Africa*. London: Oxford University Press.

Brown, A. 1996. *The Gorbachev Factor*. Oxford: Oxford University Press.

Carter, G. 1958. *The Politics of Inequality*. New York: Praeger.

—— 1980. *Which Way is South Africa Going?* Bloomington: Indiana University Press.

Caute, D. 1983. *Under the Skin: The Death of White Rhodesia*. London: Allen Lane.

Cohen, R. 1986. *Endgame in South Africa?* London: James Currey.

Connor, W. 1993. 'Beyond Reason: the Nature of the Ethnonational Bond'. *Ethnic and Racial Studies*. 16(3): July: 373–389.

—— 1994. *Ethnonationalism: The Quest for Understanding*. Princeton, NJ: Princeton University Press.

Crocker, C. 1992. *High Noon in Southern Africa*. New York: Norton.

Dobbs, M. 1997. *Down With Big Brother*. New York: Knopf.

Gann, L. and Duigan P. 1981. *Why South Africa Will Survive*. London: Croom Helm.

Giliomee, H. 1997. 'Surrender Without Defeat: Afrikaners and the South African "Miracle"'. *Daedalus*. Spring: 113–146.

Goldstone, R. 1997. 'War Crimes: When Amnesia Causes Cancer'. *Washington Post*. 2 February.

Hanf, T., Weiland, H. and Vierdag, G. 1981. *South Africa: The Prospects of Peaceful Change*. Bloomington: Indiana University Press.

Hayes, C. 1926. *Essays on Nationalism*. New York: Macmillan.

Hellmann, E. (ed.) 1949. *Handbook on Race Relations in South Africa*. Cape Town: Oxford University Press.

Horowitz, D. 1991. *A Democratic South Africa?*. Berkeley, CA: California University Press.

Johnson, R. 1977. *How Long Will South Africa Survive?* London: Macmillan.

Kane-Berman, J. 1978. *Method in the Madness*. London: Pluto.

Keppel-Jones, A. 1947. *When Smuts Goes*. Pietermaritzburg: Shuter and Shooter.

Kincaid, H. 1996. *Philosophical Foundations of the Social Sciences*. Cambridge: Cambridge University Press.

Kuhn, T. 1962. *The Structure of Scientific Revolutions*. Chicago: Chicago University Press.

Kuper, L. 1956. *Passive Resistance in South Africa*. London: Jonathan Cape.

Leftwich, A. (ed.) 1974. *South Africa: Economic Growth and Political Change*. New York: St. Martin's Press.

Lewin, J. 1963. *Politics and Law in South Africa*. London: Merlin Press.

Luthuli, A. 1962. *Let My People Go*. New York: McGraw-Hill.

Mandela, N. 1994. *Long Walk to Freedom*. Boston: Little, Brown.

Marquard, L. 1952. *The Peoples and Policies of South Africa*. London: Oxford University Press.

Marx, A. 1997. 'Apartheid's End: South Africa's Transition from Racial Domination'. *Ethnic and Racial Studies*. 20(3) July: 474–496.

Ngubane, J. 1963. *An African Explains Apartheid*. New York: Praeger.

Nolutshungu, S. 1982. *Changing South Africa: Political Considerations*. New York: Africana Publishing Company.

Patterson, S. 1957. *The Last Trek*. London: Routledge & Kegan Paul.

Rhoodie, N. and H. Venter 1960. *Apartheid*. Amsterdam: De Bussy.

Rotberg, R.I. and Barrett, J. (eds) 1980. *Conflict and Compromise in South Africa*. Lexington, MA: Lexington Books.

Sampson, A. 1999. *Mandela: The Authorized Biography*. New York: Knopf.

Sparks, A. 1995. *Tomorrow is Another Country*. New York: Hill & Wang.

Stone, J. 1973. *Colonist or Uitlander?* Oxford: Clarendon Press.

—— 1986. 'When Botha Goes: South African Society Beyond the Era of *Apartheid*'. *Ethnic and Racial Studies*. 9(3): 412–425.

Stone, J. and Mennell, S. 1980. *Alexis de Tocqueville on Democracy, Revolution and Society*. Chicago: Chicago University Press.

Taylor, P. 1994. 'South Africa Clash Smashes Old Conceptions'. *Washington Post*. 14 March.

—— 1995. 'Joe Slovo Dies: Apartheid Foe in South Africa'. *Washington Post*. 7 January.

Triffin, R. 1960. *Gold and the Dollar Crisis*. New Haven, CT: Yale University Press.

Turk, A. 1967. 'The Futures of South Africa'. *Social Forces*. 45(3): 402–412.

van den Berghe, P. 1964. *Caneville: The Social Structure of a South African Town*. Middletown: Wesleyan University Press.

—— 1965. *South Africa: A Study in Conflict*. Middletown: Wesleyan University Press.

—— 1967. *Race and Racism*. New York: John Wiley.

Waldmeir, P. 1997. *Anatomy of a Miracle*. New York: Norton.

Wilson, M. and Mafeje, A. 1963. *Langa: A Study of Social Groups in an African Township*. Cape Town: Oxford University Press.

Wolpe, H. 1988. *Race, Class and the Apartheid State*. Paris: UNESCO.

8 Sovereignty or separation?

Contemporary political discourse in Canada

John Edwards

Introduction

Among the recurring themes in Walker Connor's writings are the insistence on the continuing importance of nationalism – even in contexts in which many had come to believe it of largely historical interest – and the concern for terminological accuracy, the repudiation of Humpty-Dumpty usage. The first of these is no longer such a contentious matter; contemporary work on nationalism now forms a respectable and animated part of several academic disciplines. As far as the second theme goes, questions of verbal accuracy and precision vex us still. Indeed, Connor found it necessary to begin his *Ethnonationalism: The Quest for Understanding* (1994) with the following words: '. . . slipshod use of the key terms, nation and nationalism, is more the rule than the exception, even in works purportedly dealing with nationalism' (p. xi).

In a more accurate world, he implies, the very word *ethnonationalism* would be a prolix and redundant extension of *nationalism* itself. But in a world which confuses *state* and *nation,* and which imagines that nationalistic identification can refer to state loyalties, then the longer term is needed to avoid misunderstanding. Connor's terminological paper, 'A nation is a nation, is a state, is an ethnic group, is a . . .' (originally 1978, reprinted in Connor 1994) is of particular relevance here; in it, he discusses some important confusions (and much else, as well).

Concern with terminology need not be a narrow exercise smelling strongly of the lamp. In areas which engage powerful emotions, and in settings of contact and conflict, descriptions of reality – as variously interpreted – are of the greatest importance. The most pervasive theme in modern social psychology is the importance of *perception* and, in his own way, Connor has also underlined the centrality of social perception: as Allcock (1994) notes, he has consistently pointed out that 'what ultimately matters is not what is, but what people believe is'. We can easily see the linkage, then, between definitional matters and even more highly-charged linguistic aspects of the construction of social belief. As Daniele Conversi points out in his introductory remarks, Connor's 'linguistic' concerns encompass the accuracy and acceptability of disciplinary terminology – but they also remind us that semantic variability and, indeed, linguistic ambiguity, are at the heart of many nationalist manifestations. (We also remember that it was Renan who famously pointed out – in broader context – the importance of ambiguity or 'selective memory'.) Usage matters, often critically, where nationalism and group identity are under discussion. Influenced by Connor's attention to language-in-nationalism, this chapter is part of the contemporary focus upon nationalistic 'discourse' (for very recent examples, see Dickie 2000 and Rowley 2000) – a term which, itself, illustrates (at least) shifting terminological pillars.

The specific focus here is Quebec, a contemporary setting which is of great intrinsic interest but which also provides many *generally* illustrative examples of linguistic potency. The attempt here is *not* to construct a broadly scholarly contribution; rather, the more modest and descriptive aim is to present some worthwhile raw material, as it were, which may be refined later within the wider literature. So, while making some reference to the latter, this chapter draws heavily upon primary sources, as reported in the press. More specifically, it relies a great deal upon the Toronto *Globe & Mail* (which has some reasonable claim to be Canada's newspaper of record), more for its coverage of factual information than for 'opinion pieces' (with the exception of leaders, which are clearly indicated as such).

The 'popular' focus adopted here is, then, an intentional one. Further, the particular interest is in less subtle political comments, the main idea being to illustrate the linguistic excesses to which nationalist discourse is particularly prone or, indeed, which it can provoke. Although most of the examples are taken, for obvious reasons, from the nationalist or sovereigntist side (most from leading lights within Quebec), there are certainly examples here of federalist intemperance too. It should be noted from the outset, of course, that not all nationalists are sovereigntists, and that some of the former want radical political changes short of separation.

To conclude this section, reference should be made to several of the broad-brush treatments of the recent Canada–Quebec relationship. An excellent historical overview is provided by Bothwell (1995), in a book which interweaves formal conversations the author had with about two dozen journalists, academics and politicians. Another historical account is that of Cook (1995), in a greatly revised and expanded second edition. A political scientist's perspective on the growing tensions within the Canadian federation is that of McRoberts (1997). More focussed accounts include Carens's (1995) collection, predicated on the belief that sovereigntist aspirations in Quebec (and, indeed, nationalism *per se*) need not be illiberal; useful antidotes to some of the shriller voices can be found here. Young (1999) and Cameron (1999) are both products of reflection on the October 1995 referendum. Carment *et al.* (2001) and Young (1995) focus upon secession and its ramifications. In these books, readers will find syntheses based upon data very much like those presented in this chapter.

Setting the scene

Most people are aware of the continuing tensions in Canada, tensions centrally animated by the strained relationship between Quebec and the rest of the country.

Most people are *not* so aware, perhaps, that there are more important actors in this play than nationalist *québécois* francophones, and anglophones. It is insufficiently appreciated how the debate over the place of Quebec within (or without) the Canadian federation has drawn in *all* groups, including aboriginal and allophone populations, and has occasioned intense scrutiny of all matters dealing with language, culture and inter-group accommodation. While the purpose here is not to discuss the Canadian 'case' in detail (see, for example, Edwards 1994a, 1994b, 1995a, 1995b, 1997a, 1997b), a little contextualisation may be in order.

The major players continue to act out their (by now) familiar roles. Most Quebec francophones clearly want substantial changes in federal–provincial arrangements, and many are committed to outright independence. Anglophones and allophones debate about how much change (if any) ought to be made and, as well, argue for a reworking of their own positions in the mosaic. Aboriginal groups are adamant that if any 'distinct' status – such as Quebec has historically argued for within Canada – were to be on offer, they should surely be the first and most obvious recipients. They also argue that their members in Quebec cannot be taken out of Canada, against their will, by secessionists, thus raising interesting and vexing questions about where democratic rights of secession end. (It is clear, by the way, that Quebec nationalists who maintain that they have a right to secede – following a successful referendum – would generally deny that same course of action to (say) the James Bay Cree. *Quod licet Jovi non licet bovi* could, after all, be the motto of many nationalist groups who have to deal with internal divisions.) Thus, it is important to realise that the francophone–anglophone debate has, in fact, acted as a catalyst for broader discussions – among virtually all constituencies – about the shape of the country, about officially-sponsored programmes of social engineering (notably, bilingualism and multiculturalism), and so on. It is not unfair to suggest that all group affiliations and all identities (and all official and non-official manifestations of, and support for, them) are now in a state of flux.

In 1981–82, Canada's constitution was brought 'home' from Britain, a final act of severance. Accompanying this was a Charter of Rights and Freedoms, one of whose sections outlined minority-language rights meant to apply to all Canadians in an officially bilingual country. Quebec did not sign the new constitutional accord, largely because of the threat it was seen to pose to the province's own linguistic authority, which had moved increasingly to support French (with, for example, the 1974 law making it the official provincial language, and the famous Bill 101 of 1977 – the French Language Charter). Though not a signatory, Quebec was bound by the Canadian Charter – obviously an undesirable political state of affairs. Efforts were thus made to bring the province back into the constitutional fold, but these failed – notably with the collapse of the Meech Lake agreement in 1990, and the failure of the 1992 Charlottetown referendum, both of which aimed to somehow reconcile a 'distinct-society' status for Quebec with demands from the rest of the country that all provinces were to be treated equally. Needless to say, these failures stiffened separatist resolve in Quebec, and the *Parti Québécois* lost no time in predicting (or, rather, in *re*predicting) that an independent Quebec was the only solution to the constitutional malaise. In September 1994 they ousted the

Liberals in Quebec, taking 77 seats to the latter's 47, although their share of the popular vote was only marginally greater (44.8 per cent vs 44.2 per cent; compare, below, with the very similar results in the 1998 provincial election). While it was unclear how many supporters of the *PQ* were actually committed to the idea of a sovereign Quebec, it is clear that everyone knew that the party's leader, Jacques Parizeau, was intent on separation and that, indeed, a provincial referendum on the question would follow a *PQ* victory. The stage was thus set for the vital vote in 1995.

The referendum was held on 30 October 1995. In an extremely high turn-out, more than 4.7 million votes were cast, and the results were 49.4 per cent 'yes' (to sovereignty), 50.6 per cent 'no'. This razor-thin difference was not, however, the sole point of high drama. It was exceeded, for instance, by the number of rejected ballots (roughly 86,000 to 54,000). Many of these spoiled votes were apparently rejected for very minor technical reasons: perhaps the 'x' was too thick or too thin, too light or too dark, too shaky or too irregular; or perhaps the tick-mark was made upside down. More interesting than the extreme finickiness of the scrutineers was its apparently non-random character. For example, in Chomedy (north of Montreal), more than 11 per cent of the votes cast were rejected, in two dozen of its polling stations the figure was over 20 per cent and, in a 'handful', more than half the votes were officially classified as spoiled! Overall, about 5,400 votes were rejected, a twelve-fold increase from the previous year's provincial election. Particularly high rejection rates were also noted in Marguerite-Bourgeoys (about 5.5 per cent) and Laurier-Dorion (about 3.5 per cent). All three ridings have always had significant federalist support and a high percentage of non-francophone voters. Broader analyses revealed that, in the fifteen ridings with the most 'no' votes, the rejection rate was 2.6 per cent; in the fifteen with the most 'yes' votes cast, it was 1.5 per cent. Finally here, it was suggested that rejection rates would have been even higher if polling station clerks hadn't sometimes challenged the official scrutineers who, under Quebec's new election law, were appointed by the government – that is to say, the separatist *Parti Québécois* (see Gray 1995).

The referendum was thus lost by the Quebec sovereigntists; the country, which was at the very edge of an abyss whose nature was extremely poorly understood, was granted the thinnest of reprieves. However, since there is no doubt that most Quebec francophones voted 'yes' – even though many of them were uncertain about exactly what they were voting for, and many were using the vote to indicate broad dissatisfaction with the political status quo rather than support for Quebec independence – the issue remained (and remains) unresolved.

Since October 1995, federal regrouping has involved two 'plans' – one stressing reconciliation with Quebec, and the desire to rework constitutional and other arrangements so as to spike the sovereigntists' guns, the other a more hard-nosed assessment of future referendums. Thus, for example, in September 1996 the government asked the Supreme Court to consider (and give a ruling on) the conditions under which Quebec might leave the confederation. The Court began its deliberations in February 1998 and, in August, rejected unilateral Quebec secession; it also ruled, however, that the rest of the country would have to negotiate with Quebec were there a clear pro-separation referendum result in the future.[1]

The federal government, noting then that it would be bound to negotiate with Quebec after a 'yes' victory *only* if the referendum question were unambiguous, argued that some sort of 'clarity' legislation was called for. (This idea was given further impetus by sovereigntist arguments that Quebec would ignore the Court's references to unilateral declarations of independence: see Bellavance 2000.) It was pointed out that plain phrasing could only benefit all sides – although this was perhaps a little disingenuous, since it has been obvious for a long time that clearer, blunter questions about separation receive weaker support from Quebec voters (see below); this is of particular importance for that vital block of 'conditional' secessionists or federalists, the so-called 'swing' voters (see Simpson 1999). In December 1999, Prime Minister Jean Chrétien observed that any future question must plainly spell out that Quebec would become a separate state, that parliament would have to consider what constitutes a sufficient majority and that, in the negotiation phase, important matters would include minority and aboriginal rights within Quebec, as well as issues concerning its borders, its debt obligations, divisions of assets and liabilities, and so on. Chrétien said, 'People will be happy that we're forcing [the *PQ* government] to be honest . . . They have a referendum, they ask a crooked question, fine. So what? There will be no negotiations' (Fraser 1999b). This was naturally seen, in *Parti Québécois* circles, as yet another example of unwarranted interference, providing Chrétien with a veto on Quebec's future. When Stéphane Dion, the federal minister for intergovernmental affairs, introduced the legislation in the House of Commons, *PQ* members shouted '*traître . . . anti-démocrate . . . fasciste . . . vendu*' (Fraser 1999c; Dion also had the distinction, a little later, of being called the 'most despised politician in history' by Bernard Landry: see Séguin 2001d).

Premier Lucien Bouchard called on Quebeckers to rally against what he called 'a vulgar manoeuvre from the federal government' and, in mid-December, outlined *provincial* legislation that would reaffirm Quebec's right to decide its future without broader Canadian intervention. The main elements here were, of course, those countering the federal argument: thus, only Quebeckers can decide on their future political status, a simple majority of votes is sufficient for referendum victory, and the present territorial borders of Quebec cannot be altered (see Séguin 1999; Séguin and Ha 1999). When Bouchard visited France in April 2000, he discussed his opposition to the federal clarity legislation with President Jacques Chirac and Prime Minister Lionel Jospin, but he did not ask for any formal French support; he did, however, tell Chirac that Quebec would ignore the legislation in any future referendum – the first time, it was pointed out, that a foreign leader has been told that a 'separatist government will resort to civil disobedience' (Bellavance 2000; see also Séguin 2000a; a little later Bernard Landry, Bouchard's deputy, reiterated the sentiment: see *Globe & Mail* 2001). Temporarily withdrawn in April 2000, Quebec's legislation was adopted in the National Assembly in December, but without the support of the provincial Liberal opposition. Its passage occurred very shortly after the Canadian federal election in late November, an election in which the Liberals were returned in massive numbers – and in which, in Quebec, they took almost half of both the popular vote and of the province's 75 ridings. For its part, the federal government got the 'Clarity Act' (Bill C-20) through the House of

Commons with little difficulty, but it took until June 2000 for it to weather stormier seas in the Senate.[2]

While in France, Bouchard announced that he was abandoning his strategy of waiting for the 'winning conditions' for a successful referendum to arise, and pledging instead to 'work actively to achieve sovereignty'. But here again the linguistic exercise is central. Under continuing pressure from sovereigntist hard-liners, and with his party leadership soon coming up for review, Bouchard aimed to re-establish his own separatist credentials. The altered emphasis was generally seen, however, as the abandonment of a phrase with albatross connotations rather than any real shift in political posture. 'Winning conditions' were thus consigned to the same Orwellian memory hole that received words like *separatist* and *independence* (Picard 2000).

The *Parti Québécois* had been returned to power in the provincial election of November 1998, Premier Bouchard having announced earlier that any future referendum on sovereignty would only occur if those 'winning conditions' (see above) were in place. This delaying tactic was due, in part, to polls showing that most *Québécois* were opposed to another such vote. As well, however, a certain amount of vacillation on the matter – for, at other times, Bouchard had seemed to promise another referendum within a renewed *PQ* tenure – reflected pressure on the Premier from his hard-line *PQ* colleagues. In any event, the election gave Bouchard's party 76 of the 125 seats (the Liberals won 48); it is, at the least, an irony that the winners took 40,000 fewer votes than the losers (*PQ*: 42.7 per cent of the votes; Liberals: 43.7 per cent).

In the immediate post-election period, the 'softer' approach to unity (see above, and note 1) involved the idea of a reworked 'social union', in which programmes and policies would be more equitably arranged among the federal and provincial governments. Renewed attempts to recognise – meaningfully and acceptably – Quebec's 'distinct' status have not fared well. The so-called 'Calgary Declaration' of September 1997, in which all provincial legislatures (save Quebec's) agreed to the 'unique' character of Quebec society has been shown to be: (a) unfamiliar to most Canadians (who remain, in any event, generally opposed to any formal recognition of distinctiveness); and (b) unacceptable to Quebec nationalists because it fails to recognise Quebec as a people and a nation.

Thus, the story continues – and it is a story that has been marked, throughout, by a number of interesting and illuminating verbal and conceptual tangles. Before more directly considering some of these, we should recall that current tensions among francophones, anglophones, allophones and aboriginal groups all occur in a country in which matters of identity and self-definition – particularly, of course, *vis-à-vis* the United States – have been confused and disputatious for a long time. Within the country itself, the 'classic' Canadian panorama has often been characterised by the 'two solitudes' of French and English speakers – a phrase popularised by Hugh MacLennan in his 1945 novel of that title. Given that the term has come to signify an apparently unbridgeable chasm, it is interesting that MacLennan himself had emphasised the *original* meaning, taken from the poem by Rilke in which it is first found: 'love consists in this, that two solitudes protect, and touch, and greet each other'. Of slightly more recent vintage – but now also part of the archetypal Canadian discourse – are the famous words of Charles de Gaulle, proclaimed to the Montreal public from the balcony of the city hall (at what became the expedited conclusion to his visit of 1967): 'Vive le Québec,' said the general; and then, after a well-timed pause, 'Vive le Québec *libre!*'

Sovereignty and separation

In December 1994, Jacques Parizeau (leader of the *Parti Québécois* until just after the 1995 referendum, when he was replaced by Lucien Bouchard) introduced draft legislation to declare Quebec's sovereignty, and a poll in January suggested that about 46 per cent of Quebec voters were prepared to endorse this bill. At the same time, however, some 60 per cent indicated that they would say 'no' to the question, 'Do you want Quebec to separate from Canada and become an independent country?' This is an interesting difference – to say the least – and reveals what has been a continuing public confusion over the years, one exploited both by federalists (who, naturally enough, have wanted only a 'hard' referendum question) and by sovereigntists (who steadfastly maintained the inevitability of all sorts of ties with Canada after a declaration of independence).

In practical political terms, the difference forced upon the sovereigntists the necessity of 'softening' the referendum question, including in it an *explicit* reference to economic association with Canada. To put it another way, public volatility forced upon Parizeau – whose personal preference was clearly for a direct approach – the sort of question that an earlier Quebec government had (in 1980, under René Lévesque) presented to its constituency: one which asked merely for a 'mandate to negotiate' something called 'sovereignty-association' (which, incidentally, was rejected by a margin of 60 to 40). This time around, polls (in April 1995) revealed that, if the question offered sovereignty accompanied by economic association, more than half Quebec's voters would say 'yes'. The media were of course quick to point out that the *Parti Québécois* was presuming a great deal; federalist politicians announced that no partnership could be taken for granted, and that voters ought to have no illusions: the PQ referendum was about *separation*. The actual question asked in October 1995 was:

> Do you agree that Quebec should become sovereign, after having made a formal offer to Canada for a new economic and political partnership, within the scope of the Bill respecting the future of Quebec and of the agreement signed on June 12, 1995?

We have already noted that even this 'softened' question failed to attract 50 per cent support – but the referendum came within a whisker of success.

In fact, the volatility referred to above, and the sensitivity to the description of Quebec secession, are long-standing features of the electorate. Some useful charting of this was presented by Winsor in 1994, based upon work by Cloutier, Gay and Latouche (1992) and Lisée (1994). Their studies outline the changing levels of support for five different sovereignty 'concepts', drawing upon analyses of 165 polls taken since 1960 (see also Hamilton and Pinard 1982, for a detailed consideration of events up to the 1980 referendum, including analyses of many of the polls surveyed by Cloutier *et al.*). What is of immediate relevance (see Table 8.1) is that support is consistently higher for Quebec independence when it is described in 'softer' ways, when it is presented in conjunction with a continued and substantial association with Canada, when (in a word) it seems most non-threatening. While Pinard (1994) notes the 'paradox' that levels of support for what is, after all, the same reality, vary according to terms used, Prager points out that the various terms do not have equivalent connotations – for Quebeckers at least, 'they are not synonymous or value neutral' (1998: 574). The moral of this particular story, for those concerned with the phrasing of referendum questions and the influencing of outcomes is clearly understood (see also *Globe & Mail* 1998b; Unland 1997; Winsor 1998).[3]

Table 8.1 Changing support for concepts of sovereignty

Time period	Percentage level of support for				
	Separation	Independence	Sovereignty	Sovereignty-association	Mandate to negotiate sovereignty-association
1950–1964	8				
1965–1969	10				
1970–1974	13	27		32	
1975–1979	19	20		31	49
1980–1985		20	18	39	40
1986–1989	37	32	41	46	
1990	44	50	55	58	68
1991	42	46	53	60	
1992	33	40	45	58	
1993	33	39	49	58	

Source: After Winsor (1994).

The greatest 'threat' associated with outright independence, of course, is that of economic decline, or worse. It is clear enough that francophone nationalism was virtually as strong during the 1980 referendum campaign as it was in 1995; the difference in the actual results may be largely ascribed to a much stronger sense, now, that an independent Quebec could be an economically viable state. Nationalist impulses accompanied by economic fears often lead to frustration; if those same impulses, however, are reinforced by beliefs of economic adequacy, then change may more likely be on the cards. It could be said, then, that the frustration of twenty years ago both fuelled and evolved into the current nationalistic picture – a much more important one, as the 1995 referendum results indicated.

The 'distinct' society and *'la survivance'*

Recent attempts to bring Quebec back into the constitutional fold and, generally, to 'solve' the Quebec 'problem' have had to grapple with strengthened concerns in that province for *survivance*, for the protection of *la francophonie*. One of the great changes involved in Quebec's 'Quiet Revolution' of the 1960s – the process of modernisation, secularisation, growing nationalism and an ever-increasing sense of being *maîtres chez nous* – was a drastic fall in the provincial birthrate. Once the highest in the Western world, it now remains below the 'replacement' rate of 2.1 (children per woman). The 1956 birthrate was 3.9; this fell to 1.35 by 1987, at which point the government provided monetary incentives (since discontinued); by 1997 it stood at 1.5 (see *Globe & Mail* 1999a). The traditional Catholic *revanche des berceaux*, the old attempt to undo the 'conquest', can no longer be counted upon.

The various legislative measures to protect the French language – notably in education and the workplace – are also related to a fear of *disparition*. In particular, Quebec governments have tried, with some success, to channel non-francophone immigrants' language choices into a French stream, rather than the English one traditionally taken. And, as well, increased efforts have been made in recent years to attract newcomers from French-speaking countries. Many of these immigrants, however, are from cultures and societies very different from Quebec; many, indeed, are members of 'visible-minority' groups. They do not resemble, then, the *Québécois de vieille souche*. The attempted maintenance of a francophone society in a North American anglophone sea forty times larger makes worries about *disparition* and *survivance* understandable. One can also see why a recognition (one with some political teeth) by the rest of the country of Quebec's special status has been such an important matter. In the wake of the October 1995 referendum, Prime Minister Chrétien organised a House of Commons resolution acknowledging Quebec's distinct language, culture and civil law – but this had no constitutional force and was seen by Quebec nationalists as an empty gesture (as was the more recent 'Calgary Declaration', noted above).

In April 1996, the Quebec wing of the federal Liberal party – hoping to sidestep the 'distinct' issue – voted to settle for an acknowledgement that Quebec is the 'principal homeland' of French language, culture and legal tradition in North America. The idea, however, was met with widespread disdain. Even Daniel Johnson, then the leader of the *provincial* Liberal party (i.e., no sovereigntist), observed that the notion of a *foyer principal* implied a repudiation of many years' efforts to obtain the proper status for Quebec; in any event, he noted, 'It's like saying that Newfoundland is an island or that there are Rockies in the west' (Séguin 1996). *Parti Québécois* reaction, of course, was even more pointed: the *foyer* idea was seen to be based upon an archaic and outmoded ethnic definition (indeed, the notion of the *foyer* was adopted by hardline French-Canadian nationalists at the turn of the (twentieth) century, and has since been rejected by all modern political parties).

Nationalism in Quebec

A great deal of interesting discussion has focussed upon the *nature* of Quebec nationalism. It has always been an article of faith among sovereigntists that they were democratic in their actions and their intentions, that *all* residents of Quebec – francophones or not – were Quebeckers. Thus, for example, Parizeau reiterated in

February 1995 his commitment to the protection of minority rights. Naturally, however, the primary motivation of his *Parti Québécois* has been the protection of francophone culture, and the ultimate goal the alignment of national with state boundaries. Consequently, in the run-up to the 1995 referendum, there was in some quarters a revival of the idea that it would be manifestly unjust if the destiny of largely francophone Quebec were to hinge upon the votes of anglophones and allophones. Some ultranationalists have suggested that voting (and, indeed, citizenship) should be restricted to French speakers (or that immigrants ought to sign a contract promising to 'live and prosper in French'; see Picard 1994, 1998, and Aubin 1996 on the language *ayatollahs*).

Publicly, 'separatists get very indignant when others suggest that there is a xeno-phobic streak in Quebec nationalism' (as the *Globe & Mail* 1995a put it). But the editorial went on to report that a member of the *Bloc Québécois* (the *federal* separatist party) had asked why, 'just for once', the referendum couldn't be decided solely by 'old-stock Quebeckers' (*Québécois de vieille souche*, or *Québécois pure laine*). Most recently, the well-known poet and singer, Raymond Lévesque, argued that 'newcomers' to the province, who are typically against secession, ought not to have the right to vote; they are interlopers, he said, in a 'family dispute . . . they vote against us' (see *Globe & Mail* 2000a; Ha 2000b). Again, the old problem: who constitutes 'family' in Quebec, who is 'us'? Predictably, sovereigntist leaders denounce such outbursts, but many are clearly of like mind. (Parizeau himself had said, in 1993, that Quebec sovereignty could be achieved 'even if for the most part those who vote for it are almost exclusively Quebeckers of old stock': see El Yamani, Juteau and McAndrew 1993, on this *affaire Parizeau*). The issue came to the fore on referendum night itself. 'It's true we have been defeated, but basically by what?' said Parizeau. 'By money and the ethnic vote.'

Parizeau also spoke ominously of the 'temptation for revenge' and promised to 'exact revenge' for the referendum loss by building a francophone nation in Quebec. (Bernard Landry, Parizeau's second-in-command, noted that 'the country we want we will have soon'. He also reportedly told a Montreal hotel clerk that 'you immigrants' were to blame for the loss; see *Globe & Mail* 1996.) The day after the referendum, Parizeau remained unapologetic: 'I used words that were strong last night, but they underline a reality that exists.' A month later, Pierre Bourgault, a long-time separatist and former advisor to Parizeau, supported the Premier: 'It's the Jews, the Italians and the Greeks who vote in an ethnic block. They're the racists, not us.' Bourgault added that those groups 'don't think of themselves as Quebeckers, but as Jews, Italians, Greeks.'

For many, these sorts of comments suggested that, despite the separatists' claims that theirs was a *civic nationalism*, Quebec nationalism was, after all, essentially an ethnic phenomenon. Indeed, they have re-opened, in a sense, the debate over whether such a thing as civic nationalism really exists. It would seem that – although the concept has been taken into some English-language discourse (for example, see Ignatieff 1993; Kymlicka 1995; Smith 1995) – the idea of a civic nationalism has its strongest following in French circles (see Balthazar 1995; Breton 1988; Cahen 1994; Schnapper 1994).

The reaction to the sovereigntists' remarks can be imagined – disgust, mingled with not a little satisfaction on the part of federalists. Sovereigntist discourse also provoked some predictably vehement rejoinders. A *Globe & Mail* leader (1995b) depicted Parizeau, on the night of his referendum loss, as 'swaggering' before his 'dispirited legions'. 'From him [the leader noted] we heard nothing of reconcilia-tion . . . ever proud, ever wilful, the double-breasted Premier flailed like a tinhorn strongman and flapped like a strutting capon.' Referring specifically to Parizeau's most pointed remarks, the leader went on to observe:

> *Revenge. Money. The ethnic vote.* The words dripped like acid from Mr Parizeau's lips. This was no gaffe. This was no slip of the tongue. The Premier did not misspeak himself. In fact, he was artlessly honest and exquisitely consistent. In singling out immigrants, the English and business – all of whom largely voted no – he shouted his atavistic tribalism. In baring his bitterness, he hoped to poison any budding accommodation which might emerge.

Finally, in responding to Parizeau's 'apology', his grudging acknowledgement that perhaps his words were 'badly chosen', the *Globe & Mail* leader noted that the words, though unpleasant, were hardly surprising: 'If it is any consolation to him, they were warmly endorsed by that tribune of tolerance, Jean Marie Le Pen.' (These comments show, *inter alia*, that the intemperance produced by political fer-vour need not reside in one camp alone.)

After his widely rejected remarks about ethnic votes, Parizeau was hardly cast into the outer darkness. While demonised in many anglophone eyes, he continues to represent a no-nonsense approach many 'hard' Quebec sovereigntists applaud. In a letter to *Le Devoir* in November 1996, Parizeau returned to an arguably eth-nocentric conception of Quebec society, in which the 'real' Quebeckers – the francophones – have had their hopes frustrated by 'the others' (see Gray 1996, 1997). A year later, in November 1997, Parizeau observed that

> the Jewish Congress of Canada [Quebec section], the Greek Congress of Canada and the Italian Congress make a very good fight against sovereignty. And when I said to them, 'You've been very efficient,' they say, 'You can't say that.'

> (Stevenson 1997)

But, it may be objected, Parizeau's continuing media presence need reflect nothing of real influence. However, we find that the federal separatist party, the *Bloc Québécois*, hired Parizeau as an adviser (in January 1999) on Quebec sovereignty. His influence on the *BQ* leader, Gilles Duceppe, was clear. His straightforward com-mitment to independence began to be favourably compared to Bouchard's more tempered enthusiasm, and he himself openly criticised Bouchard's 'neglect' (see Daly 1999; Gagnon 1999; Leblanc 2000). Parizeau's appeal was not limited to hard-line sovereigntists and his arguments for 're-igniting' the sovereignty issue became increasingly popular. They certainly pushed Bouchard, in April 2000, to re-emphasise his own desires for independence – a stance that clearly impressed the *PQ* who, in a leadership review in May, gave Bouchard a very strong renewed mandate. But Parizeau's presence was felt, both in the desires of many delegates for another referendum and in Bouchard's public pronouncements about preparing for sovereignty, about promises of eventual independence, about daring to re-take the initiative. 'Our objective, our obsession, is Quebec sovereignty as soon as possible,' Bouchard told the *Parti Québécois* convention (Séguin 2000b). Following the Canadian federal election in November 2000, however, in which the *Bloc* lost Quebec seats to the Liberals – and which was, of course, also seen as a setback among the provincial *PQ* – Bouchard apparently returned to an attitude of caution about future referendums. The circle was immediately closed once more by sovereigntists of the Parizeau persuasion. An important member of the *PQ* threatened to quit, and sit as an independent, if Bouchard's 'neglect' of the issue continued. And Michel Venne, editor of *Le Devoir*, called for Bouchard to state clearly his position: 'if [he] no longer believes in sovereignty, let him say so . . . let others take up the cause . . . [otherwise] his calls to mobilize will remain a dead letter and his speeches will only bore us' (Johnson 2000).

Overall, it appears that a considerable part (at least) of the Quebec sovereigntist movement is an ethnic and not a 'civic' phenomenon. This is both understandable and unsurprising. What is of chief interest is the curious interplay among several themes. First, there are the continuing attempts by sovereigntists to argue that theirs is *not* an ethnically-specific and non-inclusive enterprise. Before the 1995 referendum, for instance, Parizeau himself (in an address to the Greek community in Montreal – 'most of whom gave him a warm welcome') made many 'inclusive' remarks, particularly rejecting the notion of 'two or three classes of citizens' (Mackie 1994a; see Mackie 1994b, for similar remarks made to a Jewish audience). Second, there is the continuing inability (or unwillingness) among Canadians at large – both 'ordinary citizens' and politicians – to understand the Quebec-as-a-nation stance and to persist, therefore, in pushing for an all-provinces-are-equal one. Third, there is the depiction by Parizeau (and others, of course) of 'us-and-them' interests and voting patterns, which is, in fact, accurate – i.e., virtually all non-francophones in Quebec are opposed to sovereignty. But it is inappropriate (at the least) to voice this as Parizeau does, to 'divide people up into mere Quebeckers and full *Québécois*' (*Globe & Mail* 1997b).

All three of these themes, of course, are reflections of nationalism in one way or another, and this is what, overtly or implicitly, animates the whole situation. Consequently, it is the underlying common factor in all the discourse treated here. It is a discourse which does not – indeed, cannot – go away. Thus, in September 1998, Bernard Landry (Quebec's deputy premier) said, in reference to the idea that any successful vote for sovereignty ought to involve more than a simple majority: 'Everyone knows well that if we put the bar too high, it's like giving a right of veto to our compatriots, brothers and sisters from the cultural communities, on our national project. That can't be done' (Ha & Séguin 1998). What could be easier here than identifying 'we', 'our compatriots' and 'our national project'?

As Charles Taylor has recently observed, the great Canadian puzzle is 'how more than one nation can live together in the bosom of a single state' (1997: 29).[4] Difficulties here are, of course, exacerbated if the very idea of two nations is not broadly accepted. Thus, Gilles Duceppe observed that 'the true problem, the real problem, remains in the obstinate, that is to say blind, refusal to recognize the very existence of the Quebec people' (Fraser 1997). Convinced of its own national integrity, the sovereigntist movement has naturally had critical views of any broader cultural connectivity. Thus, Bouchard has observed that 'Canada is divisible because it is not a real country. There are two peoples, two nations and two territories. And this one [Quebec] is ours' (*Globe & Mail* 1996). Or, we find André Joli-Coeur – the lawyer arguing the sovereigntist case in Supreme Court deliberations – stating that Canadians do not exist as a people and therefore cannot decide the future of nations like Quebec (Séguin 1998a). Similar rhetoric came from Parizeau who, in June 2000, declared Canadian culture a 'fake' or an 'invention'; the country itself, he said, is 'unworkable' since it comprises 'two nations living under the same roof'. Most recently, Diane Lemieux, Quebec's minister of culture, compared *provincial* identities: 'I believe there is no real Ontario culture' (see Leblanc 2000; Séguin 2001d). These comments – all made by important representatives of the sovereignty movement – are remarkable not for their accuracy, of course, but for the depth of feeling they represent, for the intertwining of nationalism and emotion that they portray.

There is clearly a lot of classic nationalist rhetoric in all this, but there is also some accuracy. For example, it is true that many non-francophones do not recognise Quebec as a nation – though this is more due to limitations of knowledge than to obstinacy. It is also fair to say that, while Quebec might be considered a nation, the rest of the country is something of a multicultural mix (if one built upon an anglophone base); the development of some overarching *Canadian* identity is incomplete (to say the least). If Quebec is a nation, what are its dimensions? Is it (or is it seen as, or could it be) inclusive or exclusive, 'civic' or 'ethnic'? We have thus returned to a very central theme and it is perhaps appropriate to end this section with some further consideration of relevant Quebec terminology.

Gagnon (1994) provides some developmental notes here, showing how 'sovereigntist' has replaced 'separatist' in the nationalist lexicon, and how words like 'federalist' and 'provincial' have acquired negative connotations. Most important has been the growing sense of a division between Quebec and the rest of the country, as seen in phrases like *le Québec et le Canada* or *les Québécois et les Canadiens*. Gagnon later suggests that the word *Québécois*, which should logically refer to all people living in the province, has come to have the narrower connotation of 'old-stock' francophones, and a 'real' *Québécois* is a sovereigntist (Gagnon 1997a; see also Gagnon 1997b).

The work of El Yamani *et al.* (1993) involved trawling through media coverage of majorities and minorities, of 'us' and 'them' in Quebec. They turned up about 50 terms used to describe francophones of French-Canadian background, and almost 90 for minority groups. Among the former (not including terms already presented here) we find *Québécois francophones*, *Québécois francophones de vieille souche*, *Québécois francophones du cru*, *majorité canadienne-française* and *Québécois de souche française*.

Among the latter are *autres Québécois, compatriotes d'une autre origine, communautés culturelles, membres d'origines ethniques* and *ceux de fraîche date*. The authors note that 'the term "Québécois" was always qualified when opposed [*sic*] to ethnic minorities, as if the mere presence of the "other" forces the majority in Quebec to redefine itself' (p. 15). This is counter to Gagnon's observation (above), that the current connotation of *Québécois* does not involve qualification. Given the dates of the contributions by El Yamani *et al.*, and by Gagnon, we may be seeing terminological change over a volatile five-year period.

The latest reports

The nationalist discourse – particularly in its more polemical manifestations – continues to be an important feature of the broader political debate. The most recent and egregious manifestation is *l'affaire Michaud*. Yves Michaud is a prominent sovereigntist, was the *PQ*'s delegate-general in Paris in the early 1980s, and planned to run for the party in a by-election in 2001. In December 2000, he complained that the preferences of Jewish Quebeckers in the 1995 referendum represented an 'ethnic vote against the sovereignty of the Quebec people'. Referring to the B'nai Brith, Michaud said that 'they should excuse themselves for being so anti-Quebec . . . they are the extremist anti-sovereigntists in Quebec and I don't argue with these kinds of people.' Curiously, he then attempted to compare the sovereigntist campaign for Quebec independence with the Jewish quest for a homeland; when told by a Jewish senator that the cases were not the same, Michaud said, 'It's never the same for them . . . [they are] not the only people in the world that suffered.' His remarks were widely criticised, not least by sovereigntists themselves. But some – including Parizeau and Duceppe – while distancing themselves from Michaud's statements, nonetheless opposed Bouchard's plans to block his by-election candidacy. Michaud remained uncontrite, and felt himself 'falsely demonised'. In any case, many heard in his remarks an echo of Parizeau's referendum-night statements about the 'ethnic vote'. The simple accuracy of such statements is not in question: most non-francophones do not support independence (as Parizeau reiterated during this present *affaire*). The tone, however, the resonances, the possible scapegoating, the revival of invidious distinctions between 'real' Quebeckers and others – these are of course the flashpoints (see *Globe & Mail* 2000c; Séguin 2000d, 2000e, 2000f).

Apart from its immediate and obvious significance, *l'affaire Michaud* proved to be Bouchard's Sarajevo. In January he resigned (Bouchard 2001). He was aware that his efforts to 'revive the flame' of sovereignty were unsuccessful – and many critics within the *PQ* itself, of course, felt that he had not been forceful enough, that he had never been unreservedly committed to independence, that he suffered from *attentisme* (Bouthillier 2001; Séguin 2001a); Parizeau certainly lost no time in questioning Bouchard's fervour (Séguin 2001b). As well, however, Bouchard was very much shaken by Michaud's comments and the reactions to them.

Not only did the Michaud affair prove the last straw for Bouchard, it also propelled his deputy, Bernard Landry, into the party leadership and, therefore, the premiership of the province. Landry, an unwavering separatist (see Gagnon 2001a, 2001b), immediately claimed the spotlight with some ill-chosen remarks of his own. In January he said that Quebec has 'no intention of street walking [*faire le trot-toir*] for pieces of red rag [*des bouts de chiffons rouges*]', referring to the Canadian flag. Landry's ludicrous attempts at apology included saying, first, that he hadn't meant the flag at all (but rather the cloth used to provoke bulls in the arena) and, second, that the French connotation of *chiffon* lacked the negative English aspects of 'rag' (see *Globe & Mail* 2001; Peritz 2001; Séguin 2001c). Earlier Landry discourse of note includes telling *l'Express* (in 1994) that Quebec was 'the last colony in the Western world . . . Quebeckers are . . . a little like the firemen of Chernobyl, in the centre of the cataclysm, but still standing'. In March, Landry observed that, not only is Canada of no use to Quebec, its influence has been positively harmful (he used the word *néfaste*; see Johnson 2001a, 2001b).

Conclusion

Current political discourse in Canada has thrown some light (and some dark) on perennially important issues (not all of them of only local interest): the definition of *minority group*; the logic of state divisibility (if Quebec can separate, why can't its aboriginal peoples separate from *it*, why can't Montreal anglophones engage in some 'partition' of their own?); the questions surrounding liberal-democratic support for *collectivities* rather than *individuals*; varieties of media coverage of important and controversial matters; discussions over whether or not an independent Quebec would be economically viable; the reactions to the Canadian malaise from our American cousins; and so on. This chapter has briefly hinted at some of these important matters, all of which have important linguistic components. Its main thrust, however, has been to present something of the sociopolitical discourse bearing upon conceptions of *sovereignty* and *nationalism*. Naturally, the specifics here are Canadian ones, but generalities emerge too. Two of these are particularly noteworthy.

The first is simply that terminology is never neutral and always important. Even when overt manipulation is not an issue, the lexical variations which flow, naturally enough, from different ideological wellsprings can have serious consequences. An obvious example of this occurs with the wording of questions – in polls and, indeed, in referendums! Beyond this, group designations can reveal a lot about self-concepts, about perceived social boundaries, about views of 'us' and 'them' and, consequently, can suggest likely or desired patterns of social and political action. The current Canadian scene is particularly rich in illustrative detail here, although obviously not unique in principle.

The second generality – the light that current data shed on conceptions of 'civic' versus 'ethnic' nationalism – is (only in part, of course) a more focussed variant of the first. Lexical choices and linguistic behaviour may illuminate underlying concepts of nationalism, and may (more specifically) suggest that the 'civic' variety is, after all, something of a chimera. Again, the Canadian context is clearly only one among many in which arguments about 'ethnic' versus 'civic' (or, sometimes, 'exclusive' versus 'inclusive') nationalism have occurred. But the Quebec setting is particularly relevant here, not least because sovereigntists themselves have beaten this particular drum rather loudly – although not, as we have seen in several egregious instances, always very persuasively. Stark (1995), in a piece that appeared about a month before the October referendum, cited the views of Louis Balthazar, who suggested that the Quebec 'collective identity' was based on 'aesthetic and ethical choice' rather than upon language and culture, that it was aiming for a 'non-nationalist approach to sovereignty.' Four weeks later, Parizeau was thundering about the 'ethnic vote' in the referendum!

There is a growing literature on civic nationalism and, beyond the sources that have already been mentioned, contemporary works of particular relevance include Brown (2000); Brubaker (1996); Greenfeld (1992); Keating (2001); Kymlicka (2000); McCrone (1998); Nairn (1997); Smith (1998); Touraine (1997); Yack (1999). As well, several excellent (and readable) synthetic overviews will be found in Couture *et al.* (1998). This is the literature to which the information presented here can contribute. The main questions of interest are whether the notion of 'civic nationalism' has any logical force or any unique features, whether it compromises or bastardises the continuity of 'nationalism' *per se*, whether it is a disingenuous *succédané* for 'citizenship' or perhaps 'patriotism'. This is not the place for fuller exploration but it is worth noting that the matter brings us rather neatly back to one of Walker Connor's main concerns – as Conversi points out in his introductory remarks – one of the areas in which he has attempted to correct some terminological and conceptual imprecision. The present data support Connor's contention (citing Conversi again) that 'all nationalism is ethnically predicated, and those who employ the term *nationalism* to refer to a civic identity or civic loyalty are confusing *patriotism* with nationalism.'

Two final points suggest themselves. First, part of what is sometimes a 'hidden agenda' here has to do with perceived virtue: 'civic' nationalism is inclusive and good; 'ethnic' nationalism is exclusive and bad. We could go back at least to Kohn's (1945) classic treatment here, in which there is clearly one good nationalism (state-based, democratic, rational and, indeed, essentially Western) and one bad one (cultural, undemocratic, irrational and eastern). It is entirely understandable, then, that Quebec nationalists (and others, of course) would argue that their nationalism is of the civic variety, and that critics would aim to illuminate the ethnic skeleton! But the psychological questions of interest remain potent here: if there *is* a civic nationalism, what is it, why has it become so popular a conception, in what way is it perceived to be a more attractive label than (say) patriotism, and so on? Is it, perhaps, that it seems to infuse a democratic adherence to social inclusion with a more basic sense of belonging? Is it nationalism without tears?

Second, an essentially unexplored area has to do with the relationships among 'ethnic' attachments, 'civic' ones, and social transition. Some writers, for instance, argue that 'ethnic' solidarities are *passé* (or perhaps ought to be), that some societies are now essentially cosmopolitan 'post-ethnic' ones (see, for example, Hollinger 1995). Here is an obvious point of entry, as it were, for civic loyalties. But it may be that such apparently 'de-ethnicised' societies are not stable entities at all, and that they will come to be seen as transitional. Old ethnicities break down in the American melting-pot, for instance; consequently, modern America seems 'post-ethnic' and not a nation in any traditional sense. New ethnic mixtures and attachments, however, are in the process of formation – and one day America *will* look more like a nation. Transitions between heterogeneity and (relative) homogeneity are, after all, common enough if one takes the long view. Thus 'civic nationalism' might be seen as a way-station on the road to a new version of its more full-blooded counterpart.

One day there may be no *compatriotes d'une autre origine* in Quebec. Sovereigntists would presumably endorse this idea, and even members of minority groups resisting either assimilation or exclusion from the *famille de souche* might see this as some eventual outcome – but they would surely be concerned about the type of *projet de société* that is to take them there.

Notes

1 In August 2000, a three-year-old poll (taken in October 1997) was released, one showing that many more people had favoured the 'softer' strategy (the so-called 'Plan A') than the more hard-line 'Plan B'. That is, government support for Canadian unity based upon benefits for all, the realignment of federal and provincial roles and the accommodation of Quebec in a modern society was endorsed; tougher dealings with Quebec separatism were supported by fewer than 20 per cent of the 2,000 respondents. But of course there is volatility here; for example, polls a year earlier (November 1996) – i.e., nearer the October referendum – showed most Canadians to be supportive of a *harder* line with Quebec, and unwilling to endorse any proposed constitutional recognition of Quebec as a 'distinct society' (see Aubry 2000; Winsor and Greenspon 1996).

As may be imagined, government policy has involved *both* options. Conciliation and consultation have (it is alleged) always remained on offer, while the Supreme Court ruling on separation and Ottawa's 'Clarity Bill' have been variously interpreted as hard-line or as simply commonsensical establishment of guidelines useful to all sides. Certainly, these formal procedures have provided the government with a distancing mechanism – i.e., it can argue that the Court's ruling was above politics and that its own legislation on 'clarity' is a technical necessity that logically follows the ruling (see Fraser 1999a).

2 For the text of the proposed federal 'clarity bill', see *Globe & Mail* (1999b); for a discussion of the unusual step being taken here – a country conceding that it might be broken up and then attempting to establish the rules by which this might happen, see Adams (1999); Fraser and McCarthy (1999). For notes on Quebec's Bill 99 – its 'counterattack' – see *Globe & Mail* (2000b); Ha (2000a); Séguin (2000c); Wells (2000).

3 As Fraser (1998) puts it, 'the clearer the question, the lower the Yes vote ... only about a quarter of Quebeckers say they support "independence", while maybe a third say they support "sovereignty".' A study by Nadeau, Blais, Nevitte and Gidengil (1998) is also relevant here. Respondents were asked whether they were favourable or opposed to Quebec sovereignty: some were asked this *tout court*, while for others a qualification was added (after the words 'Quebec sovereignty') – '. . . that is, Quebec is no longer part of Canada.' Across several settings, the 'qualified' version elicited lower rates of support.

4 This is something I have emphasised in my writings on Canadian issues (e.g., 'The Canadian struggle to satisfactorily house two nations in one state continues': Edwards 1997a: 108). Taylor's use of the word *bosom* reflects the words of Lord Durham, in his famous 1839 report on British North America: 'I found two nations warring in the bosom of a single state' (Craig 1963: 23).

References

In the interests of brevity, all references to pieces in the *Globe & Mail* are listed here first, without title.

Adams, P., 11 December 1999; Aubin, B. 23 November 1996; Bouchard, L., 12 January 2001; Bouthillier, G., 12 January 2001; Daly, C., 24 April 1999; Fraser, G., 25 September 1997, 8 September 1998, 10 December 1999(a), 11 December 1999(b), 14 December 1999(c); Fraser, G. & McCarthy, S., 8 December 1999; Gagnon, L., 23 April 1994, 23 August 1997(a), 30 August 1997(b), 8 May 1999, 29 January 2001(a), 5 March 2001(b); *Globe & Mail* (leaders), 1 March 1995(a), 1 November 1995b, 30 January 1996, 28 October 1997(a), 1 December 1997(b), 21 August 1998(a), 4 December 1998(b), 2 February 1999(a), 11 December 1999(b), 23 August 2000(a), 8 December 2000(b), 16 December (2000c), 25 January 2001; Gray, J., 8 November 1995, 2 November 1996, 19 February 1997; Ha, T., 2 September 1998, 6 April 2000(a), 22 August 2000(b); Ha, T. & Séguin, R., 1 September 1998; Johnson, W., 6 December 2000, 7 March 2001(a), 14 March 2001(b); Leblanc, D., 2 June 2000; Mackie, R., 14 April 1994(a), 25 April 1994(b); Nadeau, R. *et al.*, 16 March 1998; Peritz, I., 25 January 2001; Picard, A., 3 March 1994, 3 April 1998, 12 April 2000; Séguin, R., 16 April 1996, 6 March 1998(a), 4 September 1998(b), 16 December 1999, 7 April 2000(a), 8 May 2000(b), 8 December 2000(c), 15 December 2000(d), 20 December 2000(e), 21 December 2000(f), 12 January 2001(a), 13 January 2001(b), 24 January 2001(c), 9 March 2001(d); Séguin, R. & Ha, T., 11 December 1999; Simpson, J., 13 September 1996, 16 December 1999; Stevenson, J., 26 November 1997; Unland, K., 21 April 1997; Winsor, H., 13 September 1994, 2 December 1998; Winsor, H. & Greenspon, E., 16 November 1996.

Allcock, J. 1994. 'Heart of the matter'. *Times Higher Education Supplement*. 25 March.

Aubry, J. 2000. 'Liberals ignored Canadians' views on separation'. *National Post*. 7 August.

Balthazar, L. 1995. 'Within the black box: Reflections from a French Quebec vantage point'. *American Review of Canadian Studies*. 25: 519–541.

Bellavance, J.-D. 2000. 'Bouchard would disobey Clarity'. *National Post*. 6 April.

Bothwell, R. 1995. *Canada and Quebec: One Country, Two Histories*. Vancouver: University of British Columbia Press.

Breton, R. 1988. 'From ethnic to civic nationalism: English Canada and Quebec'. *Ethnic and Racial Studies*. 11: 85–102.

Brown, D. 2000. *Contemporary Nationalism*. London: Routledge.

Brubaker, R. 1996. *Nationalism Reframed*. Cambridge: Cambridge University Press.

Cahen, M. 1994. *Ethnicité politique: Pour une lecture réaliste de l'identité*. Paris: L'Harmattan.

Cameron, D. (ed.) 1999. *The Referendum Papers: Essays on Secession and National Unity*. Toronto: University of Toronto Press.

Carens, J. (ed.) 1995. *Is Quebec Nationalism Just? Perspectives from Anglophone Canada*. Montreal and Kingston: McGill-Queen's University Press.

Carment, D., Stack, J. and Harvey, F. (eds) 2001. *The International Politics of Quebec Secession*. Westport, CT: Praeger.

Cloutier, E., Gay, J. and Latouche, D. 1992. *Le virage*. Montreal: Québec-Amérique.

Connor, W. 1994. *Ethnonationalism: The Quest for Understanding*. Princeton, NJ: Princeton University Press.

Cook, R. 1995. *Canada, Québec and the Uses of Nationalism*. Toronto: McClelland & Stewart.

Couture, J., Nielsen, K. and Seymour, M. (eds) 1998. *Rethinking Nationalism*. Calgary: University of Calgary Press.

Craig, G. 1963. *Lord Durham's Report*. Toronto: McClelland & Stewart.

Dickie, J. 2000. 'Sententiousness and nationalist discourse'. *Nations and Nationalism*. 6: 3–22.

Edwards, J. 1994a. 'Ethnolinguistic pluralism and its discontents: A Canadian study, and some general observations'. *International Journal of the Sociology of Language*. 110: 5–85.

—— 1994b. 'Canadian update, and rejoinder to the comments'. *International Journal of the Sociology of Language*. 110: 203–219.

—— 1995a. 'The power of nationalism'. In W. Fase, K. Jaspaert and S. Kroon (eds) *The State of Minority Languages*. Lisse: Swets & Zeitlinger.

—— 1995b. 'Monolingualism, bilingualism, multiculturalism and identity: Lessons and insights from recent Canadian experience'. *Current Issues in Language and Society*. 2: 5–57.

—— 1997a. 'French and English in Canada: Before and after the Quebec referendum of October 1995'. In W. Wölck and A. de Houwer (eds) *Recent Studies in Contact Linguistics*. Bonn: Dümmler.

—— 1997b. 'Lengua e identidad bajo presión: Tensiones francófonas-anglófonas en Canadá en los 90'. *Revista de Antropología a Social*. 6: 53–71.

El Yamani, M., Juteau, D. and McAndrew, M. 1993. 'Towards a redefinition of ethnic boundaries in Quebec: "Us" and "them" in the media discourse on the *affaire Parizeau*'. Paper presented at the conference of the Canadian Ethnic Studies Association, October. Vancouver.

Greenfeld, L. 1992. *Nationalism: Five Roads to Modernity*. Cambridge, MA: Harvard University Press.

Hamilton, R. and Pinard, M. 1982. 'The Quebec independence movement'. In C. Williams (ed.) *National Separatism*. Cardiff: University of Wales Press.

Hollinger, D. 1995. *Post-Ethnic America: Beyond Multiculturalism*. New York: Basic Books.

Ignatieff, M. 1993. *Blood and Belonging: Journeys into the New Nationalism*. New York: Viking Penguin.

Keating, M. 2001. *Nations Against the State*. London: Palgrave.

Kohn, H. 1945. *The Idea of Nationalism*. New York: Macmillan

Kymlicka, W. 1995. *Multicultural Citizenship*. Oxford: Clarendon.

——. 2000. 'Modernity and national identity'. In S. Ben-Ami *et al.* (eds) *Ethnic Challenges to the Modern Nation State*. London: Macmillan.

Lisée, J.-F. 1994. *Le tricheur: Robert Bourassa et les québécois*. Montréal: Boréal.

McCrone, D. 1998. *The Sociology of Nationalism*. London: Routledge.

MacLennan, H. 1945. *Two Solitudes*. Toronto: Collins.

McRoberts, K. 1997. *Misconceiving Canada: The Struggle for National Unity*. Toronto: Oxford University Press.

Nairn, T. 1997. *Faces of Nationalism*. London: Verso.

Pinard, M. 1994. 'The secessionist option and Quebec public opinion, 1988–1993'. *Canada Opinion*. 2.

Prager, J. 1998. 'Seek ye first the economic kingdom! In search of a rational choice interpretation of Quebec nationalism'. In J. Couture, K. Nielsen and M. Seymour (eds) *Rethinking Nationalism*. Calgary: University of Calgary Press.

Rowley, D. 2000. 'Imperial versus national discourse: The case of Russia'. *Nations and Nationalism*. 6: 23–42.

Schnapper, D. 1994. *La communauté des citoyens: Sur l'idée moderne de nation*. Paris: Gallimard.

Smith, A. 1995. *Nations and Nationalism in a Global Era*. Oxford: Polity Press.

—— 1998. *Nationalism and Modernism*. London: Routledge.

Stark, A. 1995. 'Vive le Québec anglophone!' *Times Literary Supplement*. 21 September.

Taylor, C. 1997. 'Deep diversity and the future of Canada'. In D. Hayne (ed.) *Can Canada*

Survive? Toronto: University of Toronto Press.

Touraine, A. 1997. *Pourrons-nous vivre ensemble?* Paris: Fayard.

Wells, P. 2000. 'Childish fit of denial is Bouchard-style politics'. *National Post.* 6 April.

Yack, B. 1999. 'The myth of the civic nation'. In R. Beiner (ed.) *Theorizing Nationalism.* Albany: State University of New York Press.

Young, R. 1995. *The Secession of Quebec and the Future of Canada.* Montreal and Kingston: McGill-Queen's University Press.

——. 1999. *The Struggle for Quebec: From Referendum to Referendum?* Montreal and Kingston: McGill-Queen's University Press.

Part III

Applied Connorian perspectives

9 Federations and the management of nations[1]

Agreements and arguments with
Walker Connor and Ernest Gellner

Brendan O'Leary

The multination state faces a dual threat, consisting of demands for self-determination from below and governmental programmes of assimilation from above. Contemporary political forces, therefore, clearly move in the direction of . . . Barker's prophecy that envisages a world order in which 'each State is also a nation'.

(Connor [1967] 1994: 22)

A federal state requires for its formation two conditions. There must exist, in the first place, a body of countries . . . so closely connected by locality, by history, by race, or the like, as to be capable of bearing in the eyes of their inhabitants, an impress of common nationality . . . A second condition absolutely essential to the founding of a federal system is the existence of a very peculiar . . . sentiment . . . the inhabitants . . . must desire union, and must not desire unity.

(Albert Venn Dicey 1915: 75)

Providence has been pleased to give this one connected country to one united people – a people descended from the same ancestors, speaking the same language, professing the same religion, attached to the same principles of government, very similar in their manners and their customs, and who, by their joint counsels, arms and efforts, fighting side by side throughout a long and bloody war, have nobly established their general liberty and independence.

(Madison *et al.* 1987: 91)

Federalism as such is no guarantee for ethnic harmony and accommodation in the absence of other factors.

(Rudolfo Stavenhagen 1996: 202)

Walker Connor has never been a dedicated follower of fashion, in his thought, his life, or indeed his clothing. He has never embraced, or been embraced by, facile schools in political science, such as the behaviourists, the exponents of rational choice, or the social constructionists. He has sought, modestly, to explain, rather than to prescribe public or international policy on ethnonational matters. He has maintained a consistent focus on the depth and durability of ethnonational sentiment amongst modern peoples in modern times. In return, he been subjected to ill-considered or thought-stopping classifications, being termed a 'primordialist' or

an 'essentialist', terms often used by those with status anxieties about their cosmopolitanism and their intelligence quotients. Yet, unlike his critics, he has never
been surprised by outbreaks of ethnic sentiment or conflict, and unlike many of
them he understood and anticipated the fault-lines of the major great power to collapse in the late twentieth century. His outstanding comparative political analysis,
The National Question in Marxist-Leninist Theory and Strategy, demonstrated – to anyone
who read it – that the Soviet Union, had not 'solved' its national questions, and nor
had the People's Republics of China, Vietnam, Romania, Czechoslovakia, or
Yugoslavia. His sceptical but careful eye produced a very different vision of Soviet
history than that prevalent both amongst apologists for the regime and some
Western Sovietologists – who had come to see state socialism as an alternative industrial society, that had resolved, or was on route to resolving its national questions.

The methods Connor has deployed in his writings are those of political science
and history, buttressed by a nuanced appreciation of political geography. His typical foray has taken the form of a well-focused journal article. He has argued that
the phenomenon of nationalism, which he treats as unitary – though capable of
multiple manifestations – is one that requires understanding, rigorous clarity in terminology, and in-depth empirical and historical investigation, deploying texts,
documents, artefacts, and where possible, social surveys. He has additionally maintained that the phenomenon requires careful attention to collective and individual
perceptions, as much as facts, and to the psychology of collective identity and
homelands – though, unlike postmodernists, he has never pretended to expertise in
identity or psychological theory.

The prescriptive content in Connor's writing has mostly been methodological
and negative: he has regularly produced propositional inventories of methodological failures, which many of us have found exceptionally useful.[2] He has 'quested'
for understanding, not sought to put the world to right. He does not believe in
philosophical two-card tricks, e.g. showing that nations are social constructs, and
reasoning from that astonishingly deep insight through to the *non sequitur* that they
can easily be 're-imagined', 'de-constructed', or 're-invented', or rendered 'post-
national'. He has been relatively silent on whether constitutional engineering or
astute statecraft can ever successfully manage nationalism. He has written no essay
on 'conflict-resolution', positive or negative. His enduring scepticism towards those
who claimed to have 'solved' nationality questions, one must therefore suspect, has
become part of a wider vision: in which states, public policies and constitutional
engineers are seen as having very limited capacities to manage ethnonational conflicts. One might sum up the relevant explanatory and prescriptive implications of
Connor's work on this issue in four propositions, or 'Walker's expectations':

1   Expect secessionist movements in multi-national states, even in advanced,
    developed, prosperous industrial democracies, especially amongst peoples who
    believe themselves to be living in their homelands – and most states are 'multi-
    homeland'.
2   Expect some of these secessionist movements to succeed, despite adverse
    odds.

3 Expect state-sponsored assimilation projects, after the 'Age of Nationalism', to be increasingly politically problematic – but less so in 'immigrant states', which have either destroyed their 'first nations' through genocide, or have rendered them demographically controllable.

4 Expect what looks to be a stable multi-national state to rest, directly or indirectly, on the political preponderance of the relevant *Staatsvolk*, the dominant people; differently put, every multi-national state, upon inspection, will turn out to be a control system.[3]

The emerging political science and political sociology of national and ethnic conflict regulation generally accepts the first three propositions (see *inter alia* Horowitz 1985; Lijphart 1977; McGarry and O'Leary 1993; Nordlinger 1972), and Connor's arguments are therefore now part of a belated, though still insufficiently disseminated, wisdom. It is the last of these four *implicit* propositions that provides the focus for the present chapter.[4] In the analysis of national and ethnic conflict regulation there has always been some recognition of the limits of states, or of the capacity of politics more generally, as means for resolving or managing ethnic and national antagonisms. In that sense, Connor's injunction not to underestimate the emotional power of nationalism is accepted. But, the field has shared a common assumption that governments or states have significant capacities to shape or regulate (not necessarily 'resolve'), for good or ill, the destiny of national and ethnic relations. State officials can pursue strategies either to eliminate or to manage ethnonational differences (McGarry and O'Leary 1993). When pursuing elimination they can execute genocide or ethic expulsion; they can partition territories; or they can try to homogenise peoples through integration or assimilation programmes. Governments can, in short, try to 'right-size' their states, and to 'right-people' them (O'Leary 2001a).

We all know that modern governments have immense and awful powers to kill in genocidal or democidal programmes (Rummel 1997). And, that they expel huge numbers of people. Some even insist that nation-state and democracy-building are refugee-creating processes (Mann 1999; Zolberg 1983). Individual states and military alliances of states still consider partitions as possible means to eliminate troublesome ethnonational antagonisms. In pumping significant resources and coercive capacities into integrating or maintaining the 'right' peoples, moulding them into common citizenship, and in some cases blending them within full-scale assimilation projects, the OECD's states seem, *prima facie*, no different to the mostly newer states outside their privileged ranks. 'Nationalising states', as Rogers Brubaker (1996a) has called them,[5] are everywhere.[6]

In short, to eliminate national and ethnic differences that might become politically salient, states have exercised awesome powers and ambitions in the century just passed, and they have often done so on behalf of their dominant nation or ethnic group(s). Here there has been no death of the nation-state – though there has been a lot of dying in the war of nation against state, state against nation, and nation against nation. Nothing in this history of horror and oppression in our times is at odds with Connor's first three expectations. But, exterminations or eliminations have not been always been successful, thankfully; and not all states or governments have been exterminist or eliminationist. In the field of national and ethnic conflict regulation, theoretical, empirical and normative effort is devoted to demonstrating that states can be designed or run to steer, manage and regulate multi-national, polycultural and multi-lingual societies (Laitin 1977; 1979; 1992; 1998) in tolerable, tolerant, and democratic ways.[7] An increasing repertoire of institutional 'technologies', i.e. legal strategies, systems of rights-protection, and public policies, is being identified – and in some cases pioneered – to manage eth-nonational differences. For example, the ability of political agents, through benign or malign choices, to design electoral systems that provoke, calm, or re-channel ethnic tensions is now appraised in a literature of increasing sophistication (Reilly and Reynolds 1999).[8] One must not exaggerate: There are not too many success stories to tell. There are fewer Switzerlands than Balkan environments, and this may seem grist to the mill of Connor's fourth expectation.[9]

States do, of course, often seek to manage ethnonational differences through malign and hierarchical methods, through systems of control which organise the dominant group and which disorganise the dominated, and Connor's work on Marxist-Leninist regimes is a detailed empirical assessment of one set of such sys-tems.[10] But, it remains normatively and empirically challenging to ask whether there are limits to what states can do when seeking to manage ethnonational dif-ferences in a benign, and liberal democratic manner. That is, are there, or can there be, successful ways of stabilising democratic multi-national states? In partic-ular, we may ask whether federations can manage relations between nations in ways that we, that is egalitarian democrats, might approve? Can federations refute the pessimism of Connor's fourth expectation?

Connor and Gellner on the scale and durability of polycultural and multinational states

Let me begin an answer with a report of some mutual intellectual disrespect amongst friends, and then report a surprising agreement. Mutual intellectual dis-respect first: Walker Connor and Ernest Gellner did not have high opinions of one another's approaches to understanding nationalism.[11] Connor thinks Gellner's theory too dogmatically modernist, predicated too much on the salience of lan-guage, too functionalist, too Eurocentric, too economistic, too bereft of human sentiment, too historically ill-considered. Gellner, by contrast, thought that Connor was an undeclared exponent of ancestral 'dark gods theory', too prone to empha-sise the irrational in nationalism, too psychologistic, and that he lacked a theory to explain the modern power of nationalism. I shall not judge this mutual disrespect here, except to report that it was confined to their theories, and did not extend, in either case, to their respective persons or minds.[12] But, now note a surprising agreement. Connor and Gellner were both sceptical about the prospects of multi-national states in the modern world, though they agreed that they could be held together for long periods by coercion.[13] For those interested in prescription this important and shared inference, is, perhaps, more important than any explanatory differences between Connor and Gellner on the genesis and maintenance of nationalism. We should therefore ask whether this perhaps surprising agreement between them withstands scrutiny.

Let me first clarify a potential misunderstanding. Gellner and Connor did not, in fact, agree on all ethnonational facts about our world. Gellner wrote as if the strategic choices in the modern world were between homogenising others, or homogenisation at the hands of others. He wrote, with qualifications, as if most polyethnic or multi-national states were either disappearing, or mere shams – and as if the equilibrium condition towards which the world was rapidly headed was 'one nation, one state'. Amongst others, I questioned Gellner's apparently cavalier disregard for the facts on this matter – at best his position was premature (O'Leary 1998: 63–64). Connor, by contrast, from his earliest writings has insisted that most contemporary states are not in fact nation-states, that most states are 'multi-home-land', that there are persistent illusions about cultural homogeneity, and indeed pernicious myths about hemispheric, continental, regional and state unity (Connor 1969). Connor has also avoided making strongly dualistic judgements that suggest that peoples must either secede or be assimilated. Connor has regularly observed that it is possible for multi-national states to accommodate heterogeneity with consent: 'it would appear to be the rule that a majority of members of a homeland people are prepared to settle for [meaningful] autonomy for their homeland'(Connor 1994: 82). On these facts, and the avoidance of the dualistic judgement, Connor is the better guide.

Is there, however, a contradiction in Connor's reasoning on this matter? Is his scepticism about the stability of multi-national states belied by the recognition that they compose most of the states of the world? No, because his argument, simply put, is that nationalism and the demands of self-determination threaten the stability of *all* multi-national states, both now and in the future – an argument borne out in his lifetime by the end of the Western empires and the collapse of the Soviet Union, Czechoslovakia, Yugoslavia. There is a second reason why there is no contradiction. Though Connor observes that autonomy strategies may accommodate heterogeneity, and satisfy majorities amongst minority peoples, the hard-headed realism and historical knowledge that informs his analyses demonstrate that secessionists may prove successful despite only having initial minority support amongst their own nation, and that the holders of state power may so mismanage heterogeneity as to de-stabilise autonomy settlements. So, in short, what Connor and Gellner disagree about factually is the extent to which states have already been nationalised by one nation, or the extent to which ethnic homogenisation has occurred. They are not in disagreement about the trend, merely its velocity. Both agree that the age of empires is giving way to the age of nations.

So, what of the substantive agreement between Connor and Gellner, to which we can now devote attention? The last two centuries cast severe doubts on the stability of multi-national states, and nothing in what follows can or will refute that evidence. The bleak testimony of genocides, ethnic expulsions, coercive assimilations, partitions, secessions, and territorial restructurings following imperial collapses has demonstrated nation-building homogenisation at work, and has tempered the optimism of all but the most fanatical exponents of human progress. But, there have also been persistent liberal democratic polycultural or multinational states, federal and/or consociational in format, and persistent efforts to create new versions of such states. Surely these suggest blatant disconfirmation of Connor's and Gellner's pessimism, or, at least, imply appropriate modifications of their arguments?

But if this is granted, 'so what?' might be the riposte. Connor fairly mandates that the predispositions of the analyst be laid bare. My arguments, above and below, are motivated by the desire to reject any fundamental sociological limitations on state capacity, particularly in constitutional statecraft. Without the rejection of this premise there cannot be, at least it seems to me, a worth while prescriptive political science of national and ethnic conflict-regulation, i.e. no assurance, however qualified, that sound advice might be rendered by social scientists on ethnonational public and international policies. However, the fact that my argument is motivated should not decide its validity.

One final piece of throat-clearing is required, this time about the predispositions of Connor and Gellner. Neither of them welcomed or enthused about political instability in multi-national states, i.e. in both cases wishes were not fathers to their thoughts. Gellner, despite his experiences as a Czech, did not want to see the Soviet Union collapse, believing that a slow de-Marxification would be much the best for the welfare of the affected peoples. Nor did he favour the break-up of the federations of the Soviet Union, Yugoslavia and Czechoslovakia. He entertained hopes that advanced industrialisation might diminish national conflicts; that emerging imperatives might prompt a new global division of competencies with supra-national government to manage technological, ecological and terrorist threats in conjunction with the cantonisation of local and educational functions; and that the 'de-fetishisation' of land might be possible (Gellner 1997: 102–108). In brief, Gellner was not against federalism, or other forms of polycultural and multi-national government – or indeed the 'post-national' government foreseen by some seers who are best left alone with their seering. He was just sceptical about the prospects of multinational states, and their likely robustness. Connor too has been no political activist. One can detect in his work, by comparison with Gellner, much greater empathy for the small battalions, the small nations, the peoples-without-history, and a greater sympathy for projects of cultural autonomy, but this has not led him into any *carte blanche* public championing of secessionists. He has been deeply interested in whether a powerful ideology, Marxism-Leninism, could manage national questions; and in whether powerful world-religions, such as Islam, can manage national questions.[14] The motivation behind this research has been empirical, not based on his desires. Yes, he diagnosed the fault-lines in the Soviet, Yugoslav and Czechoslovak federations but no reader would have concluded that he would have desired their break-up after the end of communism.

What follows argues that Gellner's and Connor's implicit theses about the limited prospects for the reconciliation of nationalism with federalism are even more powerful, and more consistent with the evidence, than they seemed. I will therefore provide a theory in a manner consistent with Gellner's own propositions, if not with his words; and one with which Connor should have no difficulty, for reasons I shall explain. But, I will nevertheless be able to suggest that there is more room for constitutional statecraft than Gellner acknowledged or Connor acknowledges.

To explain what follows definitions of federalism, federal political systems, federation, and nationalism are required, together with a brief résumé of how they have been jointly treated in practical political argument. Then I elaborate and explain a theory of why stable democratic federations require a *Staatsvolk*, a dominant people. This argument is, I believe, underpinned by the work of Connor. Having done that, I present evidence in favour of the theory, together with some apparently awkward evidence. This apparently awkward evidence will then be explained, or if you prefer, explained away. Finally, I turn to the political implications of the arguments. In doing so I will confirm the thrust of Connor's arguments about the development of the European Union but from a different theoretical base. These arguments have important prescriptive implications.

Federalism, federal political systems, federations and nationalism

Federalism is a normative political philosophy that recommends the use of federal principles, i.e. combining joint action and self-government (King 1982). 'Federal political systems' is a descriptive catchall term for all political organisations that combine what Daniel Elazar called 'shared rule and self-rule'. Federal political systems, thus broadly construed, include federations, confederations, unions, federacies, associated states, condominiums, leagues, and cross-border functional authorities (Elazar 1987). Federations, with which I will be particularly concerned here, are very distinct federal political systems (Watts 1987; 1998), and are best understood in their authentic, i.e. representative, governmental forms.[15] In a genuinely democratic federation there is a compound sovereign state, in which at least two governmental units, the federal and the regional, enjoy constitutionally separate competencies – although they may also have concurrent powers. Both the federal and the regional governments are each empowered to deal directly with the citizens, and the relevant citizens directly elect (at least some components of) the federal and regional governments. In a federation the federal government usually cannot unilaterally alter the horizontal division of powers – constitutional change affecting competencies requires the consent of both levels of government. Therefore, federation automatically implies a codified and written constitution, and normally is accompanied at the federal level by a supreme court, charged with umpiring differences between the governmental tiers,[16] and by a bicameral legislature – in which the federal as opposed to the popular chamber may disproportionally represent, i.e. over-represent, the smallest regions. Elazar rightly emphasised the 'covenantal' character of federations, i.e. the authority of each government derives from the constitution, not another government.

Having defined the 'F- words' let us turn to nationalism. Nationalism is a political philosophy which holds that the nation 'should be collectively and freely institutionally expressed, and ruled by its co-nationals'(O'Leary 1997: 191). This definition is similar to Gellner's, who held that nationalism is 'primarily a political principle, which holds that the political and the national unit should be congruent' (Gellner 1983: 1). Nothing in either definition makes nationalism automatically incompatible with federalism, or federal political systems, or with federation. Both definitions are compatible with Connor's argument that a nation 'connotes a group of people who believe they are ancestrally related' though they more narrowly confine nationalism to a doctrine of political legitimacy than Connor's stipulation that it 'connotes identification with and loyalty to one's nation' (Connor 1994: xi).

Collective and free institutional expression of more than one nation may, in principle, be possible within a federation. The federation may be organised to make the regional political units and the national units 'congruent', that is to say each regional unit may have a titular nationality. Being 'ruled by co-nationals' may appear to be breached somewhat in a federation when the federal level of government involves joint rule by the representatives of more than one nation, but providing the relevant nations have assented to this arrangement, or practically assent to it, no fundamental denial of the principle of national self-determination is involved. Moreover, if we acknowledge that dual or even multiple nationalities are possible, then federations, in principle, provide effective ways of giving these different identities opportunities for collective and free institutional expression. These definitions therefore permit federalism and nationalism to be compatible political philosophies. They deliberately avoid shutting off empirical research on the relations between nationalism and federation. They do not axiomatically deny the possibility of dual or multi-national federations, and they avoid any obvious commitments on the nature or status of nations.

Nationalism and federalism in practical political design and argument

Three clear positions can be identified on the relationships between federalism and nationalism in the literature of state theory and practical politics in the last two centuries. The first holds that nationalism and federalism are mutually exclusive. The exemplary illustration of this viewpoint is that of the French Jacobins who believed that federalism was part of the counter-revolution, thoroughly hostile to the necessity of linguistic homogenisation, a road-block in the path of authentic, indivisible, monistic popular sovereignty. In his report to the Committee of Public Safety of January 1794 Barère declared that 'Federalism and superstition speak low Breton; emigration and hatred of the Republic speak German; the counterrevolution speaks Italian, and fanaticism speaks Basque' (Brubaker 1996b: 7; de Certaus *et al.* 1975: 295). On one reading of Gellner's work the Jacobins were the nationalist state-builders *par excellence*. They sought cultural assimilation; they were determined to make peasants into Frenchmen; and therefore they were deeply hostile to all forms of accommodation that inhibited this goal, including federalism.

In partial agreement with the Jacobins, many nineteenth-century federalists, notably Joseph Proudhon and Carlo Cattaneo, were resolutely hostile to nation-state nationalism (Majocchi 1991: 162), and many twentieth-century federalists, notably within the European movement, reciprocate the Jacobin view that nationalism and federalism are mutually exclusive (Bosco 1992: Part III). Such federalists have been, and are, resolutely anti-nationalist, associating nationalism with ethnic exclusiveness, chauvinism, racism, and parochially particularistic sentiments. For them federalism belongs to an entirely different co-operative philosophy, one that offers a non-nationalist logic of legitimacy, and an antidote to nationalism rather than a close relative. This viewpoint was most clearly articulated by Pierre Trudeau – educated at the LSE by Elie Kedourie, Gellner's local counterpoint – before he became Canadian Prime Minister. In an article entitled 'Federalism, Nationalism and Reason' Trudeau squarely associated federalism and functionalism with reason, nationalism with the emotions (Trudeau 1968). Trudeau regarded federalism as the denial of and solution to nationalism, though thinkers like him occasionally adopt the view that federalism must be built upon the success of nationalism which it then transcends in Hegelian fashion (Majocchi 1991: 161). In effect they echo Einstein's reported remark that nationalism is the measles of mankind.

The second perspective, by contrast, holds that nationalism and federalism, properly understood, are synonymous. This was the thesis of the Austro-Marxists, Karl Renner and Otto Bauer, in the last days of the Habsburg empire (Bauer 1907; Hanf 1991; Pfabigan 1991). Lenin, Stalin, and their colleagues in the course of Soviet state-building pressed their arguments, in a suitably bowdlerised format, into service. In this conception nationalism and federalism were to be harnessed, at least for the task of building Soviet socialism. In the words of Walker Connor, Lenin's second commandment on the management of nationalism was strategically machiavellian: 'Following the assumption of power, terminate the fact – if not necessarily the fiction – of a right to secession, and begin the lengthy process of assimilation via the dialectical route of territorial autonomy for all compact national groups' (Connor 1984: 38).

Marxist-Leninists were, of course, formal cosmopolitans, committed to a global political order, but pending the world revolution, they maintained that federal arrangements, 'national in form, socialist in content', were the optimal institutional path to global communism. This was the worldview subjected to Connor's critical research in *The National Question in Marxist-Leninist Theory and Strategy*.

The third perspective unites those who think that federalism and nationalism can intersect, and be mutually compatible, but who sensibly believe that not all nationalisms are compatible with all federalisms. But this agreement masks an important difference, one between what I shall call national or mono-national federalists, and multi-national or multi-ethnic federalists. National federalists are exemplified by the first exponents of federation in its modern form, for whom its prime function was 'to unite people living in different political units, who nevertheless shared a common language and culture' (Forsyth 1989: 4). The earliest federalists in what became the Netherlands, in the German-speaking Swiss lands, in what became the USA, and in what became the second German Reich, were national federalists. They maintained that only an autonomous federal government could perform certain necessary functions that confederations or alliances found difficult to perform, especially a unified defence and external relations policy (Riker 1964). They often advocated federation as a stepping stone towards a more centralised unitary state.

The USA may serve as the paradigm case of national federalism, subsequently imitated by its Latin American counterparts in Mexico, Brazil, Venezuela, and Argentina. The US federation shows 'little coincidence between ethnic groups and state boundaries' (Glazer 1983: 276), with one major exception: most of its original and subsequent states had white Anglo-Saxon Protestant majorities. Federation preceded the great expansion in the USA's internal ethnic diversity, and new states were generally only created when they had WASP or assimilated white demographic and electoral majorities.[17] English-speaking whites were the creators of every American state, 'writing its Constitution, establishing its laws, ignoring the previously settled American Indians, refusing to grant any [autonomy] rights to blacks, and making only slight concessions to French and Spanish speakers in a few states' (Glazer 1983: 284). National federalism was part and parcel of American nation-building (Beer 1993), aiding the homogenisation of white settlers and immigrants in the famous melting-pot of Anglo conformity (Gordon 1964), and was evident in the writing of *The Federalist Papers*. National federalism poses no problem for Gellnerian theory or for Connor's outlook. Indeed, it confirms it, because national federalists aim to make the sovereign polity congruent with one national culture; they wish to construct the federation in the image of its dominant people.

Multi-national or multi-ethnic federalists, by contrast, may pose a significant challenge to Gellnerian theory and to Connor's fourth expectation if they prove successful in their political endeavours. They advocate federation 'to unite people who seek the advantages of membership of a common political unit, but differ markedly in descent, language and culture' (Forsyth 1989: 4). They seek to express, institutionalise, and protect at least two national or ethnic cultures, often on a permanent basis. Any greater union or homogenisation, if envisaged at all, is postponed for the future. They explicitly reject the strongly integrationist and/or assimilationist objectives of national federalists. They believe that dual or multiple national loyalties are possible, and indeed desirable. Some of them make quite remarkable claims for federalism. Political scientist Klaus von Beyme, referring to Western democracies, argued in 1985 that 'Canada is the only country in which federalism did not prove capable of solving . . . ethnic conflict' (1985: 121). Multi-national federalists have been influential in the development of federations in the former British Empire, notably in Canada, the Caribbean, Nigeria, South Africa, India, Pakistan, and Malaysia. They influenced Austro-Marxists and Marxist-Leninists, and have had an enduring impact in the post-communist development of the Russian Federation, Ethiopia, and the rump Yugoslavia. The recent democratic reconstructions of Spain and Belgium also bear their imprint. The most ambitious multi-national federalists of our day are those who wish to develop the European Union from its currently largely confederal form into an explicit federation, into a 'Europe of the nation-states and a Europe of the citizens', as the German foreign minister recently urged at Berlin's Humboldt University (Fischer 2000).

Multi-national federalists have two ways of arguing that national and ethnic conflict regulation can work to harmonise nationalism and federalism. The first is an argument from congruence. If the provincial borders of the components of the federation match the boundaries between the relevant national, ethnic, religious or linguistic communities, i.e. if there is a 'federal society' congruent with the federating institutions, then federation may be an effective harmonising device. That is precisely because it makes an ethnically heterogeneous political society less heterogeneous through the creation of more homogeneous sub-units. Of the seven large-scale genuine federations in durable Western democracies, three significantly achieve this effect for some culturally distinct communities: those of Belgium, Canada, and Switzerland. The federations of Australia, Austria, Germany and the USA, by contrast, do not achieve this effect, and are not organised to do so, and in consequence this possibility in federal engineering cannot be used to explain the relative ethnonational tranquillity of Australia, post-war Austria and Germany, and the post-bellum USA (in which past genocides, the overwhelming of the indigenous populations, and/or integration/assimilation are more important in explaining ethnonational stability). In Belgium, Canada, and Switzerland the success of federation in conflict-regulation, such as it is, has not been the result of comprehensive territorial design. Rather it has largely been based upon the historic geographical segregation of the relevant communities. Post-independence India, especially after Nehru conceded re-organisation of internal state borders along largely linguistic boundaries, is an example of deliberate democratic engineering to match certain ascriptive criteria with internal political borders (see *inter alia* Arora and Verney 1995; Brass 1991; Brass 1990; King 1997; Laitin 1989; Rajashekera 1994). Post-communist Russia and Ethiopia may prove to be others.

Plainly this defence of federation as a way of managing nations – to each nation let a province be given – cannot satisfy those communities that are so dispersed, or small in numbers, that they cannot control federal units or provinces, e.g. Quebec Anglophones, Flemish-speakers in Wallonia, Francophones in Flanders, blacks in the USA; or small and scattered indigenous peoples in Australia, India and North America. Indeed, one reason federation proved insufficient as a conflict-regulating device as Yugoslavia democratised was because there was insufficient geographical clustering of the relevant ethnic communities in relation to their existing provincial borders. However, federal engineering to achieve something approximating the formula 'one nation-one province' does look like a *prima facie* challenge to the tacit Gellnerian notion that in modern times the equilibrium condition is one sovereign state, one culture (or nation). If we treat broadly the 'political unit' in Gellner's definition, to encompass regional or provincial units in a federation, then his theory can accommodate such arrangements, but at the significant concession of recognising that such federal systems are compatible with dual and possibly multiple nationalities. The same argument applies to Connor's fourth expectation – though Connor has explicitly recognised that such autonomy arrangements can work, when national minorities regard them as the most feasible forms of freedom they are likely to get, when there is good-will towards the state which encompasses them, and because national minorities are more likely to be obsessed by the desire to have freedom from the dominant nation than freedom to be wholly sovereign (Connor 2001: 123ff.).

There is a second and more subtle way in which multi-national or ethnofederalists may argue that nationalism and federalism can be harmonised, though it is rarely explicitly defended, because it is really a strategy to defeat national self-determination. It has been eloquently defended by Donald Horowitz (1985: Chapters 14–15). He suggests that federations can and should be partly designed to prevent ethnic minorities from becoming local provincial majorities. The thinking here recommends weakening potentially competing ethnonationalisms: federalism's territorial merits are said to lie in the fact that it can be used as an instrument to prevent local majoritarianism (which has the attendant risks of local tyranny or secessionist incentives). Designing the provincial borders of the federated units on this argument, should be executed on 'balance of power' principles – proliferating, where possible, the points of power away from one focal centre, encouraging intra-ethnic conflict, and creating incentives for inter-ethnic co-operation (by designing provinces without majorities), and for alignments based on non-ethnic interests. This logic is extremely interesting, but empirical support for Horowitz's argument seems so far confined to the distinctly uninspiring case of post-bellum Nigeria. In most existing federations to re-draw regional borders deliberately to achieve these results would probably require the services of military dictators or one-party states. Already mobilised ethnonational groups do not take kindly to efforts to disorganise them through the re-drawing of internal political boundaries. Belgium may, however, become an interesting exception to this scepticism: the Brussels region, created in the new federation, is neither overtly Flemish or Wallonian, and perhaps its heterogeneity will stabilise inter-national relations in Belgium, because without Brussels Flanders will not secede, and there is presently little prospect of Brussels obliging Flanders.

Multi-national and multi-ethnic federations have, of course, been developed for a variety of reasons, not just as means to harmonise nationalism and federalism. They have often evolved out of multiethnic colonies – to bind together the coalition opposing the imperial power (e.g. in the West Indies, and Tanzania). They may have been promoted by the colonial power in an attempt to sustain a reformed imperial system, but subsequently developed a dynamic of their own, as has been true of Canada, India, and indeed South Africa. A history of common colonial or conquest government usually creates élites (soldiers, bureaucrats and capitalists) with an interest in sustaining the post-colonial territory in one political unit, as has sometimes been true of Indonesia, which has recently been re-canvassed as a candidate for an authentic federation (Anderson 1998). Large federations can often be sold economically – they promise a larger single market, a single currency, economies of scale, reductions in transactions' costs and fiscal equalisation. Such instrumental discourses are the common coinage of Euro-federalists. Federations can also be marketed as geopolitically wise, offering greater security and protection than small states, indeed, William Riker rather prematurely assumed that this was the basis for the formation of all federations (Riker 1964). Finally, federations can be advertised as necessary routes to superpower status, a foreground note in the enthusiasms of some Euro-federalists. But the fact that multi-national or multi-ethnic federations may be over-determined in their origins does not affect our central question: can the stateholders of multi-national federations successfully and stably reconcile nationalism and federalism in liberal democratic ways?

The answer at first glance looks like 'yes and no'. There are federal successes and failures. Even some positive 'yes' answers, however, would be enough to counter-act the pessimism induced by Gellnerian theory and Connor's fourth expectation. But let us first do a Cook's Tour of the failures, which pose no problems for Connor's or Gellner's expectations. Many multi-national or multi-ethnic federa-tions have either broken down, or have failed to remain democratic, throughout the communist world, and throughout the post-colonial world. The federations of Latin America – Mexico, Venezuela, Argentina, and Brazil – are either national federalisms and/or have yet to prove themselves durably democratic. The federa-tions of the Soviet Union, Yugoslavia and Czechoslovakia broke down during or immediately after their respective democratisations. In the post-colonial world multi-national or multi-ethnic federations failed, or failed to be successfully estab-lished in the Caribbean, notably in the West Indies Federation. Even the miniature federation of St. Kitts-Nevis recently faced the prospect of secession by referendum by the smaller island of Nevis (Premdas 1998). Multi-national or multi-ethnic fed-erations have failed in sub-Saharan Africa – in Francophone West and Equatorial Africa, in British East Africa (Kenya, Uganda and Tanganyika), and in British Central Africa (Northern and Southern Rhodesia and Nyasaland), or have failed to remain durably democratic – Nigeria and Tanzania, or have yet to be estab-lished as durable authentic democracies – South Africa. The Mali and the Ethiopian federations in independent Africa have experienced break-ups while the Cameroons have experienced forced unitarism after a federal beginning. The Arab world knows only one surviving federation, the United Arab Emirates, which does not score highly on democratic attributes. In Asia there have been obvious federative failures, e.g. in Indochina, in Burma, and in Pakistan, and of the union of Malaya followed by the secession of Singapore. Durably democratic federations have been rare – consider the history of Pakistan. In short, new multi-national fed-erations appear to have a poor track-record as conflict-regulating devices – even where they allow a degree of minority self-government. They have broken down, or failed to be durably democratic, throughout Asia, Africa, and the Caribbean. India stands out as the major exception in Asia, but even here severe qualifications are in order: to crush or divide secessionists in Kashmir, Punjab and elsewhere, the Indian state has deployed emergency powers in a manner, to put it at its mildest, wholly inconsistent with liberal, democratic and federal norms.

These failures in federation have had multiple causes according to their analysts (Elazar 1987: 240–244; Franck 1968; Hicks 1978). In some cases minorities were outnumbered at the federal level of government; in others, notably Malaya, the rel-evant minority was not welcome at the federal level of government – Lee Kuan Yew's courting of the Malay Chinese helped break the Malay federation. In both scenarios the resulting frustrations, combined with an already defined boundary, and the significant institutional resources flowing from control of their own province, provided considerable incentives to attempt secession. Breaks from federations may, of course, invite harsh responses from the rest of the federation: the disintegration of the Nigerian and American federations were halted through millions of deaths. India, the most successful post-colonial multi-ethnic federation has so far faced down vigorous secessionist movements on its frontiers, especially in Kashmir and Punjab. The threat of secession in multi-national or multi-ethnic federations is such that the late Erik Nordlinger consciously excluded federalism from his list of desirable conflict-regulating practices (Nordlinger 1972). The recent emergent principle of international law that permits the disintegration of federations along the lines of their existing regional units is in some people's eyes likely to strengthen the belief that federation should not be considered as a desirable form of multi-national or multi-ethnic accommodation (Horowitz 1998). Integrationist nation-builders in Africa, Asia, and the Caribbean have distrusted federalism precisely because it provides secessionist opportunities. The kleptocratic Mobutu only offered federalism as a model for Zaire as his power-base collapsed. Tunku Abdul Rahman only offered federation with Singapore because he shared Lee Kuan Yew's fears of a communist take-over. Post-colonial state-builders' antipathy to federalism is now matched amongst the intellectuals of Eastern Europe, who regard it as a recipe for secession, given the Czechoslovakian, Yugoslavian and Soviet experiences.

Two final generalising statements must be added to this quick global survey of multi-national or multi-ethnic federal failures. The first is that federations appear to have been especially fragile in bi-ethnic or bi-national, or bi-regional states. In 1982 Maurice Vile could not find a single case of a surviving federation based upon dyadic or triadic structures. Pakistan's Western and Eastern divorce has been the biggest example of the instability of dualistic federations. Czechoslovakia is a more recent case. Whither Serbia and Montenegro, the last two units in Yugoslavia? Belgium may seem like a subsequently emergent exception to Vile's rule, but technically it is a four-unit federation, and it is of rather recent vintage. St. Kitts-Nevis may seem another, but as already indicated Nevis has been tempted to go. The second generalisation is that failures have occurred largely in developing or poor countries, where most theorists of democratisation would predict great difficulty in obtaining stable democratic regimes of whatever hue. This suggests that India, and the three multi-national democratic federations in the advanced industrial world (Belgium, Canada and Switzerland), are the apparently anomalous successes that Gellner and Connor need to be able to explain, or else stand overtly falsified.

A theory of the necessity of a federal *Staatsvolk*

The theory that I wish to advance and explore is that *a stable democratic majoritarian federation,*[18] *be it national federal or multi-national, must have a Staatsvolk, a national or ethnic people, who are demographically and electorally dominant* – though not necessarily an absolute majority of the population – and who must be the co-founders of the federation. This is a theory consistent with liberal nationalism, national federalism as

I presented that idea earlier, and with Ernest Gellner's theory of nationalism and Connor's fourth expectation. It is inconsistent with liberal cosmopolitan and radical multi-culturalists' hopes, and with the more optimistic beliefs of some federalists, though, I shall argue, it does not require entirely bleak conclusions to be drawn about the prospects for constitutional statecraft and state management in multi-national or multi-ethnic federations which lack a *Staatsvolk*. Let us call the theory the Dicey–O'Leary theory, as nice a compound pun as one could have.[19]

The theory states a necessary condition of stability in a liberal democratic majoritarian federation, but not a sufficient one. Its logic rests on simple micro-foundations. In liberal democratic systems the population share of an ethnonational group can be taken as a reasonable proxy for its *potential* electoral power, if its members were fully mobilised *en bloc* – admittedly a rare occurrence. The underlying idea is therefore simple: in a majoritarian federation an ethnonational group with a decisive majority of the federal population has no reason to fear federation. It has the ability simply to dominate the rest of the federation through its numbers, or to be generous – because it does not feel threatened. A *Staatsvolk*, a people who own the state, and who could control it on their own through simple democratic numbers, is a prime candidate to lead a federation, whether the federation is a national federation or a multi-national federation, to be what the Russians called the titular nationality. The theory may also give a clue as to why multiple unit federations appear at first glance to be more stable than binary or triadic federations. A preponderant *Staatsvolk* may be more willing to have its own national territory divided up into multiple regions, states or provinces, knowing that it is not likely to be coerced by minority peoples at the federal level. The theory also implies that if there is no *Staatsvolk* then majoritarian federalism, of whatever internal territorial configuration, will not be enough to sustain stability – a point to which I shall return.

Table 9.1 provides data which appear to confirm the Dicey–O'Leary theory. It lists the twenty-three currently democratic federations in the world – the data was collected before the coup in Pakistan – and it lists the share of the federation's population that I have classified as belonging to the relevant (or potential) *Staatsvolk*. I have arranged the data in descending order of the proportionate size of the relevant *Staatsvolk*. Let us take 50 per cent as our initial threshold for the existence of a *Staatsvolk*, a plausible threshold for democratic majoritarian assessment. The data suggest that all the federations which have been durably democratic for more than thirty years have, *prima facie*, a *Staatsvolk* which is significantly over 50 per cent of the relevant state's population: Australia (95), Austria (93), Germany (93), India (80) if its *Staatsvolk* is considered to be religious, the USA (74), Canada (67), if its *Staatsvolk* is considered to be Anglophones, Switzerland (64), and Malaysia (62). The African federations have not been durably democratic, but on this measure the Comoros Islands and South Africa have reasonable prospects. By contrast, neither Ethiopia nor Nigeria have a *Staatsvolk*, so the theory suggests that they are not likely to survive long if they are run as majoritarian democratic federations. The Russian Federation may not prove durably democratic but it has a *Staatsvolk*; so on the Dicey–O'Leary theory it has the necessary condition for survival. As for the other

Table 9.1 The size of the actual or potential *Staatsvolk* in current democratic federations

Name of the federation (census year, category)	Name of the Staatsvolk	% share of population
Comoros Islands (1980 ethnicity)	Comorian	97
Commonwealth of Australia (1986 ethnicity)	White Australians	95
St. Kitts and Nevis (1991 ethnicity)	Blacks	95
Federal Republic of Yugoslavia (1991 ethnicity)	Serbs	93
Federal Republic of Austria (1991 national origin)	Austrians	93
Federal Republic of Germany (1990 ethnic)	Germans	93
Russian Federation (1984 ethnicity)	Russians	85
Argentine Republic (1986 ethnicity)	Whites	85
India (1) * (1991 religion)	Hindus	80
United States of America (1994 racial)	White Americans	74
Kingdom of Spain ** (1980 ethnolingual)	Spaniards	72
Canada (1991 linguistic)	Anglophones	67
Venezuela (1993 ethnicity)	Mestizo	67
South Africa (1) *** (1994 ethnicity)	Blacks	65
Switzerland (1990 linguistic)	Swiss Germans	64
Malaysia (1990 ethnicity)	Malays	62
United Mexican States (1990 ethnicity)	Mestizo	60
Kingdom of Belgium (1976 linguistic)	Flemings	59
South Africa (2) *** (1994 ethnicity)	Blacks (excl. Zulus)	54
Brazil (1990 ethnicity)	Whites	54
Republic of Pakistan **** (1991 linguistic)	Punjabis	48
Micronesia (1980 ethnicity)	Trukese	41
Republic of India (2) * (1981 linguistic)	Hindi speakers	39.7
Ethiopia (1983 ethnicity)	Amhara	38
Federal Republic of Nigeria (1983 ethnicity)	Yoruba	21.3

Notes:
* India has two obvious candidates for the title of Staatsvolk, Hindus, who constitute approximately 80 per cent of its population, and Hindi speakers who constitute just less than 40 per cent of its population.
** Spain's status as a federation is controversial (Arend Lijphart does not think it is a federation, Juan Linz and Al Stepan think it is).
*** South Africa's blacks can be considered a potentially homogeneous category, though it is politically incorrect to say so. Since Zulus are politically differentiated between Zulu nationalists and South African nationalists the new black Staatsvolk excluding half of Zulus can be estimated at 65 per cent. If Zulus are considered an entirely separate group and all other blacks are regarded as the new Staatsvolk then the latter compose *c.* 54 per cent of the population.
**** Pakistan's recent coup makes it currently undemocratic.

Sources: United Nations, Britannica Year Book, Lane and Ersson (1976), Edmonston, CIA.

Asian cases Table 9.1 suggests that Pakistan should be on the threshold of crisis, and that India would be too if an attempt were made to construct a *Staatsvolk* out of Hindi-speakers. Of Micronesia I cannot speak because I am wholly ignorant. Likewise, I have little confidence in interpreting the Latin American data, but at first glance they appear to suggest that Mexico and Brazil are closer to the threshold of the necessary condition than might be expected, though their status as durable democracies is far from confirmed.[20] The data in Table 9.1 even suggest that Switzerland and Belgium have a *Staatsvolk* each, though doubtless this may raise eyebrows.

This attempt to test for the existence of a *Staatsvolk* based on this data may seem very crude, and the data-set (n = 23) may seem small, even if it is exhaustive of current democratic federations. Nevertheless the data are highly suggestive; there are no immediately anomalous cases. The federations without a *Staatsvolk* are of recent vintage, and are not obviously democratically stable. The data in short appear to confirm Connor and Gellner on the political impact of nationalism. Naturally they cannot prove causation: the stability of the durably democratic federations may have other causes, possibly mutually independent causes in each case, but it is suggestive that the data satisfy the necessary condition of the Dicey-O'Leary theory.

But more sophistication may be demanded before jumping to conclusions. I have been taxed with the question of whether the *Staatsvolk* is objective, or real. How exactly should we determine whether a group is a candidate for the title of *Staatsvolk?* Without subscribing to constructionist epistemological views, or social constructionism in general or particular, I want to emphasise that the notion of a *Staatsvolk* is a concept which is intended to capture what real people know, think, sense, *and* imagine about a dominant group in a state, and which describes what may or may not be present as a result of political construction in various states, i.e. a *Staatsvolk* is something that can be forged through political strategies and alliances. I am suggesting that so-called primordial elements will normally be the foundations of efforts to construct or mark off a Staatsvolk – common ancestry, race, language and common religion – though I do not insist on this. Some of these elements are ones which are relatively easy to find relatively reliable and testable data about, and to have knowledge about their salience within the relevant states. All this argument, and the data upon which it relies, may be accepted, I believe, without subscribing to any particular theories of race, religiosity or linguistics. All that my test so far does, in other words, is to check whether one of these elements – chosen on the basis of reading about the federation's history – has the possibility of having formed, or has the potential to form, the basis of a federal Staatsvolk.

It might be suggested that investigation should focus more deeply on the durably democratic and formally multi-national or multi-ethnic federations that might be considered to constitute the strongest challenges to Gellner and Connor, viz. India, Canada, Switzerland, and Belgium. If the primary division in India is linguistic rather than religious then India may appear to lack a *Staatsvolk*.[21] If Anglophones are considered too heterogeneous a category it might be suggested that Canada's real *Staatsvolk* is those of British and Irish descent – which would take the size of its *Staatsvolk* down, closer to the threshold of the necessary condition. If Swiss historic divisions were fundamentally religious rather than linguistic, then Helvetica too might appear to lack a definite *Staatsvolk*. The sheer size of the Francophone minority in Belgium and the country's long traditions of dualism might also lead us to pause before deciding if Belgium has a *Staatsvolk*.

I have no quarrel with the deeper investigation of cases to see whether my n-case argument is false in the particulars, and I intend to make such investigations. But, what I would like to suggest here is that what we may perhaps need most is an index not just of the potentially largest group, however defined, but a measure of the relative weight of groups according to any particular specific ascriptive criterion. So let me rephrase the Dicey–O'Leary theory in this way: *In a stable demo-cratic majoritarian federation the politically effective number of cultural groups must be less than 2 on the index of the effective number of ethnic groups, ENENg* (defined as the reciprocal of the Herfindahl-Hirschman concentration index of ethnonational groups).

Let me demystify this wordy mouthful. Specialists in the field of electoral analy-sis and party systems will recognise the index as an application of a measure developed by Albert Hirschman in economics, and extended to political science by Rein Taagepera and his colleagues – who were interested in finding an objective and tractable way of measuring the effective number of parties in a party system, and in whether or not one party or bloc of parties was dominant (Hirschman 1945; Laakso and Taagepera 1979; Taagepera and Shugart 1989: Chapter 8). Let me illustrate the index through an example. How might we respond to the question: how many ethnonational groups are there in Belgium? One would expect to be told that there are two big groups, Flemings and Walloons, with a smaller number of other groups, notably Germans, and recent migrants, all of whom might self-identify in these categories, especially if obliged to do so by a census. But does that mean that for politically important purposes that bear on the stability of the state, that Belgium has two, or two and an eighth, or two and a sixteenth ethnonational groups? The Herfindahl-Hirschman concentration index is designed to provide an objective way of measuring the effective number of components in a system. It does so in a way that stops analysts from following their intuitive (though often sen-sible) prejudices about what should count as a big or a small and negligible component.

The Herfindahl-Hirschman index (HHi) runs from 0 to 1. Applied to ethnona-tional groups it has the following logic. In a perfectly homogeneous nation-state, in which one ethnonational group has 100 per cent of the population, HHi = 1. If the state has an extremely polyethnic character in which every ethnonational group is vanishingly small, i.e. each person is an ethnonational group, then HHi tends towards 0. The measurement method used for the index allows each group's share of the population to 'determine its own weight', so its share is multiplied by its own share. In Belgium let us agree that the most salient definition of ethnona-tional groups is linguistic. In 1976 Flemings made up 59 per cent of the population, Walloons 39.3 per cent, and Germans 0.64 per cent (Lane and Ersson 1990: Appendix).[22] Of the total population Flemings therefore had a fractional share of .59, Walloons .393, and Germans .0064. Using the HHi index the weighted share of Flemings is determined by its own weight, i.e. by multiplying .59 by .59 = .348. Correspondingly, the share of Walloons is .393 x .393 = .153. The share of Germans is $(.0064)^2 = .00004096$. So, without imposing any arbitrary cut-off points, the political importance of the Belgian Germans is going to be discounted by this measure, which will conform to all but the most ardent Germanophiles' intuitions. The result of adding up the weighted values of all components is our Herfindahl-Hirschman concentration index:

$$HHi = \Sigma p_i^2$$

where p_i is the fractional share of the i-th ethnonational group and Σ stands for summation over all components. In the Belgian case in 1976 the HHi was therefore .501 when we reduce to three decimal places. What we shall call the effective number of ethnonational groups (ENENg) is defined as the reciprocal of the HHi index:

$$ENENg = 1/HHi = 1/\Sigma p_i^2$$

Given our Belgian data, the ENENg = $1/.501 = 1.996$, or 2 if we round it off. The somewhat elaborate procedure adopted to calculate the effective number of ethnonational groups in Belgium conforms to most people's intuitions about this case – there are two effective ethnonational groups.

The merits of the HHi and ENENg indices are straightforward. HHi provides an index that runs from 0 to 1, and ENENg provides us a measure of the effective number of ethnonational groups in a system that makes political and intuitive sense. ENENg turned out to be 2 using 1976 Belgian linguistic data. It is easy to see that a state divided into four equally sized ethnonational groups would have an ENENg of 4. These examples, of course, are neat cases, chosen to be helpful. But imagine that the demographic shares in Belgium shifted, say to the following proportions: 51 per cent Flemings, 42 per cent Walloons, 5 per cent Germans, 1 per cent British migrants, and 1 per cent Italian migrants. Then the new Belgian HHi would be .439, and new ENENg would be 2.28. The latter indicator, again, would conform with most people's intuitions about the effective number of ethnonational groups in the state – two big groups and a smaller third group, or a third clustering of smaller groups. These measures therefore provide means for potentially objective studies of the relationships between ethnonational groups and political systems. They also alert us to the importance of the size of second, third and other groups in the population, not simply the largest group.

Table 9.2 presents the HHi and ENENg scores for the current democratic federations in the world, in the same order as the federations in Table 9.1, i.e. according to the largest proportionate share held by the relevant (or potential) *Staatsvolk*. As is readily apparent, there is a close relationship between the size of the *Staatsvolk* and the HHi and ENENg scores. All the federations with ENENg scores of less than 1.9 are, in fact, majoritarian federations, with the possible exception of India.

By contrast, the bulk of the federations with ENENg scores of 1.9 and above, have often been classified as non-majoritarian federations because they have additional non-federal power-sharing or consociational features, or else they have had such institutions recommended to stabilise them. Consociational arrangements, clarified and theorised by Arend Lijphart (1977), involve four features:

- cross-community executive power-sharing;
- proportional representation of groups throughout the state sector;
- ethnic autonomy in culture (especially in religion or language);
- formal or informal minority-veto rights.

Table 9.2 The effective number of ethnonational groups in democratic federations

Name of the Federation	Staatsvolk	SV % share of population	HHi index	ENENg index
Comoros Islands	Comorian	97	.94	1.06
Commonwealth of Australia	Whites	95	.91	1.1
St. Kitts and Nevis	Blacks	95	.9	1.11
Federal Republic of Yugoslavia	Serbs	93	.89	1.12
Federal Republic of Austria	Austrians	93	.87	1.14
Federal Republic of Germany	Germans	93	.87	1.15
Russian Federation	Russians	85	.73	1.38
Argentine Republic	Whites	85	.75	1.34
India (1) *	Hindus	80	.66	1.52
United States of America	Whites	74	.57	1.74
Kingdom of Spain **	Spaniards	72	.56	1.8
Canada	Anglophones	67	.51	1.96
Venezuela	Mestizo	67	.5	1.99
South Africa (1) ***	Blacks	65	.46	2.18
Switzerland	Swiss Germans	64	.45	2.22
Malaysia	Malays	62	.48	2.10
United Mexican States	Mestizo	60	.46	2.18
Kingdom of Belgium	Flemings	59	.51	1.99
South Africa (2) ***	Blacks (excl. Zulus)	54	.36	2.74
Brazil	Whites	54	.45	2.24
Republic of Pakistan ****	Punjabis	48	.29	3.47
Micronesia	Trukese	41	.26	3.91
Republic of India (2) *	Hindi speakers	39.7	.19	5.19
Ethiopia	Amhara	38	.28	3.58
Federal Republic of Nigeria	Yoruba	21.3	.14	6.91

Notes:

* India has two obvious candidates for the title of Staatsvolk, Hindus, who constitute approximately 80 per cent of its population, and Hindi speakers who constitute just less than 40 per cent of its population.
** Spain's status as a federation is controversial (Arend Lijphart does not think it is a federation, Juan Linz and Al Stepan think it is).
*** South Africa's blacks can be considered a potentially homogeneous category, though it is politically incorrect to say so. Since Zulus are politically differentiated between Zulu nationalists and South African nationalists the new black Staatsvolk excluding half of Zulus can be estimated at 65 per cent. If Zulus are considered an entirely separate group and all other blacks are regarded as the new Staatsvolk then the latter compose *c.* 54 per cent of the population.
**** Pakistan's recent coup makes it currently undemocratic.

Sources: United Nations, Britannica Year Book, Lane and Ersson (1976), Edmonston, CIA.

All of the durably democratic multi-national federations previously identified as potentially problematic for Gellner and Connor, viz. Belgium, Switzerland, Canada, and India, have ENENg scores of 1.9 or more. But the first three of these have relatively undisputed consociational histories (Lijphart 1981; Noel 1993; Steiner 1989), and Lijphart has recently claimed that India had effective consociational traits during its most stable period under Nehru.[23] All this suggests that the Dicey–O'Leary theory should have a corollary – *where there is no Staatsvolk, or where the Staatsvolk's position is precarious, a stable federation requires (at least some) consociational rather than majoritarian institutions if it is to survive*, though of course its survival is by no means guaranteed.

The microfoundations of this theory are straightforward: where no group has a clear majority, a balance of power among ethnonational groups is likely to exist, and such a balance of power is conducive to consociational settlements – though it is of course also conducive to warfare and secessionism. The corollary has both strong predictive and prescriptive power: Malaysia, South Africa with autonomous Zulu organisation, Pakistan, India (with regard to its linguistic cleavages), Ethiopia and Nigeria may not endure as democratic federations without some consociational devices.[24] In India consociational add-ons have been most apparent in the development of ethnic autonomy in culture: the granting of provincial or to coin a phrase, *Ländervolk* status, to major non-Hindi speaking peoples.

Analytical conclusions

If the arguments developed here are correct then the Dicey–O'Leary theory seems, thus far, unfalsified: a majoritarian democratic federation requires a *Staatsvolk*, a demographically, electorally and culturally dominant nation. This lends weight to Ernest Gellner's theory about the power of nationalism and Walker Connor's expectations about the power of ethnonationalism. It also suggests an important socio-political limit on what states can do, consistent with Connor's fourth expectation, i.e. they cannot design and run successful majoritarian democratic and stable federations without having, or building, a *Staatsvolk*. However, the theory has an important corollary, which leaves room for political initiative and statecraft. The absence or near absence of a *Staatsvolk* does not preclude democratic federation, but a democratic federation without a clear or secure *Staatsvolk* must adopt (at least some) consociational practices if it is to survive. This suggests that we are entitled to have greater (if not intense) optimism than Gellner or Connor allow about statecraft in the management of multi-national and multi-ethnic units.

Perhaps I should emphasise, for those who remain sceptical of the positivist cast of this chapter, or who dislike monocausal emphases, that federations can be destabilised for other reasons than the lack of a *Staatsvolk*, and that multi-national federations may be de-stabilised for reasons that have nothing to do with the absence of consociational practices. What the theory and its corollary state are necessary conditions for stability in democratic federations. There may be other necessary conditions for stable federations – e.g. voluntary beginnings, a favourable external environment, and appropriate matches between peoples and territories – but these causal arguments have not been defended or evaluated here. This is an initial statement: I plan to do more detailed research on the agenda suggested. But, I do want to observe that Connor's *The National Question in Marxist-Leninist Theory and Strategy* contains the building blocks of a political explanation of the role of the *Staatsvolk* in federations and other types of multi-national states.

In Chapter 11 of that book Connor sums up his assessment of Lenin's policy on the national question in communist systems. He maintained, in a spirit of detachment, that nowhere had the policy been given a fair testing. In practice, control systems had been implemented – in language policy, cadre policy, the movement of populations, and the location of boundaries within the federated units – all of which belied Lenin's proscription against coercion. But, Connor proceeded to ask himself an important hypothetical question: what would multi-national states require to be stable?[25]

From the perspective of minorities they would require the state to be based on national equality and involve no coercive pressure to assimilate. Connor riposted that 'if nearly any decision involving language, education, the movement of peoples, and the geographic distribution of investments is apt to be viewed as violating the principle of national equality and/or the principle of noncoercive assimilation' (Connor 1984: 481), how could this formula be compatible with the needs of a re-distributive industrialised state? He then observed that 'were minorities dispersed evenly throughout a country, the goal of national equality could be achieved (at least theoretically) through antidiscrimination policies, without causing economic dislocation', but 'the fact that national groups populate distinct regions of a country introduces a complicating element' (ibid.: 484) because there is a law of regional uneven economic development – which operates independently of policy-makers' intentions, and of discriminatory or anti-discriminatory endeavours. Then, he noted the 'difficulty, if not the impossibility, of discovering a universally acceptable formula to achieve equality between unequals' (ibid.: 485). Quotas, for example, will always be controversial in the eyes of those adversely affected by them, and 'if the *lingua franca* (the language of success) is the traditional language of another group, that group and its culture are automatically endowed with favoured status' (ibid.: 487). These are, in Connor's eyes, the considerations which might make minorities happy or unhappy with multi-national states.

But, what of the dominant nation, if it exists? Here Connor observed that many communist party leaders consistently and explicitly proclaimed a vanguard or *primus inter pares* role for the dominant nation, e.g. the Russian, Han, Rumanian and Vietnamese peoples within the states within which they predominated (ibid.: 490), and asked himself why these leaders felt compelled to adopt themes, histories, and capital cities, that would necessarily irritate their respective minorities. One explanation was that the theme of the superiority of the dominant nation represented the convictions of the power élite themselves, mostly members of the most favoured nation; another explanation, to which he gave greater weight, was the need 'to ensure the fidelity of the dominant group' to the regime (ibid.: 491). Connor then drew the obvious conclusion: the difficulty, for communist leaders, of reconciling the demands of national minorities to have equality with that of giving the dominant nation the esteem and leadership role necessary to ensure its fidelity.

In Connor's analysis in *The National Question*, which I have truncated, I detect an implicit theory: in a multi-national state, with a dominant nation, there will always be tensions between the need to appease the esteem of the dominant nation (where there is one) and the demands of national minorities for equality; whereas in a multi-national state without a dominant nation political life will be dominated by a politics of the balance of power. In the first type of multi-national state a federation may prove stable, so long as it is constructed around the consent of the dominant nation, and so long as a mixture of coercion and consent retains the less wholehearted allegiance of national minorities – and it will be the more secure the more dispersed is each national minority throughout the state. The second type, by contrast, mandates the use of consociational formulae for stability in democratic conditions – but will be subject to the difficulties to which consociational systems are prone, perhaps especially where the different national minorities are territorially concentrated. Connor's implicit theory is, I submit, consistent with the argument I have sketched above, and provides an important research agenda.

Practical political conclusions

If the arguments sketched above are broadly correct, then they have powerful practical political implications for what states can do with regard to re-engineering or re-inventing their institutional and constitutional formats. Let me conclude with two examples, the UK and the European Union.

The British unionists who want to federalise the UK have nothing to fear from these arguments: the UK has a *Staatsvolk*, the English. The English, because they are overwhelmingly dominant, electorally, demographically and in resources, could live with either a national federation, e.g. the Federation of the English-speaking peoples, or with a multi-national federation, e.g. The Federation of England, Scotland and Wales. The English often fail to distinguish English and British identities, often happily embrace both, and do not regard the current name of the state as an offence to their esteem, viz. The United Kingdom of Great Britain and Northern Ireland. For them, the scale of redistribution of resources required to appease their national minorities has been, to date, tolerable. The dispositions of the peoples of Scotland, Wales and Northern Ireland are, of course, rather different. Scottish and Welsh nationalists would not warmly accept a national federation which explicitly treated the English as the *Staatsvolk*, but, they could, I submit, be reconciled to a multi-national federation – albeit with the tensions predicted by Connor – especially if such a federation granted greater autonomy to Scotland and Wales than exists under the new asymmetrical devolution arrangements. The peoples of Northern Ireland, by contrast, would divide sharply. British Ulster unionists would be happiest with an integrated unitary state which ruled out the possibility of Northern Ireland joining Ireland. Absent that foreclosed option, they could live with a multi-national federation, and be loyal advocates of the maintenance of the federation. Irish nationalists in Northern Ireland would be most unhappy with a federation which explicitly ceded dominance to the English as a Staatsvolk. They would be less unhappy within a multi-national federation, especially if Britain was its name. Most of them could live with it, provided that: they maintained the existing right of Northern Ireland to unification with Ireland if they obtain a local majority for that option; they are not subject, in the interim, to local majoritarian dominance by British Ulster unionists; and they maintain the full consociational rights as a national minority, including cross-border institutions with Ireland, recently negotiated in the Belfast Agreement (O'Leary 1999a; 1999b).

None of the foregoing should be too surprising to those who follow politics in Britain and Ireland. However, the theoretical arguments considered here have important and surprising implications for the European Union, especially strong for those Euro-federalists who wish to convert the European Union from a con-federation into a federation. The European Union lacks an obvious potential *Staatsvolk*. Its largest ethnonational people, the Germans of Germany, compose just over a fifth of its current population, about the same proportionate share as the Yoruba and Hausa have each in Nigeria. The European Union's ENENg score is presently 7.23, higher than Nigeria's 6.69, and it will go higher on the accession of the Poles, Hungarians and Ernest Gellner's Czechs. On the Dicey–O'Leary theory, to put it bluntly and insensitively, there are just not enough Germans for the European Union to function effectively as a majoritarian federation. This would still be true, even if we, causing mutual outrage, were to treat Austrian, Dutch, and Swedish people as honorary Germans!

The Dicey–O'Leary theory suggests, by implication, that calls to have a fully-fledged European federation, with the classic bicameral arrangements of the USA, or to have a directly elected and powerful EU President, all to address the so-called 'democratic deficit' in the European Union, may be a recipe for institutional dis-aster *unless* such calls are accompanied by strong commitments to consociational governance devices. Consociational governance would mean mechanisms to ensure the inclusive and effective representation of all the nations of the European Union in its core executive institutions; proportionate representation of its nations in its public bureaucracies and legal institutions; national autonomy in all cultural matters deemed of profound cultural significance (e.g. language, religion, educa-tion), and last, but not least, national vetoes to protect national communities from being out-voted through majoritarian rules – vetoes that would be most vigorously represented through referendums to veto EU proposals, or, less strongly, through rights to 'opt out' of such proposals. What I am arguing, to put it bluntly, is that many of the current consociational and confederal features of the EU, which fed-eralists want to weaken or temper in their pursuit of formal European federation, are required to ensure the EU's prospects as a multi-national democratic federation.

This is not a Euro-phobic argument. The European Union has been correctly defended as one forum that has helped resolve the security and ethnoterritorial dis-putes between France and Germany; that has facilitated the possible and actual resolution of British–Irish and Italian–Austrian border and minority questions; that is a means through which Irish nationalists, Tyrolese Germans and Austrians, and Spanish and French Basques can be interlinked with their co-nationals and co-eth-nics in trans-frontier and functional cross-border programmes and institutions; and that may encourage its multi-national member-states to permit a fuller flour-ishing of internal regional autonomy. All this is true, though the EU's therapeutic powers should not be exaggerated, as they standardly are.[26]

But one of the EU's greatest current dangers may stem from its ardent majori-tarian federalists, who forget that it was forged partly as a means to control Germany, to stop it from ever again trying to become the *Staatsvolk* of Europe.

Given that the European Union is falsely seen by many as the exemplary illustration of the death of the nation state or of its transcendence, the full irony of my argument should be apparent. Only a European Union constructed from secure nation-states, or better, nation-states and their *ethnies*, co-operating within either a confederal or consociational federal format, will have reasonable prospects of development and maintenance as a democratic political system. It is, of course, possible that the Dicey–O'Leary law is wrong, but, if so, then a majoritarian federal democratic European Union will genuinely be unique.

This argument about the European Union is one with which Walker Connor should rest easy. He has observed, and a lot earlier than thousands of European political scientists, including those in receipt of European Union research funds and titles, that the European Union, insofar as it strays beyond economic integration, does so without the consent of most European peoples (Connor 1976; 1993; 1995; 1998; 2001: 126ff.). We owe to him the thesis that the iron law of oligarchy is alive and well in the European Union, that the real democratic deficit is that which lies between the promoters of the European Union and their citizens. Walker Connor's observations should be compulsory reading for those who would rush the nations of Europe into a federation that cannot work on their elitist and 'post-national' – for which read anti-national – axioms.

Notes

1 This chapter adapts and extends ideas first presented in the 5th Ernest Gellner Memorial lecture (O'Leary 2001b), and is dedicated to my friend, mentor and fellow Irishman, Walker Connor.

2 In *Explaining Northern Ireland* John McGarry and I were, in effect, Connorians because we argued against erroneous explanations of the conflict that: relied upon tangible markers (e.g. religion), exaggerated the influence of materialism upon human affairs, favoured explanations based on class, improperly analogised from the experience of the USA and the (rest of the) UK, and that assumed that increased interaction and integration necessarily increase the likelihood of harmonious ethnic relations (McGarry and O'Leary 1995). We took to heart Connor's injunctions to observe the 'predisposition of the analyst', and tried, as best we could, to ensure that our own predispositions were scrutinised. For the salutary inventory see Connor (1987), reprinted in Connor (1994: especially 69–71).

3 The warrants for the first three of these propositions, can be found in Connor (1994: Chapters 3–7) and Connor (2001: 115), and the last in Connor (1984: Chapters 9–11).

4 The wording is deliberately circumspect. The last proposition is, I believe, implicit in Connor's work, but not stated as such.

5 Brubaker's otherwise pioneering work is vitiated by its epistemic prejudices, which lead the author to deny the reality of nations. His desire to avoid contamination by nationalist convictions, leads him into strange waters – denying the reality of nations, on his premises, would, *mutatis mutandis*, render 'unreal' such collective entities as classes, men, women, states, i.e. it would dispense with classical sociology.

6 Influenced by realism and Gramscian Marxism Ian S. Lustick has argued that states have and may continue to develop 'hegemonic projects' which, if successful, will incorporate territories and their peoples (Lustick 1993; O'Leary *et al.* 2001).

7 Some go further and claim that polyethnic states are the norm in world history, one to which we shall inevitably return, e.g. William H. McNeill (1986).

8 For a humane attempt to construct a manual see Harris and Reilly (1998).
9 In his 'Self-Determination: The New Phase' (1967), Connor dealt astringently with the history of the 'successful' examples of multi-nationalism cited by J.S. Mill, Acton, Barker and Cobban (reprinted in Connor (1984: 11–16)).
10 The opening article here is Lustick (1979). In 'Reinforcement for the forms', Connor provides a lucid overview of Marxist-Leninist strategies in language policy, the recruitment and purging of élites, and the redistribution and gerrymandering of national groups, which is, by some margin, the best exemplification in the annals of comparative communism, of what Lustick calls control (Connor 1984: 254–387).
11 Separate conversations with Brendan O'Leary, Budapest, Hungary November 1995 (Gellner), Belmont, Vt, USA (Connor), November 2000, August 2001.
12 This formula is still too sharp: Connor respected Gellner as a philosopher, and his field work in Morocco; Gellner respected Connor's demonstration of Soviet Marxism's failure with the national question.
13 For the evidence on Gellner's views see O'Leary (2001b).
14 When Connor's work on religion and nationalism is completed it will make a fascinating counterpoint to Gellner's work on nationalism and Islam.
15 The Soviet Union, Yugoslavia, and Czechoslovakia were not democratic federations. Citizens' 'choices' of representatives in all governmental tiers were fictional until the late 1990s. When their choices became more democratic the relevant states disintegrated largely mostly around the territorial units of the previously sham federations. The 'federal republics' offered opportunity-structures for old and new political élites as the communist systems opened. The fact that the republics had titular nationalities, mostly substantive, made this prospect even more likely. Their experience offers additional confirmation of the generalisation that 'the dissolution of authoritarian structures cannot possibly save a supranational entity; instead it initially destroys it and helps to create new national entities that then need to be laboriously democratized' (Pfabigan 1991: 63). What might have happened had the centres of these federations been democratised first, as suggested in the works of Juan Linz and Alfred Stepan, must remain a matter for speculation. The argument developed here suggests that the Soviet and Yugoslav cases would have required consociational federations to have had any prospects of endurance.
16 The judicial constructions of the relevant Supreme Court may radically affect the nature of the federation and the distribution of effective competencies. Despite an avowedly centralised federal constitution the Canadian provinces are more powerful and the federal government weaker than in any other federation, while the Australian federal government has become much more powerful and state powers have waned, despite operating a constitution designed to create a weak federal government. In both cases these outcomes are the result of judicial decision-making (Zines 1991: 79, and Chapter 7 *passim*).
17 There were some exceptions to this pattern as Glazer points out. Moreover, a fully correct description of the USA's constitutional form enumerates it as consisting of 50 states, 2 federacies, 3 associated states, 3 local home rule territories, 3 unincorporated territories, and 130 Native American domestic dependent nations, cf. Watts (1996: 10).
18 By a majoritarian federation I mean a non-consociational one —- this makes sure that the argument rests on clear antonyms. The federation is intended, at the federal level, to enable at least one branch of the federal government to have a clear federation-wide mandate based on some notion of a popular majority of the people established through a winner-take-all electoral formula of some kind. Normally both a president and a congressional house of representatives embody these notions, but so may a premier-cabinet. A majoritarian federation does not follow the principle of ethnic proportionality as a rule in its representative, bureaucratic, electoral and judicial institutions; it does not officially recognise ethnic community as opposed to territorial autonomy; and it does not permit veto-rights to belong to ethnic groups – as opposed to territorial governments.
19 When I first had this idea I thought it original, and wrong - indeed probably wrong

because it was original: surely someone had thought of it, and demonstrated it to be wrong? Having read comparative federalist literature I could find no clear statement of the theory, though I found hints of it (e.g. in Forsyth 1989, and in Franck 1969) or of its falsehood. Later I came to believe the idea might be true. Mads Qvotrup subsequently told me of Dicey's remarks in the *Law of the Constitution* (cited in the epigraph to this chapter). This partly disappointed me, because Dicey is fairly far from my (Irish) political tastes. But if the theory is a false trail I can at least blame the Victorian bigot.

20 My LSE colleague Dr Francisco Panizza observes that the non-*mestizo* minority in Mexico is both ethnically very heterogeneous and shares a common Catholic culture with the rest of the population. Mestizo dominance is therefore much greater than the raw figures for the *Staatsvolk* suggest. In Brazil race is not as a deep a cleavage as it might appear – blacks are dispersed throughout the country, and racial, ethnic and cultural mixing are significant, despite significant differentials in advantages between non-blacks and blacks. Though Brazil's federalism has some consociational devices these are intended to accommodate regional-territorial rather than ethnonational differences.

21 If one accepts that the dominant cleavage is linguistic then it is interesting to note that India's linguistic arrangements have been seen both as highly federal *and* highly consociational in character (for various discussions see Laitin 1989; Lijphart 1996).

22 The authors provide data on no other linguistic groups in Belgium. Their source is Stephens (1976).

23 See Lijphart (1996). The classification of India now, and through time, is, of course, highly contentious. India's numerous federated units interact with the centre in different ways; India has exercised rigorous and oppressive control in Kashmir, and elsewhere; both its federal and consociational traits have been inconsistent.

24 As for Mexico and Brazil, see note 20.

25 Connor explicitly addressed the question to communist systems, but it is of universal import.

26 Rigorous treatments of Northern Ireland and the European Union are available (McGarry 2001; Tannam 1999).

References

Anderson, Benedict 1998. *The Spectre of Comparisons: Nationalism, Southeast Asia and the World.* London: Verso.

Arora, Balveer and Verney, Douglas V. 1995. *Multiple Identities in a Single State: Indian Federalism in Comparative Perspective.* New Delhi: Konark Publishers PVT Ltd.

Bauer, Otto 1907. *Die Nationalitétenfrage und die Sozialdemokratie.* Vienna: Wiener Volksbuchhandlung.

Beer, Samuel H. 1993. *To Make a Nation: The Rediscovery of American Federalism.* Cambridge, MA: Belknap Press.

Bosco, Andrea (ed.) 1991. *The Federal Idea: The History of Federalism from Enlightenment to 1945.* Vol. 1. London: Lothian Foundation Press.

—— (ed.) 1992. *The Federal Idea: The History of Federalism since 1945.* Vol. 2. London: Lothian Foundation Press.

Brass, Paul R. 1990. *The Politics of India Since Independence.* New Delhi: Cambridge University Press.

—— 1991. *Ethnicity and Nationalism: Theory and Comparison.* New Delhi: Sage.

Brubaker, Rogers 1996a. 'National Minorities, Nationalizing States, and External National Homelands in the New Europe'. In *Nationalism Reframed: Nationhood and the National Question in the New Europe.* Cambridge: Cambridge University Press: 55–76.

—— 1996b. *Nationalism Reframed: Nationhood and the National Question in the New Europe.* Cambridge: Cambridge University Press.

Connor, Walker 1967. 'Self-Determination: The New Phase'. *World Politics*. xx: 30–53.

—— 1969. 'Myths of Hemispheric, Continental, Regional and State Unity'. *Political Science Quarterly*. lxxi: 555–582.

—— 1976. 'The Political Significance of Ethnonationalism within Western Europe'. In A.A. Said and L.R. Simmons (eds) *Ethnicity in an International Context*. New Brunswick: Transaction Books.

—— 1984. *The National Question in Marxist-Leninist Theory and Strategy*. Princeton, NJ: Princeton University Press.

—— 1987. 'Ethnonationalism'. In M. Weiner and S.P. Huntington (eds) *Understanding Political Development*. Reprinted in Connor 1994.

—— 1993. 'Europe: Where Nationalism Began and Where It Still Thrives'. In Justo G. Beramendi, Ramón Máiz and Xosé M. Núñez (eds) *Nationalism in Europe: Past and Present*. Santiago de Compostela: Santiago de Compostela University Press: 1(1994): 167–198.

—— 1994. *Ethnonationalism: The Quest for Understanding*. Princeton, NJ: Princeton University Press.

—— 1995. 'European Union and the Iron Law of Oligarchy'. In *Annual Meeting of the Political Science Association of Ireland*. Drogheda, Ireland.

—— 1998. 'Address: Nationalism in Post-National Western Europe'. Middlebury College, VT, USA.

—— 2001. 'From a Theory of Relative Economic Deprivation towards a Theory of Relative Political Deprivation'. In M. Keating and J. McGarry (eds) *Minority Nationalism and the Changing International Order*. Oxford: Oxford University Press: 114–133.

De Certaus, Michel, Dominique, Julia and Revel, Jacques 1975. *Une Politique de la Langue. La Révolution Française et les patois: L'enquête de Grégoire*. Paris: Gallimard.

Dicey, Albert Venn 1915. *Introduction to the Study of the Law of the Constitution*. London: Macmillan.

Elazar, Daniel 1987. *Exploring Federalism*. Tuscaloosa: University of Alabama.

Fischer, Joschka 2000. 'Apologies to the UK, but "Federal" is the Only Way'. *Independent*. 16 May: 4.

Forsyth, Murray 1989. 'Federalism and Nationalism'. Leicester: Leicester University Press.

Franck, Thomas M. 1968. *Why Federations Fail: An Inquiry into the Requisites for Successful Federation*. New York: New York University Press.

Gellner, Ernest. 1983. *Nations and Nationalism*. Oxford: Basil Blackwell.

—— 1997. *Nationalism*. London: Weidenfeld and Nicolson.

Glazer, Nathan 1983. 'Federalism and Ethnicity: The American Solution'. In N. Glazer (ed.) *Ethnic Dilemmas, 1964–82*. Cambridge, MA: Harvard University Press: 274–292.

Gordon, M. 1964. *Assimilation in American Life: The Role of Race, Religion and National Origins*. New York: Oxford University Press.

Hanf, Theodor 1991. 'Reducing Conflict Through Cultural Autonomy: Karl Renner's Contribution'. In U. Ra'anan, M. Mesner, K. Armes and K. Martin (eds) *State and Nation in Multi-Ethnic Societies: The Break-up of Multi-National States*. Manchester: Manchester University Press: 33–52.

Harris, Peter and Reilly, Ben 1998. 'Democracy and Deep-Rooted Conflict: Options for Negotiators'. Stockholm: International Institute for Democracy and Electoral Assistance.

Hicks, Ursula K. 1978. *Federalism, Failure and Success: A Comparative Study*. London: Macmillan.

Hirschman, Albert O. 1945. *National Power and the Structure of Foreign Trade*. Berkeley, CA: University of California Press.

Horowitz, Donald 1985. *Ethnic Groups in Conflict*. Berkeley, CA: University of California Press.

—— 1998. 'Self-Determination: Politics, Philosophy and Law'. In M. Moore (ed.) *National Self-Determination and Secession*. Oxford: Oxford University Press: 181–214.

King, Preston 1982. *Federalism and Federation*. London: Croom Helm.

King, R. 1997. *Nehru and the Language Politics of India*. New Delhi: Oxford University Press.

Laakso, M and Taagepera, Rein 1979. 'Effective Number of Parties: A Measure with Applications to West Europe'. *Comparative Political Studies*. 12.

Laitin, David D. 1977. *Politics, Language and Thought: The Somali Experience*. Chicago: University of Chicago Press.

—— 1979. 'Language Choice and National Development: A Typology for Africa'. *International Interactions*. 6: 291–321.

—— 1989. 'Language Policy and Political Strategy in India'. *Policy Sciences*. 22: 415–36.

—— 1992. *Language Repertoires and State Construction in Africa*. Cambridge: Cambridge University Press.

—— 1998. *Identity in Formation. The Russian-Speaking Populations in the Near Abroad*. Ithaca, NY: Cornell University Press.

Lane, Jan Erik and Ersson, Svante O. 1990. *Politics and Society in Western Europe*. London: Pinter.

Lijphart, Arend 1977. *Democracy in Plural Societies: A Comparative Exploration*. New Haven and London: Yale University Press.

—— 1981. 'Conflict and Coexistence in Belgium: The Dynamics of a Culturally Divided Society'. Research Series, No 46. Berkeley, CA: Institute of International Studies University of California.

—— 1996. 'The Puzzle of Indian Democracy: A Consociational Interpretation'. *American Political Science Review*. 90: 258–268.

Lustick, Ian 1979. 'Stability in Deeply Divided Societies: Consociationalism Versus Control'. *World Politics*. 31: 325–44.

—— 1993. *Unsettled States, Disputed Lands: Britain and Ireland, France and Algeria, Israel and the West Bank-Gaza*. Ithaca, NY: Cornell University Press.

McGarry, John 2001. 'Globalization, European Integration, and the Northern Ireland Conflict'. In M. Keating and J. McGarry (eds) *Minority Nationalism and the Changing International Order*. Oxford: Oxford University Press: 295–324.

—— and O'Leary, Brendan 1993. 'Introduction: The Macro-Political Regulation of Ethnic Conflict'. In J. McGarry and B. O'Leary (eds) *The Politics of Ethnic Conflict Regulation*. London and New York: Routledge.

—— and O'Leary, Brendan 1995. *Explaining Northern Ireland: Broken Images*. Oxford and Cambridge, MA: Basil Blackwell.

McNeill, William H. 1986. *Polyethnicity and World History: National Unity in World History*. Toronto: Toronto University Press.

Madison, James, Hamilton, Alexander and Jay, John 1987 [1788]. *The Federalist Papers, edited and with an introduction by Isaac Kramnick*. Harmondsworth: Penguin.

Majocchi, Luigi Vittoria 1991. 'Nationalism and Federalism in 19th Century Europe'. In A. Bosco (ed.) *The Federal Idea: The History of Federalism from Enlightenment to 1945*. Vol. 1. London: Lothian Foundation Press.

Mann, Michael 1999. 'The Dark Side of Democracy: The Modern Tradition of Ethnic and Political Cleansing'. *New Left Review*. May–June: 18–45.

Noel, Sid 1993. 'Canadian Responses to Ethnic Conflict: Consociationalism, Federalism and Control'. In J. McGarry and B. O'Leary (eds) *The Politics of Ethnic Conflict-Regulation*:

Case Studies of Protracted Ethnic Conflicts. London: Routledge: 41–61.

Nordlinger, Eric 1972. *Conflict Regulation in Divided Societies.* Cambridge, MA: Center for International Affairs, Harvard University.

O'Leary, Brendan 1997. 'On the Nature of Nationalism: An Appraisal of Ernest Gellner's Writings on Nationalism'. *British Journal of Political Science.* 27: 191–222.

—— 1998. 'Gellner's Diagnoses of Nationalism: A Critical Overview *or* What is Living and What is Dead in Gellner's Philosophy of Nationalism?' In J.A. Hall (ed.) *The State of the Nation: Ernest Gellner and the Theory of Nationalism.* Cambridge: Cambridge University Press.

—— 1999a. 'The Nature of the Agreement'. *Fordham Journal of International Law.* 22: 1628–1667.

—— 1999b. 'The Nature of the British-Irish Agreement'. *New Left Review.* 233: 66–96.

—— 2001a. 'The Elements of Right-Sizing and Right-Peopling the State'. In B. O'Leary, I.S. Lustick and T. Callaghy (eds) *Right-Sizing the State: the Politics of Moving Borders.* Oxford: Oxford University Press: 15–73.

—— 2001b. 'An Iron Law of Federations? A (neo-Diceyian) theory of the Necessity of a Federal Staatsvolk, and of Consociational Rescue'. *Nations and Nationalism.* 7: 273–296.

——, Lustick, Ian and Callaghy, Thomas 2001. *Right-Sizing the State: The Politics of Moving Borders.* Oxford: Oxford University Press.

Pfabigan, Alfred 1991. 'The Political Feasibility of the Austro-Marxist proposal for the Solution of the Nationality Problem of the Danubian Monarchy'. In U. Ra'anan, M. Mesner, K. Armes and K. Martin (eds) *State and Nation in Multi-Ethnic Societies: The Break-up of Multi-National States.* Manchester: Manchester University Press.

Premdas, Ralph R. 1998. *Secession and Self-Determination in the Caribbean: Nevis and Tobago.* St. Augustine, Trinidad: The University of the West Indies.

Rajashekera, H. 1994. 'Nehru and Indian Federalism'. *Indian Journal of Political Science.* 55: 135–148.

Reilly, Ben and Reynolds, Andrew 1999. *Electoral Systems and Conflict in Divided Societies.* Washington, DC: National Academy Press.

Riker, William H. 1964. *Federalism: Origin, Operation, Significance.* Boston: Little, Brown.

Rummel, Rudolph J. 1997. *Death by Government.* London and New York: Transaction Publishers.

Stavenhagen, Rodolfo 1996. *Ethnic Conflicts and the Nation-state.* Basingstoke: Macmillan.

Steiner, Jurg 1989. 'Power-Sharing: Another Swiss Export Product?' In J. Montville (ed.) *Conflict and Peacemaking in Multiethnic Societies.* Lexington, MA: Lexington Books.

Stephens, M. 1976. *Linguistic Minorities in Western Europe.* Llandysul: Gomer Press.

Taagepera, Rein and Shugart, Matthew Soberg 1989. *Seats and Votes: The Effects and Determinants of Electoral Systems.* New Haven and London: Yale University Press.

Tannam, Etain 1999. *Cross-Border Cooperation in the Republic of Ireland and Northern Ireland.* Basingstoke: Macmillan.

Trudeau, Pierre 1968 (1965). 'Federalism, Nationalism and Reason'. In P.E. Trudeau (ed.) *Federalism and the French Canadians.* Toronto: University of Toronto Press: 182–203.

Vile, Maurice 1982. 'Federation and Confederation: The Experience of the United States and the British Commonwealth'. In D. Rea (ed.) *Political Co-operation in Divided Societies.* Dublin: Gill and Macmillan.

Von Beyme, Klaus 1985. *Political Parties in Western Democracies.* Trans. E. Martin. Aldershot: Gower.

Watts, Ronald L. 1987. 'Federalism'. In V. Bogdanor (ed.) *The Blackwell Encyclopaedia of Political Institutions.* Oxford: Basil Blackwell: 228–230.

—— 1996. *Comparing Federal Systems in the 1990s*. Kingston, Ontario: Institute of Intergovernmental Relations/Queen's University.

—— 1998. 'Federalism, Federal Political Systems, and Federations'. *Annual Review of Political Science*. 1: 117–137.

Zines, Leslie 1991. *Constitutional Change in the Commonwealth*. Cambridge: Cambridge University Press.

Zolberg, Aristide R. 1983. 'The Formation of New States as a Refugee-Generating Process'. *Annals of the American Academy of Political and Social Science*. 467: 24–38.

10 Ethnic conflict and third-party mediation

A critical review

William Safran

In recent years, Western political scientists have been increasingly concerned with the resolution of ethnic conflicts by peaceful means. There are a number of reasons for this: (1) the growth in the number of violent conflicts in Western Europe, ex-Communist Eastern Europe, and the Third World; (2) the belief that the alternatives to a peaceful resolution of ethnic conflict that have been tried – expulsion, forcible assimilation, ghettoization, and genocide – do not accord with civilized norms of behavior; and (3) the conviction that if ethnic conflicts are allowed to fester, they will interfere with the processes of democratization and globalization, and introduce regional and global instability.

A reflection of this pattern of thinking is the widespread interest in the involvement of outsiders in the resolution of ethnic conflicts. There is a growing belief that third parties, such as international organizations and/or major powers, have both the obligation and the ability to mediate such conflicts and that such mediation generally produces positive results. This belief is born of a mixture of idealism, *Realpolitik*, domestic pressures, and vested research interests.

Since the end of the Cold War, many international politics specialists, informed by the notion that the 'nation-state' is the major unit of international action, have discovered the reality of ethnic politics. While the Cold War lasted, they had tended to ignore that reality, either because ethnic communities had been overshadowed by 'national interests' – that is, *state* interests – or because such communities had been, would eventually be, or ought to be eclipsed by more dynamic social units in the interest of modernization and 'nation-building'. The indifference to ethnic communities was reflected in the conflation of the concepts of state and nation. As Walker Connor has put it, 'The League of Nations, the United Nations, and, indeed, the expression of international relations are but a few of the many available illustrations of the fact that statesmen and scholars are inclined to the indiscriminate interuse of the two concepts' (1972: 330–332). The discovery of the continuing, or reviving, ethnic reality and the investigation of ways in which this reality can be managed by external forces has been helped along by the existence of institutes and grants devoted to international 'conflict management,' peacemaking, and peacekeeping.

This chapter is not intended to duplicate the work that has been done on institutional responses to demands for ethnic justice, responses that are seen as alternatives to secession. My purpose is neither to add to the burgeoning literature about the successes of third-party mediation in resolving ethnic conflicts nor to denounce all third-party interventions. It is, rather, to caution against false expectations, to bring some critique to bear on exaggerated claims, and to introduce a modicum of modesty into the discussion of the issue. The argument presented here is essentially this: by and large, the record of external (third-party) intervention, either by international organizations or major powers, has been a record of failure. In most cases, such intervention has been useless. In many instances where intervention might have been useful, it has not taken place, because the cost to the third party, in terms of its own national (or state) interest, would have been higher than it was willing to pay. In some instances, the consequences of intervention have been perverse and the situation of threatened ethnic communities has ended up worse than before, in the sense that their safety has been weakened and existing injustices have been preserved or magnified. This assessment is based on an examination of some two dozen interethnic disputes, from the end of World War I to the present.

Ethnonational self-determination and third parties: a note on the historical record

From the nineteenth century to the end of World War II, an important rationale for the involvement of the major powers has been to promote the self-determination of peoples. This rationale became particularly important with the collapse of multinational dynastic empires at the end of World War I. However, that rationale had to accord with the self-interest of the intervening powers, among which was the desire to prevent the domination of one or another country, especially in Europe. For that reason, international conferences in which outside mediators got together to settle problems of ethnic or national claims tended to restrict their agendas in such a way that matters touching upon their own national interests were left out. At the Congress of Vienna, for example, the French participated only when they were assured that the problems of Egypt, Syria, and Tunis would not be discussed (Cohen and Cohen 1974: 11–14).

At the Congress of Berlin in 1878, the major issue was, ostensibly, to revise the terms of the Treaty of Paris (1856) that had settled the Crimean War between Russia and Turkey. At that congress, several Balkan ethnonational communities were given (or promised) autonomy, and the Armenians and other religious minorities were promised protection. These solutions were imposed upon the Turks by Germany, Austria, and Britain acting in concert – with Bismarck acting as the 'honest broker' – and in their respective national interests. The British ended up with their own prize, which had nothing to do with self-determination (or any other approach to ethnic justice), namely, Cyprus. When the Ottoman Empire collapsed, the British and French jointly carved out the remains to form independent states based on selective self-determination for Syrians, Lebanese, and Iraqis; but the British got the sheikhdom of Transjordan as a buffer state. The signatories of the Treaty of Sèvres (1920) had promised the Armenians independence, but these promises came to naught. Armenian statehood was nullified by the Russo-Turkish

Treaty of 1921, under which the Soviet incorporation of several million Armenians was officially recognized, while other Armenians remained scattered in various countries of the Middle East. The Treaty of Sèvres had also promised the Kurds, who were spread over Turkey, Iraq, and other countries, 'a scheme of local autonomy' and recognized their entitlement to an independent state (to be carved out of eastern Turkey), but, due to the resistance of Kemal Atatürk, the treaty was never implemented; and the Treaty of Lausanne, imposed by the Allies on Turkey in 1923, made no mention of Kurdish claims (Sciolino 1991). At the Munich Conference in 1938, Britain, France, Italy, and Germany imposed the cession of Sudetenland, a region in Czechoslovakia dominated by Germanophones, to Hitler's Third Reich. They acted ostensibly in the name of self-determination, but for the leaders of Britain and France the fear of facing Germany was paramount.

Selective interventions: saving lives and other good causes

Ceteris paribus, major powers tend to intervene in order to resolve ethnic conflicts on the basis of self-determination, prevent the outbreak of ethnic wars, and contain the damages inflicted on victims of ethnic wars. The means used have included the imposition of treaties to protect minority languages; externally imposed partition schemes; the provision of peacekeeping forces; a variety of collective agreements and security guarantees; and finally, 'peace processes'.

Such intervention has been highly selective. The genocide of Armenians committed by the rulers of Ottoman Turkey evoked little reaction on the part of the major powers and certainly no intervention (Melson 1996).[1] The Holocaust had met with similar indifference. Before the mass killings of Jews had begun, there was an international conference on refugees – it took place at Evian in 1939 – but the pious verbal concerns of the United States and other major powers were not followed by the granting of a haven to Jews trying to escape. While the mass murder of Jews and Gypsies was in full progress, the United States refused to bomb the Auschwitz killing sites, on the grounds that it lacked sufficient aircraft and the ability to target with precision; and it also argued that winning the war had to have priority. The paramount goal of achieving victory for democracy was also used to account for our indifference to the fate of Volga Germans in the Soviet Union and for our own injustice vis-à-vis an ethnic minority – the internment of Americans of Japanese descent. The problems of the Hmong refugees in Southeast Asia were overshadowed by Khmer Rouge massacres; but the massacres themselves provoked only limited interest on the part of the Western powers and the United Nations.

To be sure, there are occasions when third parties lack effective means to intervene in behalf of an ethnic minority. Often enough, however, they lack the will. The willingness to intervene is influenced by subjective factors, such as their cultural affinities with the ethnic minority in question. In the Greek-Turkish war of 1897, the Greeks were militarily defeated; but the major European powers intervened, forcing the Turks to halt their operations and to sign a peace treaty under which the Turks gave up their territorial gains and agreed to make Crete an autonomous province (Cohen and Cohen 1974: 6). This action was inspired in large part by the fact that the powers were less sympathetic to the Muslim Turks than to the Greeks, a Christian nation with a classical past that became part of the heritage of the Western powers. In the recent Bosnian crisis, the Russians were on the side of the Serbs, largely because of a common Eastern Orthodox religion. Conversely, several Western nations favored the Croats over the Serbs, although the former were as guilty of 'ethnic cleansing' as the latter. For some countries, the explanation of this preference is the fact that there have been more Catholics among their inhabitants than Eastern Orthodox, and for Germany, the additional empathy for a country that was once an ally.[2] The inaction of the Vatican, the International Red Cross, the US State Department, and the various Western European foreign offices in the face of the Shoah could be attributed to traditional anti-Semitism. In our own day, the widespread indifference among leaders of major powers regarding the fate of Cambodians, southern Sudanese, Gypsies, and Tutsis has been due in no small measure to our lack of affinities with these peoples. In the current civil war between the Muslims of northern Sudan and the Christians and other non-Muslims of southern Sudan, the latter, who are fighting for cultural and religious freedom, are starving to death, but there is general indifference on the part of the international community, probably because one side is clearly losing anyway.[3] There is no evenly matched conflict to resolve, and the national security of any potential intervenor is not threatened by the outcome.

Selective sympathy based on cultural or ideological grounds is reflected today in the attitudes of the major third parties regarding the crisis in Kosovo. Most of the French intellectual and political élite (especially in the Foreign Office) has opposed independence for the Albanian majority in that province for Jacobin dogmatic reasons, that is, the belief that the territorial integrity of a country should be maintained, especially if membership in the 'national' community of that country is based on a political or civic (as opposed to an organic or ascriptive) definition of citizenship. US opposition, however, has been justified on the grounds that Kosovo has emotional significance for the Serbs as the cradle of their Christian civilization. It is curious that when it comes to Jerusalem, the factor of the emotional significance of that city for Jews as the focus of their religious/national consciousness is minimized, if not ignored.[4]

In some ethnic conflicts, human lives – as opposed to the fate of *communities* and the maintenance of *collective identities* – are not directly at stake. In such situations humanitarian considerations do not intrude directly, and it is easier to justify selective nonintervention. In that selectivity, a number of principles seem to apply:

1   Third parties generally refrain from attempts to mediate in favor of an oppressed minority if the 'host' country is a powerful authoritarian regime or if the minority is backed by country that is as powerful as the potential intervening third party. Conversely, it is always easier for third parties to impose solutions to ethnic conflicts upon losers, who are less able to resist intervention, rather than upon winners. This explains why the Irish claim for independence

from Britain was not considered by the Paris Peace Conference in 1919; why
the Kurdish and Armenian claims for independence were rejected, after
having benefited from initial support (Rugman and Hutchings 1996); and
why a large number of Magyars were consigned to minority status outside the
redrawn boundaries of Hungary (with the result, however, that irredentist
sentiment continued to fester). In 1918 Russia lost the war, and Estonia,
Latvia, and Lithuania got self-determination; in 1944 Russia won the war, and
the Baltic peoples lost their self-rule.

2   Both intervention and non-intervention are easier if justified in terms of positive goals, such as (a) preserving the territorial integrity of state; (b) helping to
secure the right to self-determination, either by some form of autonomy (Sisk
1996) or by secession (Carment 1994); (c) fostering democracy and liberty; and
(d) promoting regional peace and stability.

3   In the majority of cases, third-party intervention in behalf of ethnic rights
must yield to a *force majeure*, the most important of which is the national interest of the potential intervenor. The third party may hide its true aims behind
high-sounding rhetoric; these aims may be pursued selectively and in a contradictory fashion; and the policies that emerge may have the opposite results
from the ones ostensibly intended (as, for example, the Munich Agreement of
1938, which led, not to 'peace for our time', but to war). The arrangement
arrived at may not promote more individual liberty, democratic participation, or prosperity for the ethnic minority than it now possesses, and may, in
fact, promote fewer of these benefits – an outcome very likely for the
Chechens, Kosovar Albanians, and Palestinian Arabs. In that case, there
would be what the Germans call a *Verschlimmbesserung* – corrections that are
worse than the defects.

Outsiders have refrained from supporting claims of autonomy by the
Spanish Basques, the Corsicans, the Québécois, and even the Chechens
(except, in the latter two cases, in the form of lip service), not only because of
an unwillingness to interfere in the internal affairs of Spain, France, Canada,
and Russia respectively, but also, it has been argued, because as democracies,
these countries have provided sufficient liberties for the expression of the cultures of their minorities. Similarly, the aspirations of Kurds for meaningful
autonomy, let alone independence, have not been seriously supported by third
parties, lest they offend Turkey (in the case of the United States) or Iraq (in the
case of France).

In many Third World countries that are not democratic and in which ethnic
minorities are treated unequally, non-intervention has been rationalized in a different manner. Outside intervention in favor of one or another ethnopluralistic
institutional arrangement might produce a modicum of ethnic justice, but it would
also serve to maintain 'backward' minorities and interfere in 'nation-building', a
process that, although 'nation-destroying' (Connor 1972), was thought to be associated with democratization and economic development. That position was
supported by the majority of Western intellectuals in a number of cases, as, for

example, during the attempt by the Ibos in Biafra to gain autonomy from Nigeria. Many of the opponents of independence for the Ibos were inspired by developments in Western Europe, which they considered a developmental model to be followed by the Third World. In the words of Connor:

> If Cornishmen, Scots, and Welsh had become thoroughly British; if Basques, Catalans, and Galicians had become Spanish; if Flemings and Walloons had become Belgian; if Alsatians, Bretons, and Corsicans had become French, then why should not Ibo, Hausa, and Yoruba become Nigerian; or Baluchi, Bengali, Pashtun, and Sindhi become Pakistani?
>
> (1979: 20)

Those who used such arguments were apparently not bothered by the fact that the boundaries of Nigeria were survivals of Western colonialism. Moreover, they ignored the fact that the 'national' transformation of many European ethnonational communities has been far from complete, even after many generations. Curiously, both the 'autonomists' and the 'nation-builders', while using democratic rhetoric, accused each other of ignoring the real motivation of third parties: securing easier access to raw materials (Heraclides 1991: 80ff.).[5]

The paramount importance of the quest for oil and other resources and of markets is reflected in a number of positions regarding ethnic conflicts. The United States and other Western countries have not seriously raised the issue of Tibetan self-determination with China, in order not to interfere in profitable commercial opportunities; for many years they showed considerable indifference with regard to the East Timorese, so as not to offend Indonesia, a major Asian power and trading partner of these countries; and they have not intervened to protect the rights of the Armenian minority in Azerbaijan, in order not to jeopardize access to recently discovered oil in the Caspian Sea area.[6] More recently, the United States decided not to intervene in Chiapas province in behalf of of the Zapatista Indian rebels, who were being killed by government forces, in order not to endanger the profitable economic relations with Mexico, where many US factories have been relocated since the establishment of the North American Free Trade Association (NAFTA) (Preston 1998). In 1998 the European Parliament condemned the massacre of the Zapatistas – a condemnation that, from an economic point of view, was relatively risk-free – and members of the US government expressed their 'indignation' (Marion 1998a, 1998b). Western European countries have justified these inactions in terms of 'critical dialogue', and the United States, in terms of 'constructive engagement'.

Sometimes, intervention and non-intervention are decided upon on the basis of criteria that go beyond narrow economic interest, namely those of regional and global stability and peace. After World War I, when Polish forces occupied Vilnius, the capital of Lithuania, the Western powers did not intervene, largely because newly independent Poland was regarded as a bulwark against Bolshevik Russia. During the Cold War, US rhetoric about the 'liberation of captive nations' was not followed by concrete action; similarly, the United States refrained from intervening in the interethnic conflict in Cyprus in order not to annoy the Greeks (who had an important domestic lobby) or the Turks (who had a powerful military force bordering the Soviet Union). When, as a result of the Ta'if accord (1989), Lebanon became a virtual province of Syria, both France and the United States pretended that Lebanon was still a sovereign country – the former because it wished to retain its position as a 'privileged interlocutor' of the Arab countries, and, subsequently, the latter because it needed Syria as an ally during the Gulf War.

Such actions or inactions are often justified in terms of rationality, which predisposes a country to give pride of place to the protection of its own national security, regardless of how serious the complaints of ethnic minorities. However, not all third-party interventions can be explained in terms of that kind of rationality. There are instances when a third party intervenes (a) to promote the ego of a politician (e.g., Jimmy Carter's interventions in the Bosnian and Middle East conflicts); (b) to enhance the global visibility of a country (e.g., French meddling in conflicts in the Middle East and Sub-Saharan Africa); (c) to distract the populace of a major power from domestic problems and compensate for the failure of its government to address them; or (d) to garner an easy foreign-policy victory, usually by 'solving' a conflict within a relatively powerless country, usually to the disadvantage of the latter.

Two recent events may serve to illustrate the difficulty of explaining third-party interventions in terms of national security (or other 'reasons of state'): the German involvement in the break-up of Yugoslavia and the French involvement in Rwanda. In 1991, a newly reunited Germany, supported by Austria, unilaterally encouraged the disaggregation of Yugoslavia in the name of self-determination (Binder 1991), and pursued a policy of favoring Croatia.[7] The Germans have not been particularly interested in the self-determination of the Kurds in Iraq, the Corsicans in France, or the Basques in Spain.[8]

For more than a generation, France has continued its interest in developments in Sub-Saharan Africa because even after its former colonies there gained independence, France considered these states part of its 'backyard' *(prècarré)*. This interest extended to Rwanda, a former Belgian colony that seemed to be sliding into the 'Anglo-Saxon' sphere of influence. It is still a matter of controversy whether France – or the United States and the UN – knew about the genocide of the Tutsis in 1990; but there is general agreement that France did nothing to stop it and that it supported the genocidal Hutu leaders.[9] The UN, too, was implicated; according to several sources, the UN had been warned about an impending massacre by the Rwandan government, but had ignored these warnings (Prunier 1995; McKinley 1998).[10]

Sometimes, a third party's concrete reasons for intervening in ethnic conflicts, such as national security, economic interests, or regional stability, are counterbalanced by equally concrete reasons for *not* intervening. For instance, the major powers might be tempted to intervene in Algeria in order to protect the linguistic rights of the Berbers in Kabylia, who are threatened by the current campaign of 'Arabization', which is becoming increasingly violent. The problem is that the government waging that campaign is a secular one, which is fighting Islamic fundamentalist terrorism, presumably a much greater problem than the cultural oppression of an ethnic minority. Conversely, a too active campaign by Western powers against Islamic fundamentalism would be opposed by the UN, in which Islamic countries wield enormous power. Similarly, neither the Western powers nor the UN is predisposed to intervene in behalf of the Coptic Christian community in Egypt, because neither wishes to alienate a country that is viewed as a regional stabilizing force, whose role in any settlement of the Arab–Israeli dispute is indispensable. That dispute itself illustrates the dilemma for third parties. In terms of pure economic rationality, most Western countries have had no difficulty in supporting the Arab countries and the Palestine Liberation Organization (PLO), and would have little hesitation in sacrificing Israel or imposing an unfavorable *diktat* on Israel that would ultimately facilitate its destruction as a state. Certain US decision-makers would go along with this policy, but they are hampered by another concrete (and relatively short-term) interest – the electoral considerations of politicians – and for that reason refrain from alienating domestic supporters of Israel.

Such dilemmas are sometimes resolved by the introduction of subjective criteria. It is a moot question whether the Western powers' professed concern for Israel's well-being is influenced by their frequently proclaimed interest in securing the survival of 'the only democracy in the Middle East'; there is somewhat less doubt about the subjective aspect when it comes to countries that have cultural, linguistic, or religious affinities with a claimant ethnic community. This is particularly true of a powerful country that adjoins a region in which such conflicts take place, especially if one of the parties to the conflict is an ethnic kin. Intervention by a 'big neighbor' is probably motivated by a combination of national interest and subjective impulses. The most recent example is that of Russia, which is inclined to side with the Serbs in the dispute over Kosovo, largely because they are fellow Slavs. Both the intervenor's national interests and its biases may be accentuated in international peacekeeping operations to the extent that the various components of multinational military forces are answerable to their own governments.

One should also not underestimate the importance of the cultural egos of third parties, and the place of ideology in them. For example, in a contest between Romania and Hungary, the French are likely to side with Romania, one reason being its Romance language and the allegedly 'Latin' nature of its culture. In the Arab–Israeli conflict, the traditional anti-Semitism of Western foreign offices continued for years to influence their attitudes (Loftus and Aarons 1994).

Common kinship is not always the decisive factor, despite a subjective temptation to invoke it. Such a temptation was particularly apparent in the case of India, in view of the cultural similarity between the Tamils of Sri Lanka and the people of the southern Indian state of Tamil Nadu. India, however, has endeavored not to intervene too directly in behalf of the Tamils in Sri Lanka, because such intervention might lead to secession; and the truncated state of Sri Lanka that would result from it would be tempted to ally with India's enemies and threaten India's own security.[11] Indeed, India's increased pressures on Sri Lanka in the 1980s had been followed by Pakistan's support of the government of Sri Lanka in its efforts at protecting the country's territorial integrity as well as the support of China, which supplied arms to the Sri Lanka government (Navaratna-Bandara 1995: 69). These developments explain India's gradual disengagement from the conflict. The same reasoning explains Australia's refusal to intervene in Indonesia's takeover of East Timor. An additional constraint against an excessive role by Australia and New Zealand in resolving ethnic disputes may be the fear of contributing to a 'contagion' effect on their own indigenous minorities. Similarly, the decision by Syria (so far) to refrain from a formal incorporation of Lebanon can be attributed to Syria's reluctance to provoke countermeasures by Israel. Conversely, there are times when a big neighboring state has little choice about intervention. The conflictual relationship between Turkey and Greece goes back to the nineteenth century; however, the proximate cause of Turkish intervention in Cyprus in behalf of their ethnic confreres was virtually provoked by the Greeks' promotion of *enosis*. Turkey's military occupation of northern part of the island, however, did not resolve the ethnic conflict.

Peace processes and other facilitations

If third parties cannot resolve ethnic conflicts, they can at least initiate a process whereby conflicting ethnic communities can be brought together. There is a widely held conviction that outsiders can be useful in facilitating a dialogue between the conflicting communities; in helping them to get to know each other; and in persuading one party to make concessions to the other in order to improve the atmosphere.[12] This conviction is found in particular among professional peacemakers, such as the Carnegie Foundation, the Friends Service Committee, and social psychologists who hold that personal contacts between representatives of conflicting ethnic groups enable them to learn of each other's problems and fears and help them to factor out the elements accounting for their ethnic orientations.

Herbert Kelman (1997) refers to the importance of symbolic gestures, bull sessions, and other 'confidence-building measures'. But such gestures may mislead an adversary and create false hopes. Similarly, 'getting to know your adversary', an approach based on 'the optimistic belief that increased ties between groups are both symptomatic and productive of harmonious relations' (Connor 1987: 197), may be wasted, and having personal encounters, especially when these are forced by outsiders, may not improve the contending parties' impressions of each other. Moreover, it is doubtful whether such encounters have led to a sincere mutual acknowledgment of 'national narratives'. In most cases, conflict resolution through outside mediation has been difficult, not because the parties do not know each other, but rather because they – the Israelis and Arabs, the Serbs and Kosovar Albanians, the Greeks and Turks, the Romanians and Hungarians, and the Tamils and Sinhalese – know each other too well. Personal dialogue may simply enable one side to learn about the weaknesses of the other side and to exploit these. Handshakes, White House Lawn ceremonies, and even continued negotiations over concrete issues between the Israelis and Palestinians, while persuading some Israelis of the good will of the PLO, have so far not caused the latter to give up its ultimate aim: the destruction of Israel (an aim that Yasir Arafat, the president of the Palestinian Authority, has repeatedly affirmed in his remarks to Arab inter-locutors).

A widespread assumption of believers in third-party mediation is that most ethnic conflicts are based on irrational factors, and hence that the first step to solving these conflicts is to recognize them as such. Getting a party to an ethnic conflict to act 'rationally' involves convincing it to acknowledge that its collective consciousness is a false one because it is based on faulty perceptions of the past. Thus, many scholars committed to problem-solving through mediation denigrate ethnic claims as irrational because they are based on history rather than concrete reality – because, in short, they reflect 'the fear of the future, lived through the past'. As David Lake and Donald Rothchild have put it:

> The polarization of society is magnified by such non-rational factors as political memories and myths, on the one hand, and emotions, on the other. Political myths can lead groups to form distorted images of others and see others as more hostile and aggressive than they really are. Such myths are often rooted in actual events, and probably could not be long sustained without a historical basis. Yet historical events can, over time, evolve into legends that justify the superiority of one group over another, stimulate desires for retribution, or sustain group hatreds.
>
> (1996: 55)

Lake and Rothchild refer specifically to Slobodan Miloševic, whose control of the media 'allowed him to present a one-sided view of Croat violence toward Croatian Serbs'. Whether genocide is rational or irrational is a matter of controversy, depending upon the perspective of the perpetrator or the victim; for the families of the numerous Gypsies, Jews, and Serbs who faced the mass slaughter perpetrated by Croat Ustaše forces during World War II, such memories are still real, and the families in question would be acting irrationally if they discounted them, especially in view of the presence of Ustaše supporters in the Tudjman regime and the fact that that regime engaged in as much ethnic cleansing as has the Miloševic regime. Making the distinctions mentioned here betrays the ahistorical view of many American social scientists; and it may also betray the bias of the third party in favor of one side or another: in this particular case to come down on the side of the Croats rather than the Serbs. Similarly, the memory Jews in Israel have of six million of their ethnic kin being killed without any serious third-party attempt at 'mediation' remains quite vivid.

Lake and Rothchild do raise a number of important points. They are aware of the limits of international intervention, arguing that it often serves merely to facilitate rather than resolve ethnic conflicts; that it is bounded by the credibility of the international commitment; and that it is sometimes worse than no intervention at all. But their analysis tends to downplay the 'national-interest' agenda of the mediator. Furthermore, their analysis, like that of many others, tends to equate the problems of ethnic minorities with those of 'nation-states', when they speak of the 'security dilemma'. Such a dilemma arises when a state is confronted with hostile external powers that might threaten its territorial integrity.[13] What concerns ethnic minorities is not the protection of territorial boundaries but sheer survival, both as members of a cultural community and as individuals, because the most rational choice, that of 'exit' from the ethnic community in order to take care of their personal interests, is not always available.

The discussion above illustrates the assumptions about 'nations' and 'ethnonations' that have informed both decision-makers and academicians – the former in determining whether, and in what way, to intervene; and the latter, in minimizing ethnonational concerns. These assumptions have been convincingly called into question by Connor. He has criticized both economic factors as determining ethnic aspirations and the widespread belief that class consciousness necessarily trumps ethnic consciousness (Connor 1984b); and the failure of outsiders to take into account the historical roots and emotional depth of ethnonational identity (Connor 1987).

Methods, processes, and incentives

In theory, many approaches are available to third parties in their attempts to help resolve ethnic conflicts. These include both 'carrot' and 'stick' incentives, among them economic aid, security guarantees, and formal alliances. All of them present problems, however. Big power mediators often promise payoffs to small countries in exchange for accommodating actions, especially territorial concessions, toward ethnic contenders. One of these payoffs is economic aid, such as that provided by the United States to Israel, Egypt, and Jordan to encourage them to adopt negotiating modes, or that provided by Germany to Russia and Poland in return for cultural autonomy for *Volksdeutsche* residing in these countries. Sometimes, monetary payoffs involve a one-time lump sum. Often, however, economic aid is a continuing commitment; in that case, the donor is held hostgage to the good behavior of the recipient, because the latter may withdraw his commitments once the money has been spent and there is no prospect of getting more.

Other approaches are collective security arrangements and 'guarantees'. Collective security alliances, however, may not last, as was demonstrated by the meaninglessness of the inter-war Locarno agreements (guaranteeing the integrity of the frontiers of the successor states) when Czechoslovakia was dismantled. Similarly, the various treaties signed by the US federal government with Native American tribes were frequently violated. Unwritten 'guarantees' have a way of vanishing even more quickly, as was demonstrated when, in 1956, the tripartite guarantees to Israel of 1950–51 proved to be inoperative, and again in 1967, when US guarantees to Israel made in 1957 could not be found. Moreover, territorial concessions exacted by side A in exchange for promises and commitments by side B may be 'salami tactics' that encourage the latter to ask for more, and they do not guarantee that the promises will be kept. Such concessions are sometimes called 'peace *processes*', which are open-ended and do not necessarily achieve *peace* as an end state. In fact, 'process' may even be a substitute for a desirable end state. As Donald Horowitz has said, 'Mediators have a process bias that keeps them from focusing on good institutional arrangements, in favor of "getting to yes," any yes' (quoted in Sisk 1996: 94).

In order to get results, mediators prefer to negotiate with spokespersons who agree with them and who are malleable, and mediators may encourage divisions within a society to weaken the position of less accommodating negotiators – those who, in Timor Kuran's words, are not 'ethnic activists [who] can drive individuals to represent falsely their true preferences' (quoted in Lake and Rothchild 1996: 54). A recent example is provided by Kosovo, where the openly expressed preference of the six-nation Contact Group was to negotiate, not with the Kosovo Liberation Army or other representatives of the Albanian majority, but with Ibrahim Rugova, the Sorbonne-educated pacifist leader. In making these choices, third parties tend to substitute incentives to ethnic leaders – academic appointments, Nobel Peace prizes, and co-optation into a transethnic élite – for concrete benefits to an ethnic community's rank-and-file members.

There are instances when third parties are unable to convince ethnic communities, or their 'host' countries, to make concessions ostensibly for their own good, but in reality in conformity with the mediator's own agenda. In such cases, the stick may replace the carrot. Such an approach – it comes under the rubric of 'power mediation' (Harris and Reilly 1998: 109–110) – consists of cutting off aid to a recalcitrant party; embargoes and other economic sanctions; withdrawing peace-keeping forces; or arming the adversaries of those who do not want to be helped. It is sometimes argued that in order for an ethnic conflict to be properly mediated by outsiders, the ethnic community or, as the case may be, the host country harboring it, must be ready, or 'ripe', for compromise. Such ripeness, which is often a reflection of exhaustion that produces 'a mutually hurting stalemate', may be the result of third-party pressures or similar constraints (Pruitt 1997).

All of these methods have been used, and they have not added up to a solid narrative of success. One study listed 90 (ethnic and other) conflicts at the end of the Cold War, and asserts that by 1993, 47 of them remained active (Wallensteen and Axell 1994). The 43 conflicts that were dropped from the list had two kinds of resolution: victory of one side or mutual agreement. Ethnic conflicts were ended (or at least suspended) in Romania when Ceausescu was killed and in Ethiopia when Mengistu was defeated. The six cases in which an amicable settlement was reached were Lebanon, Mali, Morocco/Western Sahara, Mozambique, El Salvador, and Nicaragua. But a note of caution is in order: in some cases, such as Mozambique, the UN was involved; in other cases, such as Nicaragua, agreement was reached because both sides appeared to be exhausted; in still other cases, such as Lebanon, the 'amicable' settlement (the Ta'if agreement) was virtually imposed by Syria.

In most, if not all, these cases, renewed conflict is possible if one party feels that it has a chance of victory, or is persuaded by third parties that it has such a chance. Where third-party involvement is important is in areas in which agreements (or at least cease-fires) have been reached, and where the UN or NATO 'guarantees' them by means of peacekeeping forces (as in the Golan Heights, and in Bosnia, Kosovo, and Cyprus). Such agreements, however, are likely to collapse the moment such forces are withdrawn. The continuing involvement of third parties in these and other conflicts is questionable, largely because of the end of the Cold War, which has made intervention to contain regional conflicts less important than before. Moreover, to the extent that third-party involvement does take place, it is motivated by the third party's national interest. Often national interest seems to dictate a third party's acceptance of the suppression of an ethnic or religious community's rights, as in the cases of Tibetans in China, Kurds in Turkey and Iraq, Chechens in Russia, and Copts in Egypt. Where no such interest is demonstrable, there is indifference, as in the cases of the Nubian tribes in southern Sudan and the Berbers in Kabylia.

In sum: with rare exceptions, the record of third-party interventions in ethnic conflicts has been of more failures than successes. One of the exceptions is sub-Saharan Africa, where big-power or international mediation has seemed to work better than elsewhere. Perhaps one of the major reasons for that success is that the African countries are weak and that, as a Department of Defense document declared in 1995, the United States has 'very little traditional strategic interest in Africa' (*United States Security Strategy* 1995: 3). To be sure, the United States has sent military forces to Africa more than a dozen times since 1990; but that was to ensure regional stability, to protect US economic interests, and to stem terrorism and illegal narcotics trade rather than to help resolve the ethnic conflicts behind the instability, for such intervention generally is beyond the capability or interest of intervening military forces.[14] This is not much different from France's intervention, which has to do with symbolic benefits, such as spreading *francophonie* and asserting the country's 'presence'. In short, the solutions arrived at in that region have not necessarily been in terms of ethnic justice; on the contrary, they have permitted dictators to deny ethnic claims. As illustrated by Zaire (Katanga) and Nigeria (Biafra), intervention has often been *against* the ethnic claims of minorities, and has tended to keep the autocratic system intact, under the pretext that it constituted a bulwark against Communist influence. Another exception is South Africa, where the groundwork for third-party mediation was laid by a relatively effective economic boycott as well as by the political change of heart of members of the white élite.

A third instance of possible success is Northern Ireland, where the United States did not openly take positions in favor of either the Catholic side, given the fact that Britain is our ally, or the Protestant one, given the powerful Irish Catholic lobby in United States. George Mitchell was a successful mediator because he was not perceived to be on one side or the other; moreover, both sides compromised because each thought it was a rational move in terms of its particular expectations of the final resolution of the conflict. Another explanation for the success of Mitchell's mediation – if, indeed, it proves to be a success – was the fact that the personal interests of David Trimble, the leader of the Ulster Protestants, and Gerry Adams, the leader of Sinn Fein, happened to coincide: each felt that, by compromising, he would protect his own leadership position. In the end, the Northern Ireland conflict will be 'solved' as soon as one of two conditions is achieved: (a) the complete secularization of Northern Irish political culture (an unlikely outcome); or (b) a significant natural growth rate of the Catholic population, so that it will outnumber the Protestant one.

The cases dealt with above, however, are exceptions and do not provide sufficient grounds for optimism. A major problem is the inconsistency and selectivity with which third parties approach ethnic claims, emphasizing sometimes the primacy of self-determination and sometimes the territorial integrity of states. In view of this inconsistency, outside intervention may be less desirable than no intervention at all. In fact, outside intervenors, or mediators – international organization or powerful countries – may be conflict *multipliers*. The UN has had particularly questionable credibility as a third-party mediator, since it has rarely been exercised about the oppression of ethnic minorities (or citizens in general) in Third World countries, and since it is dominated by coalitions of countries with their own vested interests. The few 'successes' of the UN – in stopping the fighting between Iran and Iraq, facilitating the withdrawal of Soviet troops from Afghanistan, establishing a broad coalition in Cambodia, and ending the civil war in El Salvador – were due to exceptional circumstances, such as the exhaustion of the warring parties or the unwillingness of external powers to support local clients; and some of these achievements (such as the coalition in Cambodia) were to fall apart later (Touval 1994). Where UN secretaries-general have played personal roles, these have often been neither objective nor constructive. U Thant, for instance, had an anti-Western bias, and Kurt Waldheim an anti-Israel and (on occasion) a pro-Soviet one. What is true for the UN is true, *a fortiori*, for individual countries. India has supported the suppression of Tamil claims in Sri Lanka for its own strategic reasons; France has compromised its role as a mediator by its one-sided positions on the Arab–Israeli conflict, and its role in Rwanda has been that of a spoiler, if not as an instigator of ethnic violence. As we have seen in the case of certain peace conferences, such as Vienna (1815), Berlin (1878), and Paris (1918–1919), third-party negotiators have managed to take care of their own interests first.

A big power may try to resolve a regional ethnic conflict because it wishes to secure its supply of petroleum; in that case, it is likely to intervene on the side of the ethnic community that contributes to the securing of that supply. Its intervention may also be motivated by primary goals other than the resolution of an ethnic conflict: minimizing the spread of conflict to neighboring countries; providing a *raison d'être* for a regional system of which it is a member, such as NATO (which explains, at least in part, the belated bombing of Serbia in 1999); shutting out undesirable ideological influences (for example, Communism or Islamic fundamentalism); or promoting economic globalization.

Above I have referred to some of the national agendas of mediating powers. One may add other instances where, especially during the Cold War, major powers functioned, not as resolvers of ethnic conflict, but as agents *preventing* resolution. Thus, the United States supported the Pakistanis in suppressing the Bengalis in East Pakistan and (together with other Western countries) was on the side of the Indonesian government as its leader, Suharto, engaged in the slaughter of thousands of East Timorese; and the Soviet Union helped the Ethiopian government in its suppression of the separatists in Eritrea. The collapse of the Soviet Union in 1991 and the end of the Soviet arms supply weakened the central government of Ethiopia, thereby strengthening the position of Eritrean secessionists. The United

States, too, had earlier supported the Haile Selassie government and, later, the idea of a unified Ethiopia. But in 1991, the United States changed its position, arguing that Eritreans deserved independence on the basis of the right to self-determination (Taras and Ganguly 1998: 116). Before the Gulf War, the United States supported Iraq in its conflict with the Kurds; during that war, the United States encouraged the Kurds to fight for autonomy, but as soon as the war ended, it abandoned them.

One of the problems making the work of third parties difficult is the 'spoiler' problem – the sabotaging of attempts at the resolution of ethnic conflicts for reasons of narrow commercial interest. Thus, Russia sold missiles to the Greek Cypriots, thereby reducing their incentive to negotiate with the Turkish Cypriots for a communalist solution. Conversely, interference by governmental or non-governmental forces may exacerbate ethnic conflicts (Stedman 1997). In order not to be sidetracked from their work, and eager to achieve the resolution of an ethnic conflict, third parties may ignore the existence of spoilers; sometimes, in fact, a third party may *encourage* the work of terrorists and other spoilers, either because their work may help to make one or the other conflicting communities more impatient and more amenable to compromise, or because the third party may be less interested in a fair solution than in extending its regional influence. Among the examples is Russia's funding of terrorist activities against Israel while participating in international conferences dealing with the Arab–Israeli conflict.

Choosing fair criteria and neutral agents of third-party involvement: a possible agenda

My analysis is not intended to suggest that third-party interventions should be abandoned. In order for them to succeed, however, they should be based on more honest and more neutral bases and be guided by criteria that may provide a modicum of justice and fairness. Providing for its own national security, facilitating access to economic resources for itself, and enhancing global or regional stability are understandable motives for a mediating power, but these do not necessarily serve the interests of the contending ethnic communities.

After World War I, the motivation behind League of Nations interventions had a democratic element; to the extent that ethnopolitical conflict resolution was seen in terms of national self-determination, it was believed that that aim could be best achieved by the creation of independent states, to be carved out of decaying empires – the Ottoman, the Czarist, the Austro-Hungarian. Since these empires were absolute monarchies, independence for the ethnic minorities they contained was regarded as a necessary condition for the development of democracy. For that reason, the 'Austro-Marxists' deviated from Marxist orthodoxy, which at that time had little use for the articulation of ethnic consciousness (Connor 1984a: 29, 534). Today, it is doubtful whether the promotion of democracy in areas of ethnic conflict is a priority item on the agenda of outside intervenors.

A variety of concerns, conditions, and constraints have determined the intervention of third parties, among which, as indicated above, the concerns of ethnic minorities as such have played a subsidiary role. Among them have been regional security concerns, the maintenance of the traditional ties and friendship of a country in which a minority is situated, and the belief that some ethnic groups are more deserving of protection than others. These constraints have often been dealt with by reference to more or less acceptable principles, such as the principle of non-interference in the internal affairs of a persecuting nation or the principle of self-determination. That latter principle, however, tends to be invoked selectively.

Several generations ago, entitlement to self-determination was based on the democratic nature of a politically mobilized ethnic group or its presumed readiness for democracy. Today, it is considered more rational to favor the protection or promotion of the cultures and languages of large communities rather than small ones ('primordial groups') because the former tend to be 'nation-building' and 'modernizing' and can develop greater capacities to fulfill the economic needs of everyone, including members of ethnic minorities. In deciding which ethnic group deserves independence (or at least autonomy), Western intellectuals have used certain 'politically correct' criteria, such as what Allan Buchanan has called 'saltwater' and 'pigmentation'. Under the saltwater test, colonies separated from their mother country by an ocean require, if not separation, at least territorial autonomy; under the 'pigmentation' test, claimants for secession have increased legitimacy if they are 'of a different color from those from whom they wish to secede' (Buchanan 1992: 345). Such criteria have often been misapplied. Thus, third-party mediators (or potential mediators) have stressed the rights of the Palestinians to independence, but not those of the Tibetans or Kosovar Albanians. In fact, in the latter case, Robert Gelbard, an American negotiator, has reiterated that 'independence [was] out of the question'. Furthermore, the advocacy of the rights of some nations or ethnonations has taken place under a more or less well-hidden agenda: thus France under President de Gaulle promoted a 'free' Québec in part in order to annoy the 'Anglo-Saxons'; and during the Cold War the United States maintained its (largely rhetorical) interest in the rights of the Baltic nations to independence in order to annoy the Soviet Union.

To be effective, mediators must be credible. First, they must be clear about their basic motivations, which must be the achievement of just solutions. Second, they must develop a thorough knowledge of the local economic, geographic, and social conditions of all the conflicting ethnic groups and the nature and causes of their grievances. Thus the third party must not refer to the activities of some ethnic communities as 'terrorism' and of others as 'armed struggle for liberation'.[15] Third, they must show an equal sensitivity to the history and collective identity, or (in the ahistoricist vocabulary of protagonists of rational-choice approaches) the memories or myths of all the parties.[16] Specifically, this means an avoidance of the tendency of third parties toward a 'too exclusive concentration on the dominant group in the case of societies with a *Staatsvolk*, [a concentration often manifested in] statewide . . . culture studies that make no reference to the . . . cultures of ethnic minorities' (Connor 1987: 199). Fourth, they must take the 'particularist' concerns of *all* the contending ethnic groups seriously. This is important because the claims of ethnic minorities tend often to be minimized, if not denigrated, especially by scholars who have grown up in countries where nationhood is defined functionally rather than organically, and where minority cultures have had to give up their identities to assume those of the majority, which, having achieved dominance, are considered *ipso facto* superior.

In order to prevent global balkanization, not all ethnic claims can be, or should be, satisfied by independence or even territorial autonomy, and choices must be made. Heraclides has enumerated the 'attributes for a qualified right to secessionist self-determination' that might guide mediators. These are (1) a pattern of systematic discrimination or exploitation against a sizable, self-defined minority; (2) the existence of a distinct community or society that compactly inhabits a region within a state and that overwhelmingly supports separatism; (3) a realistic prospect of conflict resolution and peace within and between the new and old state as a result of the envisaged self-rule or partition; and (4) the rejection of compromise solutions by the central government (Heraclides 1992: 400–401). It is not clear what third parties can do if one or more of these conditions are not met; and it is equally unclear what they can do to affirm the right to a solution short of separatism, that is, to some form of autonomy, especially if the 'host' society does not accept the self-definition of a categoric group as an ethnic community. That would be the case in France and Bulgaria, where the Corsicans and the Pomaks, respectively, are not considered minorities; in Romania, which refers to the Magyars of Transylvania as 'Hungarian-speaking Romanians'; and in Turkey, whose government insists that the Kurds in the western region of the country are 'Mountain Turks'.

These examples illustrate Connor's complaints about the conceptual confusion that results from variable and inconsistent use of terminology (1978, 1991). Some of the labeling is done by dominant leaders or groups within a country for their own purposes. Bosnian Muslims were accorded the label of 'nation' by Tito because he had reasons to do so, i.e., to achieve an internal balance by reducing the relative power of the Serbs. Under Napoleon, the *nation juive* that existed in pre-revolutionary France was dissolved into the *culte israélite* to which Jews might belong as individuals – all in the interest of building a politically defined nation without intermediary communities. In the Soviet Union, the Jews were defined as a 'nationality', but without the cultural and institutional appurtenances permitted other nationalities. In Hitler's Germany, Jews were redefined as a race – in order to make it easier to exclude them from the German nation.

Often the granting or withholding of the label of 'nation' is done by outsiders, who may do so for reasons of their own. Thus the Palestinians are widely considered a nation (separate from other Arabs), but not the Tibetans; the East Timorese, but not the Kabyle Berbers, the Kosovar and, more recently, the Macedonian Albanians. Nor do third parties insist on regarding the Bretons or Corsicans as anything other than inhabitants of a given region in France, or at best members of groups with certain folkloric characteristics (including *dialectophonie*). The Lebanese nation, insofar as the term applies to the residents of the Levant, was created by the Western Allies after World War I. Conversely, the Macedonian nation has had some difficulty being recognized as such by its neighbor, Greece, which continues to refer to the 'Former Yugoslav Republic of Macedonia (FYROM)'. At this writing, the European Union, as a third party, appears to be playing a more positive role, insofar as it makes the legitimation of the ethnonational rights of minorities in the former Communist countries in Eastern Europe a condition of membership.

Before embarking on mediation, third parties must have definitional clarity; they must be consistent in their use of criteria for determining what is a nation and 'when'. Furthermore, in order for mediating third parties to have greater success than before, both they and the conflicting ethnonational groups must be bound by the premise that agreements will be honored. International agreements have meaning only for those states or communities that share Western notions about the sanctity of contracts. Where some of the parties do not, those who do are at a disadvantage, and internationally arranged agreements may be prescriptions for future conflicts. The Soviet Union's commitments to hold democratic elections in Eastern Europe did the ethnic minorities little good, since that country did not abide by agreements. Second, mediators must demonstrate their neutrality by refraining from taking advantage of the asymmetry of players – the unequal position of conflicting groups – and must not favor one contender over another. They must show that they are immune to pressures from military, religious, ethnic, and economic lobbies. Finally, in order for third-party intervention to succeed, conflicting ethnonational groups must be convinced that the intervention is guided less by the national agenda of the intervenor and more by moral considerations and by political norms that have a universal appeal. According to Leonard Binder, these norms should include protection against foreign invasion and internal anarchy, the right of every ethnonational community to self-determination, and the notion that democratic government is preferable to all other kinds (Binder 1996). Some of these norms may be incompatible; in that case, mediators may have to determine to what extent an externally suggested solution to an ethnic conflict is preferable to the existing situation. An acceptable resolution would be one in which the ethnic group in question will have more individual liberty, more democracy, more justice, and more economic opportunity than it has now. It would also be an outcome in which the culture of the ethnic community is better protected than it is now. A credible mediator would have to convince the contending ethnic groups that minority identities are as entitled to protection as majority ones and that minority cultures are intrinsically worth preserving; at the same time, such cultures would have to be compatible with the values of individual liberty and democracy.

Timothy Sisk argues that the most fruitful 'entry points' for international intervention are democratic systems, because they are more tolerant, more open to reasoning, and more likely to compromise than non-democratic systems, and they are also more likely to make institutional provisions for the expression of ethnic identities, with third parties doing little more than 'facilitating' negotiations (Sisk 1996: 92). This explains why the conflict between Austria and Italy over Alto Adige was resolved amicably and why the conflict in Northern Ireland is (one hopes) likely to be resolved. What happens, however, when one of the parties to the conflict is democratic and the other is not? In such a situation, the latter has the advantage because it will be less bound by agreements. For that reason, Serbian,

Palestinian, or Iraqi signatures to internationally 'facilitated' agreements are less likely to be honored once peacekeeping forces are removed than signatures by such post-Communist regimes as Hungary that are in process of democratization. Paradoxically, it is in the latter countries that mediation has the greatest prospect of success because it is least necessary.

Notes

1 It was only in 1998 that the French National Assembly acknowledged officially that such a genocide had taken place. In February 2000, however, the French Senate refused such acknowledgment lest it offend the Turkish government.

2 It has been pointed out that the Christian Social Union (CSU), a coalition partner in Helmut Kohl's government, was close to President Franjo Tudjman, and that two-thirds of the 700,000 Yugoslavs living in Germany were Croatian Catholics.

3 The 'Christian affinity' with the southern Sudanese is in part neutralized by the fact that they are even darker skinned than the northern Sudanese and that the latter control the oil resources that are of interest to Western powers.

4 The US State Department has opposed the extension of the Jerusalem municipal boundaries westward into *Israeli* territory so as not to upset the population balance of the city in favor of Jews. Yet it has not encouraged the Arabs in east Jerusalem to reduce their birthrate, which has a much greater impact on the population balance on the Arab side.

5 See Heraclides (1991: 80–106). For a discussion of the economic agendas behind French support of Katanga and US-British-French support of Biafra, see also MacNamara (1989: 176–180).

6 In July 1998, the State Department asked the US Congress to end the economic sanctions on Azerbaijan that it had imposed in retaliation for the Azeris' blockade of Armenia and Nagorno-Karabagh.

7 For a more updated and critical approach on the issue of German–Croatian relations and German foreign policy toward the Yugoslav successor states, see Ramet and Coffin (2001).

8 It is interesting to note that about the same time that conditions for Balkan 'ethnic cleansing' were set in motion as an unintended consequence of Germany's policies, German Foreign Minister Genscher called upon the Western powers to prevent a genocide of the Kurds in Iraq. Genscher also argued that (according to UN Resolution 688) a state that tramples on human rights, oppresses its own citizens, and forces them to flee would in future not be able to invoke the principle of the non-interference in its internal affairs on the part of the world community (*Deutschland-Nachrichten* 1991: 1–2).

9 See Rémy Ourdan, 'Au pays des âmes mortes: Rwanda, Enquête sur un génocide,' *Le Monde*, 31 March 1998, and subsequent articles in the same journal. According to an article in *Le Figaro* (12 January 1998), France supplied weapons to the Rwanda government during the genocide, the latest instance being 18 July 1994.

10 On the French and Rwanda, see Prunier (1995: 103–107), which discusses in detail the considerations of national interest, and especially the cultural motivations, behind France's involvement in the crisis.

11 Another possibility, however remote, was that a Tamil secession from Sri Lanka might encourage Tamil Nadu nationalist elements to secede from India (Navaratna-Bandara 1995: 63 ff.: 130–131).

12 For an example of this sort of idealistic approach, see the articles by Herbert Kelman and others in 'Psychological Obstacles to Peace: The Arab–Israeli Conflict', *Internasjonal Politikk* (Norway), no. 1B—Supplement 1980.

13 The notion of 'security dilemma' is taken from international relations theory and

applied to ethnic conflict, see Saideman (1996). In international relations, all actors (states) live in a state of nature and its security is constantly at risk. Therefore they take whatever measures they can to ensure their existence, e.g., engaging in arms races, making alliances, and occasionally resorting to preventive wars. Others argue that ethnic groups behave the same way once empires that had controlled their behaviors fall apart: they make alliances, secure weapons, and fight each other, and they view every improvement in the condition of other ethnic groups in the region as a threat to their own existence. This sort of analogy is exaggerated, because (1) ethnic groups do not enjoy the legitimacy as international actors that states enjoy; (2) it is unclear whether ethnic groups should be more or less worried about their 'security'—i.e., their existence as a community—in a post-imperial situation, especially since empires, rather than mediating fairly between ethnic groups, often suppress ethnic consciousness (e.g., Prussia, Czarist Russia, Nazi Germany); (3) an ethnic community's policy of securing its existence does not require a zero-sum solution: such a community may accept the idea of a peaceful (and often cooperative) coexistence of several ethnic groups.

14 See Henk and Metz (1997: 13–14). The booklet refers to alleviating hunger and refugee problems, sustainable development, the encouragement of democracy, technical advice, and acting as a broker in fights between warlords, but not resolving ethnic conflicts.

15 For instance, French decision-makers and their supporters refer to the Palestinians as 'liberators' and the Kurdish separatists as 'terrorists'. See Jacques Amalric, 'Un défi pour l'Europe', *Libération*, 30 December 1997. Moreover, since the French prefer 'integrated' countries, they refer to the Turks who have occupied northern Cyprus as 'invaders' and to Albanian Kosovars as 'rebels'.

16 It is currently held that the identity of Palestinians must be protected by a separate state because their identity is decidedly different from that of a neighboring Arab state; at the same time, it is argued that although the Kosovar Albanians have a clear identity that is different from that of the Serbs, Kosovo should not be permitted to secede because that province is the cradle of Serb civilization and Serb memory. But this criterion is not applied to Jerusalem, which has been the focus of Jewish collective identity for more than 2000 years. See Vladan Radoman, Aris Fakinos, and Louis Schittly, 'Le Kosovo comme Jérusalem', *Libération*, 19 March 1998.

References

Binder, David 1991. 'Some Western Nations Split Off on Yugoslavia'. *New York Times*. 7 March.

Binder, Leonard 1996. 'The Moral Foundations of International Intervention and the Limits of National Self-Determination'. *Nationalism and Ethnic Politics*. 2(3) (Autumn): 325–359.

Buchanan, Allen 1992. 'Self-Determination and the Right to Secede'. *Journal of International Affairs*. 45(2) (Winter): 349–365.

Carment, David 1994. 'The Ethnic Dimension in World Politics: Theory, Policy, and Early Warning'. *Third World Quarterly*. 15(4): 551–582.

Cohen, Raymond and Cohen, Stuart 1974. *Peace Conferences: The Formal Aspects*. Jerusalem: Hebrew University, Jerusalem Papers on Peace Problems.

Connor, Walker 1972. 'Nation-Building or Nation-Destroying?' *World Politics*. 24 (April): 319–355.

——— 1978. 'A Nation is a Nation, is a State, is an Ethnic Group, is a . . .' *Ethnic and Racial Studies*. 1 (October): 377–400.

——— 1979. 'Ethnonationalism in the First World'. In Milton J. Esman (ed.) *Ethnic Conflict in the Western World*. Ithaca, NY: Cornell University Press.

—— 1984a. *The National Question in Marxist-Leninist Theory and Strategy*. Princeton, NJ: Princeton University Press.

—— 1984b. 'Eco- or Ethno-Nationalism'. *Ethnic and Racial Studies*. 7 (October): 342–59.

—— 1987. 'Ethnonationalism'. In Myron Weiner and Samuel P. Huntington (eds) *Understanding Political Development*. New York: Little, Brown. Reissue 1994. Prospect Heights, IL: Waveland Press: 196–220.

—— 1991. 'From Tribe to Nation'. *History of European Ideas*. 13(1–2): 5–18.

Deutschland-Nachrichten 1991. 'Genscher: Völkermord an Kurden verhindern'. 19 April.

Harris, Peter and Reilly, Ben (eds) 1998. *Democracy and Deep-Seated Conflict: Options for Negotiators*. Stockholm: Institute for Democracy and Electoral Assistance.

Henk, Dan and Metz, Steven 1997. *The United States and the Transformation of African Security*. Carlisle, PA: US Army War College.

Heraclides, Alexis 1991. *The Self-Determination of Minorities in International Politics*. London: Frank Cass.

—— 1992. 'Secession, Self-Determination, and Nonintervention: In Quest of a Normative Symbiosis'. *Journal of International Affairs*. 45(2) (Winter): 399–420.

Kelman, Herbert 1997. 'Social-Psychological Dimensions of International Conflict'. In I. William Zartman and J. Lewis Rasmussen (eds) *Peacemaking in International Conflict: Methods and Techniques*. Washington, DC: US Institute of Peace Press: 191–237.

Lake, David A. and Rothchild, Donald 1996. 'Containing Fear: The Origins and Management of Ethnic Conflict'. *International Security*. 21(2) (Fall): 41–75.

Loftus, John and Aarons, Mark 1994. *The Secret War Against the Jews: How Western Espionage Betrayed the Jewish People*. New York: St. Martin's Press.

MacNamara, Francis T. 1989. *France and Black Africa*. Washington, DC: National Defense University Press.

Marion, Georges 1998a. 'Plus de 10,000 manifestants: Mexico protestents contre le massacre du Chiapas'. *Le Monde*. 14 January.

—— 1998b. 'Mexique, les leçons d'un massacre'. *Le Monde*. 24 January.

McKinley, James C. 1998. 'General Tells Rwanda Court Massacre Was Preventable'. *New York Times*. 28 February.

Melson, Robert 1996. 'The Armenian Genocide as Precursor and Prototype of Twentieth Century Genocide'. In Alan S. Rosenbaum (ed.) *Is the Holocaust Unique?* Boulder, CO: Westview Press: 87–100.

Navaratna-Bandara, Abeysinghe M. 1995. *The Management of Ethnic Secessionist Conflict: The Big Neighbor Syndrome*. Aldershot: Dartmouth Publishing Co.

Preston, Julia 1998. 'Both Carrot and Stick Fail in Chiapas'. *New York Times*. 17 May.

Pruitt, Dean G. 1997. 'Ripeness Theory and the Oslo Talks'. *International Negotiation*. 2(2): 337–250.

Prunier, Gérard 1995. *The Rwanda Crisis: History of a Genocide*. New York: Columbia University Press.

Ramet, Sabrina P. and Coffin, Letty 2001. 'German Foreign Policy toward the Yugoslav Successor States, 1991–1999'. *Problems of Post-Communism*. 40(1): 48–64.

Rugman, Jonathan and Hutchings, Roger 1996. *Ataturk's Children: Turkey and the Kurds*. London: Cassell.

Saideman, Stephen M. 1996. 'The Dual Dynamics of Disintegration: Ethnic Politics and Security Dilemmas in Eastern Europe'. *Nationalism and Ethnic Politics*. 2(1) (Spring): 18–43.

Sciolino, Elaine 1991. 'Kurds: Stateless People with a 70-Year Grudge'. *New York Times*. 28 March.

Sisk, Timothy D. 1996. *Power Sharing and International Mediation in Ethnic Conflicts*. Washington, DC: US Institute of Peace Press.

Stedman, Stephen 1997. 'Spoiler Problems in Peace Processes'. *International Security.* 22(2) (Fall): 5–53.

Taras, Raymond C. and Ganguly, Rajat 1998. *Understanding Ethnic Conflict: The International Dimension*. New York: Longman.

Touval, Saadia 1994. 'Why the U.N. Fails'. *Foreign Affairs.* 73(5) (September–October): 44–57.

United States Security Strategy for Sub-Saharan Africa 1995. Washington, DC: Department of Defense Office of International Security Affairs (August): 3.

Wallensteen, Peter and Axell, Karin 1994. 'Conflict Resolution and the End of the Cold War, 1989–93'. *Journal of Peace Research.* 31(3) (August): 333–349.

11 Religion and nationalism in the First World

John Coakley

Introduction: religion and society

It is now three decades since Walker Connor warned us that 'ethnic strife is too often superficially discerned as principally predicated upon language, religion, customs, economic inequality, or some other tangible element' (1972: 341), and more than two since he suggested that this warning has particular application in respect of studies of nationalism in Europe (1979: 40–41). That scholars have sought at least partial explanations of ethnonationalism in 'objective' factors of these kinds is hardly surprising, since this pursuit is part of the stock-in-trade of the social scientist; but, as Connor points out, our expectation of success must be realistic – and low. It is nevertheless the case that some relatively measurable human characteristics, such as language, have a powerful impact on ethnonational sentiment, and an enormous body of literature has engaged in further analysis of this relationship.[1] The object of the present contribution is to explore the significance for ethnonationalism of another factor, religion – one to which much less attention has been given in the literature.

This imbalance is not particularly surprising given the fact that ethnonationalism commonly has a linguistic basis. Conversely, linguistic tension almost always has an ethnonational dimension (though there are a few exceptions, such as Ireland, Norway and Greece).[2] By contrast, many of the sharpest religious-type conflicts (such as those in several contemporary Islamic societies) are not at all obviously ethnonational in character. Europe's most bitter 'religious' wars took place in an age that would conventionally be seen as pre-national, and their echoes continue into the contemporary period, most of them still devoid of ethnic content. It is clear that in the twentieth century most religious conflicts in Europe were not ethnonational in nature, and that most ethnonational conflicts did not have a significant religious dimension.

As the Introduction to this volume reminds us, the study of nationalism has been seriously challenged by definitional confusion; similar difficulties beset the study of religion. One of the biggest challenges is the central term itself. Recourse to a classic – but by no means uncontroversial – definition offers at least a stop-gap solution. Emile Durkheim (1915: 47) defined religion as 'a unified system of beliefs and practices relative to sacred things, that is to say, things set apart and forbidden – beliefs and practices which unite into one single moral community called a Church, all those who adhere to them'.[3] This draws attention to the combination of belief and ritual that lies at the centre of the concept of religion. It also takes us a little further. Ritual is not exclusive, in that an individual may participate (at least externally) in the ceremonial aspects of different religions, for example by attending the mosque on Friday, the synagogue on Saturday and church on Sunday. But subscription to more than one set of religious beliefs is much more difficult: in their finer theological points, Islam, Judaism and Christianity are incompatible.

In exploring the character of religion further, it is instructive to bring to bear a perspective that has been utilised in the study of the relationship between *language* and the state; the similarity of linguistic and religious communities is, indeed, sometimes explicitly noted (Kloss 1969: 31–34). Approaches to the analysis of the spatial dimension of language can resemble strikingly approaches to the spatial dimension of religion. The framework adopted by Jean Laponce (1987) in his study of language and territoriality shares certain distinctive features with that of Chris Park (1994) in his study of the geography of religion. From the sets of questions that both address, it is possible to abstract a set of three more general questions: about the nature of religious differentiation, the normative content of religious belief and its political implications, and the spatial distribution of religious groupings and its societal consequences (including those for ethnonationalism).

The first question arises from the fact that religious belief varies qualitatively within the individual. Membership of a religious denomination may be easily measurable in terms of participation in an inauguration process such as baptism, but this will tell little about intensity of commitment, and individuals may opt out entirely from membership of *any* religious group.[4] By contrast, mastery of language is virtually a requirement of the adult human condition and, unlike religion, its importance has increased over time. There are few circumstances where it is possible for an individual to 'opt out' of language; indeed, the modern citizen needs not only oral fluency but also command of the written language, and one's life chances are strongly influenced by one's linguistic competence. The frontiers between languages in the oral domain (for example, between Norwegian and Swedish) may, of course, be gradients rather than lines; but written norms are more clearly differentiated. It is also true that adherence to language is much less exclusive than adherence to religion: additional languages may be learned with more or less difficulty, though in most cases a single language, the mother tongue, will also be the language of everyday use, with other languages consigned to a subordinate position. There are circumstances – admittedly, not many – where simultaneous commitment to two religions is possible. Shintoism and Buddhism, for instance, are said to comprise respectively 79 per cent and 75 per cent of the population of Japan.[5] The great Western religions can and do form a blend with various folk religions and beliefs in certain societies, just as Christianity in early modern England was able to accommodate, however uncomfortably, magic, witchcraft and astrology (Thomas 1973). The reality is that language has grown in importance as society and the state have developed: the competent individual *must* be fluent in at least one language. The significance of religion for the individual has diminished at the same time: as states have forsaken their religious trappings, even external conformity has become less important, and wide variations in intensity of religious commitment have evolved.

The second point at which the character of religion departs from that of language lies in the political domain. Both religion and language may be described as systems in which symbols are shared for purposes of communication, but in its developed sense this is *par excellence* a characteristic of language. Yet, no matter how elaborately developed a language is, it remains in an important sense politically neutral. In all languages, particular words, phrases, stories or corpuses of literature may be redolent with political content; but this is socially generated, and not inherent in any particular language. Politically alternative words and phrases exist (or may be coined), and alternative stories and texts may be created. Language is, then, simply a medium; but it may incidentally be the bearer of a powerful political message. One of the more important types of such message is the religious one. Unlike language, religion can rarely be said to be politically neutral. The teachings of many of the great world religions (such as Islam and the main strands of Christianity) have clear public policy implications, sometimes vigorously expressed. Other groups (such as Mennonites) may seek to opt out of the political world, but this, far from being a politically neutral position, is likely to lead to conflict with the state. Even religious systems that are apparently passive politically (such as Confucianism) may be *de facto* supportive of the political regime, simply by occupying a space that would otherwise fall to alternative and potentially hostile religious perspectives.

The third contrast between religion and language relates to their capacity for boundary maintenance. Purely personal and individualistic forms of religion may and indeed do exist but a language requires a minimum of two adherents, and in practice languages require large communities. Geographical isolation may ensure the continued existence of small language communities, but in the modern world linguistic survival depends on critical mass: the community must possess the demographic resources to survive disruptive patterns of migration and leakage through exogamous marriage. Furthermore, it must also possess the sociolinguistic resources to resist the threat of assimilation by more powerful linguistic communities; this implies not just a high degree of linguistic development (in the sense of standardisation of syntax and orthography, and elaboration of vocabulary) but also a wide measure of use by economic, social, cultural and political élites. The development of the modern state has placed a particular premium on certain languages: those associated with the state tend to enjoy a very considerable advantage, and if, as is the case in most states, there is a single official language, fluency in this language is an imperative (even to those who wish to resist it). In the case of religion, the trend over time has been precisely the reverse. When religion and politics were integrated, political community required religious conformity, and the European principle *cuius regio, eius religio* found its echoes in other parts of the world. But the separation of church and state legitimated adherence to minority religions, or to none, preparing the way for the complex pattern of religious adherence or non-adherence that is now so characteristic of the Western world. As religion was relegated to the private sphere, in other words, religious pluralism became a realistic possibility, and members of diverse religious communities could coexist peacefully. It should also be pointed out that, like languages, religions may be internally differentiated (with theological tendencies corresponding to dialects), but they may also have extensive external links (the ecumenical movement, for instance, linking the Christian denominations, or the more ambitious global efforts to find common pan-religious moral principles). This is not to say that spatial considerations have become irrelevant. For those to whom access to religious buildings and services is important, residence close to a cluster of co-religionists is a practical consideration (since this is the only realistic way in which a church infrastructure can be provided); but there is no powerful impetus towards integration along spatial lines of the kind that is characteristic of language.

In assessing the consequences of religion for ethnonationalism, the two last questions are arguably the most important, and they are addressed in the next two sections of this chapter, which deal respectively with the impact of religion on politics in general and its impact specifically in the area of ethnonationalism. The concluding section provides some illustrations of the religion–nationalism relationship, and offers some tentative generalisations. The discussion throughout aims to address these questions in a global context, but, due to the complexity of the subject, most illustrative material is drawn from Europe, the continent which the generalisations best fit.

The polity: religion and the public sphere

How, then, may we generalise about the political significance of religion? It has been suggested that the religious vision of the world can result in an ethical position consisting of four parts: *piety*, a set of cultural operating norms that constrain political leadership; *polity*, a model of the 'right order' of the political domain; *policy*, a distinctive understanding of those social and cultural programmes that are considered most appropriate; and *political action*, the formation, in certain circumstances, of specifically religious parties or movements (Stackhouse 1987: 411–413). This list dovetails neatly with four of the five aspects of secularisation identified by Donald Smith (1974: 7–17): *polity separation*, the termination of church–state links and of the religious identity of the state; *polity expansion*, extension of the state into sectors formerly regulated by religion; *political culture secularisation*, the replacement of religious by secular notions of politics; and *political process secularisation*, decline in the political saliency of religious élites (the fifth aspect, *polity dominance* or elimination of all areas of religious autonomy, in reality reflects an intensification of the other four processes and is being set aside here). The first four aspects identified by Smith may be seen as corresponding respectively with Stackhouse's four categories: polity, policy, piety and, more loosely, political action. These four features suggest a useful framework for the examination of the impact of religion on politics. The two gateposts of this framework are two ideal types – complete linkage of religion and the state, and complete separation of the two. But the interesting features are the cross-bars that span these: the conflicts that develop in the struggle to move from one of these positions to the other. The complexity of these movements depends on the confessional structure of the state, so we may look separately at the position in unidenominational and multidenominational societies.

Politics and religion in unidenominational societies

Complete fusion of religion and politics implies a unified church–state structure; regulation of all aspects of public policy by the state religion; full popular endorsement of the religious value system of the state; and absence of differentiation between religious and political élites. Full-bodied secularisation implies complete separation of church and state; unqualified secular control of public policy and complete absence of distinctively religious influence in this area; popular rejection of the notion that religious values should have a role in the public sector; and complete differentiation between civil and religious élites, with the latter entirely deprived of political influence. These two ideal types represent, of course, polar positions that are not necessarily represented in reality; indeed, it is difficult to find clear-cut examples of complete secularisation, as defined here, and impossible to find examples of the complete fusion of religion and politics. As with all ideal types, empirical cases are to be found in the interesting continuum that lies between these two extremes.

The key to religio-political tensions lies in the third and fourth areas, those of popular values and élite perspectives. Church–state separation and secularisation of public services imply the existence of a public opinion that has been substantially deconfessionalised and of secular élites with the resources to mount a successful challenge to clerical or religious privileges. This was the pattern of development in Catholic Europe following the French Revolution, in the course of which tensions between clerical and 'liberal' (or, in effect, anticlerical or secular) tendencies were crystallised. The political history of France, Belgium, Austria and Italy in the nineteenth and early twentieth centuries illustrates the evolution of this conflict, as the role of the Catholic Church as a state church was challenged, secular education, health and welfare systems were introduced and social legislation increasingly ignored the efforts of religious élites to provide guidance. Conflict between Christian democrats on the one hand and liberals and their left-wing secular tactical allies on the other became an enduring feature of the politics of these countries (Whyte 1981), and it was to be found, in different form, also in Spain and Portugal.

In the Protestant states of northern Europe, on the other hand, intimate links between the independent state churches and the political system survived until much later, even though the level of secularisation of public opinion has arguably proceeded further and the status of religious élites is less powerful than in Catholic societies. Yet the role of the Protestant state churches (in Scandinavia and the United Kingdom, for instance) has not been subjected to the same degree of secular challenge as that attracted by the Catholic Church elsewhere in Europe – perhaps because the very close links between church and state in these countries has resulted in a partial secularisation of the church itself, or because of

Protestantism's weaker institutional structure. Politically oriented Protestant religious movements tended in the past to have rather different priorities than their Catholic counterparts. Fundamentalist Protestants trusted the capacity of the individual to adhere to biblically enjoined sexual norms to a much greater extent than Catholics did, and did not share the zeal of the latter to ensure that this was protected by legislation; but, unlike Catholics, they utterly mistrusted the capacity of the individual to remain sober in the face of temptation from 'the demon drink' and to keep holy the sabbath, demanding legislative intervention in these areas, particularly in the era of prohibition and strict sabbatarianism.

It would be misleading, however, to see secularist pressure as the only source of political tension in the domain of religion. Resistance to secularism – an effort to slow down or roll back the separation of church and state – has been a distinctive feature of political mobilisation in many societies. Within Protestant societies, religious fundamentalist movements (however described) have sought to restore religious values to political systems criticised for ignoring biblical precepts, and in certain societies – notably Northern Ireland and, until recently, South Africa – conservative Protestantism has been a powerful force in shaping the character of public policy (see Wallis and Bruce 1986: 227–359); the southern United States could be added to this list. In recent decades conservative Protestantism has even found common ground with conservative Catholic movements in such areas as the struggle against the liberalisation of legislation in the area of sexual morality. Within many Islamic societies, the political appeal of fundamentalism has been even more striking, resulting in new linkages between the political and religious worlds (Piscatori 1986).

Politics and religion in multidenominational societies

Tensions between different perspectives on the appropriate place of religious values and symbols in political life are, then, to be expected in unidenominational societies, or in societies where a substantial haemorrhage from religious to secular (or agnostic, or atheistic) positions has taken place. But the potential for such conflict in bi- or multidenominational societies is even greater, since the range of distinct perspectives is likely to increase. There are reasons for expecting religions whose origins lie in the Middle East (Judaism, Christianity and Islam) to make more far-reaching demands on the political system than those whose origins lie in what is now India (including Buddhism and Hinduism): their belief in a single god with whose moral will the political system should comply contrasts with the emphasis of the eastern religions on societal harmony rather than the political order (Stackhouse 1987: 415). But different religions, and even different variants of Christianity, interpret God's will differently, leading to conflicting perceptions in each of the areas we have been considering. Thus, in denominationally divided societies the main religions compete for status in the political system; they may disagree on the colour of public policy and the character of service provision; they seek to protect and reinforce the value systems of their adherents; and their élites may be forced to jockey for positions of power and privilege.

While geography helps to keep religions apart today, history helped in the past. So central was the political role of religion in post-Reformation Western Europe that an extremely high level of conformity between political borders and religious frontiers was achieved. Nevertheless, by the nineteenth century a number of major bi-religious societies had emerged by different routes, all of them, incidentally, following a very similar pattern: a state imbued with Protestant values housing a predominantly Protestant population, but also acting as host to a significant Catholic minority. Germany, Switzerland, the Netherlands and the United Kingdom are the outstanding examples, but it is interesting to note that this pattern was reproduced outside Europe in such British colonies or former colonies as the United States, Canada, Australia and New Zealand. In each of these cases, religion played a role in political life comparable with that which it played in secularising Catholic states. Catholic élites, like the clericalist élites in France, Belgium and Austria, fought for the preservation of Catholic values, if necessary by carving out a distinct Catholic segment of the public sector (including the health and welfare systems but, in particular, the schools) which would be informed by distinctively Catholic values. Almost everywhere, this was a recipe for political conflict, with Protestants or secularists arguing that services provided and paid for by the state should be subject to state regulation alone, and rejecting demands for Catholic control.

Although these tensions were most visible in the case of the Protestant–Catholic relationship in Western Europe, they were not altogether absent elsewhere. Thus, in the twentieth century, Protestant Latvia found itself with a sizeable Catholic minority in the south; Orthodox Ukraine with a significant Uniate (Greek Catholic) minority in the west; Orthodox Bulgaria with a Muslim minority in the south; Orthodox Romania with Calvinist, Lutheran, Catholic and Uniate minorities in Transylvania; Muslim Albania with a small Catholic minority in the north, and a larger Orthodox one in the south; and the religious complexity of the former Yugoslavia is well known. Although some of these relationships had considerable potential for conflict, this was eclipsed by the threat from an ideology that dismissed religion as 'the opium of the people', and that posed a greater threat to religious élites than any of them posed to each other. The secularising (and, in the case of Albania, aggressively atheistic) menace of communism thus entirely eclipsed what might otherwise have become interdenominational differences of some political significance.

The nation: religion and boundary maintenance

The significance of religion for ethnonationalism is, as we have seen, widely acknowledged. It is frequently listed among the factors that are associated with nationalism in general, especially in the case of early nationalist movements. But one of the most perceptive of the founding fathers of the study of nationalism, Carlton Hayes, put his finger on a crucial dilemma three quarters of a century ago: nationalism may well have had religious roots in many cases, but it was itself remarkably similar to religion, constituting a new creed, with its own gods, rituals, theological system, holy days, and other classical accoutrements of conventional religion (Hayes 1926: 93–125). Indeed, many years later he was to entitle his summary of his lifetime's reflection on the subject *Nationalism: A Religion* (Hayes 1960). Other influential early scholars in the field came to a similar if less categorical conclusion (Kohn 1944, esp. pp. 23–24), or argued that nationalism, because of its own religion-like character, could easily find itself in conflict with conventional religion (Hertz 1944: 121). This interpretation remains of central importance to the present, with leading scholars reminding us that, as a 'political religion', nationalism has been associated with both the politicisation of religion and the messianisation of politics (Smith 2000). In this respect, nationalism can resemble other phenomena such as Marxism in being a type of secular religion, or 'civic religion' as it has been described (Llobera 1994: 134–137).[6]

The concept of a 'secular religion', however, is an oxymoron, at least if we are to start from a conventional definition of religion. Furthermore, as John Hutchinson (1994: 66–77) has pointed out, notwithstanding the extent to which nationalism depends on religion, certain intrinsic characteristics of the latter push in quite a different direction. Unlike nationalism, the great religions are universalistic and transethnic; their orientation is towards the spiritual world rather than towards this world; and their written languages have historically been 'dead' ones. How, then, can religion feed in to nationalism? Anthony Smith's perceptive analysis of the contribution of organised religion to the ethnonational process identifies three aspects of this relationship that are of particular significance: a close relationship, in many cases, between ethnic origin myths and religious belief; religious sectarianism as a potential support for nationalist separatism; and the contribution of a particular religion's organisational base, in terms of educated personnel and communication channels, to the nationalist project (Smith 1986: 34–37). This suggests a possible framework for further exploration of this relationship. Taking Smith's last point first and interpreting all three freely, we may identify three areas in which religion has an impact on ethnonationalism: social infrastructure, ideological roots and political organisation.

The social contribution of religion

The impact of religion on society is to be felt not merely in the areas of ideas and rituals; the dissemination of ideas and, in most cases, the management of ceremonies depend on the existence of a relatively sophisticated organisation. They also imply an effective communication system, one capable of disseminating a complex religious message, with a mixture of narrative and normative content, to all potential adherents of the faith. Of course, oral lore and family socialisation have a role to play, especially in local religions, but they need to be reinforced by other agencies in the case of the great religions. In many religions, the task of disseminating the precepts of the faith to the masses is carried out indirectly, through the services of preachers, priests or other intermediaries. But there are others where this need is seen as entailing, in turn, a requirement that members of the church be able to read. This is in particular a characteristic of what Gellner

(1997: 75–78) has termed 'Protestant-type' religions (the main Protestant faiths are indeed the most obvious examples of this concern).

The historical distinction between the Catholic and Protestant traditions owes much to the differences between these approaches. The Catholic Church, with its commitment to a moral code whose origins are said to lie in reason but to which access is most obviously provided by a hierarchical pyramid with parochial clergy at the bottom, bishops in the middle and the pope at the top, is, by comparison with the Protestant churches, a highly organised monolith. Protestantism, by contrast, with its commitment to personal salvation though the word of God, to which access is gained by reading the Bible, is much more decentralised and emphasises the importance of individual interpretation of the religious message (even if this encourages sectarian rifts). Profound consequences flow from this: for political cultural values, and even for educational priorities. It is striking, and by no means accidental, that the creation of mass education systems in Catholic southern Europe lagged significantly behind the pace of development in Protestant northern Europe, and wide gaps in literacy levels arose between these two types of society (and, indeed, between Catholics and Protestants within denominationally mixed societies).[7] These differences within Christianity are reproduced in the differences between the major world religions, which place greatly varying emphasis on the importance of literacy.

There is another respect in which the indirect consequences of different religions have implications for nationalism. Protestantism implies not just literacy, but, to a much greater degree than Catholicism, use of the vernacular language. Translation of the Bible into the languages of the people was a major project of the post-Reformation period, resulting in the provision of an extensive devotional literature. Protestant communities, such as the Estonians and the Latvians, thus found themselves with a more developed school system and a more extensive vernacular literature by the nineteenth century than their Catholic Lithuanian neighbours. Given the more recent vigour of Lithuanian nationalism, it is easy to forget that until World War I its pace of development was much slower than its Estonian and Latvian counterparts (see Loit 1985). In Europe's Celtic fringe, extensive state support failed to prevent the near-extinction of the Irish language in Catholic Ireland, and Catholic Brittany has experienced an even more dramatic process of assimilation (if not yet complete) to the French language; but the Welsh language, though it exists in the shadow of one of the world's most vigorous cultures, has been much more successfully maintained, with the democratic tradition of Protestant nonconformism offering significant assistance.[8] Factors other than religion were, of course, important in all of these cases.

Religions tend, then, to play a considerable role in breaking down barriers of communication between communities that adhere to the same belief system. At a very minimum, shared ritual and geographically transposable religious practice highlight similarities within the community of believers and differences between them and outsiders. The phenomenon of the pilgrimage in Catholic, Hindu, Buddhist and especially Islamic traditions reinforced this sense of community of belief (Barber 1991). But the solidarity of the religious community is also enhanced by dissemination of shared religious values and perhaps by the use of a common language (even if this is confined to a clerical élite). The importance of Latin, Old Church Slavonic, Arabic, Hebrew and Sanskrit respectively for the Catholic, Orthodox, Islamic, Jewish and Hindu faiths illustrates this point. In addition to establishing common reference points for believers, religions also, in varying degrees, provide a vital organisational infrastructure: a network of clergy imbued with a commitment to the central values of the faith and capable of acting as an effective medium for communication with the masses.

The contribution of religion in this respect plays a central role in preparing the path for nationalism: it has the capacity to provide essential organisational resources, ones whose penetrative power is a central ingredient in the formation of ethnic identity (Enloe 1980; Armstrong 1982: 201–206). But it must be emphasised strongly that there is nothing deterministic about this. In serving as facilitator of at least symbolic communication and as provider of a vital social infrastructure, religion may be paving a path for movements or ideologies that are *incompatible* with nationalism – ones that, for example, are international in character. This aspect of religion prepares the ground, then, for ethnonationalist mobilisation; but this ground may be occupied by alternative political forces.

The ideological contribution of religion

In assessing the ideological contribution of religion to nationalism, it is important to revert to a long-standing distinction between two types of religion: the *universalistic* religion whose message, it is claimed, is valid for all humankind and which is open to engaging in proselytist or missionary activity, and the *ethnic* religion whose message relates to a specific group. Of course, not all ethnic religions are particularly supportive of nationalism: tribal or folk religions may have local or regional focuses, ones that impede larger-scale ethnonational integration. Like tribal languages or local patois, they tend to be seen by nation-building élites as dysfunctional to the ethnonational project and as, at best, dispensable. Of course, one person's region is another person's nation; but this is not the place to deviate into a discussion of the issues of scale and definition.

The importance of major ethnic religions for nationalism, however, is clear. Hinduism has been central to the growth and development of Indian nationalism (van der Veer 1994), and Shinto has played a major role in promoting Japanese nationalism (Brown 1955: 114–117; Fridell 1983). The role of religion in the Jewish nationalist movement and in contemporary Israeli nationalism is well known (see Cohen 1987: 42–63). The reasons for this kind of association are obvious: the sacred religious tracts are also revered national texts, and religious tradition and ethnonational myth are inextricably intermingled. By contrast, to the extent that they embrace missionary ambitions and realise their objectives of conversion over a wide geographical area, universalist religions undermine their own capacity to contribute to processes of nation formation. It does not follow that universalistic religions tend to promote only patterns of transethnic loyalty that conflict with ethnonational ones. There are three ways in which they may depart from their universalistic logic: by falling victim to doctrinal secession, to organisational fragmentation, or to frontier conflict. Although the second and to some extent the third of these processes belong to the political rather than to the ideological domain it is appropriate to discuss them at this point.

Doctrinal secession – withdrawal from the parent religion because of a conflict over fundamental religious beliefs – need not be associated with any kind of ethnonational protest, but it very frequently is. The Protestant Reformation itself is a good example: the reformers were in general geographically distant from Rome, and there was an important political dimension to their protest. In fact, there were several strings to this secession, with Lutheranism dominant in Germany and Scandinavia, Calvinism in the Netherlands, Scotland and parts of Hungary, and a distinctive variant, Anglicanism, in England. Earlier, even before the reformation, the Hussite secession, though ultimately crushed by the military and political might of the Habsburgs, provided Czech nationalism with an evocative historical myth that was rediscovered in the nineteenth century (at a time when almost all Czechs were Catholic). At the end of the eighteenth century, the Methodist secession from the Anglican Church was to find particular appeal in Wales, where it was of long-term significance for nationalism. Though less traumatic in impact than the divisions that were to emerge within Christianity, Tibetan and Theravada Buddhism were regional variants of one of the great religions of Asia, and were associated with ethnonational distinctiveness in their territorial domains. But perhaps the clearest example of all is the emergence of Sikhism out of Hinduism in the fifteenth century – a development that amounted, in effect, to the creation of a new ethnic religion (see Ahmed 1996).

Doctrinal secession led to organisational secession, but was not a precondition for this. Thus, the Reformation in Europe was associated not just with the rise of Protestantism but also with the rise of national churches. The new Protestant monarchies were entirely independent of each other, each constituting a separate church and sharing doctrinal perspectives and ritual practices in varying degrees. Their appearance was crucial in the development of state-centred nationalism in these countries. The phenomenon of galicanism in southern Europe – the attempt, especially in France, to establish organisational autonomy for the Catholic Church under the control of the king – was less significant, but not without implications for French nationalism. In Orthodox Europe, organisational secession was more politically loaded: in the last century of Ottoman rule, the Orthodox patriarchate of Constantinople was forced to recognise 'autocephalous' (in effect, independent) Orthodox churches in Greece (1850), Serbia (1879) and Romania (1885), and an independent Bulgarian exarchate was established in 1872 (Petrovich 1980). The trend has indeed continued into the more recent period: there were movements for the independence of the Macedonian Orthodox Church in the 1960s and of the Montenegrin Orthodox Church in the 1990s (Bruce 1996: 97).

The third set of circumstances in which religion may promote ethnonationalism arises at interdenominational interfaces. It frequently happens that major political borders fail to coincide with lines of religious division, leaving large minorities on the 'wrong' side of a border in terms of their religious affiliation. Some such minorities conform to pressures from their political rulers. Most of the Orthodox leaders of Polish Western Ukraine recognised the pope as their head in 1596 (becoming 'Greek Catholics' or Uniates), a change whose consequences are still to be felt in the Ukraine (Johnston 1992).The Orthodox Romanians of Transylvania followed the same path in 1697 (Oldson 1992). In these cases, later nationalist movements (Ukrainian and Romanian) had to cope with what was essentially a negative consequence of religion, which disrupted their unity (Hann 1993). But the consequences could also be supportive of ethnonationalism: for Polish Catholics in Protestant Germany and Orthodox Russia down to 1918, for Irish Catholics in the United Kingdom before 1922 and to some extent for Belgian Catholics in the Protestant Netherlands in 1815–30, the Catholic Church offered a reassuring bulwark against a hostile culture. The Orthodox minorities in the Balkans, already mentioned in connection with their struggle for autocephalous status, also had an interest in encouraging political ethnonationalism, and the two movements tended to reinforce each other (Jelavich and Jelavich 1977: 14–16).

There is a risk, in thus discussing the relationship between religion and ethnonationalism in the domain of ideology, of confusing cause and effect. The discussion above has focussed on the impact of religion on nationalism; but the symbiotic nature of this relationship should be borne in mind. Ethnic religion may well promote ethnonationalism, but ethnonationalism is also likely to encourage ethnic religion; and although the pursuit of autocephalous status may encourage political nationalism, it is also in part a consequence of the latter (just as linguistic differentiation may be a consequence rather than a cause of political separatism). Except in the case of ethnic religions, the processes just discussed *may* encourage nationalism, but they cannot fully define its contours: they may help to separate members of the nation from persons of other denominations, but they also link them with the rest of what is claimed to be a universal church. We need, therefore, to look further in accounting for the more intense patterns of ethnonationalism with which universalistic religions are sometimes associated.

The political contribution of religion

The discussion above of the impact of religion on nationalism in the ideological sphere has already taken us close to the issue of political organisation: the defence of religious values by clerical élites may, in certain geopolitical circumstances, encourage the endorsement of nationalism. This was, as we have seen, an important factor in the nineteenth century in the case of Irish and Polish nationalism (taking the form of defence of Catholicism against alien creeds), and in a much more complex way in the case of Serbian, Romanian and Bulgarian nationalism (where the Islamic Turkish political rulers posed little threat to their Orthodox minorities in the area of religion, but the Greek phanariot religious élites of the Ottoman empire were a rather more considerable cultural threat). Catholicism played a similar role in Quebec, where it helped to reinforce the identity of the Francophone community against Anglophone, Protestant Canada (Grand'Maison 1970; Guindon 1988).

But religion can play a more direct role in ethnonationalism even when it is removed from the context of its beliefs and practices: simple religious labelling can have significant ethnic connotations, and can play a classical boundary defining role of the kind discussed by Conversi (1999). It could be argued that being Irish, Polish or Lithuanian implies being Catholic; that being Russian, Bulgarian or Serbian implies being Orthodox; or that being English, Finnish or Estonian implies being Protestant. But these associations weaken as the intensity of religious belief weakens, as movement to other religions (or altogether out of religious adherence) proceeds, and as long-established immigrants of alien religious backgrounds seek assimilation. Nevertheless, the echoes of this image of an intimate link between religion and national identity persist, even in the case where it has by now become most tenuous, England.[9]

This linkage is especially problematic in the case of 'lapsed' adherents of the national religion. Does exiting from religious belief imply opting out of national identification? The answer, of course, is 'no'; national identification is much more emotionally profound and more complex in its origins than rational subscription to confessional principles. Atheistic Muslims in Bosnia and non-believing Protestants in Northern Ireland seem capable of the most intense forms of ethnic attachment. But in such cases there is typically a perception of loose affiliation – genealogical rather than ideological in character – to a denominationally defined community, to the ancestral faith, though consciousness of this may be other-imposed, or it may itself be a consequence and not merely a cause of conflict (Lynch 2000). Efforts to monitor ethnicity in Northern Ireland have thus moved away from religious adherence to identification with a culturally defined religious community as the only feasible way of taking account of the large numbers who now claim to have no religious belief.[10]

But if the identification of religion with 'the nation' is problematic for the confessionally uncommitted, it is much more difficult for those who subscribe to other faiths. In many cases, the weakening of the bonds between religion and nationality have eased this problem. English Catholics were once a suspect minority (Clayton and McBride 1998); now their ethnonational loyalty is generally accepted. But the evidence of certain other religious minorities (typically small, and geographically marginal) is instructive. Can one be a Protestant Pole, a Protestant Lithuanian, an Orthodox Estonian or a Muslim Bulgarian provided one's mother tongue is that of the majority? Not, apparently, in all cases. Thus we find a tendency, at least in the past, for Protestants in Polish Masuria to identify as 'Masurs' or even as Prussians or Germans rather than Poles (Blanke 1999); for Protestants in Lithuanian Klaipeda to identify as 'Memellanders' rather than Lithuanians (Misiunas 1968); for Orthodox residents near Estonia's eastern frontier to be described as 'Setus' rather than Estonian (Hurt 1904; Jääts 2000); and for Muslims in Bulgaria's Rhodope Mountains to be described as 'Pomaks' (Apostolov 1996; Konstantinov 1997) – even though these groups traditionally spoke, respectively, dialects of Polish, Lithuanian, Estonian and Bulgarian.

We do not need to rely on the dramatic cases of Northern Ireland or former Yugoslavia, then, for evidence of the capacity of religious differences to promote ethnic differentiation: there are circumstances where religious denominational and ethnic boundaries seem entirely to coincide. It has even been suggested that nationalism has been assisted in the past by variations in intensity of belief in unidenominational societies. The images of the Catholic Bretons remaining true to the faith of their fathers in secular France, of the religious zeal of the Catholic Flemish within secular Belgium and of the traditional Catholicism of the Slovaks within secular Czechoslovakia, for instance, are said to have had some impact on Breton, Flemish and Slovak nationalism, and an image of this kind occasionally flickers elsewhere, as in the case of the Basques.

There is, however, a more fundamental factor that commonly underlies apparently denominationally based nationalism: religion may be a surrogate for some other characteristic, such as ethnic or at least regional origin. Thus, in Northern Ireland being a Protestant is not simply a matter of religious belief: it evokes memories of the British heritage among those who see themselves as descendants of seventeenth-century Scottish or English colonists, and acts as a badge of differentiation in respect of the 'native Irish' Catholic population with its indigenous Gaelic roots. In the Balkans, the gap between Croats and Serbs, which divides a single linguistic community, coincided with the long-established frontier between the Habsburg and Ottoman empires, whose Christian populations became divided in loyalty between Rome and Constantinople (with the descendants of those Serbs who converted to Islam constituting a third group, the ethnic Muslims). Before the establishment of independent Poland and Lithuania, the Masurs and Memellanders had been separated for centuries from the main areas of Polish and Lithuanian settlement through their political and administrative inclusion in Lutheran East Prussia. The Setus, though speaking Estonian, had lived for centuries in Russia proper, just outside the boundary of the Baltic provinces. Outside Europe, East Timorese nationalism set a predominantly Christian population against its Islamic Indonesian rulers, but the legacy there of long-established Portuguese rule that helped solidify the frontier between East Timor and the west of the island (and, indeed, the rest of Indonesia), with its Dutch heritage, was, perhaps, the critical factor.

In each of these cases, then, religion pointed to a long history of separate paths of geopolitical orientation; it was seen as a marker of the ethnic community to which one belonged. These examples might be multiplied if we were to include cases where ethnic communities are defined not only in religious denominational terms but also linguistically. In Sri Lanka, the two sides also compete in terms of origin myths – the issue of who first settled the island. In Israel, the conflict owes much of its bitterness to similarly conflicting settlement myths. The capacity of religion to function as an agent of political activism in these instances may be seen as a special case of its more general potential as an instrument of mobilisation: it offers political élites a powerful weapon in generating committed mass support, especially to the extent that it promotes values of self-sacrifice and group solidarity in respect of other religious groups (Hasenclever and Rittberger 2000).

Conclusion: religion and conflict

This chapter has argued, then, that religion has had a major impact on politics in a number of respects: through its historical linkage with the world of politics, as expressed in the image of the traditional monarch who personified the union of political and religious life; by moulding the shape of public policy; by providing a cadre of competent élites; and through its contribution to mass political culture. With political modernisation and the growth of secular values, strains between clerical and secular priorities were fought out in a number of domains, with different outcomes in different contexts. But while this aspect of religion – the political implications of the religious message and the societal consequences of religious organisation – may have been of some significance for ethnonationalism, there are other aspects of religion whose role is even greater. Religion can play a major role in the creation and maintenance of ethnonational boundaries when the religion in question is an 'ethnic' one; but universalistic religions can also play this role. The reality is that the spatial boundaries of such religions frequently cut across established political borders, creating zones of potential conflict and denominationally distinct pockets. In these circumstances, religion may acquire considerable ethnic significance, and it may act as an effective ethnonational marker by coinciding with some other defining characteristic – whether this is more visible, as in the case of language, or, more importantly, less visible, as in the case of descent or region of origin.

When we turn to look at the capacity of religion to lead to violent political conflict the balance sheet is rather more modest than that associated with, say, language-related conflict. One survey of the position in the early 1990s identified 20 such conflicts (though one of these was in reality a cluster of five). Only two of these were categorised as non-ethnonational in character, deriving from attempts to enforce strict religious law (in Sudan and Afghanistan). Of the remaining cases, three were identified as ones where religion was closely linked to efforts to establish independence or an ethnic state (Tibet, Palestine and the Punjab), and in the remaining 15 cases religion was identified as only one factor in the conflict, alongside territorial, political and ethnic issues. The instances where religion was regarded as most significant included Kashmir and four other Indian cases, Northern Ireland, Bosnia, Sri Lanka and Lebanon (O'Brien and Palmer 1993: 66–67). Additional cases could be added to this list if we move to a different time period.

		Salience of religion	
		High	Low
Salience of language	High	Bulgaria Sri Lanka Israel	Spain Finland Belgium
	Low	Northern Ireland Bosnia Lebanon	Great Britain South Africa Rwanda

Figure 11.1 Religion, language and ethnic conflict: a typology.

The relationship between conflicts of this kind and linguistic-based conflict is summarised in Figure 11.1. This assumes that states where ethnonational conflict is an issue may be classified along two dichotomous dimensions: high or low salience of religion, and high or low salience of language (an obvious but functionally necessary oversimplification). Cross-classifying these gives us four categories. The easiest category to illustrate is the top right-hand one. There are so many cases of ethnonational conflict based primarily on language that it is easy to find examples, and those included here draw attention to three different types of context: a state dominated by one linguistic group but with indigenous minorities (Spain); one dominated by one linguistic group but with a minority related linguistically to an adjacent state (Finland); and one straddling the line of division between two major languages (Belgium). There are also many instances where linguistic divisions are reinforced by religious ones, and the three examples given here again illustrate different contexts: in Bulgaria the Bulgarian-Orthodox versus Turkish-Muslim division is the predominant one (if we leave aside the Pomaks); in Sri Lanka the Sinhalese-Buddhist versus Tamil-Hindu division is the most obvious, but the Tamil-speaking Muslims constitute an important additional group; and in Israel and the territories it occupies the Hebrew-Jewish versus Arabic-Muslim is the major line of conflict, but there are non-Hebrew-speaking Jews on one side and non-Muslim Arab speakers on the other.

The number of cases available for the bottom left category is low, and the three listed again illustrate rather different patterns: the bipolar pattern of Northern Ireland (though there are significant internal divisions on the Protestant side); the trilateral pattern of Bosnia (where the ethnonational focus of two of the three groups lies outside the territory); and the complex position of the Lebanon (with deep divisions within both the Christian and Muslim sides). Finally, it is difficult to find cases for the bottom right category, where ethnonational identification does not have a clear-cut linguistic or religious basis, and the instances given illustrate the problem. In Great Britain, it is difficult to find either a linguistic or a religious basis for Scottish nationalism, though neither of these issues is absent; in South Africa language and religion were of central importance, but they have now been overshadowed by ethnonational tensions whose roots lie elsewhere; and in Rwanda the sources of the deep Hutu–Tutsi division lie in social rather than in linguistic or religious factors.[11]

This chapter began with a warning from Walker Connor about the risk of seeking to explain ethnonationalism in terms of 'objective' factors such as language and religion. While a good deal of evidence may be cited to show the close correlation, in many cases, between ethnonationalism and religion, explaining this relationship remains a fundamental challenge. It is, then, appropriate to close by recalling another of Connor's pieces of advice, one expressed at the very end of his major anthology, when he again warned students of nationalism of the subject's inherent complexity and of the need to treat as suspect 'rational' explanations of its nature (Connor 1994: 210). Religion is not a phenomenon to which the adjective 'rational' can comfortably be applied; but it is nevertheless a highly visible and clear-cut, if complex, social reality. Attempts to articulate its implications for nationalism, including this one, are likely to be imperfectly successful. In this, however, the project tackled in this chapter is little different from others in this subtle and fascinating subfield of the social sciences.

Acknowledgements

I would like to thank Padraic Conway, Kevin Howard and Tobias Theiler for comments on an earlier draft.

Notes

1 An account of this vast literature is both impossible here and in any case unnecessary; but see Fishman (1999) for an overview.
2 In Norway and Greece disagreement over linguistic norms (use of Nynorsk or Bokmål, or of Katharevusa or Demotic Greek) divided the community in the past, while in Ireland disputes between supporters and opponents of the revival of the Irish (Gaelic) language have taken place; but these tensions have been mild, and the opposing sides have clearly been drawn from the same ethnonational community.
3 For a critical discussion of Durkheim's definition, see Pickering (1984: 177–187); and for a more general discussion of the definition of religion see Aldridge (2000: 13–32). This approach is not incompatible with a broader 'social' understanding of religion, one that offers a crucial insight into Europe's post-Reformation religious conflicts (Thomas 2000).
4 Statistics regarding adherence to the major world religions are frequently provided in the same manner as statistics relating to languages, but this does not imply that the challenge in the two cases is the same. Park (1994: 36) lists the world religions as follows, in terms of percentage of the world population: Christians, 32.4 per cent; Muslims, 17.1 per cent; Hindus, 13.5 per cent; Buddhists, 6.2 per cent; and he lists six other religions, four groupings (such as ('tribal religions') and two non-religious groups (the non-religious, and atheists); see also Barrett (1982). Laponce (1987: 67–68) provides a similar listing in the case of languages, headed by Chinese, English, Hindi/Urdu, Spanish and Russian.
5 Calculated from *Statesman's Yearbook* (2001: 920, 928).
6 This should be distinguished from the much more specific form of 'civil religion' that Fawcett (2000: 9–10) has identified in the case of Ulster Protestants and Calvinist Afrikaners, and which was expressed in such para-religious offshoots as the Orange Order and the Broederbond. This quasi-religious quality may also help to explain the phenomenon of nationalist martyrdom.
7 Lawrence Stone (1969: 77) summarised the difference between the two main religions in a memorable expression: 'The Catholics were fearful of heresy because of Bible study, whereas the Reformers were fearful of superstition because of lack of Bible study'; but for an alternative interpretation based on the German experience see Strauss (1984).
8 See Rokkan and Urwin (1983: 85–86), for a comparative political perspective; Durkacz (1983) explores the significance of religion in language maintenance in Ireland, Scotland and Wales; Broudic (1995) provides a general survey in the case of Breton and Lachuer (1998) draws attention to the ambiguous role of the Breton clergy in the nineteenth century. The more general role of religion in the development of nationalism in England and its neighbours is reviewed in Hastings (1997).
9 Discussion of the distinction between English and British nationalism is being avoided here; for a discussion of the political significance of religion in this respect, see Colley (1991).
10 See Fair Employment Commission for Northern Ireland (1998: 5).
11 On these cases, see respectively O'Leary and McGarry (1996); Malcolm (1994); Odeh (1985); McCrone (1992); Marks and Trapido (1987); Uvin (1998).

References

Ahmed, Ishtiaq 1996. 'Religious nationalism and Sikhism'. In David Westerlund (ed.) *Questioning the Secular State: The Worldwide Resurgence of Religion in Politics*. London: Hurst: 259–285.

Aldridge, Alan 2000. *Religion in the Contemporary World: a Sociological Introduction*. Cambridge: Polity Press.

Apostolov, Mario 1996. 'The *Pomaks:* a religious minority in the Balkans'. *Nationalities Papers* 24(4): 727–742.

Armstrong, John A. 1982. *Nations before Nationalism*. Chapel Hill, NC: University of North Carolina Press.

Barber, Richard 1991. *Pilgrimages*. Woodbridge, Suffolk: Boydell Press.

Barrett, David B. 1982. *World Christian Encyclopedia*. Oxford: Oxford University Press.

Blanke, Richard 1999. '"Polish-speaking Germans"? Language and national identity among the Masurians'. *Nationalities Papers* 27(3): 429–453.

Broudic, Fañch 1995. *La pratique du breton de l'Ancien Régime à nos jours*. Rennes: Presses Universitaires de Rennes.

Brown, Delmer M. 1955. *Nationalism in Japan: An Introductory Historical Analysis*. New York: Russell and Russell.

Bruce, Steve 1996. *Religion in the Modern World: From Cathedrals to Cults*. Oxford: Oxford University Press.

Clayton, Tony and McBride, Ian 1998. 'The trials of the chosen peoples: recent interpretations of protestantism and national identity in Britain and Ireland'. In Tony Clayton and Ian McBride (eds) *Protestantism and National Identity: Britain and Ireland, c. 1650–c. 1850*. Cambridge: Cambridge University Press: 3–29.

Cohen, Mitchell 1987. *Zion and the State: Nation, Class and the Shaping of Modern Israel*. Oxford: Blackwell.

Colley, Linda 1991. *Britons: Forging the Nation, 1707–1837*. New Haven, CT: Yale University Press: 19–45.

Connor, Walker 1972. 'Nation-building or nation-destroying?' *World Politics* 24(3): 319–355.

—— 1979. 'Ethnonationalism in the first world: the present in historical perspective'. In Milton J. Esman (ed.) *Ethnic Conflict in the Western World*. Ithaca, NY: Cornell University Press: 19–45.

—— 1994. *Ethnonationalism: The Quest for Understanding*. Princeton, NJ: Princeton University Press.

Conversi, Daniele 1999. 'Nationalism, boundaries and violence'. *Millennium: Journal of International Studies* 28(3): 553–584.

Durkacz, Victor Edward 1983. *The Decline of the Celtic Languages: A Study of Linguistic and Cultural Conflict in Scotland, Wales and Ireland from the Reformation to the Twentieth Century*. Edinburgh: John Donald.

Durkheim, Emile 1915. *The Elementary Forms of Religious Life*. Translated Joseph Ward Swain. London: George Allen and Unwin.

Enloe, Cynthia M. 1980. 'Religion and ethnicity'. In Peter F. Sugar (ed.) *Ethnic Diversity and Conflict in Eastern Europe*. Santa Barbara, CA: ABC-Clio: 347–371.

Fair Employment Commission for Northern Ireland 1998. *Profile of the Monitored Workforce in Northern Ireland: Summary of the 1998 Monitoring Results*. Belfast: Fair Employment Commission for Northern Ireland.

Fawcett, Liz 2000. *Religion, Identity and Social Change*. Basingstoke: Macmillan.

Fishman, Joshua A. (ed.) 1999. *Handbook of Language and Ethnic Identity*. Oxford: Oxford University Press.

Fridell, Wilbur M. 1983. 'Modern Japanese nationalism: State Shinto, the religion that was "not a religion"'. In Peter H. Merkl and Ninian Smart (eds) *Religion and Politics in the Modern World*. New York: New York University Press: 155–169.

Gellner, Ernest 1997. *Nationalism*. London: Weidenfeld and Nicolson.

Grand'maison, Jacques 1970. *Nationalisme et religion*. Vol. I: *Nationalisme et révolution culturelle*. Montréal: Beauchemin.

Guindon, Hubert 1988. 'The crown, the Catholic church, and the French-Canadian people: the historical roots of Quebec nationalism'. In *Quebec Society: Tradition, Modernity and Nationhood*. Toronto: University of Toronto Press: 94–111.

Hann, C.M. 1993. 'Religion and nationality in central Europe: the case of the Uniates'. *Ethnic Groups* 10(1–3): 201–213.

Hasenclever, Andreas and Rittberger, Volker 2000. 'Does religion make a difference? Theoretical approaches to the impact of faith on political conflict'. *Millennium* 29(3): 641–674.

Hastings, Adrian 1997. *The Construction of Nationhood: Ethnicity, Religion and Nationalism*. Cambridge: Cambridge University Press.

Hayes, Carlton 1926. *Essays on Nationalism*. New York: Macmillan.

Hayes, Carlton 1960. *Nationalism: A Religion*. New York: Macmillan.

Hertz, Frederick 1944. *Nationality in History and Politics: A Psychology and Sociology of National Sentiment and Nationalism*. London: Routledge and Kegan Paul.

Hurt, J. 1904. *Über die pleskauer Esten oder die sogennanten Setukesen*. Helsingfors: Drückerei der Finnischen Litteratur-Gesellschaft.

Hutchinson, John 1994. *Modern Nationalism*. London: Collins.

Jääts, Indrek 2000. 'Ethnic identity of the Setus and the Estonian-Russian border dispute'. *Nationalities Papers* 28(4): 651–670.

Jelavich, Charles and Jelavich, Barbara 1977. *The Establishment of the Balkan National States, 1804–1920*. Seattle: University of Washington Press.

Johnston, Hank 1992. 'Religious nationalism: six propositions from eastern Europe and the former Soviet Union'. In Bronislaw Misztal and Anson Shupe (eds) *Religion and Politics in Comparative Perspective: Revival of Religious Fundamentalism in East and West*. Westport, CT: Praeger: 67–79.

Kloss, Heinz 1969. *Grundfragen der Ethnopolitik im 20. Jahrhundert: die Sprachgemeinschaften zwischen Recht und Gewalt*. Wien: Wilhelm Braumüller.

Kohn, Hans 1944. *The Idea of Nationalism: A Study in its Origins and Background*. Toronto: Collier.

Konstantinov, Yulian 1997. 'Strategies for sustaining a vulnerable identity: the case of the Bulgarian Pomaks'. In Hugh Poulton and Suha Jahi-Farouki (eds) *Muslim Identity and the Balkan State*. London: Hurst: 33–53.

Lachuer, Valérie 1998. *L'état face à la langue bretonne*. Rennes: Presses Universitaires de Rennes.

Laponce, J.A. 1987. *Languages and their Territories*. Toronto: University of Toronto Press.

Llobera, Josep R. 1994. *The God of Modernity: The Development of Nationalism in Modern Europe*. Oxford: Berg.

Loit, Aleksander 1985. 'Die nationalen Bewegungen im Baltikum während des 19. Jahrhunderts in vergleichender Perspektive'. In Aleksander Loit (ed.) *National Movements in the Baltic Countries during the 19th Century*. Stockholm: Centre for Baltic Studies, University of Stockholm: 59–81.

Lynch, Cecelia 2000. 'Dogma, praxis and religious perspectives on multiculturalism'. *Millennium* 29(3): 741–759.

McCrone, David 1992. *Understanding Scotland: The Sociology of a Stateless Nation*. London: Routledge.

Malcolm, Noel 1994. *Bosnia: A Short History*. London: Macmillan.

Marks, Shula and Trapido, Stanley 1987. *The Politics of Race, Class and Nationalism in Twentieth-century South Africa*. London: Longman.

Misiunas, Romould J. 1968. 'Versailles and Memel'. *Lituanus* 14(1): 65–93.

O'Brien, Joanne, and Palmer, Martin 1993. *The State of Religion Atlas*. New York: Simon and Schuster.

Odeh, B.J. 1985. *Lebanon: Dynamics of Conflict: A Modern Political History*. London: Zed Books.

Oldson, William 1992. 'Tradition and rite in Transylvania: historic tensions between East and West'. In Richard Frucht (ed.) *Labyrinth of Nationalism, Complexities of Diplomacy: Essays in Honor of Charles and Barbara Jelavich*. Colombus, OH: Slavica: 161–179.

O'Leary, Brendan and McGarry, John 1996. *The Politics of Antagonism: Understanding Northern Ireland*. 2nd edn. London: Athlone Press.

Park, Chris C. 1994. *Sacred Worlds: An Introduction to Geography and Religion*. London: Routledge.

Petrovich, Michael B. 1980. 'Religion and ethnicity in Eastern Europe'. In Peter F. Sugar (ed.) *Ethnic Diversity and Conflict in Eastern Europe*. Santa Barbara, CA: ABC-Clio: 373–417.

Pickering, W.S.F. 1984. *Durkheim's Sociology of Religion: Themes and Theories*. London: Routledge and Kegan Paul.

Piscatori, James P. 1986. *Islam in a World of Nation-states*. Cambridge: Cambridge University Press.

Rokkan, Stein and Urwin, Derek 1983. *Economy, Territory, Identity: Politics of West European Peripheries*. London: Sage.

Smith, Anthony D. 1986. *The Ethnic Origins of Nations*. Oxford: Basil Blackwell.

—— 2000. 'The "sacred" dimension of nationalism'. *Millennium* 29(3): 791–814.

Smith, Donald E. 1974. 'Religion and political modernisation: comparative perspectives'. In Donald E. Smith (ed.) *Religion and Political Modernisation*. New Haven, CT: Yale University Press: 3–28.

Stackhouse, Max L. 1987. 'Politics and religion'. In Mircea Eliade (ed.) *The Encyclopedia of Religion*. Vol. 11. New York: Macmillan: 408–423.

Statesman's Yearbook 2001. *The Statesman's Yearbook, 2001*. London: Macmillan.

Stone, Lawrence 1969. 'Literacy and education in England 1640–1900'. *Past and Present* 42: 69–139.

Strauss, Gerald 1984. 'Lutheranism and literacy: a reassessment'. In Kaspar von Greyerz (ed.) *Religion and Society in Early Modern Europe 1500–1800*. London: George Allen and Unwin: 109–123.

Thomas, Keith 1973. *Religion and the Decline of Magic: Studies in Popular Beliefs in Sixteenth- and Seventeenth-century England*. London: Penguin [first edn 1971].

Thomas, Scott M. 2000. 'Taking religious and cultural pluralism seriously: the global resurgence of religion and the transformation of international society'. *Millennium* 29(3): 815–841.

Uvin, Peter 1998. *Aiding Violence: the Development Enterprise in Rwanda*. West Hartford, CT: Kumarian Press.

Veer, Peter van der 1994. *Religious Nationalism: Hindus and Muslims in India*. Berkeley, CA: University of California Press.

Wallis, Roy, and Bruce, Steve 1986. *Sociological Theory, Religion and Collective Action*. Belfast: Queen's University.

Whyte, J. 1981. *Catholics in Western Democracies: A Study in Political Behaviour*. Dublin: Gill and Macmillan.

Part IV
Wider implications

12 Homeland making and the territorialization of national identity

Robert J. Kaiser

> The ethnic homeland is far more than territory. As evidenced by the near univer-
> sal use of such emotionally charged terms as the motherland, the fatherland, the
> native land, the ancestral land, land where my fathers died and, not least, the
> homeland, the territory so identified becomes imbued with an emotional, almost
> reverential dimension.
>
> (Walker Connor 1986: 16)

When Serb nationalist troops recently engaged in an ethnic cleansing campaign
against Albanians in Kosovo, the Kosovo Liberation Army – through the use of the
Homeland Calling fund – was very successful not only in convincing members of
the Albanian diaspora living in Europe and the United States to contribute large
sums of money for weapons and supplies, but also in recruiting forces from among
them to take up arms against the Serbs. During the six-week period in 1999 following NATO air-strikes, over 10,000 'ethnic Albanians professionals, laborers, and
hotel workers from the Balkans, Western Europe and the United States flooded
into Albania . . . .vowing to help the rebel army liberate Kosovo' (Rupert 1999). In
the words of Mati, an Albanian with US citizenship who left his construction firm
in New York and enlisted in the Kosovo Liberation Army (KLA), 'This is a fight for
all Albanians, wherever we're from' (Rupert 1999).

The 'call of the homeland' continues to resonate at the start of the twenty-first
century. It remains one of the most effective instruments in nationalists' efforts to
mobilize their members, even when those members no longer live 'at home'. The
homeland idea has certainly not lost its potency in an era of globalization and
increasing transnational migration.[1] Indeed, as Connor's work on ethnic homelands and diasporas demonstrates, the rising number of people living in diaspora
(i.e., outside their perceived ethnic homelands) has itself become a significant catalyst activating an exclusionary national territoriality among ethnonational
members of the homeland group. This in turn has worked to reinforce national
and homeland sentiments among diasporic communities toward their original
homelands and nations (Connor 1986).[2]

This chapter examines the ways in which homeland images, myths and symbols
have been used to nationalize space and territorialize national identity. In doing so,

it picks up on a number of themes raised by Connor in his exploratory work on perceptions of homelands, ethnonationalism and interethnic relations in the contemporary world system.[3] After a brief review of the reasons for the centrality of homeland making in nationalization projects, the chapter focuses on the instruments through which national homeland images are constructed, maintained, and communicated to populations undergoing nationalization. In the final section, the chapter assesses the impact of globalization, transnationalism and the rising numbers of people living in diaspora on national homelands and territorialized nations.

Homeland making

The process of homeland making, the role of territory and territoriality in nationalization projects, and the relationship between exclusionary claims to places as homelands and interethnic conflict have been all but ignored in the scholarly literature on nationalism. If the term homeland is dealt with at all, it tends either to be used as a synonym for state or country of origin, or alternatively to be taken for granted as the historical spatial container of equally unproblematized ethnic groups. This latter use of the term is found not only in modernist works whose authors tend to dismiss both ancestral homelands and ethnic groups as anachronistic things of the past,[4] but also in ethnographic works on indigenous peoples whose authors tend to treat homeland and ethnic identity as unchanging and almost invariably positive phenomena until the evils of capitalism, 'modernization' and Westernization – usually in the form of imperialism or neoimperialism – made their appearance (Gupta and Ferguson 1997: 43–45).

If the scholarly literature on nationalism has tended largely to ignore homelands, they are much more prominently featured in the popular press and in nationalist discourse. Nationalists mobilize myths and images of a primordial homeland to reinforce the depiction of the nation as an ancient community of belonging; an organic singularity 'rooted' to a particular place.[5] An alternative nationalistic narrative represents the homeland as a sacred place set aside by God for the nation, now represented as God's 'chosen people'. Narrating nation and homeland in this way naturalizes the linkage between blood and soil, and so strengthens the legitimacy of nationalist claims to the land itself, at least among in-group members. The ancestral homeland is not only portrayed as the geographic cradle of the nation, it is also depicted as the only place where the nation truly belongs, as the one place where it can survive and thrive in the future (Kaiser 1994). The homeland thus tends to be perceived by members of the nation as exclusively theirs, consigning all nonmembers to the status of foreigners or outsiders who do not properly belong. Connor (1986) rightly identifies those out-of-place ethnic Others as diasporas who are unlikely ever to feel truly 'at home'. Though at first glance the relationship seems paradoxical, given this definition, it should perhaps not be surprising that the rising number of people living in diaspora in recent years corresponds with the increasing utilization of exclusionary homeland discourses in nationalist movements.

Although homelands are most often depicted as politically neutral, cultural spaces that are both 'natural' and 'eternal', in reality homelands are politically constructed places toward which the population is territorialized. Homelands are constructed to instill not only a sense of spatial identity or emotional attachment to an ancestral homeland among the population being territorialized, but also a sense of exclusiveness (Kaiser 1994). Homeland making is thus inseparable from nationalization, defined here as the politicization and territorialization of the population represented as the indigenous or autochthonous ethnic community. Homelands and homeland making need to be seen for the dynamic, integral parts of nation making that they are, rather than as objective historical facts, as natural and eternal parts of the ethnocultural landscape which nationalists simply utilize in their favor or seek to overcome.

The pervasive representation of homelands as ancient if not primordial places belies the recency of homeland making itself. It is not difficult to show objectively that a sense of homeland toward geographically expansive national motherlands or fatherlands is a modern social construct, an 'invention of tradition' (Hobsbawm and Ranger 1983). Prior to the late nineteenth century, an overwhelming majority of the population throughout the world lived highly localized lives, and homeland – if the term was used at all – referred to the locale of one's birth (Weber 1976; Kaiser 1994). The primordialist images of ancestral national homelands produce a striking disjuncture with the reality of life and the relationship to land and identity experienced by the vast majority of the population, and raise serious questions as to how primordial homeland images can work to mobilize popular support for nationalist movements. Why do these emotional appeals to the ancestral homeland resonate, when they are of such recent vintage?

To answer this question, I do not intend to devote serious attention to the question of why nationalistic élites construct such images of primordial homelands. Instead, this chapter focuses attention on the representations of places as national homelands that resonate at a popular level, because 'nationalism is a mass phenomenon, and the degree to which its inciters are true believers does not affect its reality. The question is not the sincerity of the propagandist, but the nature of the mass instinct to which he or she appeals' (Connor 1994: 198). In examining national homeland making and the construction of a mass-based homeland consciousness, this chapter investigates the mutually constitutive ways in which national homelands are socially constructed and nations in turn are territorialized.

Nationalizing space/territorializing the nation

Homelands do not come ready-made, but rather are the outcomes of the 'national construction of social space' (Williams and Smith 1983). Nationalism is fundamentally an ideology and political action program designed to convert land into national territory.

Whatever else it may be, nationalism is always a struggle for control of land; whatever else the nation may be, it is nothing if not a mode of constructing and interpreting social space. Quite often, the territorial dimensions of such struggles are reduced to crude economic or sociobiological factors which stress the conflict over scarce resources like land and minerals, or the need to satisfy a species-wide 'territorial imperative,' such as Ardrey (1960) posits. But 'the land' occupies a much more pervasive place in the ideology and enterprise of nations and nationalism, and manifests itself in ways that go far beyond such simple explanations, being intrinsic to the very concept of a national identity (Williams and Smith 1983: 502).

First and foremost, this conversion of land into a national ancestral homeland must occur internally, in the perceptions of the group being nationalized. [6] This territorialization of the nation is not a one-time change resulting in a static end state (i.e., the territorialized nation), but is a dynamic process through which homeland images are constructed, contested and negotiated within a set of parameters accepted by all competing voices within the nation. This is truly the primary purpose of nationalism – to construct and maintain the past, present and future images of nation and homeland within a set of mutually understood and accepted parameters over time, so that members of the nation and homeland being made perceive both as 'natural' and 'eternal'. This territorial bounding and perceptual binding of nation to homeland or 'blood' to 'soil' is critical to nation-making, in that it delimits not only those people and places that belong within the nation, but also and perhaps more importantly marks off ethnonational Others that do not. Boundary making is an other-forming process, and plays a vital role in the construction of Us and Them. In this way, the goal of national territoriality – to secure the future of the nation by gaining control over the homeland – may be realized. Political control over the homeland itself, which is typically viewed as the principal goal of nationalism, is of secondary importance. It is merely a means to an end, since if the 'nation' politically controls 'its homeland' the task of national and homeland image construction, maintenance and stabilization is greatly facilitated (Kaiser 1994).[7]

Instruments of homeland making

Nationalists employ a wide variety of mechanisms in the social construction of national homelands. While to some extent the specific instruments of homeland making depend upon the ethnocultural, historical, socioeconomic and political contexts within which nationalization occurs, a number of homeland images, symbols and representations have been prominently featured by nationalists throughout the contemporary world system. Maps and other cartographic representations, motherland and fatherland images, symbolic national landscapes, and national monuments and commemorative sites all work to nationalize space and territorialize the nation. In addition, nationalists have employed localized place attachments in order to reterritorialize identity toward more geographically expansive notions of homeland.

Map-making, presenting a nationally particularistic image of place as homeland, is among the most widespread and persuasive of instruments.[8] Maps delimiting the boundaries of 'ancestral homelands' and the geographic extent of 'primordial nations', with sites of historical significance to the nation well marked, and frequently with text in the national language, all combine to create a powerful tool for re-imagining places as national homelands and peoples as nations. Maps of the national homeland help to naturalize and historicize the images being created of the 'primordial nation' and its intimate connection to the sacred soil of its ancestral homeland. Beyond this, the boundaries of the historic homeland have frequently been logoized and reproduced on stamps, flags, posters and in school textbooks to further cement this homeland image in the minds of the population being nationalized. Even in cases where cartographers are not nationalizers *per se*, the creation of maps and border delimitation can have a profound impact on homeland and nation-making. For example, British imperial cartographers drawing political borders around Siam unintentionally created a cartographic expression of the nation or 'geobody' within which a Thai nation could be imagined (Winichakul 1994).[9]

Along with cartographic representations, those engaged in nationalizing space also frequently personify the homeland with the invention of allegorical masculine and feminine characters. Motherland images (e.g., Mother Latvia, Mother Georgia, the Maid of Finland, Marianne), often depicted alongside logoized images of the homeland, reinforce a personal connection between the population and the land being nationalized, in an effort to weave together the two major elements of blood and soil in nationalist discourses. These symbols of nation and homeland appear to be especially prominent before national independence; afterward the symbols of state themselves (e.g., flag, anthem, constitution) tend to diminish their importance, and the initial purpose of motherland and fatherland images tends to be supplemented by alternative uses, such as promoting tourism and marketing consumer goods (Paasi 1996: 153–157).[10] In these ways, motherland and fatherland images become banal, and continue to do the work of nationalizing space by constantly 'flagging the homeland' (Billig 1995, Crameri 2000).

According to recent work on motherland and fatherland images (e.g., Hage 1996; Kristof 1994), representations of fatherland tend to be more nationally particularistic and ethnically exclusionary, and dominate nationalist discourse during national self-determination movements, or when nationalistic élites perceive the status of the nation in its homeland to be in jeopardy. This results in a hardening of borders between us and them, and between ours and theirs. Motherland images are more ethnically inclusive and tend to become more prominent following a successful national self-determination movement, as nationalist élites from the dominant group seek to create more harmonious interethnic conditions in an effort to gain the compliance – if not the outright support – of subordinate ethnic others living in the state.[11] However, even the more inclusionary motherland images that are constructed ethnically stratify society in such a way that the dominant status of the homeland nation is secured; motherland representations are discourses of hegemony (Hage 1996). For example, *Rossiya* is a more ethnically inclusive image of Russia as a multicultural state, and Rossiyan is promoted by the state as a civic national identity shared by members of all ethnic groups. However, at the core of this multicultural Rossiyan representation of the state lies the image of Russia as the homeland of ethnic Russians, who have a right to preferential treatment in 'Mother Russia' (Bokov and Alekseyev 1996: 56–57).

This (*Rossiyskaya*) ideology cannot fail to take into account the exceptional role that the Russian people play in Russia, both as a numerically large group and one that is found in all the territorial homelands of the peoples of Russia; consequently (the *Rossiyan* idea) must be an organic extension of the Russian national ideology – the Russian idea.

The Rossiya homeland narrative thus represents a hegemonic discourse that is designed to stabilize and strengthen Russia primarily as the homeland of ethnic Russians, where ethnic Others also belong, assuming that they know and accept their place as subordinate minorities.

In Kazakhstan, a 'multicultural' Kazakhstani identity or 'civic nation' is promoted by the state at the same time that policies and the changing interethnic relations of daily life are remaking Kazakhstan into a more ethnically exclusionary Kazakh homeland. At a more localized scale, the republic of Tatarstan within the Russian Federation is also creating a more inclusive motherland image of Tatarstan as the land of all *Tatarstanis*, while at the same time privileging ethnic Tatars in their own homeland. This duality of motherland and fatherland discourses is not a reflection of internal conflicts as to whether the state (or substate republic) should be a more ethnically inclusive or exclusive homeland. Rather, the motherland discourse of interethnic or 'civic' national identity formation is in reality a rhetorical device for consumption by foreign audiences and ethnonational Others in order to help stabilize interethnic relations in the state and enhance state legitimacy within the sovereign state system. In practical daily life these states – and most other multinational states for that matter – have favored more ethnically exclusionary fatherland reterritorialization policies that privilege members of titular national communities. The two homeland discourses work together to satisfy both the sense of exclusiveness that nationalists feel toward their homelands, and also the need for intra-homeland security and external legitimacy in the world system. However, when a choice must be made, exclusionary fatherland images predominate.

National poets, writers, artists and composers have also been significant agents in territorial nationalization projects through works paying homage to the homelands being constructed. Some of the images of homeland created in this way depict the land in all its variety (i.e., a 'unity in diversity' image). However, it is frequently the case that a particular landscape – one likely to evoke nostalgic feelings about the land, the people, and its past – is chosen as the symbolic representation of the homeland in its entirety. For example, in a recently published Russian history textbook appropriately titled *Our Homeland* (Borozheykina 1999), a chapter entitled 'Russia is my homeland' is filled with pictures of meadows and birch tree forests, transmitting the well-known Russian symbolic national landscape to fourth grade students. It is only in a subsequent chapter dealing with 'local homelands' that the diversity of physical geographic settings in Russia is displayed.[12] In this way too, Russia is represented primarily as the exclusive homeland of the Russian nation.

The creation of the symbolic national landscape of England and Englishness, an image well known inside and outside Britain, is described by Rose (1995: 106) as follows:

Images of place are central to ideas of Englishness . . . The way in which the land has been imagined as England has varied historically, but, as the nineteenth century progressed, England was more and more often being pictured in terms of a landscape still symbolically resonant today: a landscape of green rolling hills, shady nooks, copses, winding lanes and nestling thatched villages. The soft hills, small villages around a green, winding lanes and church steeples of the English southern counties came to represent England and all the qualities the culturally dominant classes desired.

The selection of symbolic national landscapes in homeland representations also frequently involves a conscious effort at differentiation from the symbolic landscapes and homeland images of ethnonational others. This is particularly likely if those national others are dominant and/or are perceived as a threat. For example, if England became symbolically associated with gentrified agrarian lowlands, the more rugged and barren

> West of Ireland came to symbolize the whole of Ireland to some Irish nationalists in the early twentieth century. Nationalist Irish writers initially developed a great interest in the region towards the end of the nineteenth century, partly because it was seen as the area least affected by the processes of Anglicization, but also because its bare and rugged landscape seemed to contrast so breathtakingly with the more pastoral landscapes through which contemporary England was imagined.
>
> (Rose 1995: 91)

Similar reasoning went into the selection of the mountainous regions of northwestern Wales as the symbolic national landscape of the Welsh ancestral homeland (Pyrs Gruffudd 1995).

The construction of national monuments and commemorative sites are also crucial to the success of homeland and nation making. The selection and commemoration of historic figures, events and sites help to ground the fiction of nation and homeland in specific places and times. Monuments in the landscape help to project an image of permanence onto the nation and its relationship to the land, and thus reinforce the imagery of primordialism and 'rootedness'.

In cases of national revivals, the linking together of history and territory is essential for the conceptualization of a land as a national homeland. The spatialization of historical myth and the mythologization of space in terms of history are two sides of the same cultural coin. The outcome is that space is invested with historical meanings and mythical associations, while history and memory are concretized as locations; memorial spaces and historical places make history visible and therefore tangible. In many cases, they are not intended by their builders or custodians to provide historical analysis – instead, their power of evocation lies in their ability to integrate historical myth into the texture of the landscape, to conflate history and geography and to weave historical memory into the spatial configuration of nationhood. In this capacity, sites of memory and history forge a national geography of historical myth (Azaryahu and Kellerman 1999: 111).

Both the selection of a symbolic landscape and the choice of historic figures, events and sites to commemorate are rarely uncontested; the national construction of social space is a process of contestation and negotiation, as various nationalist voices compete to have their image of homeland and nation attain dominance (Johnson 1995a; 1995b). This intra-national contestation does not end with the creation of a commemorative site or the selection of a symbolic national landscape, since each is reinterpreted to suit competing nationalist interests and perceived needs at different points in time. As an example of this, Edensor in his study of the commemorative sites to Robert the Bruce and William Wallace – who currently stand as the two most notable figures who fought for Scottish independence – notes that

> neither Bannockburn nor the Wallace Monument was originally designed to resonate with a separatist nationalism but, rather, were held to memorialize the qualities that Scotland had brought to the Union. Bruce and Wallace were thus imagined as embodying the military attributes of *imperial* adventurers.
>
> (1997: 180)

Even today, the meaning of these sites continues to be reinterpreted both by nationalists in charge of the official representations of these monuments and commemorative sites, as well as by the population that visits these sites. External events can also have a dramatic influence on the meaning and significance attached to historic figures and events. In the case of the Wallace Monument, for example, the movie *Braveheart* resulted in a dramatic increase in the number of visitors to the site, and undoubtedly altered the meaning of Scotland and Scottishness that many visitors brought with them (Edensor 1997: 177). Viewed in this way, the national construction of ancestral homelands must be seen as a dynamic, contingent and contentious process, rather than as an internally harmonious project that puts into place a universally accepted set of images and perceptions about the nation and homeland being made.[13]

Even while the meaning and image of homeland undergo modifications over time and space, a national ancestral homeland consciousness is stabilized and maintained in numerous subtle ways in everyday life – through flags, anthems, symbolic national landscapes depicted in various art forms, monuments, commemorative sites, in schools, in media, and by politicians in government (Billig 1995; Paasi 1999). This is obviously the case for members of the dominant state nations, whose political and cultural élites frequently control school curricula, media messages, and government. But it is also true for members of subordinate groups, whose subordination and/or 'foreignness' is 'flagged' just as pervasively. Feelings of being 'out of place' that are brought on by the exclusionary homeland discourses of the dominant state nation most often lead to feelings of homesickness or a longing for homeland among émigré members of ethnonational communities.[14] Among members of indigenous ethnonational communities living in areas perceived to be their ancestral homeland, even the 'banal nationalism' of the dominant group is likely to serve as a potent catalyst activating the national territoriality of subordinate group members, in a process that Hennayake (1992) refers to as 'interactive ethnonationalism'. For this reason, even though representatives of state-nations are able to dominate discourses of nation and homeland within the boundaries of the state, few have been successful in reconstructing and maintaining the state as a place with one and only one nation and homeland, i.e., the idealized nation-state.

In states that have expanded to incorporate the homelands of ethnic others, members of the dominant nation frequently come to perceive the territory of the entire state as their homeland. This was apparently the case in the USSR, where Russians during the 1970s and 1980s overwhelmingly identified their homeland as the Soviet Union in its entirety (Connor 1986). This sense of homeland remained in place even after the disintegration of the USSR; during the first half of the 1990s a majority of Russians living in Central Asia continued to say that their homeland was the former USSR (Chinn and Kaiser 1996). This obviously placed Russians at odds with scores of indigenous non-Russian groups living in the USSR, whose members had experienced a reterritorialization of identity toward particular republics as 'ancestral homelands' during the Soviet era (Kaiser 1994). In the Russian Federation today, élites affiliated with the state are seeking to reterritorialize Russian national identity toward the boundaries of the Russian state, and Russians outside the borders of the Russian Federation are officially treated as members of the nation living in diaspora (Kaiser 2001; Smith *et al.* 1998: 12–13). However, the image of the Soviet Union as homeland continues to resonate for many Russians even a decade after its demise.

It is also the case that there are some places even within the boundaries of the state toward which members of the state-nation do not feel a strong sense of homeland. For example, few Russians feel that the retention of Chechnya in the Russian Federation is worth the loss of Russian life. Even though the government was willing to engage in a bloody conflict from 1994–96 – mainly due to a fear that Chechen independence would result in the disintegration of 'Mother Russia', the war and the loss of Russian life were extremely unpopular among the Russian public. There were daily news reports of Russian mothers going to Chechnya to take their sons out of the army and *bring them home*. The 1999–2000 war in Chechnya was by contrast highly popular among the Russian public, and was crucial to Putin's rise to the presidency. However, this does not reflect a change in the Russians' perception of Chechnya as an inalienable part of Mother Russia. The popularity of the 1999–2000 conflict was due to the belief held by Russians and promoted by the government that Chechnya outside of Moscow's control poses a serious threat to the security of Russians in their homeland, a perception that was reinforced by the terrorist bombings of apartment buildings in Moscow and other Russian cities that were attributed to Chechen militants.[15]

On the other hand, areas beyond the borders of the state may also be perceived as integral parts of the national homeland. Serb nationalists under Milosevic sought to create a Greater Serbia through the gathering in (and ethnic cleansing) of pieces of the perceived Serbian homeland from Croatia and Bosnia. Croatian nationalists under Tudjman fought to retain the borders of the republic against Serbian encroachments while at the same time seeking to gain Croatian lands in Bosnia. Russian nationalists continue to argue for the need to reconnect at least Belarus, Ukraine and northern Kazakhstan, if not the entire former USSR, to Mother Russia. Jewish nationalists' homeland perception regarding the occupied lands; Armenian nationalists' feelings regarding Nagorno-Karabakh, not to mention Mount Ararat; Romanian nationalist claims to Moldova, and Hungarian nationalists' sense of homeland toward Transylvania, southern Slovakia and Vojvodina all indicate that nationalist perceptions of homeland do not end at the borders of the state within which that particular nation predominates.

The global sovereign state system is a world of nationalized places and territorialized nations, in spite of the fact that ethnically homogeneous nation-states are a rarity. It is a world system whose legitimacy rests on the naturalization of ethnonational and ethnoterritorial boundaries. The specific boundary lines of nation and homeland are subject to conflict and contestation within the nation and without. But this conflict and contestation occur only 'within the parameters that take nationhood for granted as the natural context of the universe' (Billig 1995: 87).

Localizing the nation/nationalizing localities

Identification with the territory of the state has typically been depicted as a process that supplants a more localized sense of place. This was particularly true during the 1950s and 1960s, when the modernization thesis held that a local sense of place became irrelevant with 'development' (Agnew 1987). The inappropriately labeled state-sponsored 'nation-building' was also seen as an assimilative process that made ethnocultural and geographic areas of origin obsolete. Connor's seminal work on this topic in 1972 provided conclusive evidence that interethnic mixing in urban industrial settings and 'nation-building' efforts by political and cultural élites in multiethnic states led people not to emphasize the similarities that bound them to ethnic others, but to stress the differences that made their ethnonational community distinct.

Although the modernization thesis and 'developmentalism' have lost their position as dominant social theories since the 1980s, the issue of geographic scales of identity, and particularly the role played by a local sense of place in the nationalization of space and the territorialization of the nation has been largely overlooked. The generally accepted position in studies of nationalism is that the local scale of identity gives way to a more geographically expansive national sense of homeland with nation making. This view of the loss of localized identity with national homeland making does not appear to accord well either with the intentions of nationalizers or with the experiences of the population being nationalized. Instead, a localized sense of place is frequently reinforced along with the promotion of images of a national homeland, and the most successful homeland making projects are those that work to interconnect local and national scales of identity – to localize the nation through the use of local symbolic landscapes, folklore, historical events and heroes in representations of the national homeland, while at the same time nationalizing localities through the standardization of language, national myths and histories throughout the territory of the homeland, and by siting national symbols, emblems and monuments in the localities being nationalized.

During the late nineteenth and early twentieth centuries, the development of a love of place toward one's locality and home region was frequently seen as a prerequisite for the development of a national sense of homeland. According to Paasi (1996: 138–139):

> The construction of an identity on the national scale did not take place independently of the production of identities on other territorial scales . . . Lofgren argues that the province or region has provided a micro-level model for patriotism: 'by learning to love your region – one part of the national whole – you prepared yourself for national feelings on a higher level'.

The belief that a growing love of one's locality and localized home region would strengthen a national sense of homeland was held by geographers throughout Europe at the turn of the twentieth century. For example, Helge Nelson, chair of the Geography Department at Lund University, Sweden, stated in 1913:

> The increased knowledge of the home-area will strengthen the feeling for it and make it warmer and richer. But the increased knowledge will also widen the eyes and let the home-area emerge as the small part in the big whole, in fatherland. Then the love of home area can grow to include all our land and people.
>
> (as quoted in Buttimer 1994: 162)

Support for the mutual reinforcement of locality, localized home region and national homeland all at the same time was also championed in Germany by Friedrich Ratzel, the preeminent political geographer of his time (Sandner 1994). This is not surprising given the recency of German unification and the felt need to co-opt localized and regional identities to the mission of German nationalism. *Heimatkunde*, or the knowledge of home areas, became a centerpiece of geographic education and textbooks in Germany by the end of the nineteenth century. The term *Heimat* itself, a premodern expression that had fallen into disuse, was resurrected for the purposes of conflating the existing localized sense of place with a sense of national homeland that political and cultural élites in the state sought to instill.

The idea of *Heimat* celebrated Germany's decentered structure as fully compatible with a forward-moving and modernizing nation. *Heimat* translated a more ancient sense of place into a modern sense of nation, suggesting that the boundaries of loyalty and affection between locality and supra-local state were not just unproblematic but nonexistent. A typical expression of such locally rooted nationalism was the 1909 declaration of a *Heimat* association in Schleswig-Holstein that it was not political but 'German national', with the goal of 'awakening the love of

Heimat and thereby also serving the larger Fatherland, in other words, doing the work of the nation' (Applegate 1992: 67). German national identity was also being grounded in the familiarity of local landscapes during the same time period beyond the boundaries of Germany proper, especially in Austria-Hungary (Judson 1996).

The importance of localized homeland identities in the making of nations and national homelands does not end, since nationalizing space and territorializing the nation are ongoing processes. As a recent example of this, emphasizing love of the local or 'little homeland' (*malaya rodina*) as a means through which Russians come to know and love Mother Russia has emerged as a major theme in newspaper articles, school textbooks, the construction of commemorative sites, and in films (Kaiser 2001). Ceremonies celebrating the love of local homelands, their famous native sons and daughters, as well as the historic events and even the physical geographic features for which they are known, are all seen as means through which love of Russia as the national homeland will be enhanced. Local patriotic song contests, frequently held in schools, and patriotic song festivals celebrating love of locality, were also prominently featured throughout the latter half of the 1990s. In these ways, pride in one's local homeland is being inculcated as part of national reterritorialization toward the Russian Federation as homeland. This celebration of local homelands was promoted to some extent even during the soviet era of developed socialism, when local place attachment had supposedly been overcome (Arutyunyan *et al.* 1992: 322–323). Since 1991, love of one's 'native place' (*rodnoy kray*) has become a significant aspect of national homeland-building.

The mutually constitutive way in which national homelands are localized while localities are nationalized is a critical topic for understanding the power of homeland images, myths and symbols to reterritorialize identity at both the local and national scales, and deserves much greater attention than it has received to date. In addition, national homeland images and identities are constructed and maintained not only through dialogues between the local and the national geographic scales, but also through the creation of global–national discourses. The global scale, and its relationship to homeland making and national identity, provides the subject for the final section of this chapter.

A postnational world?

During the 1990s, in the wake of the collapse of the socialist bloc of states and in anticipation of the coming millennium, an increasing number of authors have proclaimed the 'end of the world as we know it'. While some authors argue that the world political and economic system ushered in during the fifteenth century is about to end (Taylor 1996; Wallerstein 1999), others argue that globalization – frequently ill-defined – is leading to the demise of states and/or nations as power and identity become increasingly deterritorialized and transnational (Appadurai 1996; Basch *et al.* 1994). One strand of this research is reminiscent of the conclusions reached at the height of modernization theory's popularity, i.e., that the demise of states along with their deterritorialization is on the horizon (e.g., Herz 1957). The inaccuracy of earlier predictions has apparently not dissuaded several authors from making similar forecasts in the mid-1990s that the days of the state (usually inappropriately labeled the 'nation-state') are already, or at least nearly, at an end (Ohmae 1995; Guehenno 1995).[16]

The growing literature on cosmopolitanism, transnationalism and the rise of diasporic identities appears to predict a similar fate for nations, homelands and nationalism. Transnationalism is defined as 'the processes by which immigrants forge and sustain multi-stranded social relations that link together their societies of origin and settlement' (Basch *et al.* 1994: 7). The image of 'transmigrants' portrayed in this and other works on transnationalism is one of an internationally mobile population that is equally at home in two or more places. They maintain multiple homelands in the world, and 'take actions, make decisions, and develop subjectivities and identities embedded in networks of relationships that connect them simultaneously to two or more nation-states' (ibid.).

According to Basch, Appadurai, and others, transnationalism has also tended to engage the 'homeland' or sending states in new global scale or at least transnational efforts at nationalization, as they seek to retain the loyalty and resources of the new 'transmigrant' or diasporic communities. The decision taken by India's government in March 1999 to offer 'Persons of Indian Origin Cards' to individuals born in India but who currently hold citizenship in another country is only the latest example of this growing trend.[17] Basch cites this type of behavior as evidence of the deterritorialization of states, as sending states seek to include 'as citizens those who live physically dispersed within the boundaries of many other states, but who remain socially, politically, culturally, and often economically part of the nation-state of their ancestors' (1994: 8). On the other hand, Appadurai concludes that it is the nation rather than the state that has become deterritorialized as a result of globalization and transnationalism. 'Territory and territoriality are increasingly the critical rationale of state legitimacy and state power, while ideas of nation seem increasingly driven by other discourses of loyalty and affiliation – sometimes linguistic, sometimes racial, sometimes religious, but *very rarely territorial*' (1996: 48).

There are several problems associated with transnationalism and the predicted demise of nations, homelands and states, as portrayed in this literature.[18] First, the idea that transmigrants feel equally at home in their new places of settlement was challenged as early as 1986 by Connor, who found that diasporic communities in a wide variety of political, economic and cultural contexts were rarely if ever made to feel at home by members of the homeland nation, even if they were originally invited and welcomed in by the host states. More recently, Hage (1996) found that even in immigrant states such as Australia, which are relatively more accommodative of transmigrants, the non-Anglo-Celtic population – and especially recent non-European immigrants – were unable to acquire sufficient cultural capital to fully participate in their newly adopted home state and nation. Even if transmigrants wish to develop second and third homeland identities, it is almost certain that they will be made to feel 'out of place' by members of the nations that perceive these second and third places as their primary homelands.

Second, the claim that transnational migration represents a deterritorialization of national identity appears to be based on the faulty assumption that emigrating from one's national homeland is a reflection of (or results in) a deterritorialization of identity. Most of those living in diaspora did not leave by choice, and enter their new places of settlement not intending to fit in, but rather to return home as soon as possible. In fact, Safran, taking Connor's definition of diaspora as his starting point, uses group attitudes, values and beliefs about the homeland and return as the central criteria in his definition of diasporas as:

> expatriate minority communities whose members share several of the follow-
> ing characteristics: 1) they, or their ancestors, have been dispersed from a
> specific original 'center' to two or more 'peripheral', or foreign, regions; 2) they
> retain a collective memory, vision, or myth about their original homeland – its
> physical location, history, and achievements; 3) they believe that they are not –
> and perhaps cannot be – fully accepted by their host society and therefore feel
> partly alienated and insulated from it; 4) they regard their ancestral homeland
> as their true, ideal home and as the place to which they or their descendants
> would (or should) eventually return – when conditions are appropriate; 5)
> they believe that they should, collectively, be committed to the maintenance or
> restoration of their original homeland and to its safety and prosperity; and 6)
> they continue to relate, personally or vicariously, to that homeland in one
> way or another and their ethnocommunal consciousness and solidarity are
> importantly defined by the existence of such a relationship.
>
> (Safran 1991: 83–84)

These expatriate communities come bringing homeland images and identities with them into diaspora, and frequently attempt to reconstruct their homelands of origin in their new areas of resettlement (e.g., Ostergren 1988). Furthermore, the in-migration of ethnic others more often than not serves as a catalyst activating national territoriality in receiving areas, which tends to nationalize and territorial-ize the identities of both the indigenous population and the immigrants (Connor 1986; 1972; Kaiser 1994; Weiner 1978). As evidence of the latter, migrants return-ing to their homeland states after living in diaspora are frequently at the forefront of nationalistic organizations and movements upon their return (Chinn and Kaiser 1996). While transmigrants clearly represent distinctive (though not necessarily new) reconfigurations of the interaction between place and identity, the claim that either states or nations are deterritorializing as a consequence of transnationalism and transmigration is unfounded.

Third, there is a tendency in much of the transnationalism literature to use evi-dence from the United States and Western Europe, or evidence drawn from the lives of intellectual cosmopolitan élites (frequently the academics doing the writing) as if it was universally applicable to all those living in diaspora (Newman and Paasi 1998). If the degree of transnationalism is on the rise in these core regions of the world system and among the intellectual élites living in diaspora (both highly debatable assumptions), this is still unlikely to tell us much about trends among the millions living in diaspora in the rest of the world. More broadly, Connor has consistently stressed the need to distinguish between the American case on the one hand and other ethnonational and ethnoterritorial contexts in much of the rest of the world on the other, due to the lack of comparability in homeland sentiments between 'homeland states' and 'immigrant states' (Connor 1972; 1984; 1986).[19]

Fourth, even within a seemingly transnational region such as the European Union, the deterritorialization of states represented by European integration has been accompanied by a reterritorialization of identities at more localized geographic scales, often at the scale of sub-state homelands and nations. For example, national separatist campaigns waged by the Scottish National Party during the 1990s promoted 'Independence in Europe', and viewed a deepening of European integration as a process that enhanced their prospects for national self-determination. In addition, surveys conducted within the European Union indicate that identification with more localized 'scales of immediacy' is growing, not disappearing, as the European Union becomes more integrated (Hedetoft 1998). Furthermore, the same surveys provide convincing evidence that a transnational European identity is strongest in those very places where national identities are most secure, and therefore that rising internationalism does not supplant but corresponds to strong nationalism. Just as the national scale of homeland identity is strengthened and reinforced by being grounded within local homeland narratives, national homeland narratives that tend to situate each particular nation and homeland at the epicenter of Europe also make use of the international scale of identity to stabilize and maintain images of nation and homeland. In this way, national homeland discourses operate at a multiplicity of geographic scales, such that local, national and international homeland narratives mutually reinforce one another, rather than diminish each other in a zero sum fashion.

Finally, in assessing the impact that the new phase of globalization is likely to have on homelands and nations, it is important to keep in mind that deterritorialization and reterritorialization across geographic scales are ongoing, historically contingent processes that are certainly not new. While globalization may affect the geographic scales at which power, place and identity intersect it cannot result in a deterritorialization of identity, since identity formation and maintenance are inherently territorial processes. As Murphy concludes (1996: 109): 'Attachments to territory are as old as human society, and there is little to suggest that the powerful ideological bonds that link identity, politics, and territory will be loosened.'

In conclusion, national homeland images continue to exert a powerful influence on popular perceptions of identity and remain among the most effective instruments that nationalists have at their disposal to mobilize their national communities. Transnationalism and the rising number of people living in diaspora have not undermined the ability of national homeland myths and symbols to territorialize identity and call the nation to action, and may actually have enhanced their potency in these regards, not least among the diasporas themselves.

The irony of these times is that as actual places and localities become ever more blurred and indeterminate, *ideas* of culturally and ethnically distinct places become perhaps even more salient. It is here that it becomes most visible how imagined communities (Anderson 1983) come to be attached to imagined places, as displaced peoples cluster around remembered or imagined homelands, places, or communities in a world that seems increasingly to deny such firm territorialized anchors in their actuality.

Remembered places have, of course, often served as symbolic anchors of community for dispersed people. This has long been true of immigrants, who use memory of place to construct their new lived world imaginatively. 'Homeland' in this way remains one of the most powerful unifying symbols for mobile and displaced peoples, though the relation to homeland may be very differently constructed in different settings (Gupta and Ferguson 1997: 37).

Notes

1   Several authors (e.g., Appadurai 1996) have argued that national identity has been deterritorialized as a result of these trends. This issue is taken up below.

2   The chapter returns to these issues in the final section.

3   Connor was one of only a handful of scholars of nationalism writing in the 1970s and 1980s whose work devoted serious attention to the homeland as a mobilizing factor in ethnonationalist movements. Although he published only one article dealing exclusively with the 'homeland question' (1986), several of his articles as well as his 1984 book highlighted the importance of homeland sentiments in ethnonationalist mobilization. My own research and writing on the role played by homelands and homeland making in nationalist mobilization owes much to Connor's groundbreaking work in this area, and so it is a sincere privilege to honor him with a contribution to this volume.

4   This tendency to ignore the role of the homeland is true of place generally, which Agnew (1987), Agnew and Duncan (1989) and MacLaughlin (1986) see as related to the dominant status of modernization theory during the post-WW II period within Western social science.

5   On the use of botanical terminology such as 'roots' and 'rootedness', see Malkki (1992).

6   The emphasis here on the subjective or perceptual way in which identity is territorialized and and reterritorialized over time, rather than on objective geographic criteria, parallels Connor's subjective definitions of nation and nationalism: 'The essence of the nation is not tangible. It is psychological, a matter of attitude rather than of fact (Connor 1994: 42). 'It is not *what is* but what people perceive as is which influences attitudes and behavior' (ibid. 197).

7   Nevertheless, for many nationalists the line between 'means' and 'end' in this regard becomes blurred, so that control over the national homeland can become equated with gaining control over the past representations and future direction of the nation (Kaiser 1994). Sack (1986) has noted this tendency within human territoriality more generally.

8   For a general discussion of the relationship between map-making and power, see Harley (1988; 1992).

9   See also Anderson (1991: 163–185).

10   However, the recent contestation in France over the most appropriate way to update the image of Marianne indicates that these motherland symbols retain the capacity to evoke strong emotional responses at a popular level.

11   Although the shift from fatherland to motherland images with independence may be seen as the norm, this has not always been the case. For example, the shift from more inclusive motherland representations of Sri Lanka at the end of the colonial era toward more exclusionary fatherland discourses promoting Sinhala-only policies after independence resulted in the withdrawal of Tamil support in the state, and the rise of a Tamil national separatist movement in a process that Hennayake describes as 'interactive ethnonationalism' (Hennayake 1992). More inclusive motherland discourses that

either were imposed by a withdrawing colonial power, or were constructed to mobilize the interethnic population in the former colonies in support of a decolonization movement during the 1950s and 1960s, have frequently been replaced by more exclusionary fatherland representations of the state following independence and the seizure of power by élites of one ethnonational community.

12 'Local homelands' in this context refer to local places toward which Russians feel emotionally attached, and not to the non-Russian republics (e.g., Chechnya, Tatarstan) within which nation and homeland making toward the titular groups are also occurring. I return to this issue below under the section: localizing the national/nationalizing localities.

13 This view of homeland making accords Anthony Smith's (1986) discussion of the flexible way in which historical events and individuals are selected and altered within the myth-symbol complex in order to reset the future trajectory of the nation.

14 More inclusive motherland discourses can enable ethnic others to 'feel at home' by 'knowing their place' (Hage 1996: 472).

15 No credible evidence has ever been provided by the Russian government to support these claims.

16 On the tendency to confuse nation and state, and to treat all states as 'nation-states', see Connor (1978). An alternative definition of nation-state as states operated of, for and by members of the dominant state-nation, is also useful as presented by Hennayake (1992).

17 These cards would allow their holders to travel to India without a visa, to buy and sell real estate, to invest in government bonds, and to apply for admission to colleges in India. The Hindu nationalist Bharatiya Janata Party favors the more radical step of granting dual citizenship to 'persons of Indian origin' (Dugger 1999).

18 Nearly all of the twelve analytical errors identified three decades ago by Connor in his rebuttal to Deutsch and the nationalization thesis (1972) appear once again within the transnationalism literature.

19 Connor's work has also highlighted the dangers associated with analytical bias introduced due to the 'predispositions of the analyst' (e.g., Connor 1994: 57).

References

Agnew, John 1987. *Place and Politics*. Boston: Allen & Unwin.

—— and Duncan, J. (eds) 1989. *The Power of Place*. Boston: Unwin Hyman.

Anderson, Benedict 1983. *Imagined Communities*. Revised edn. London: Verso.

Appadurai, Arjun 1996. 'Sovereignty without territory: notes for a postnational geography'. In P. Yaeger (ed.) *The Geography of Identity*. Ann Arbor: The University of Michigan Press: 40–58.

Applegate, Celia 1992. 'The question of *Heimat* in the Weimar Republic'. *New Formations*. 17: 64–74.

Ardrey, Robert 1966. *The Territorial Imperative*. New York: Dell.

Arutyunyan, Yuri *et al.* 1992. *Russkiye: Etno-sotsiologicheskiye Ocherki*. Moscow: Nauka.

Azaryahu, Maoz and Kellerman, Aharon 1999. 'Symbolic places of national history and revival'. *Transactions of the Institute of British Geographers*. 24: 109–23.

Basch, Linda *et al.* (eds) 1994. *Nations Unbound*. Langhorne, PA: Gordon and Breach.

Billig, Michael 1995. *Banal Nationalism*. London: Sage.

Bokov, Kh. and Alekseyev, S. 1996. *Rossiyskaya Ideya i Natsional'naya Ideologiya Narodov Rossii*. Moscow: Zhizn' National'nostey.

Borozheykina, N. *et al.* 1999. *Nasha Rodina i Sovremennyy Mir. Besedy o Rossii: Uchebnik dlya 4 klassa nachal'noy shkoly*. Smolensk: Assotsiatsiya XXI Vek.

Buttimer, Anne 1994. 'Edgar Kant and Balto-Skandia: *Heimatkunde* and regional identity'. In D. Hooson (ed.) *Geography and National Identity*. Oxford: Blackwell: 161–183.

Chinn, Jeff, and Kaiser, Robert 1996. *Russians as the New Minority*. Boulder, CO: Westview Press.

Connor, Walker 1972. 'Nation-building or nation-destroying'. *World Politics*. 24 (April): 319–355.

—— 1994. *Ethnonationalism: The Quest for Understanding*. Princeton, NJ: Princeton University Press.

—— 1986. 'The impact of homelands upon diasporas'. In G. Sheffer (ed.) *Modern Diasporas in International Politics*. London: Croom Helm: 16–45.

—— 1984a. *The National Question in Marxist-Leninist Theory and Strategy*. Princeton, NJ: Princeton University Press.

—— 1984b. 'Eco- or ethnonationalism'. *Ethnic and Racial Studies*. 7: 342–359.

—— 1978. 'A nation is a nation, is a state, is an ethnic group, is a . . .'. *Ethnic and Racial Studies*. 1 (October): 377–400.

Crameri, Kathryn 2000. 'Banal Catalanism?' *National Identities*. 2: 145–157.

Dugger, Celia 1999. 'India offers rights to attract its offspring's cash'. *New York Times*. 4 April.

Edensor, Tim 1997. 'National identity and the politics of memory: remembering Bruce and Wallace in symbolic space'. *Environment and Planning D: Society and Space*. 29: 175–194.

Gruffudd, Pyrs 1995. 'Remaking Wales: nation-building and the geographical imagination 1925–50'. *Political Geography*. 14: 219–239.

Guehenno, J. 1995. *The End of the Nation-state*. Minneapolis: University of Minnesota Press.

Gupta, Akhil and Ferguson, James 1997. 'Beyond "culture": space, identity, and the politics of difference'. In A. Gupta and J. Ferguson (eds) *Culture, Power, Place*. Durham, NC: Duke University Press: 33–51.

Hage, Ghassan 1996. 'The spatial imaginary of national practices: dwelling-domesticating/being-exterminating'. *Environment and Planning D: Society and Space*. 14: 463–485.

Harley, J. 1988. 'Maps, knowledge and power'. In Denis Cosgrove and Stephen Daniels (eds) *The Iconography of Landscape*. Cambridge: Cambridge University Press: 277–312

—— 1992. 'Deconstructing the map'. In Trevor Barnes and James Duncan (eds) *Writing Worlds*. London and New York: Routledge: 231–247.

Hedetoft, Ulf 1998. 'Constructions of Europe: territoriality, sovereignty, identity'. In S. Immerfall (ed.) *Territoriality in the Globalizing Society*. Berlin: Springer: 153–171.

Hennayake, Shantha 1992. 'Interactive nationalism: an alternative explanation of minority ethnonationalism'. *Political Geography*. 11: 526–549.

Herz, John 1957. 'Rise and demise of the territorial state'. *World Politics*. 9: 473–493.

Hobsbawm, Eric and Ranger, Terence (eds) 1983. *The Invention of Tradition*. Cambridge: Cambridge University Press.

Johnson, Nuala 1995a. 'The renaissance of nationalism'. In R. Johnston *et al.* (eds) *Geographies of Global Change*. Oxford: Blackwell: 97–110.

—— 1995b. 'Cast in stone: monuments, geography, and nationalism'. *Environment and Planning D: Society and Space*. 13: 51–65. Reprinted in John Agnew (ed.) *Political Geography: A Reader*. London and New York: Edward Arnold 1997.

Judson, Pieter 1996. 'Frontiers, islands, forests, stones: mapping the geography of a German identity in the Habsburg Monarchy, 1848–1900'. In Patricia Yaeger (ed.) *The Geography of Identity*. Ann Arbor, MI: The University of Michigan Press: 382–406.

Kaiser, Robert 1994. *The Geography of Nationalism in Russia and the USSR*. Princeton, NJ: Princeton University Press.

—— 2001. 'Reterritorializing Russian national identity during the 1990s'. Paper presented at the Annual Meetings of the Association of American Geographers, New York, 1 March.

Kristof, Ladis 1994. 'The image and the vision of the Fatherland: the case of Poland in comparative perspective'. In D. Hooson (ed.) *Geography and National Identity*. Oxford: Blackwell: 221–232.

MacLaughlin, James 1986. 'The political geography of "nation-building" and nationalism in social sciences: structural and dialectical accounts'. *Political Geography Quarterly.* 5: 299–329.

Malkki, Liisa 1992. 'National geographic: the rooting of peoples and the territorialization of national identity among scholars and refugees'. *Cultural Anthropology.* 7: 24–44.

Murphy, Alexander 1996. 'The sovereign state system as political-territorial ideal'. In T. Biersteker and C. Weber (eds) *State Sovereignty as Social Construct*. Cambridge: Cambridge University Press: 81–120.

Newman, David and Paasi, Anssi 1998. 'Fences and neighbours in the postmodern world: boundary narratives in political geography'. *Progress in Human Geography.* 22(2): 186–207.

Ohmae, K. 1995. *The End of the Nation State*. New York: Free Press.

Ostergren, Robert 1988. *A Community Transplanted*. Madison, WI: University of Wisconsin Press.

Paasi, Anssi 1996. *Territories, Boundaries and Consciousness*. New York: John Wiley & Sons.

—— 1999. 'Nationalizing everday life: individual and collective identities as practice and discourse'. *Geography Research Forum*. University of Oulu, Finland.

Pred, Allan 1984. 'Place as historically contingent process'. *Annals of the Association of American Geographers.* 74: 279–297.

Rose, Gillian 1995. 'Place and identity: a sense of place'. In D. Massey and P. Jess (eds) *A Place in the World? Places, Cultures and Globalization*. Oxford: The Open University: 87–132.

Rupert, James 1999. 'Albanians worldwide answer the rebels' call'. *The Washington Post.* 10 May.

Sack, Robert 1986. *Human Territoriality*. Cambridge: Cambridge University Press.

Safran, William 1991. 'Diasporas in modern societies: myths of homeland and return'. *Diaspora.* 1: 83–99.

Sandner, Gerhard 1994. 'In search of identity: German nationalism and geography'. In D. Hooson (ed.) *Geography and National Identity*. Oxford: Blackwell: 71–91.

Smith, Anthony 1981. 'States and homelands: the social and geopolitical implications of national territory'. *Millennium: Journal of International Studies.* 10: 187–202.

—— 1986. *The Ethnic Origins of Nations*. Oxford: Basil Blackwell.

Smith, Graham *et al.* 1998. *Nation-building in the Post-Soviet Borderlands*. Cambridge: Cambridge University Press.

Taylor, Peter 1996. *The Way the Modern World Works*. Chichester: John Wiley & Sons.

Wallerstein, Immanuel 1999. *The End of the World as We Know It*. Minneapolis: University of Minnesota Press.

Weber, Eugen 1976. *Peasants into Frenchmen*. Stanford, CA: Stanford University Press.

Weiner, Myron 1978. *Sons of the Soil: Migration and Ethnic Conflict in India*. Princeton, NJ: Princeton University Press.

Williams, Colin 1989. 'The question of national congruence'. In R. Johnston and P. Taylor (eds) *A World In Crisis? Geographical Perspectives*. 2nd edn. Oxford: Blackwell. Reprinted in John Agnew (ed.) *Political Geography: A Reader*. London and New York: Edward Arnold 1997.

——, and Smith, Anthony 1983. 'The national construction of social space'. *Progress in Human Geography.* 7: 502–518.

Winichakul, Thongchai 1994. *Siam Mapped: A History of the Geo-Body of a Nation*. Honolulu: University of Hawai'i Press.

13 Ethnicity and nationality[1]

The twin matrices of nationalism

Thomas Spira

Nationalism is the world's most intriguing and pervasive ideological force in the modern world. In our determination to study it, we have often tended to take for granted *ethnicity* and *nationality*. These are the twin matrices out of which nationalism has normally emerged and will continue to do so, in the developing as well as the developed portions of the globe. Nationalist movements have arisen seemingly from nowhere, out of soil which only a few decades ago seemed ethnically barren. Ethnicity and nationality are two indispensable forces which, under favorable social, economic, and psychological conditions, are likely to engender nationalism.

A brief retrospective of these two formative phenomena might prove useful on behalf of the continuing research into the causes, developments, successes and failures of contemporary nationalisms. It also might be of interest to note the striking resemblances – and the differences – that ethnicity and nationality share. Many of their features intertwine and overlap, whereas a few characteristics diverge. Scholars have not succeeded – and perhaps have not even tried – to identify at which point ethnicity and nationality diverge. Such research is necessary in order to lend precision and accuracy to investigations in the etiology of nationalism (Carr *et al.* 1939: xvi–xx; Connor 1981: 201–203). This chapter reviews the results of recent and less recent research on this topic, and makes a few recommendations of its own concerning the incongruity which governs the scholarly terminological usage of these two phenomena.

Ethnicity

Five propositions inform the nature of ethnicity: (1) It always originates in specific historical circumstances that are simultaneously structural and cultural. (2) It describes a set of relations and a mode of consciousness. (3) Its meaning and salience vary for different social groupings according to their positions in the social order. Yet, as a firm consciousness it is only one among many, produced as particular historical structures impinge themselves on human experience and condition social action. (4) It has its origins in the asymmetric incorporation of structurally dissimilar groupings into a single political economy. (5) It is the product of specific historical processes, but it tends to assume the natural appearance of an autonomous force – inasmuch as it is a concept capable of determining the course of social life, where it becomes an identified item in the collective consciousness of a society. Ethnicity may be perpetuated by factors that differ from those that caused its emergence, and may have a direct and independent impact on the context in which it arose (Comaroff and Comaroff 1992: 49ff.; 54).

The origins of ethnicity

According to Anthony D. Smith, the origins of ethnicity must be sought in the way ethnic crystallization came about. In premodern times, this process hinged on the gain or loss of a particular piece of territory regarded as the homeland, the vicissitudes of struggle with enemies, and organized religion that generated the rituals and traditions that formed channels of ethnic continuity, and the power of the myth of ethnic chosenness (Smith 1983: 31–32). In modern times, crystallization occurred as the consequence of the varied activities of the modern state, such as the behavior of the secular polity's political intelligentsia and the rebuttals by the ethnic intelligentsia, the cultural and civic activities of the modern state, and the ideologies of modern nationalism (ibid.: 32–34). Two opposing views persist regarding the practical origins of ethnicity. Ethnic identity and modern nationalism have tended to arise out of specific types of frequently negative interactions between the leadership of centralizing states and élites from non-dominant ethnic groups, especially but not exclusively on the peripheries of their resident states. According to the other view, ethnic mobilization and nationality-formation in centralizing multiethnic states and the particular forms they assume when they do occur depend upon the kind of alliances that centralizing and regional or other non-dominant élites tend to conclude (Brass 1991: 8–9).

Perspectives of ethnicity

The phenomenon of ethnicity may be studied from the perspectives of the environment, namely, culture, trends of change and assimilation pressures, levels of operation, notably the prevailing social structure, the sophistication of symbols and personality patterns, operative levels, such as physical traits, group interaction, family structures, sense of ethnic honor, art, approved ethnic modification, as in assimilation and adaptation, causes and functions of ethnicity, and functional modes, including crisis reactions (Reminick 1983: 62–63). The key to the understanding of how ethnic groups react to their environment has been provided by Walker Connor, who identified modernity and its consequences as the chief causes for the growth of ethnic sentiments. In his view, a modern trend tends to increase the cultural awareness of minorities by making their members more aware of the distinctions that separate them and others. Not only do ethnic individuals grow more cognizant of alien ethnic groups, they also become more conscious of those who share their identity (Connor 1972: 329).

Properties of ethnicity

The properties of ethnicity may be grouped under several headings. Biologically, members draw from a certain genetic pool over time. Culturally, they share what to do and how to perform certain tasks. Linguistically, they communicate most easily among themselves and express similar thoughts. Structurally, they organize their relations differently from those of others, evolve different social roles and pattern these variables differently (Foltz 1982: 103).

Anthropological properties of ethnicity may be explained as a biologically self-perpetuating population, a sharing of culture values and forms, a field of communication and interaction, and as a grouping that identifies itself and is identified by others as constituting a category different from others of the same type (Barth 1969: 9, 13).

Persistence of ethnicity

The persistence of ethnic identity has three major causes. According to the structural argument, ethnicity is a valuable identity, because it promotes social mobility, protects status, and serves economic and political interests. According to the cultural argument, ethnicity is basically a primordial sentiment, with its sources embodied deep in the socialization process. Ethnicity is often attached to a distinctive religion and language, both of which are crucial sources of a person's world view. Despite acculturation, deep layers of primordial cultures persist and are passed along within intimate family circles. According to the characterological argument, many ethnic people feel dislodged from their moorings, immersed in anomie, with emphases on universality, rationality and instrumentality predominating. Ethnicity serves as an escape route for people mired in the negative morass of modernity (Yinger 1994: 3ff.).

Common characteristics of ethnicity

The five common characteristics of ethnicity are its strengthening in the late 1960s; the revival of ethnic sentiments among passive ethnic minorities; the professionalization of ethnic activism; the movement to the Left; and the tendency by many governments to respond sympathetically to ethnic demands (Allardt 1979: 16, 30). Ethnicity promotes national integration in four ways. It tends to assume some of the functions of the extended family and hence, it diminishes the importance of kinship roles; it serves as a mechanism of resocialization; it helps to keep the class structure fluid, and thereby prevents the emergence of castes; and it serves as an outlet for political tensions (Wallerstein 1960: 134).

Components of ethnicity

Certain essential components embody ethnicity. A combination of factors unites phenotype, faith, language, origin, or population concentration in a given region, clustered over time and passed from generation to generation, all of which must serve to demarcate a given community. Members of the collectivity must also share a sense of solidarity, and participate in a common subjective identification. Purported ethnic groups must be in active contact with one another in the same society (Segal 1979: 10). Ethnicity depends on self-identification or self-categorization, descent, distinctive cultural patterns, especially language use, and social organization involving interethnic engagement (Allardt 1979: 16, 30).

Varieties of ethnicity

Cultural background

Ethnicity primarily implies a cultural heritage shared by members of a group. It is a form of social organization that functions to achieve certain common ends, and combines cultural and social dimensions subject to a dialectical development (Keyes 1981: 4, 11). Ethnicity is that dimension of corporate identity which exists independently of any repertoire of customs, beliefs, or institutions, because these are ever contingent and changing, and hence they cannot account for group continuity and persistence. Ethnicity and nationalism are reflections of primordial identities formed throughout recorded history. For a group to have a history and tradition, it must be rooted in some such essential element prior to the evolution of that history and tradition. This essential element is ethnicity (Cohen 1974a: 92; 1974b: ix–x; 1978: 386–387; Alverson 1979: 13). Reference to common origins and a conception of distinctiveness underscore the necessity that ethnicity is relevant only when two or more categories of people are involved in the same social system (Hicks and Leis 1977: 3). It is this status upon which individuals and groups in all societies – developed or developing, democratic or totalitarian, open or closed – tend to base their definitions and interpretations of social reality (Segal 1979: 10).

Cultural boundaries

These delineations point to an identity that reflects the cultural experiences and feelings of a particular group. For an ethnic group to exist there must be cultural practices or beliefs that define it as being different qualitatively from other groups in society (Spoonley 1988: 40–41). Members of a segment of a larger society are thought by themselves and/or others to have a common origin and to share important segments of a shared culture (Vincent 1974: 376; Smith and Kornberg 1969: 341–357), in addition to participating in joint activities, in which the common origin and culture are significant ingredients (Simpson and Yinger 1985: 10–11). In the course of this process they use their difference to enhance the sense of distinctiveness for purposes of organization or identification. Ethnicity can exist only at the boundary of 'us', in contact or in confrontation with 'them'. As the sense of 'us' alters, so the boundary between 'us' and 'them' shifts. Not only does the demarcation fluctuate, but the criteria which mark it change as well (Wallman 1979a: 202; 1979b: 3).

Commonly, such cultural differentiations may include language, territory, political unit, or common cultural values and symbols (Young 1976: 47ff.). The union of a relatively large number of people who are socially defined as belonging together because of the belief in their being demarcated from common ancestors tends to produce the essential ingredients of a sense of identity and shared sentiments of solidarity (Francis 1976: 382). These common feelings are primarily a cultural heritage shared by a group, a form of social organization that functions to achieve certain joint objectives for a people. This psychological combination takes the cultural and social dimensions of ethnicity into account (Keyes 1981: 4, 11). It is also a vehicle for value dissensus and disengagement from an inclusive sociopolitical arena, that is, a venue for pursuing major cultural values deemed not shared by others in the field (Aronson 1976: 13–15).

The primordial qualities of culture

The real or perceived primordial qualities that accrue to a group by virtue of a shared race, religion, or national origin, including linguistic and other cultural attributes, are associated with a common territorial ancestry (Alexander 1980: 10–11). The members of a group with such a shared cultural tradition and a sense of identity differ regarding certain cultural characteristics from the other members of their society. They may have their own language and religion as well as certain distinctive customs. Probably most important is their feeling as a traditionally distinct group (Theodorson and Theodorson 1969: 135). These cultural values and norms thereupon distinguish the members of a given group from others, and these joint sentiments can share a direct awareness of a common cultural identity separating them from other groups around them (Giddens 1989: 726).

The essence of belonging

That aspect of the culture of a group accounts for its origin and character, thereby differentiating it from other groups within large-scale political units and setting the tone for its relationships with those groups and with the government (Greenwood 1994: 83). Such a cultural individuality of people would not be possible unless they had been educated together under a particular cultural roof. They share the same ways of behavior, the same beliefs and institutions, the same language and historical background, the result not of biological or genetic traits but of part of their cultural heritage, formed out of common responses to common needs in the historical experience of their group (Bernard 1972: 3). This is the quintessential state of being ethnic, of belonging to an ethnic group, of being part of an ethnicity (Kellas 1991: 4–5).

This individuality clearly demonstrates that a group is to be defined not only by the sum total of objective cultural traits, but in terms of those features which its members regard as significant. These aspects constitute the boundary between groups, which determines intra- and interethnic group social relations (Leggon 1979: 2). This notion requires a central experiential concept or focal point around which all others can be clustered, namely, paternity in the broadest sense, or the putative biological origins of the primordial ancestor (Fishman 1989: 5; 1977: 17). Through the awareness of an ancestral forebear of this type, the members of a self-perceived group likely maintain a common set of traditions not shared by others with whom they are in contact (De Vos 1975: 9).

Objective and subjective elements

Ethnicity is a matter of the impact of objective and subjective elements, insofar as members of ethnic groups survey the world of the majority peoples among whom they dwell, and depending on how the latter perceive representatives of the subordinate peoples who live in their midst. Objective elements involve ethnic members distinguishing themselves and being distinguished by others on the basis of such diacritical features as facial marks, dress, language, life style and value orientations, which transmit exclusive forms of coded information and maintain a distinct kind of communication (Leach 1976: 9–10). Membership of an ethnic group therefore implies having a basic identity and the claim to judge and be judged by standards relevant to that reality (Barth 1969: 9, 13). Subjective elements consist of the attitudes, opinions, sentiments and stereotypes which ethnic members hold both about themselves and other ethnic groups, and also the views that superordinate neighbors maintain in their own subjective criteria concerning the ethnics in question (van den Berghe 1973: 222; 1976: 243).

Political action

Whether objectively or subjectively perceived by themselves and by others, ethnic groups situated at the ethnicity stage of development are inevitably confronted with the need to resort to political action. Such a political mobilization is always a reaction to perceived sociocultural threats. This decision often consists of wishing to protect or restore a traditionally suppressed native language that serves as the symbol of unity, and which cuts across ethnic internal divisions, confrontational vested interests, and generalized feelings of inferiority (Khleif 1985: 187). Such conditions are induced by a self-defined and/or other-defined, presumed or factual, common descent (Weber 1961: 305–309; Weber 1968: 389; Connor 1994: 103), and by relationships between groups which consider themselves, and are regarded by others, as being culturally distinctive, possibly inferior (Eriksen 1993: 4).

Both judgmental alternatives hinge on a set of relations and a mode of consciousness. It is only one among many sets, each of which is produced as particular historical structures that impinge themselves on human experience and precipitate social action (Comaroff and Comaroff 1992: 49ff., 54). The process involves a primary focus of group identity, that is, the organization of plural persons into distinctive groups, and second, the solidarity and the loyalties of individual members of such groups (Parsons 1975: 53–83; Parsons *et al.* 1961: 243). It must also be kept in mind, as a number of observers have pointed out, that ethnicity is not necessarily the most general or widest scaled identity but rather that it can be narrowed or broadened in boundary terms in relation to specific needs of political mobilization (Fried 1968: 3–20; Smith and Kornberg 1969: 341–357; Vincent 1974: 376). A number of observers have noted the incipient political nature of ethnicity, often expressed as regionalism. This is evidenced by a desire for a degree of political autonomy or independence on the basis of identities rooted in a variety of emotional, historical and politico-economic realities, as perceived and defined by members of the national group (Connor 1973: 1; Knight 1983: 119).

Culture and ethnicity

Culture has a large and broadly differentiated role to play in ethnicity. Owing to the divergent nature of the meaning of culture, and thanks also to the thoroughgoing interrelatedness of culture with other kindred and cognate concepts, it is difficult to relate the influence of culture on ethnicity, and vice versa, without encountering semantic and other difficulties. Ethnicity may be regarded as a structural and situational concept. The contents of ethnic interaction are related to specific situations, as determined by the group structurally in relation to others, and culturally in relation to the prevailing situation (Vincent 1974: 376).

The character, quality or condition of ethnic group membership, based on an identity with and/or a consciousness of group belonging, is differentiated from others by symbolic markers, including cultural, biological or territorial ones, and is reinforced by bonds of a shared past and perceived ethnic interests. Ethnicity is responsive to external and subjective circumstances, which makes gradual change an inherent attribute. For this reason alone, ethnicity cannot be understood apart from the broader sociocultural system. Although ethnicity is moored to individual and group properties, it is not itself interethnic or intergroup *per se*. Rather, ethnicity can serve as a catalyst for such relationships (Burgess 1978: 270).

Structure and ethnicity

Structurally, it is possible to envision a model combining ethnicity and culture (Freedman 1976: 181–188). Every society has observable customs, lifestyles, and institutions – a distinctive set of cultural forms – through which meanings and ascribed goals are enumerated, and social life is regulated. The totality of these cultural forms is often regarded to comprise the ethnicity of a particular group. A model defining culture encompasses a set of observable behaviors which occur independently of a group's relationship to the means of production and exchange. In this manner, indicators of religious affiliation or linguistic behavior may be considered to be cultural variables. If we elaborate a model defining ethnicity as the sentiments which bind individuals into solidary groups on some cultural basis, then ethnicity alludes to the quality of relations existing between individuals sharing certain cultural behaviors. Cultural variables cannot be used to indicate the strength of ethnic solidarity within groups, or vice versa (Hechter 1974: 1152).

The product, such as class, of an interplay of objective and subjective factors is always primordial and highly changeable. The very fact that language and culture are media of interaction and barriers thereto makes objective ethnic characteristics a partial determinant of ethnic consciousness. Objectively trivial differences can cause profound social cleavages and savage conflicts, e.g., in the former Yugoslavia (van den Berghe 1973: 222; 1976: 243).

Consciousness in ethnicity

A self-and-other aggregative definitional dimension of culture dealing with 'us' versus 'them' and with 'them' versus 'them', is close enough in awareness and contractive experiences to be called a consciousness. It is a self-contained, self-sufficient, culturally autonomous basis of aggregation that strains toward and is experienced as being societally complete, intergenerationally continuous and historically deep (Fishman 1977: 17). A reaction occurs when two sets of people, or individual members of two sets of people, come into contact or confrontation with each other. A felt boundary between them involves the difference and the meaning placed upon distinctions (Wallman 1979a: 202; 1979b: 3). Cultural continuity and identity, which are believed to rest on a common descent and a unique relationship with the divine or revelation, find their expression in the fund of customs and myths about the origins and history of the group (Smith 1972: 10). A phenomenon may be regarded as cognitive or cultural, wherein actors themselves may structure their experiences (Mitchell 1974: 16) and patterns of human interaction form the basis for categorical social relations with observable, or projected, economic consequences (Whitten 1975: 60).

Essentially, this ethnic consciousness encapsulates the process by which a people's difference is used to enhance the sense of 'us' for purposes of organization and identification (Wallman 1979a: 202 ; 1979b: 3). A type of cultural discontinuity may also intersect class and territorial segmentation, especially when it is linked to the perception that the members of the ethnic group possess a symbolically different geographic origin than the dominant population, as well as having other cultural differences, and that these perceptions are largely a case of ascription by self and/or others (Thompson and Rudolph 1986: 32). Cultural ethnicity is consequently a composite of shared values, beliefs, norms, tastes, consciousness of kind within the group, shared in-group memories and loyalties, certain structural relationships within the group, and a trend toward continuity by preferential endogamy (Singer 1962: n. 11; Schermerhorn 1974: 2).

The ultimate determinant of consciousness in ethnicity and its practical consequences has been described by Walker Connor as the notion that what ultimately matters is not what exists but what people believe to be true. A subconscious belief in the unique origin and evolution of the group is an important component of national psychology, and seldom accords with factual data, nor does it need to (Connor 1978: 377, *passim*).

Tribalism and ethnicity

Discrimination and strife based on differences in interethnic symbols can resemble tribalism, in that an ethnic group embraces one or more related tribal units, both of which emphasize group identity and exclusiveness. Nonetheless, tribalism and ethnicity are not interchangeable terms – ethnicity is the more inclusive concept (Otite 1975: 119–130). Like kinship, ethnicity appears as one of the few domains of social theory privileged by its fusion of biosocial constraints and universal cultural expression to justify its claim to the status of essential scientific building blocks for the analysis of society. The series of kinship, clanship and ethnicity recapitulate the natural relationship among these groups, with ethnicity serving as the apex (Galaty 1982: 1–2).

Ethnicity as a means of national integration

Ethnicity promotes national integration when ethnic groups usurp some of the functions of the extended family and hence diminish the importance of kinship roles. Ethnic groups serve as a mechanism of resocialization, especially when ethnic groups help to keep the class structure fluid. Thereby they prevent the emergence of castes. Ethnic groups, far more so than families and castes, serve as an outlet for political tensions (Wallerstein 1960: 134).

Another factor to be considered is one that has arisen as the consequence of the upsurge of ethnonationalism, or the belief that a nation is a self-differentiating ethnic group based on the psychological mindset of individuals sharing a sense of nationhood which exemplifies a high degree of independence from such variables as geographic situation, level of economic development, forms of government, degree of urbanization, sociopolitical philosophy, literacy rate or living standard (Connor 1973: 2).

Summary

Ethnicity expresses a shift to multicultural, multiethnic interactive contexts wherein attention is focused on an entity – the ethnic group – which is marked by a heightened degree of cultural and social commonality. Membership criteria by members and non-members may or may not be identical, and the creation and maintenance of the ethnic boundary within which members function can evolve according to kindred and continuing unifying roles as a major aspect of the phenomenon (Cohen 1974a: 92; 1974b: ix; 1978: 386). Ethnicity is the intermediate product of a sense of common descent extending beyond kinship and political solidarity *vis-à-vis* other groups, and even beyond common customs, language, religion, values, morality and etiquette (Weber 1961: 305ff.; 1968: 389). It is that condition of perceived unity wherein some or all members of a society consciously decide to emphasize certain assumed or real cultural or somatic traits as their most meaningful bases of primary extra-familial identity (Patterson 1975: 308; Patterson 1977: 104–109; Kunstadter 1981: 119–163).

Nationality

Nationality is a human group that, in most cases, may exist without having a political identity or lacking the exercise of political autonomy. Most frequently, nationality is joined by specific ties of cultural homogeneity, animated by consciousness of kind, and by fundamentally similar, shared mores, but it need not necessarily possess complete uniformity in all cultural traits, excepting language, religion, clothing styles and unique ornamentations, types of recreation, a unique moral code, a recognizable, rudimentary political system, a distinctive family pattern and ethical ideas, as well as reciprocal bonds of sympathy and a desire for a commonly experienced lifestyle (Fairchild 1962: 201; Connor 1970: 92).

Nationality may also denote the expression of a social system whose members share certain common cultural elements – a joint history, or some national symbols and a shared language, and who, on this basis, want to stress their peculiarity and gain some kind of recognition as a group, but who, nonetheless, do not necessarily desire a separate political entity as their primary goal (Elklit and Tonsgaard 1992: 83). Anthony D. Smith successfully bridges the span of the chronological-topical division that distinguishes ethnicity from the nation-state. This connection entails the operations of a myth-symbol complex, enshrined in the ethnie, or ethnic community, reinforced by its historical memories and central values, responsible for the growth of the nation-state since antiquity and the early Middle Ages that pervaded social and cultural life (Smith 1986: 89) in Western Europe. Somewhere along the continuum separating ethnicity from the nation-state lies nationality.

Properties of nationality

Despite, and perhaps because of, this apparent set of structural contradictions, nationality is a complex, mercurial, social fact comprising several properties bound into a unique, socially vital phenomenon (Lamser 1971: 183). These properties consist of a common blood line, a recognizable race, a perceived origin, and a unique language. The other qualities are nothing but the consequences of the other three variables, most specifically, the first (Linz 1973: 37). According to another view, the chief qualities or interests upon which the foundations of nationality rest are a race, a language, and a territory – as effectively occupied, not as politically owned, as Poland during 1795–1918, common economic interests, a unique culture, characteristic standards and modes of life, a religion that is clearly associated with the nationality it represents, considerable political unity at least on a hypothetical level, a recognizable political tradition, political subjection by a superordinate group, and the latter's political domination of such a collectivity (MacIver 1970: 95–96). Nationality also pertains to a national-feeling group regarded as such by others. This occurs when the national consciousness of members of a nationality has not yet achieved a national state, or when it exists as a minority group within a superordinate sovereign nation (Sulzbach 1943: 72), e.g., the Palestinians. Nationality is a subjective phenomenon. A group of people constitutes a nation when members feel that they do. These sentiments may be related, as cause and effect, to the group's observable characteristics. No uniform or necessary pattern of objective factors whence national feeling is derived or in which it manifests itself need exist (Claude 1969: 2).

Anthony D. Smith cogently summarizes the nature of the properties of nationality. In his view, sentiments, consciousness, attitudes, aspirations and loyalties, as opposed to doctrines, ideologies, programs, organizational activities and nationalist movements, frequently prevail, in the case of nationalities. A sentiment of supreme loyalty to the nation, and an aspiration for its purity, autonomy and strength, generally dominate the feelings of a people embarked on a transition from ethnicity to desiring its own sovereign state (Smith 1983b: 168, 174).

Elsewhere, Anthony D. Smith amplified these characteristics in reference to nationhood, which might as well apply to the study of nationality. He explains that nationhood is a status sought by most nationalist movements, characterized by autonomy and self-government for the group, *but not necessarily in a sovereign state* (italics not in the original), solidarity and fraternity of the group in a recognized and recognizable territory or homeland, and a distinctive culture and history unique to the group in question (Smith 1976: 2).

Most definitions of nationality fail to resolve the dilemma of a people torn between the decision to remain within their present host-state or whether actively to seek sovereignty and full independence. Louis L. Snyder's view on this topic is apposite. According to him, nationality comprises a group of persons speaking the same language and observing the same customs, *but often lacking their own states* (italics not in the original) (Snyder 1968: *passim*). In numerous respects, therefore, ethnicity and nationality seem to overlap in their characteristics and meanings, as do nationality and nationalism.

The common beliefs of nationality

As in ethnicity, the self-determined nature of nationality is indisputable. Nationality embraces a people which, because of the belief in their common descent and their mission in the world, by virtue of their common cultural heritage and historical career aspire to exercise sovereignty over a territory or seek to maintain or enlarge their political and/or cultural influence in the face of opposition by a dominating power (Wirth 1936: 723). Nationality is such a deeply-rooted social-psychological concept, defined by the way that people feel about each other and about their government, that it need not be defined legal dicta (Rose 1967: 728), so that human groups that are united by a community of civilization need not necessarily be joined by a political bond. The attraction is more a matter of a community of natural and physical affections and instincts (Acton 1956: 163) that are essentially spiritual in character. This affinity implies the sense of a special unity which separates those who share in it from the rest of humanity. That unit is the outcome of a common history, of victories won and defeats suffered, and traditions created by a corporate effort, a sense of kinship all of which binds people into oneness. Members recognize their likeness, and emphasize their difference from others (Laski 1967: 219–220).

The history of nationality

After the final Partition of Poland in 1795 and during the French Revolution of 1789, the sense of nationality was a collective sentiment. Thereafter, definitions of nationality diverged. In the early nineteenth century, nationality applied to peoples who lived under foreign domination and who did not constitute independent states, such as the Czechs. Later in the nineteenth century and in early twentieth-century Central Europe, the designation was that of a rank below the nation, or that of a community of a superior category. Karl Marx had the Irish and the Magyars in mind as nationalities that deserved to have their own independent governments. In British usage, nationality connotes state citizenship, or an ethnic group to which some subordinate peoples belong (Seton-Watson 1977: 4). In the early twentieth century, nationality acquired two differing senses. When used concretely, it referred to a group of persons united by certain common attributes, and when used abstractly, it was meant in relation to a certain group consciousness, and the idea of the gathering of persons in national groups. In the latter sense, the meaning of nationality also incorporated the quality of uniting peoples of the same nation (Joseph 1929: 20–23).

More currently, nationality is generally used as a condition, attributed to a person or group of persons in virtue of membership in a nation. Its meaning varies with that of the latter word. It is used as well in a sense that is equivalent to nationalism, as in the rise of nationality to statehood. In a strictly legal sense, nationality is equivalent to membership, or citizenship, in a state. It also serves to describe a people potentially but not actually a nation (Carr *et al.* 1939: xvii), such as the Kurds or Tamils. The attitude of a person toward a people, engendered by having ideas concerning its welfare, honor, and position among other peoples, is still another designation of nationality that is of relatively recent vintage (Handman 1921: 104; Chadwick 1966: 1).

The political essence of nationality

Even though a nationality is not politically bounded, it must, of necessity, demonstrate the hypothetical feasibility of such a unison derived from mutual links, such that sociocultural units have to develop ideas that go beyond the fulfilment of primarily local self-concepts, concerns and integrative bonds. The unit envisioned in this manner must presuppose a higher level of sociocultural integration than that enjoyed by an ethnic group, yet it still has to be characterized to a degree by the quality and essence of its ethnic roots. To be more specific, nationality (Fishman 1968: 39; 1972: 3) is an imperfect or unaccomplished nation consisting of ethnic units (Francis 1976: 389). It is also a community defined historically and by its behavior on the international scene in the political field, albeit not necessarily as an independent unit (Munck 1986: 7). Paradoxically, nationality is a group joined by a sentiment of unity required to constitute a nation, without needfully possessing an independent government, being either divided among several different regimes, as the Kurds, or united under one government along with persons of different nationality, as the Magyars of the defunct Austro-Hungarian Monarchy (Sidgwick 1919: 224).

The early Bolshevist state in Russia functioned on the premise that nationalities existed as a reality and that they had to be vested with certain cultural-political concessions to be applied internally within the Soviet state. Under V.I. Lenin's pluralist system, national relations would be predicated upon absolute national equality. Any blending of the involved cultures would be voluntary and devoid of coercion by the government. The harmonization process would eventually result in the creation of an entirely new identity, a socialist individual, or the Soviet person (Connor 1984: 201). Presumably, the nationalities would survive under this system, albeit as strictly cultural units enjoying a certain modicum of administrative self-determination.

Soviet anthropology has labeled this stage in national development *narodnost,* or a pre-capitalist social formation (Arutuniov and Bromley 1978: 11). In the Western sense, nationality is an ethnic community which, by its own efforts, has succeeded in achieving any one of the numerous goals of autonomist development, either within an existing state or in a state of its own, as the ultimate stage of development (Brass 1976: 227). What, then, is the *raison d'être* of a nationality? It consists of an alignment of large numbers of individuals, largely from the middle and lower classes, linked to regional centers and leading social groups by channels of social communication and economic intercourse, both indirectly from link to link and directly with the center (Deutsch 1969: 101). These are a people among whom there exists a significant movement toward the regional exercise of political economics and of cultural autonomy (Deutsch 1961: 493–514).

What Anthony D. Smith has written in connection with the formation of the nation applies as well to the underlying roots of a nationality. Smith claims the effects of the fusion of three distinct elements, an ethnic principle, which emerged originally from kinship organization, a territorial component, which derived historically from dynastic and colonial units, and a norm of political community found in the city-states of ancient Greece and medieval Italy (Smith 1976: 2). Here, too, there is a clear avoidance of the issue as to whether the members of a nation, or a nationality, are capable of, or desire to, preside over a modern territorial, sovereign, state of their own.

The solidarity of nationality

The discriminenda of nationality are essentially at the level of authenticity and solidarity of group behaviors and group values, rather than at the niveau of governmental, politico-geographical realizations and/or implementations (Fishman 1968: 39; 1972: 3). Such realities arise solely out of the group relationship. They impress themselves on the individual, but by no means ineradicably. Nationality is acquired by having its ideology socially transmitted (Fairchild 1962: 201). As Walker Connor aptly observed, 'the nation, in its pristine form, is predicated upon a myth of common origin and is therefore analogous to the family writ large, observable by how propagandists interchange the words nation', or nationality, 'to refer, for example, to the Arab nation or Arab family' (Connor 1983: 282, n. 1). In actual fact, nationality is an artificial product derived from racial raw material, which, as a finished product, confers distinctiveness on a modern group based on racial and historical association, as well as attachment to the soil. Nationality is the joint product of people and ideas, a heritage of ideals and traditions held in common and accumulated during the centuries (Dominian 1917: 4).

Anthony D. Smith points out the fragility of ethnic or national(ity) solidarity. He cautions that modern collectivity is hybridized and fragmented. Contained in anxiety-ridden states, every national identity is ambivalent and precarious, inasmuch as it is composed of fragments from the periphery that refuses to be integrated and assimilated (Smith 2001: 23). If cohesion is achieved at all, it is through the application of a basic process whereby national identities are reconstituted out of ethnic connections and characteristics, and then replicated and modified. Reconstruction occurs in every generation, altering, but never eliminating, the basic patterning of the dominant ethnoheritage underlying popular and recognized national identity (Smith 2001: 32).

In Leninist, i.e., Communist, parlance, nationality involves a people in a prenational state of development who, for some reason, have not yet, and may never, achieve the one step higher designation of nationhood. Or, nationality might be a segment of a nation living outside the state where the major body of the nation resides, e.g., Magyars residing in Slovakia, Romania and former Yugoslavia (Connor 1984: xiv). Nationality is a nebulous concept in Western thought as well. It is a subjective, psychological force, a condition of the mind, a spiritual possession, a way of feeling, thinking and living (Zimmern 1918: 51), an abstract concept that represents the spiritual experience and the self-expression of a people. It signifies a willingness to cooperate in its structure and to contribute to its development (Greenberg 1937: 14–16, 18–20).

The spiritual essence of nationality

The attachment to a nationality because of its humanitarian values and its contributions to the cause of humankind constitutes the beginnings of spiritual nationalism (Greenberg 1937: 14–16, 18–20). It is therefore a tight, uniform and unified grouping which does not necessarily exist as a primary, or even as a societally organized, collectivity. Its members are unified by an array of specific ties, such as the possession of a present or past common territory, a homeland, a belief in their common origin, a history and destiny and the desire to share a common life (Hertzler 1965: 233). They have a high mutual regard and a pronounced sense of 'we-feeling', and also a sharp sense of difference and demarcation from other nationalities. What Walker Connor asserts as a verity concerning the viability of the nation and nationalism also applies to the *raison d'être* of nationality. In his view:

> Membership in some groups may be a matter of rational self-interest. But self-identification with the nation and its fortune lies in the non-rational (not

necessarily irrational) sphere of emotions . . . . It is important, therefore, to remember that when we discuss nationalism's place in a hierarchy of values assigned to various group-identities, we are not concerned with rational calculations and describable formulae, but with an emotional, non-rational response, capable of overcoming all rational considerations.

(Connor 1983: 278)

Anthony D. Smith's view partially overlaps with the evaluation of Walker Connor. As he explains the success of the nation and nationality, the bases of nations were laid by the fund of myths, symbols, memories, and values that were transposed from generation to generation throughout the community and down the social scale. The chief mechanism of transmission, in his opinion, is organized religion with a sacred text liturgy, rites and clergy. These ensure the persistence and shape the contours of demotic *ethnies* (Smith 1994: 151). The criteria stipulated by Walker Connor and Anthony D. Smith might just as well have been framed as the causation of the rise of ethnicity.

Nationality of this type is a product of historical development, an essentially subjective, active sentiment of unity, discernible within a fairly extensive group, a feeling based upon real but diverse political, geographical, physical, and social factors, any or all of which may be present in this or that case, but not one of which must necessarily be present in all instances.

(Buck 1916: 45)

The eclectic nature of nationality

Nationality is, in many instances, an unstable mixture compounded of concrete, abstract, political and cultural ingredients, with objectives that differ widely and are seldom absolutely convincing or clear. Nevertheless, nationality does have certain assumed characteristics upon which it is possible to erect some sort of a structure. Nationality is a social group which regards itself as having evolved from the status of an ethnic minority, primarily because its members speak the same language and because they observe the same customs, and desire recognition as a unique cultural community. What it often does not wield is *de facto* political power in its own sovereign state. It strives most of the time only for cultural, and only sometimes for political autonomy within the framework of a broader state accommodation, and almost without exception on the basis of either linguistic or civic criteria. Members of a nationality, whether independentists or autonomists, as the Québécois prior to the Silent Revolution, want to be a people that is distinguished from other peoples by one or more common cultural traits (Coleman 1971: 423).

   Based on the evidence, nationality is an inadequate, general term which does not always accurately connote the various possible combinations of its specific factors. It has a concrete and abstract ideal, with political and/or cultural connotations. All that may be said of nationality, in view of the foregoing, is that the desire of a community is formed by the will of its people to be a nation (Hertz 1950: 8–14, 31).

The essential element of nationality resides in possessing a living and active corporate will, formed by the decision to form a nationality (Kohn 1967: 16–17).

Nationality is therefore a puzzling phenomenon, even a mysterious one. Large groups of people may not constitute political societies, yet they nevertheless possess a non-corporeal unity, e.g., Poland and Finland before 1918 and 1917, respectively. These human groups are united by a community of civilization without being linked by a political bond, groups which are either former states that have not surrendered the notion of reconstituting themselves, or are states in the process of becoming (Giddens 1986: 206).

Conclusion

The final word on the essential differences that distinguish these two terminologies may reside in the relative absence of certain key words which seldom appear in connection with both. Putative ancestry, presumed or factual consciousness, basic identity, traditional identity, myths and tribalism arise almost exclusively in connection with the phenomenon designated as *ethnicity*. It is a well-known fact that ethnicity serves as the womb in which a putative *nationality* slumbers until some societal impetus causes it to be awakened. It would assist the study of nationalism if it could be ascertained what precisely those societal impulses are, and to determine at which exact point in time or development it is possible to speak of nationality instead of ethnicity.

There are certain incongruities regarding the study of nationality. Presently, nationality is so broadly defined that it overlaps with ethnicity at one end, and with nation (Spira 1999: 384–389) at the other. It should be possible to distinguish nationality from ethnicity by invoking a more rigorous *dimensionalistic* approach to the problem, wherein the items measured are given values according to the intensity of the standard against which they are judged – as Emory S. Bogardus pointed out with reference to a different problem (1954: 549).

Walker Connor expressed his dissatisfaction and provided the appropriate corrective to remedy the prevailing confusions. In the final analysis, he believes, the coincidence of the customary tangible attributes of nationality, such as a common language or religion, is not determinative. The prime requisite is subjective and consists of the self-identification of people with a group (Connor 1967: 30). To this might be added a clarification regarding whether a people demands the possession of a sovereign political state of its own, such as the Basques, or whether the group merely wishes to preserve an existent recognized status within a nation-state of which it is a member, e.g., the Puerto Ricans or Catalans. The designation of nationality ought to be confined to the former example. The latter category ought to be called an *incipient nationality*.

Note

1 This chapter is an adapted and expanded version of some of the entries that appear in Thomas Spira (ed.) (1999) *Nationalism and Ethnicity Terminologies: An Encyclopedic Dictionary*

and Research Guide, with a Foreword by Walker Connor, Volume 1, Gulf Breeze, FL: Academic International Press, e-mail:bevon@gulf.net, and from Volumes II and III, forthcoming.

References

Acton, L. 1956. *Essays on Freedom and Power*. London: Thames and Hudson.

Alexander, J.C. 1980. 'Core solidarity, ethnic outgroup, and social differentiation: a multi-dimensional model of inclusion in modern societies'. In J. Dofny and A. Akiwowo (eds) *National and Ethnic Movements*. Beverly Hills, CA: Sage: 5–28.

Allardt, E. 1979. 'Implications of the ethnic revival in modern, industrialized society: a comparative study of the linguistic minorities in Western Europe'. Helsinki: *Societas Scientiarum Fennica*.

Alverson, H.S. 1979. 'The roots of time: a comment on utilitarian and primordial sentiments in ethnic identification'. In R.L. Hall (ed.) *Ethnic Autonomy*. New York: Pergamon: 13–17.

Aronson, D. 1976. 'Ethnicity as a cultural system: an introductory essay'. In F. Henry (ed.) *Ethnicity in the Americas*. The Hague: Mouton: 9–19.

Arutuniov S.A. and Bromley, Y.V. 1978. 'Problems of ethnicity in Soviet ethnographic studies'. In R.E. Holloman and S.A. Arutuniov (eds) *Perspectives on Ethnicity*. The Hague: Mouton: 11–13.

Barth, F. 1969. 'Introduction'. In F. Barth (ed.) *Ethnic Groups and Boundaries: The Social Organization of Cultural Differences*. Boston: Little, Brown: 9–38.

Bernard, W.S. 1972. 'Integration and ethnicity'. In W.S. Bernard (ed.) *Immigrants and Ethnicity: Ten Years of Changing Thought. An Analysis Based on the Special Seminars of the American Immigration and Citizenship Conference 1960–1970*. New York: American Immigration and Citizenship Conference: 1–7.

Bogardus, E.S. 1954. *Sociology*. 4th edn. New York: Macmillan.

Brass, P.R. 1976. 'Ethnicity and nationality formation'. *Ethnicity*. 3: 225–41.

—— 1991. *Ethnicity and Nationalism: Theory and Comparison*. New Delhi: Sage.

Buck, C.D. 1916. 'Language and the sentiment of nationality'. *The American Political Science Review*. 10: 44–69.

Burgess, M.E. 1978. 'The resurgence of ethnicity: myth or reality?' *Ethnic and Racial Studies*. 1: 265–285.

Carr, E.H. *et al.* (eds) 1939. *Nationalism: A Report by a Study Group of Members of the Royal Institute of International Affairs*. Oxford: Oxford University Press.

Chadwick, H.M. 1966. *The Nationalities of Europe*. Cambridge: Cambridge University Press.

Claude, I.L., Jr. 1969. *National Minorities: An International Problem*. New York: Greenwood Press.

Cohen, A. 1974a. *Two-Dimensional Man: An Essay on the Anthropology of Power and Symbolism in Complex Society*. Berkeley, CA: University Press of California.

—— 1974b. 'Introduction: the lesson of ethnicity'. In A. Cohen (ed.) *Urban Ethnicity*. London: Tavistock: i–x.

Cohen, R. 1978. 'Ethnicity: problem and focus in anthropology'. *Annual Review of Anthropology*. 7: 379–403.

Coleman, J.S. 1971. *Nigeria: Background to Nationalism*. Berkeley, CA: University of California Press.

Comaroff, J. and Comaroff, J. 1992. *Ethnography and the Historical Imagination*. Boulder, CO: Westview Press.

Connor, W. 1967. 'Self-determination: the new phase'. *World Politics*. 20: 30–53.

—— 1970. 'Ethnic nationalism as a political force'. *World Affairs*. 133: 91–97.

—— 1972. 'Nation-building or nation-destroying?' *World Politics*. 24: 319–355.

—— 1973. 'The politics of ethnonationalism'. *Journal of International Affairs*. 27: 1–21.

—— 1978. 'A nation is a nation, is a state, is an ethnic group, is a . . .'. *Ethnic and Racial Studies*. 1: 377–400.

—— 1981. 'Nationalism and political illegitimacy'. *Canadian Review of Studies in Nationalism*. 8: 201–228.

—— 1983. 'Nationalism: competitors and allies'. *Canadian Review of Studies in Nationalism*. 10: 277–282.

—— 1984. *The National Question in Marxist-Leninist Theory and Strategy*. Princeton, NJ: Princeton University Press.

—— 1994. *Ethnonationalism: The Quest for Understanding*. Princeton, NJ: Princeton University Press.

Deutsch, K.W. 1961. 'Social mobilization and political development'. *The American Political Science Review*. 55: 493–514.

—— 1969. *Nationalism and its Alternatives*. New York: Knopf.

De Vos, G. 1975. 'Ethnic pluralism: conflict and accommodation'. In G. De Vos and L. Romanucci-Ross (eds) *Ethnic Identity: Cultural Continuities and Change*. Palo Alto, CA: Mayfield: 5–41.

Dominian, L. 1917. *The Frontiers of Language and Nationality in Europe*. New York: American Geographical Society.

Elklit, J. and Tonsgaard, O. 1992. 'The absence of nationalist movements: the case of the Nordic area'. In J. Coakley (ed.) *The Social Origins of Nationalist Movements: The Contemporary West European Experience*. London: Sage: 81–98.

Eriksen, T.H. 1993. *Ethnicity and Nationalism: Anthropological Perspectives*. London: Pluto.

Fairchild, H.P. (ed.) 1962. *Dictionary of Sociology*. Patterson, NJ: Littlefield, Adams.

Fishman, J.A. 1968. 'Nationality-nationalism and nation-nationism'. In J.A. Fishman *et al.* (eds) *Language Problems of Developing Nations*. New York: Wiley: Vol. 2: 39–51.

—— 1972. *Language and Nationalism: Two Integrative Essays*. Rowley, MA: Newbury House.

—— 1977. 'Language and ethnicity'. In H. Giles (ed.), *Language, Ethnicity and Intergroup Relations*. London: Academic: 15–57.

—— 1989. *Language and Ethnicity in Minority Sociolinguistic Perspective*. Clevedon: Multilingual Matters.

Foltz, W.J. 1982. 'Ethnicity, status and conflict'. In W. Bell and W.E. Freeman (eds) *Ethnicity and Nation Building: Comparative International and Historical Perspectives*. Beverley Hills, CA: Sage: 103–116.

Francis, E.K. 1976. *Interethnic Relations: An Essay in Sociological Theory*. New York: Elsevier.

Freedman, M. 1976. 'Ethnic puzzles'. *New Community*. 5: 181–188.

Fried, M.H. 1968. 'On the concepts of "tribe" and "tribal society"'. In J. Helm (ed.) *Essays on the Problem of Tribe: Proceedings of the 1967 Annual Spring Meeting of the American Ethnological Society*. Seattle, WA: University Press of Washington: 3–20.

Galaty, J.G. 1982. 'Being Masai: being people-of-cattle: ethnic shifters in East Africa', *American Ethnologist*. 9: 1–20.

Giddens, A. (ed.) 1986. *Durkheim on Politics and the State*. Trans. W.D. Halls. Stanford, CA: Stanford University Press.

—— 1989. *Sociology*. Cambridge: Polity Press.

Greenberg, L.S. 1937. *Nationalism in a Changing World*. New York: Greenberg.

Greenwood, D.J. 1994. 'Continuity in change: Spanish Basque ethnicity as a historical process'. In M.J. Esman (ed.) *Ethnic Politics*. Ithaca, NY: Cornell University Press: 81–102.

Handman, M.S. 1921. 'The sentiment of nationalism'. *Political Science Quarterly*. 36: 104–121.

Hechter, M. 1974. 'The political economy of ethnic change'. *The American Journal of Sociology*. 79: 1151–1178.

Hertz, F. 1950. *Nationality in History and Politics: A Psychology and Sociology of National Sentiment and Nationalism*. 3rd edn. New York: Humanities Press.

Hertzler, J.O. 1965. *A Sociology of Language*. New York, NY: Random House.

Hicks, G.L. and Leis P.E. (eds) 1977. *Ethnic Encounters: Identities and Contexts*. North Scituate, MA: Duxbury.

Joseph, B. 1929. *Nationality: Its Nature and Problems*. London: Allen and Unwin.

Kellas, J.G. 1991. *The Politics of Nationalism and Ethnicity*. New York: St Martin's Press.

Keyes, C.F. 1981. 'Introduction'. In C.F. Keyes (ed.) *Ethnic Change*. Seattle, WA: University Press of Washington: 1–23.

Khleif, B.B. 1985. 'Issues of theory and methodology in the study of ethnolinguistic movements: the case of Frisian nationalism in the Netherlands'. In E.A. Tiryakian and R. Rogowski (eds) *New Nationalisms of the Developed West: Toward Explanation*. Boston: Allen and Unwin: 176–199.

Knight, D.B. 1983. 'The dilemma of nations in a rigid state-structured world'. In N. Kliot and S. Waterman (eds) *Pluralism and Political Geography: People, Territory and State*. London: Croom Helm: 114–137.

Kohn, H. 1967. *The Idea of Nationalism: A Study in its Origins and Background*. 2nd edn. New York: Collier.

Kunstadter: 1981. 'Ethnic group, category and identity: Karen in Northern Thailand'. In C.F. Keyes (ed.) *Ethnic Change*. Seattle, WA: University Press of Washington: 119–163.

Lamser, V. 1971. 'A sociological approach to Soviet nationality problems'. In E. Allworth (ed.) *Soviet Nationality Problems*. New York: Columbia University Press: 183–210.

Laski, H.J. 1967. *A Grammar of Politics*. 4th edn. London: Allen and Unwin.

Leach, E. 1976. *Culture and Communication*. London: Cambridge University Press.

Leggon, C.B. 1979. 'Theoretical perspectives on race and ethnic relations: a socio-historical approach'. In C.B. Marrett and C. Leggon (eds) *Research in Race and Ethnic Relations: A Research Annual*. Greenwich, CTL JAI: Vol. 1: 1–15.

Linz, J.J. 1973. 'Early state building and late peripheral nationalism against the state: the case of Spain'. In S.N. Eisenstadt and S. Rokkan (eds) *Building States and Nations: Analysis by Region*. Beverley Hills, CA: Sage: Vol. 2: 32–116.

MacIver, R.M. 1970. *On Community, Society and Power: Selected Writings*. Chicago: University Press of Chicago.

Mitchell, J.C. 1974. 'Perceptions of ethnicity and ethnic behaviour: an empirical exploration'. In A. Cohen (ed.) *Urban Ethnicity*. London: Tavistock: 1–25.

Munck, R. 1986. *The Difficult Dialogue: Marxism and Nationalism*. London: Zed Books.

Otite, O. 1975. 'Resource competition and inter-ethnic relations in Nigeria'. In L.A. Despres (ed.) *Ethnicity and Resource Competition in Plural Societies*. The Hague: Mouton: 119–130.

Parsons, T. 1975. 'Some theoretical considerations on the nature and trends of change of ethnicity'. In N. Glazer and D.P. Moynihan (eds) *Ethnicity, Theory and Experience*. Cambridge, MA: Harvard University Press: 53–83.

———. et al. 1961. *Theories of Society: The Foundations of Modern Sociological Theory*. Vol. 2. New York: Free Press.

Patterson, O. 1975. 'Context and choice in ethnic allegiance: a theoretical framework and Caribbean case study'. In N. Glazer and D.P. Moynihan (eds) *Ethnicity, Theory and Experience*. Cambridge, MA: Harvard University Press: 305–349.

—— 1977. *Ethnic Chauvinism: The Reactionary Impulse*. New York, NY: Stein and Day.

Reminick, R.A. 1983. *Theory of Ethnicity: An Anthropologist's Perspective*. Washington, DC: University Press of America.

Rose, A.M. 1967. *Sociology: The Study of Human Relations*. 2nd rev. edn. New York: Knopf.

Schermerhorn, R.A. 1974. 'Ethnicity in the perspective of the sociology of knowledge'. *Ethnicity*. 1: 1–14.

Segal, B.E. 1979. 'Ethnicity: where the present is the past'. In R.L. Hall (ed.) *Ethnic Autonomy – Comparative Dynamics: The Americas, Europe and the Developing World*. New York: Pergamon: 7–17.

Seton-Watson, H. 1977. *Nations and States: An Inquiry into the Origins of Nations and the Politics of Nationalism*. Boulder, CO: Westview.

Sidgwick, H. 1919. *The Elements of Politics*. 4th edn. London: Macmillan.

Simpson, G.E. and Yinger, J.M. 1985. *Racial and Cultural Minorities: An Analysis of Prejudice and Discrimination*. 5th edn. New York: Plenum.

Singer, L. 1962. 'Ethnogenesis and Negro Americans today'. *Social Research*. 29: 419–432.

Smith, A.D. 1972. 'Ethnocentrism, nationalism and social change'. *International Journal of Comparative Sociology*. 13: 1–20.

—— 1976. 'Introduction: the formation of nationalist movements'. In A.D. Smith (ed.) *Nationalist Movements*. London: Macmillan: 1–30.

—— 1983a. 'The ethnic sources of nationalism'. In M.E. Brown (ed.) *Ethnic Conflict and International Security*. Princeton, NJ: Princeton University Press: 27–41.

—— 1983b. *Theories of Nationalism*. London: Duckworth.

—— 1986. *The Ethnic Origins of Nations*. Oxford: Basil Blackwell.

—— 1994. 'The origins of nations'. In J. Hutchinson and A.D. Smith (eds) *Nationalism*. New York: Oxford University Press: 147–154.

—— 2001. 'Interpretations of national identity'. In A. Dieckhoff and N. Gutiérrez (eds) *Modern Roots: Studies of National Identity*. Aldershot: Ashgate: 21–42.

Smith J. and Kornberg, A. 1969. 'Some considerations bearing upon comparative research in Canada and the United States'. *Sociology*. 3: 341–357.

Snyder, L.L. 1968. *The Meaning of Nationalism*. New York: Greenwood.

Spira, T. 1999. *Nationalism and Ethnicity Terminologies: An Encyclopedic Dictionary and Research Guide* with a foreword by Walker Connor. Gulf Breeze, FL: Academic International Press.

Spoonley: 1988. *Racism and Ethnicity*. Auckland, NZ: Oxford University Press.

Sulzbach, W. 1943. *National Consciousness*. Washington, DC: American Council on Public Affairs.

Theodorson, G.A. and Theodorson, A.G. 1969. *A Modern Dictionary of Sociology*. New York: Crowell.

Thompson R.J. and Rudolph, J.R., Jr. 1986. 'Ethnic politics and public policy in Western societies: a framework for comparative analysis'. In D.L. Thompson and D. Ronen (eds) *Ethnicity, Politics, and Development*. Boulder, CO: Lynne Rienner: 25–63.

van den Berghe, P.L. 1973. *Power and Privilege at an African University*. London: Routledge and Kegan Paul.

—— 1976. 'Ethnic pluralism in industrial societies: a special case?' *Ethnicity*. 3: 242–255.

Vincent, J. 1974. 'The structuring of ethnicity'. *Human Organization*. 33: 375–379.

Wallerstein, I. 1960. 'Ethnicity and national integration in West Africa'. *Cahiers d'études Africaines*. 3: 129–139.

Wallman, S. 1979a. 'The boundaries of "race": processes of ethnicity in England'. *Man.* 13: 200–217.

—— 1979b. 'Introduction: the scope of ethnicity'. In S. Wallman (ed.) *Ethnicity at Work.* London: Macmillan.

Weber, M. 1961. 'Ethnic groups'. In T. Parsons *et al.* (eds) *Society: The Foundations of Modern Sociological Theory.* New York: Free Press: 305–309.

—— 1968. 'Economy and society: an outline of interpretive sociology'. In G. Roth and C. Wittich (eds) *Economy and Society: An Outline of Interpretive Sociology.* New York: Bedminster.

Whitten, N.E., Jr. 1975. 'Jungle Quechua identity: an Ecuadorian case study'. In L.A. Despres (ed.) *Ethnicity and Resource Competition in Plural Societies.* The Hague: Mouton: 41–69.

Wirth, L. 1936. 'Types of nationalism'. *The American Journal of Sociology.* 41: 723–737.

Yinger, J.M. 1994. *Ethnicity: Source of Strength? Source of Conflict?* Albany, NY: State University Press of New York.

Young, C. 1976. *The Politics of Cultural Pluralism.* Madison, WI: University of Wisconsin Press.

Zimmern, A.E. 1918. *Nationality and Government: With Other War-Time Essays.* London: Chatto and Windus.

14 Resisting primordialism and other *-isms*

In lieu of conclusions

Daniele Conversi

If the study of nationalism has reached academic maturity, the main reason may be that it is now predicated on more solid definitional and conceptual grounds – a task for which Walker Connor's work has been highly relevant. However, some great obstacles remain. This concluding chapter will try to identify some of them.

One of this book's distinctive outcomes has been the collection of several chapters canvassing on an open 'primordialist' approach, including a few attempts to engage in a debate with primordialist approaches. Most contributions have referred in one way or another to 'primordialism'. This chapter will deal with the possible problems stemming from this, while proposing new ways of identifying old problems.

Although 'primordial' has been identified by Anthony D. Smith (1996, 1998) as 'preceding state organization', 'primordialism' as a scholarly approach or trend still eludes scholarly scrutiny. So what is 'primordialism'? As expected, not a single unanimous definition of the term has emerged and the very concept remains shrouded in ambiguity. What have emerged instead are the following three competing meanings (possibly ranging from the most to the least benign ones):[1]

1   Primordialism as a belief-system, as a passionate and deeply-felt attachment to one own's ethnic values and identity. This may be compatible or not with any rational endeavours and attitudes. This approach has been highlighted by Joshua Fishman' s chapter.
2   Primordialism as abdication, reflected in the erstwhile academic attitude of dismissing ethnic and other attachments as irrational relics of a bygone past, contrary to 'rational' nation-building and hence not worth studying or defining. This is the 'renounciative' view sketched, among others, by Shils and Geertz. It was assumed by most modernization theorists in the 1960s and 1970s, and has been well identified in Donald Horowitz's chapter.
3   Primordialism as *essentialism*, the idea that groups are clearly identifiable actors which can be transparently recognized by the author(s) as self-perpetuating homogeneous units with specific interests and agendas. This is the approach considered, at least in part, by William Safran.

Is any of these three meanings identifiable in Walker Connor's work? In the name of clarity and precision, Connor has always rejected all forms of compartmentalization, name-calling, and labelling. He has done so because, as an anti-essentialist, he is well aware that realities are more complex and nuanced than they appear to the external eye, that individuals and groups are situated in a continuum of shaded and, very often, incoherent positions. Yet, these and similar themes permeate the literature referring to Connor's writings, including many of this book's chapters. Let us therefore briefly examine each of the three views in relation to Connor.

1   Connor's focus on emotions is very distinct from Joshua Fishman's own defence of these emotions. Both may reflect Blaise Pascal's dictum that 'the heart has its reasons which reason knows nothing of'. But Connor's task is to highlight the powerful impact of non-rational behaviour and attitudes, rather than to uphold them. However, Fishman's piece, which partakes openly this viewpoint, is also in line with Connor's critique of elitism, insofar as 'primordialism' is meant to challenge top-down constructivist propositions. By focusing on the emotions of intellectuals, artists, leaders and followers, old ivory towers are more likely to crumble.

2   Walker Connor's entire work is a critique of point 2 above, especially as associated with the modernization theory, namely the idea that ethnic sentiments are quaint remains of a bygone age. If by 'primordialism' we mean a view of ethnic sentiments as casual relics of a pre-modern past, then we fail to see them as actually and modernly viable – which is far from the truth. As we have seen, Connor has turned modernization postulates topsy-turvy. But, by emphasizing the non-rational character of nationalism, he has certainly not asserted that this feature should, or may, preclude its scholarly study.

3   Connor has avoided as much as possible essentialist inclinations. No homogeneity of culture is inferred, although a certain coherence of intentions, beliefs, values and behavior, is ascribed to national groups. Even though nationalism is a mass phenomenon and mobilizes groups as cohesive communities reflecting an inner perception of homogeneity, the task of the scholar should not be to indulge in the belief of its subjects and groups as organic wholes. This is still in line with Kant's and the positivists' vision of the ideal scholar as immune from ideologies, power and cultural constraints. As both O'Leary and Kaiser remind us, Connor (1994: 57) has stressed the need to recognize the analytical bias introduced by the 'predispositions of the analyst'. The arbitrary identification of Connor with primordialism stems mostly from an article, 'Beyond Reason' (Connor 1993), where the non-rational essence of nationalism is underscored. Yet, as explained in the introduction, his one is not an apotheosis of irrationality.

Of the three forms of primordialism so far identified, I feel that the first two have been sufficiently covered in this book, but the third one (essentialism) needs further exploration. Therefore, what follows is the identification of some trouble spots still plaguing the study of ethnicity and nationalism, as also reflected in some of the book's chapters. It is therefore an implicit call to overcome these obstacles, straighten the discipline and make it more scholarly sound.

The *-isms* which follow should be intended as potential trends rather than as closed boxes or rigid categories. But their pervasive use should not be seen as being in flagrant contradiction with Connor's methodological premises. Connor has stressed the need to avoid 'name-calling' and the temptation to essentialize and simplify his colleagues' ideas. Scholarly categories are indeed more fluid and nuanced than outer ascription to over-simplifying categories can allow: no single scholar can be easily put in a conceptual box or definitional heading as most authors span several categories. Yet, this endeavour is necessary for any discipline to advance – although unpalatable and distasteful to some. Therefore the theoretical taxonomies I propose below should not be intended as blocs to confine the quoted authors.

Essentialism

Essentialism is often recognizable by the reiterated and totalizing use of *ethnonyms*: entire groups are hypostatized as cohesive entities obeying self-perpetuating mandates and enduring injunctions.[2] In this way they appear to be ensnared in their historical legacy.[3] For instance, some authors write about 'the French', 'the Arabs', 'the Croats', 'the Serbs', 'the Armenians', etc. and other peoples as if they were coherent homogeneous entities endowed with their own collective will and goals. There is a tendency, perhaps understandable, to over-generalize and ascribe attitudes to the population at large for which there is no real evidence. However, this is different from saying that this population does not share some myths of common descent to maintain social cohesion. Moreover, essentialists usually fail to identify the substantial actors of ethnic processes, such as the French political élites or a particular person or group of persons (rather than 'the French').[4]

The essentialist view has been bestowed an evolutionary rationale in Donald Horowitz's chapter, which discusses Brewer and Miller's 'evolutionary primordialist' approach (Chapter 4). However, the application of essentialism in the academia was preceded by its celebration in the media and among politicians. This has been, and is, true of US media dealing with international affairs: academics have simply followed the political leaders' lead mostly remaining uncritical towards such mainstream usages.

Essentialism is often approached with the best of intentions, but eventually with unintended results: as well illustrated by Robert Kaiser, 'map-making' is among the most essentializing projects and it is central to nation-making, despite the existence of compatible localized homeland identities. Essentialism is hence quintessential *reification*, the transformation of beliefs, ideas and perceptions into animated entities and inherent 'wholes'. It displays an innate tendency to homogenize, to impose patterns, and, more dangerously, to ignore what does not fit the paradigm employed.

A particularly essentialist construct is the concept of '*self-determination*'. As famously expressed by Ivor Jennings in 1956, the problem is that in order to apply this principle you have to establish first who is the 'self' to be 'determined'. Any third-party intervention based on such a vaporous concept is bound to essentialize the 'self' as a coherent whole. At the same time, self-determination is also predicated on social engineering as it imposes rigid patterns upon plural environments.

But, although the concept of self-determination is based on essentialist postulates, it would be impossible to discard it altogether, lest half of mankind might be subjected to some form of unwelcome domination. The task of the scholar, the theoreticians and the international lawyer, should hence be either to dismantle the concept, or to find suitable applications, flexible enough to be adapted to human diversity, plurality, overlapping boundaries and ethnoterritorial mixing.

This is precisely one of the aspects appraised throughout the book's third section, with its emphasis on the practical implications of Connorian analysis. Brendan O'Leary has discussed the varieties of territorial federalism, while William Safran has dealt with self-determination as a plausible tool of international relations and conflict resolution. But other formulas are available to policy makers – with disparate results: pillarization or consociation (Lijphart 1977, 1996), cantonization (Henders 1997), hegemonic control (Lustick 1979) and various forms of non-territorial autonomy (Coakley 1994).[5] There is no need to recur to extreme solutions, be they either secession or centralization (Guibernau 1999, Keating 1999, Loughlin 2000).[6]

Essentialism may be naïve, but it becomes detrimental if applied to any dimension of foreign policy analysis.[7] It forces upon reality a rigidity of patterns which makes ultimately impossible any plural accommodation except by means of war or total victory. To essentialize the outsider is to prepare for war. In more academic terms, to infer a homogeneous and widespread popular feeling from élites' and political minorities' decisions is reversing elitism top-down, thereupon performing a parallel deformation of reality. As essentialism is the utmost version of primordialism, it prompts an abdication of etiology, of the study of the causes of ethnic conflict. Conflicts are simply seen as irrational and unaccountable. For the essentialist, conflicts occur because they do: they are inscribed in groups' primordial instincts. But if the study of the causes is so promptly relinquished, how could one even identify any possible path to conflict resolution?

Once the roots of ethnic conflicts are analysed in depth, their evolution and profile usually change and the panorama becomes less shallow. Once names and actions of single individuals pop up, generalizations become harder, while clues as to the strategic or tactical choices of élites or proto-élites begin to emerge. In this way it is feasible to ascertain why some leaders, groups or organizations 'adopt violent strategies'.[8]

Finally, essentialism is linked with at least two form of fashionable determinism. First, it is associated with *cultural*, or *ethnocultural*, *determinism*, the view that we are all intrinsically enslaved in our petty cultural habits and that these are ethnically (in extreme cases, biologically) determined, rather than determined by culture *per se*. Second, it is often associated with *historical determinism*, the view that the past has got a hold on the present, and that you cannot escape its grasp. There are obviously other forms of determinism, some moribund (racial determinism), other persisting (economic determinism), but the ensuing two have acquired in the 1990s an aura of respectability which needs to be tested and challenged.

Cultural determinism

In popular and scholarly literature, ethnicity and culture are often seen as intrinsically linked, one reinforcing the other. This confusion indicates not only a lack of precision, but also that essentialism is alive and kicking. Of the two concepts, culture is by far the most difficult to grasp. It remains still largely undefinable, as noticed already in the 1950s by US anthropologists Alfred Louis Kroeber and Clyde Kluckhohn, who identified over 100 competing definitions of 'culture' (Kroeber and Kluckhohn 1952). But, for the sake of clarity, I shall re-state a cardinal distinction: *ethnicity* can be easily defined as a group's shared and subjective belief in common descent, whereas *culture* can be identified in the objective existence of an innerly coherent, yet plural, set of tangible outputs (including material artifacts) whose proper crafting is passed on through generations (and renewed with each generation) within a system of values and codes conveyed by its own symbolism.[9] Of course, culture needs reproduction and inter-generational transmission in order to survive and thus is permeated by ethnicity. But, although culture is attached to ethnic continuity, the two concepts should always be distinguished.

The confusion between ethnicity and culture is particularly pervasive in what I defined above as cultural determinism. The latter comes in at least two main variants, ethnocultural and 'civilizational', both of which have recently witnessed a resurgence in US media and academia. The very use of the term *ethnocultural* indicates confusion between the two. Precisely because this approach is essentialist, ethnicity and culture are conflated as nearly synonymous. Thus, ethnic wars become culture wars.

On the other hand, 'strict' cultural determinists may be aware of the distinction between ethnicity and culture, since they argue that national conflicts are rigorously cultural in origin. Communication gaps arising from 'cultural' differences are seen as conflict-engendering and being at the heart of misunderstandings. They thereby focus on pretentiously unbridgeable 'fault lines' derived by the imprint of greater, mostly non-ethnic, cultural blocs or civilizations. Conflicts occur at the intersection between culture and modernization: It is the latter's disruptive impact, together with the devastating repercussions of an all-mighty Western culture, which generates the unavoidable collision.

The most famous interpretation in this line comes from Samuel Huntington (1995) and his theory of the 'clash of civilizations'. Accordingly, the new post-Cold War world order has been reshaped no longer along ideological cleavages, but along cultural fault lines – where ethnicity plays a merely interstitial role as a sub-component of civilization. In other words, instead of competing nationalities or the two blocs, we have now entered an era in which being either Western, Muslim, Christian Orthodox, Latin American, Confucian, African, Hindu, Buddhist or Japanese matters more than ever before. This is occurring despite increasing secularism and modernization, indeed, precisely as a result of that: religions are not to be taken as they were in the past, that is, as belief systems, but rather as civilizational aggregates. But this view of the strength of civilizations reveals that religion has been secularized, at least in ethnic conflicts. As shown by John Coakley, secularism, rather than other-worldly faith, nurtures the political use of religion.[10] In his study of Muslim society, Gellner (1981) defines Islamic fundamentalism as a regional variant of Western modernism and nationalism. Brought to its logical conclusions, even Osama Bin Laden's ideology can be seen as a form of patriotism, religious in form, but nationalist in substance. Bin Laden himself has built his political career in the fight against US military presence in his native Saudi Arabia. He can be seen alternatively as an Arab nationalist or as a pan-Islamic irredentist.

Huntington has applied this approach to, and was probably inspired by, the Yugoslav wars. All the 'warring' parties of the Yugoslav drama were merely re-enacting ancient civilizational alliances and obeying the lust of primordial dictats. Thus, for instance, Greece was viewed as unshakably tied to, say, Serbia and Russia by virtue of its Christian Orthodox legacy (Michas 2002). Centuries of common cultural heritage and interactions between Orthodox and non-Orthodox within the Ottoman Empire fold were ignored or elided.

An avalanche of critiques has submerged this thesis.[11] Civilizational determinists overlook many exceptions: for instance, Serb nationalists have not always been pro-Greek and erstwhile versions of pan-Serbianism claim the region of Greek Macedonia, including Thessaloniki, as part of Southern Serbia.[12] In the Caucasus, Christian Armenia has forged a highly favorable relationship with the Islamic Republic of Iran, whereas Christian Georgia has created preferential links with Muslim Azerbaidjan and Turkey, rather than with Armenia.

Various reasons can be advanced for the emergence of this vision in the 1990s and these should be the subject of a separate investigation. The emergence of civilizational approaches could also prosper because it had the explicit support of the *éminence grise* of US foreign policy, the Cold War strategist Henry A. Kissinger (Hitchins 2001). In tune with Huntington's postulates, Kissinger claimed that

> [t]he war in Kosovo is the product of a conflict going back over centuries. It takes place at the dividing line between the Ottoman and Austrian empires, between Islam and Christianity, and between Serbian and Albanian nationalism. The ethnic groups have lived together peacefully only when that coexistence was imposed – as under foreign empires or the Tito dictatorship.[13]

Early US policy on Bosnia was indeed influenced by what can be named the 'Kissinger–Milosevic–Bin Laden' approach to international relations. For instance, two Kissinger associates, Lawrence Eagleburger and Brent Scowcroft, were strongly linked to Belgrade's élites, including Milosevic, as advisers on Yugoslavia to James A. Baker III, US Secretary of State and former Secretary of the Treasury (Almond 1994: 39).

The myth of innate antagonisms and perennial hatred rests on the modern vision that people following different religious creeds decimated each other for thousands of years. But this totally ignores the much longer periods of peace and mutual coexistence, as well as the endless forms of hybridization, syncretism and *métissage* that took place throughout the ages and all over the world. The need to emphasize the importance of 'fading' ethnic conflicts, as well as of accommodation and coexistence, has been pointed out in Horowitz's chapter.

Yet, the 'ancient hatred' distortion lingers on, seemingly impermeable to rational reasoning. Most historical research demonstrates that it is untenable. One of the breeding grounds of primordialist interpretations has been Bosnia, where warfare has been explained away as a result of deeply embedded primordial and age-old animosities. But we tend to forget that a rich tradition of diversity, pluralism and tolerance developed here over many centuries and flourished until quite recently, only to be shattered at the closing of the millennium by Milosevic's war machine with US, French and British blessing (Conversi 2002; Malcolm 1994; Simms 2001). Everyday practices and traditions of consensus were echoed in the political sphere by coalition-building and a habit of pragmatic compromise (Donia and Fine 1994). Bosnia's pluralist heritage in terms of syncretic movements and 'religious bridge-building' dated back at least to the late Middle Ages (Norris 1994: 263–268). Yet, recently, the media's, the politicians' and the scholars' abuse of cultural determinism and vilification of reality has reached paroxistic levels ever since Bosnia (Bennet 1994). Even in Kosovo, a long tradition of coexistence has been all but forgotten (Malcolm 1999), while many US commentators have been suddenly re-reading the Macedonian conflict as a re-enactment of ethnic or civilizational incompatibilities.

In other words, Yugoslavia's collapse was not resulting from atavistic ethnic tensions (Bennett 1994; Ramet 1999). On the contrary, a lingering negative memory of imperfect coexistence was artfully revived by Belgrade television with technicolor effects. Sheer propaganda is essential for ethnic exclusivist regimes, from the Young Turks to the Nazis or Serbia's ethnic cleansers. As a framework for interpreting ongoing events, cultural determinism was a clumsy but effective deceit: It simultaneously became a cause and an effect of the West's tragic failure in the Balkans.[14] It was also an effective strategy aimed at pulverizing the multiethnic fabric of Bosnia and other societies. Its greatest 'success' was to turn neighbours and friends into mortal enemies, almost overnight.

Historical determinism

Historical determinism is the view that the past has got a hold on the present, and that we cannot escape its grasp. Each nation is condemned by its own yore, even to the point of repeating the past itself. In analysing current ethnopolitical conflicts, historical determinists assert that there are unshakable geo-political alliances which endure over the years and these determine domestic politics as well as international relations.

Historical determinism differs from cultural determinism in that it relies on historical memories and legacies as causal factors, rather than on culture or religion. Thus, even people sharing the same religion or 'grand civilization' may collide simply because they have already collided in the past. Each conflict is explained as a recurring pattern of historical alliances of the type which we saw, for instance, when Bulgaria clashed with Serbia and Greece. Accordingly, Greece has 'always' been an ally of Serbia and Russia, but has also been an antagonist of Bulgaria, despite sharing a common Orthodox faith. Accordingly, the intermittent anti-Serbian attitudes in Bulgaria are supposed to revive old time alliances dating back at least to the Second Balkan War (1913).

Historical determinists are often nationalists themselves, and pretend to explain the current conflict as a *longue durée* epic battle, rooted in age-old enmities. Many contemporary nationalists simply see modern conflicts as instances of never-ending, perennial patterns of persecutions (Takei 1998): negative events are perceived as befalling in recurring cycles which escape logic and cannot sensibly be explained if not in term of atavistic idiosyncrasies. This is in contrast with most modernist approaches. Indeed, a full-blown theory of modernity would claim that things could never be the same again after the spread of industrialization, accompanied or preceded by state militarism (Gellner 1983). For instance, the Armenian genocide can be seen as the earliest avatar of a tragically novel trend that would become the hallmark of the twentieth century.[15] Many Holocaust scholars describe genocide as an entirely modern occurrence with its unprecedented systematic technological aspects (Bauman 1989).[16]

But historical determinism can lead even further: we learn that, in case of an irredentist war pitting Hungary against Romania, France will instinctively side with Romania in virtue of their shared 'Latin' heritage. Should we equally expect that the Finns and the Estonians will enlist their armies in defence of their distant kinsmen, the Hungarians? Not to count the 'civilizational' factor that 'the French' are not part of the 'Orthodox civilization' while Rumania is. Likewise, Germany's early recognition of Croatia was allegedly dictated by historical alliances dating back to the Third Reich and even further. In the early 1990s, possibly the most influential coterie promoting this view in international fora consisted in Milosevic's own cronies. The fiction that a freshly reunited Germany in 1991 supported Croatia's independence for 'historic' reasons (that is, as a former 'ally' during World War II) percolated through the media, notably in the *New York Times*, whose lines and editorials Edward Herman and Noam Chomsky have clearly identified as being 'based on major falsifications, but in keeping with their propaganda function' (Herman and Chomsky 1988: 141).[17]

If all this were true, we should anticipate an extremely unstable world ruled by memory and emotions mingled with sheer egotistic interests, rather than cold impartiality. Once it is conceded that each nation cannot escape its historical mission of conquest and subjugation, no nation can act as a fair, dispassionate arbiter, or as neutral, detached 'third party'. This would first and foremost apply to the USA, a country most vulnerable to both ethnic lobbying and civilizational crusades.[18]

Of course, alliances in the Balkans have shifted over the centuries in unpredictable ways. Some more enduring coalitions may be discernible, but there is scarcely a relationship which has been able to withstand the vicissitudes of history. For instance, the historical (rather than cultural) alliance between France and Serbia may have been radically altered by post-1999 developments.[19] A parallel tradition of Serbophilia has been hard hit and castigated in Britain, at least after 1999.[20] There is much to dispute even about the most discussed alliance, the supposedly quasi-mystical bond between Russia and Serbia, originally conceived in the framework of Pan-Slavism.[21]

The sudden emergence of historical determinism in Western political discourse during the 1990s recapitulated the dominant attitude prevailing in Belgrade's chanceries and environs. In the case of Serbia, the watershed date was 1389, the mythical recurrence of the defeat of 'the Serbs' at the hand of 'the Turks' in Kosovo Polje (Anzulovic 1999).[22] 'History' here directly replaced culture and even ethnicity: the Albanians' distinctive origins were obliterated, their culture made irrelevant. What is central to this case of historical determinism (which is entirely able to turn history on its head) is the Albanians' and other groups' arbitrary association with the historical enemy of Serbia: 'the Turks'. Contemporary Serbian massacres against Bosnians, Sandjakis and Kosovars were often referred to as the latest chapter of an epic struggle against 'the Turks'. The effects on the ground of this dominant past-oriented discourse became immediately discernible, as recounted by many courageous reporters who engaged in high-risk investigative journalism: 'When one went into a village where fighting had taken place, it was often easier to get a history lesson than a reliable account of what had occurred earlier the same day' (Rieff 1995: 69). As casualties mounted, history came to the fore and gave major impetus and justification to an endless chain of crimes, revenge and counter-revenge.

In recent years, historical determinism has typically plagued academic endeavours, governmental rhetoric, and popular discourse, particularly over the Yugoslav conflict. There have been repeated references to a supposed tradition of endemic warfare and relentless bloodshed in the Balkans. This has served to create an aura of historical inevitability that has in turn been used to justify ongoing events.

The resurgence of historical determinism is an indication that many scholars and politicians, as well as ordinary people, are moving in an interpretive vacuum. Refusing or lacking more rational and convincing explanations, they fall back onto primordialist accounts of war and conflict. Yet, the past offers only part of the explanation. Present political developments have much more bearing on our understanding.

Institutionalism vs culturalism?

Most of the issues raised above relate to a crucial question: 'what are ethnic conflicts made of?' A second line of investigation involves the major ingredients giving rise to nationalist mobilizations: 'what are the factors triggering their formation and crystallization?' Many competing views have emerged and they have centered alternatively on economy, politics, history, culture, institutions, and so on. Economy as a significant key factor has been analysed consistently, and eventually ruled out, by Connor (1984, 2001; see also the Introduction: 6ff). Among alternative factors, we have seen various deterministic approaches putting culture or history at the centre stage. Institutions, and in particularly the state, are key variables analysed by several authors.

One of the major contemporary controversies revolves around the tension between institutionalists and culturalists (Lecours 2000). In contrast with other sets of oppositions and dichotomies, these two are clearly compatible: it is possible to focus on the centrality of culture in shaping institutions,[23] while simultaneously focusing on the opposite direction, the capacity of institutions to influence culture, and on how both fashion ethnopolitical mobilization.[24]

Followers of the modernization paradigm believed in the doctrine of nation-building, the idea that institutions (usually the state) can shape and even spawn nations, while quelling impertinent ethnic cleavages. Walker Connor has recognized this extreme form of institutionalism as political-institutional determinism, and has effectively moved in the opposite direction: from ethnicity to institutions, via the nation. Nations cannot be fashioned or forged at élite's will. Rather, they are responses to modernization and increasing inter-ethnic contacts. The latter events transform previously unaware ethnic groups into fully mobilized nations, which in turn require legitimate institutions, notably the control of the state, that is, the modern institution *par excellence.*

Nor can Connor be defined as a *culturalist*, since culture belongs to the realm of tangibility and objectivity, while ethnicity is predicated upon subjective feelings and has on its side the light power of elusiveness. Connor's critique of strict culturalism (culture as a causal factor) has been well explored in Coakley's chapter. In other words, Connor is neither an institutionalist nor a culturalist.

Some authors have argued that Connor's emphasis on ethnicity is at the expenses of institutions. By radically rejecting the 'nation-building' school with all its flagrant mistakes, prejudices, elitism, Euro-centrism, and chrono-centrism, one risks succumbing to the opposite illusion, namely a disregard for the long-term influence of institutions on all aspects of material and emotional life: patterns of behaviour, attitudes, beliefs and, not to be forgotten, cultural artifacts.

Probably in no area of the ecumene can this be discerned more clearly than in one of Connor's regions of expertise, the former Communist bloc.[25] In particular, the deep-rooted impact of erstwhile Communist institutions is most visible in the country which first of all has re-drawn its boundaries according to the ethnic principle, namely Germany. In many respects, German unification remains a fiction in the wider socio-cultural and attitudinal sphere. The unification process has led to more problems and tensions that could have been originally predicted. Instead of boosting Germany's self-image, unification has been widely regretted from the moment Bonn had to face the hard task of dismantling a fossilized bureaucracy in the East. After the initial enthusiasm, unification has come under hefty attack among West Germans. Popular perceptions of German unity have become adverse, while negative 'ethnic' stereotypes of East Germans have emerged (Behrend M. 1995; Panzig 1995). The popular dichotomy between *Ossies* (East Germans) and *Wessies* (West Germans) has correspondingly increased (Behrend H. 1995). This gap has been institutionalized by the massive support enjoyed by the reformed Communist Party (PDS) in East Germany, in spite of the deep anti-communist sentiment of the local population. The gap is sufficiently wide that some Germans decline to identify the *Ossies* as Germans. On the other hand, Eastern intellectuals had accused West Germany's establishment of cultural colonialism (Blankenburg 1995).[26] All this despite the fact that the flight of ethnic Germans from Eastern Europe into Germany has emptied many areas of its German minorities, making it possible an unprecedented overlap between *Reich* and *Volk*.

The rift was evident even in Berlin, the new capital of united Germany. Data from the 1996 City Registry is straightforward, and unambiguous: only 562 of the 16,383 marriages in Berlin occurred between West and East Berliners; 22 per cent of all marriages were between Berliners and foreigners, and only 4 per cent between East and West Berliners. Typically, West 'Berliners find more in common with Slavs, Africans, Turks . . .'.[27]

Given also the spate of racial attacks occurring in East Germany,[28] as compared with the anti-racist candlelight demonstrations packing West Germany's streets,[29] one is tempted to declare that we are confronting two entirely different societies, endowed with dissimilar cultural baggages and perceptions of reality, but dwelling under the same ethnonational roof – and, now, the same state. It is relatively common to hear that *Ossies* and *Wessies* form two distinct peoples, with not much in common except an imposed standardized high culture and a (probably misguided!) belief in common descent.

After over ten years of unification, this expanding gap tells a lot about the legacy of institutions (in particular state-sanctioned Communist institutions) on people's emotions, attitudes, perceptions and behaviour (Bunce 1999). Of course, it would be exaggerated to declare that German ethnicity and sense of common 'brotherhood' are weaker than the cultural–ideological divide, but certainly the legacy of institutions has proven to be quite impressive, profound and long-lasting.

As demonstrated by classical psychiatric investigation, Communist state terrorism had a far-reaching impact: techniques of indoctrination and interrogation used by Communist regimes often led to depressive stupor, a sense of total helplessness and uncertainty, impairment of critical capacities and disruption of mental functioning. This often ushered in a loss of personal and individual attributes by increasing dependence upon the regime (Hinkle and Wolff 1956). The end result was self-destructive conformism, a will to emulate the powerful, and contempt for the powerless. This led to unparalleled degrees of submission and torpidity, which made it subsequently easier for post-Communist societies to accept passively the unyielding power of mafias, MTV and fast-food giants, as well as nationalism. As Ernest Gellner (1994) has rightly pointed out, consumerism was much more enthusiastically endorsed than any meaningful ratio of substantial democracy.

To date, after over a decade of 'free-market' diktats, basic attitudes have only tenuously changed in many post-communist countries. In some areas they have indeed deteriorated or even vanished, notably in inter-ethnic relations and grassroots democracy (both of which remain awfully fragile). As democratic practices stay elusive, ethnic exclusivism triumphs. Mass ideology from the Soviet era has been directly supplanted by mass consumerism as 'globalization' holds sway. In this context, globalization becomes a more subtle form of totalitarianism, accepted passively by most people as it lands on them another salvational promise. Such a post-communist *Weltanschauung* has nothing to do with civilizational, ethnic, cultural, historical, perhaps even economic, legacies, but simply with the fresher inheritance of 40 to 70 years of Communist manipulation.

Institutions may not matter more than popularly held myths of ethnic descent, but by underscoring the latter one risks ignoring the former at the expense of accuracy.

Looking at the future: where to go from here?

Walker Connor has established some firm bases for the future study of nationalism. Once laid its conceptual grounding, nationalism studies have become a self-standing discipline. Courses of nationalism are now available in most English-language universities; only ten years ago they were still a rarity. Most of these courses use Connor"s classical articles as compulsory reading – some of which are included in his textbook (Connor 1994). It will be up to the responsibility of the single author whether to consider or disregard Connor's conceptual and theoretical foundational work. In doing so they will have once more to deal with the terminological conundrum, only to begin again or to indulge in weak, or risky, scholarship.

One of the hot themes and contexts which is going to grab scholarly attention in the forthcoming years is likely to be globalization or, more meaningful still, the intellectual and popular response to it. The sudden rise of the 'no global' movement will no doubt propel a great amount of academic research (Hertz 2000; Klein 2000). This is especially impelling since 'national sovereignty', the key ingredient in the nationalism studies staple, has been seized by multinational corporations: As George Monbiot has illustrated with richness of details, corporations have taken over the function of government in many crucial areas, thereby menacing the very core of the *demos* (Monbiot 2000). However, this relatively new field still proceeds in a conceptual–terminological vacuum – more or less, as nationalism studies were moving a few years ago: there is no yet coherent or universal definition of globalization. Some definitions focus on mere economic aspects, other on financial flows, other on policy-making and the law, and so on.

At least for our purpose, cultural globalization is the most visible form of globalization, and hence perhaps the most effective one. But in its current shape, cultural globalization can be broadly understood as one-way massive import of standardized cultural items and icons from a single country, the United States of America. For large portions of the ecumene, it is hence synonymous with Westernization, or, more accurately, Americanization. 'Americanization' should be understood here in its most superficial, incoherent, fractional, and deficient sense, as aping and mimicking something one does not even grasp the value of, and as the spread of quite trivial and commercial aspects of industrialized US mass-directed products. Because the process is one-way, top-down and unidirectional, there is scarce fusion or amalgamation between nations and ethnic groups.

The main challenge for the scholar of nationalism will be first of all to define the relationship between the two phenomena. Does nationalism reinforce globalization or can it rather represent a challenge to globalization? Is globalization reinforcing nationalism or can it in some way be channelled in the opposite direction? What kind of nationalism is most likely to emerge with, or as a response to, globalization? Is globalization a causal factor in the explosion of ethnic conflict, xenophobia and racism?

The last question is of particular importance, since most evidence seems to point to an affirmative response, namely the existence of a direct link between cultural globalization and the rise of racist and xenophobic nationalism. This follows in part from Connor's (1994) postulate, also expressed in this book's Introduction and reiterated in many of the chapters, that some forms of international contacts are bound to create more clashes than encounters, or further separation rather than fusion. But which kind of contacts? Certainly, not all forms of contacts are 'ethnogenetic' or bound to invigorate ethnic awareness and militancy. Otherwise, we could only expect a world in perpetual conflict. So, which type of international contacts are bound to generate conflict? This question points towards an entire new range of possibilities in the expansion of scholarly research. Connor would agree that those contacts leading to a sense of group *threat* are the most conflict-engendering ones. Specifically, a threat to the group's culture, way of life and sense of continuity is likely to lead to increasing group mobilization. But this rules out the possibility that a sense of threat can be also artfully fabricated by political élites (Zulaika and Douglass 1998). Similarly, I would add, a real threat can be easily hidden to public opinion by media and political manipulation. Therefore the focus needs to be, again and again, on political élites – which does not rule out Connor's overall critique of elitism in academia.

Or, is it rather the case that cultural globalization does *not* really represent a genuine increase in inter-personal, inter-ethnic and inter-cultural contacts? In fact, in most areas of public life there is no cultural globalization at all in the real sense. The process is rather pyramidal, top-down, with a few individuals and groups, nearly all in the USA, establishing the patterns to be followed by the rest of mankind. If this 'brave new global world' had its own capital, this would likely be Hollywood, rather than Washington. Political globalization may still seem remote to some vintage scholars of nationalism so sentimentally attached to their object of study, but 'Hollywoodization' has become a daily routine for millions of peoples all over the world. Indeed, for increasing numbers it is the only known reality. The most primary tools of socialization, erstwhile in the firm hands of the family (nuclear or extended), then assumed by the state in the industrialization 'phase' of compulsory schooling, have become, with post-modernity, at the mercy of uncontrollable cash-driven corporate powers and media tycoons. If a group can no longer socialize its children according to its culture and traditions, then the very basis of nationhood is visibly at stake – although nationalism itself may not only persist and resist, but be perceived as a response to the onslaught.

By relying on Hollywood *et similia* as unique conveyors of 'globalization', inter-ethnic communication automatically drains away. There are instances where communication has virtually vanished: in many post-communist societies, the explosion of chauvinism, racism, neo-fascism and xenophobia goes hand in hand with a blind faith in mass consumerism. As diagnosed by LSE political philosopher John Gray (1998), free market dogmas have already heralded the triumph of 'anarcho-capitalism' and its atomic mafias in the MacDonaldized East. But there is a more important factor: the collapse of real, effective inter-ethnic and international communication as a direct consequence of superficial Americanization. Let's take an example: until 1989, it was relatively easy to see on Hungarian television and in many of Budapest's cinemas, movie masterpieces from France, Russia, Italy, Britain and many other countries. This is no longer possible. Only the worst (and the best) of Hollywood can now be seen every day on every Hungarian channel and cinema screen. Data on this 'cultural suicide' or 'self-genocide' begins now to be available – albeit largely undebated in Hungary itself.[30]

Rather than representing a bridge between cultures, such an unilateral planetary drive has eroded the basis for mutual understanding, hampering inter-ethnic and international communication. This has been facilitated by the persisting legacy of totalitarianism which had already turned communist societies into a cultural *tabula rasa* (Conversi 2001). But in Hungary (and the entire East) 'Americanization' has not simply meant the eradication of Hungarian (and other) cultures in all possible aspects bar language (in the former case semantically and philologically impenetrable, hence unavailable to non-Hungarian speakers). It has also meant the effacement and undoing of neighbouring cultures. And two self-destructions add up to each other in incremental ways: from no culture and no inter-communication, through a twofold negative relationship, to likely conflict.

Yet, if cultural globalization can be simply identified as naked 'Americanization', then the equation is simpler and scholars of nationalism *may* find something new to ponder about and begin theorizing anew. In this case, globalization would be automatically associated with colonialism and/or imperialism (depending on ideological inclination). *Il re' e' nudo.* It would follow that nationalism and ethnicity could potentially become vehicles of resistance to US-led globalization. But this has mostly not yet been the case. On the contrary, nationalism has often reinforced globalization, and vice versa. Therefore their relationship needs to be scrutinized more in depth, knowing that an apparent acceptance of US iconography is no proof that either the surface or the substance will be passively accepted in the long term.

Three lines of research on this relationship can be tentatively proposed. A first line of interpretation may focus on the long-term political effects of socio-cultural change: Benjamin Barber's (1985) pioneering view that 'McWorld' harbors in itself the seeds of a planetary 'Jihad' belongs to a wider tradition which sees massive social uprooting as leading to widespread social unrest, and cultural destruction as ushering social disintegration. This approach can be associated with a classical 'cause-effect' model or, borrowing from medicine and chemistry, an *homeostatic* view of social change (Conversi 1995). For instance, Ernest Gellner (1983) saw nationalism as an inevitable consequence of, and reaction to, industrialization – although within functionalist parameters and in a different socio-historical context. But it was particularly Walker Connor (1994) who emphasized the underlying, persistent and pervasive force of oppositional ethnicity against the 'grand' projects of nation-builders.

A second interpretive framework might come from what can be called 'failed communication' view expressed in the preceding sections. The key argument is that the current 'world order' has a vertical, indeed pyramidal, structure, where groups have less and less opportunities to inter-communicate or interact in a meaningful way and know each other's traditions. For increasing numbers of individuals, a US-manufactured mass consumerist culture remains the only 'window on the world'. Consequently, to know and appreciate one's own neighbours has become an ever arduous task. 'Free-market fundamentalism', spearheaded by cultural American-ization has led not only to environmental catastrophe, but also to an incremental rise in nationalism and xenophobia.

A third line of analysis should focus on a more concrete and actual form of glob-alization, which can work independently from Americanization: the expanding role of *diaspora* in international politics and the rise of 'e-mail nationalism' – a term coined by Benedict Anderson (1992). In an increasingly uniform world, ethnic identities have not only resisted, but are being unremittingly emphasized. The expansion of the Internet has prompted the creation of global ethnopolitical net-works which can be constricted by state boundaries only at the price of curtailing fundamental human rights.[31] Although increasingly monitored by state agencies, mobile phones have at the same time reinforced ethnic exclusivism, family ties and parental control by increasing communal contacts and decreasing the chance of new inter-personal encounters.

Conclusions

None of the above *-isms* or trends listed in this epilogue can be ascribed to Walker Connor. Even though Connor has not directly confronted them, his prose has carefully eschewed any of the above traps, eluding most forms of determinism. Yet, the latter are pervading the literature at large and have even emerged in some of this volume's contributions.

It is generally difficult to situate a particular scholar within any of these fields, unless s/he is a self-declared nationalist. In particular, most primordialists them-selves resist any definition of primordialism, as they thrive on indefiniteness and ambiguity. On the other hand, name-calling is recurrent in academia and some of the contributions do indulge in this practice. This editor has deliberately chosen not to be immune from it. And Smith's chapter defines Connor as a 'late modernist', while referring to his own approach as 'ethnosymbolist'. Although this epilogue's many *-isms* may lead some readers to raise their eyebrows, labelling and categor-ization are built-in in scientific, humanistic, even artistic, enterprise. Taxonomies are not tedious reorderings of disciplinary knowledge, but can be creative and syn-cretic endeavours needed for the very advancement of human learning and scholarship. In this respect, they may serve to identify underlying, even emerging, trends in the social science.

The most recurrent theme in this volume has been that of ethnic persistence and continuity. The emphasis on the unfathomable and elusive character of ethnicity should hence be part of a wider sociology and history of human unpredictability. As with other social movements, ethnic mobilizations and conflicts have frequently surprised scholars and journalists for their sudden, 'unexpected' appearance. As a recent example, a (truly global) anti-global movement has unanticipatedly emerged in dispersed locations of the ecumene, from Seattle to Prague, from Quebec City to Gothenborg and Genoa, ostensibly without announcing itself. Yet, a popular reaction against the excesses of globalization, perceived by many as all-pervasive US colonialism, was fully predictable – and some have anticipated both its emergence and its initially contradictory, disorganized, 'anarchical' modalities (Barber 1995).

Likewise, the evidence accumulated from many case studies over the past thirty years point to the possibility of predicting or at least expecting, the explosion of ethnic conflicts in specific situations. There is, for instance, ample evidence to say that the role of the state is essential in prefiguring ethnic conflict, which largely depends on the state's (either conflictive or tolerant) response to, and relationships with, multiculturalism, religious pluralism, and ethnic dissent (Williams 1994).

Of course, primordialism and essentialism can be identified as part of a political agenda or as a weapon at the disposal of both nationalists and empire-builders. In particular, the 'fiction' of pure irrationality dissimulates a political goal: once a group or person is described as totally irrational, unmanageable to reason, therefore unreasonable, it/s/he is automatically pushed at the fringes of humanity. Authoritarian regimes and anti-terrorist 'experts' refer extensively to the reasonless, illogical 'essence' of their foes.[32] Unreason implies fallacy and error, thus untruth and falsehood, eventually leading to insanity and aberration. The results are ostracism, exile and banishment for entire peoples, as well as for individual ideologically or ethnically associated with non-governmental views.

Yet, ethnic sentiments have an inarguably non-rational (perhaps even 'irrational') bent and the actors involved in ethnic disputes seem often impermeable to reason, at least universal reason. This remains the core of the dilemma and makes a radical rejection of primordialism difficult (Grosby 1994). In general, it is easier to reject the other, above described, forms of determinism on both scholarly and ethical grounds. Primordialism can be more easily rejected on purely methodological grounds. It fails because of its unreliability, since it is prevalently based on unproven assumptions. This book has collected fellow travellers on Connor's pioneering road, a good scholarly generation, plus a few new voices, advancing possible new directions of research.

Notes

1 Following Clifford Geertz's lead, Eller and Coughlan (1993) identify primordialism's three main attributes: *apriority* (the anti-sociological idea that primordial attachments are 'given' and 'prior to all experience of interaction'), *ineffability* (the idea that primordial attachments are overpowering and 'ineffable', and therefore escape sociological scrutiny), and *affectivity* (the idea that primordial attachments are quintessentially emotional and predicated on affective bonds, which again makes them quite impermeable

to social research, given the poor advancement in the study of emotions). Each of these three dimensions relate to my second definition of primordialism, insofar as they all advocate a renunciation of scholarly sociological analysis in front of the overpowering irrationality and elusive emotionality of the phenomenon. For a critique to this position, see Grosby (1994).

2 Essentialism is sometimes opposed to *constructivism* (more than instrumentalism). Whereas essentialists reify the nation as an organic whole, constructivists see it as constructed by *fiat* of man, rather than God. Hence constructivists include prototypical *instrumentalists*, such as *élite-manipulation theorists* (Hobsbawm and Ranger 1983), who see nations as the top-down creation of political leaders either élites or proto-élites.

3 A cautionary note: I have generally avoided this use – bar in the book's title, *The Basques, the Catalans and Spain*, chosen by the publisher (Conversi 1997).

4 US media commentators and the public at large do often engage in the belief that, outside the US, entire groups are naturally inclined to rehearse atavistic battles, scrimmages and civil or civilizational wars.

5 For a typology of these formulas, see Coakley (1992).

6 Secession has been the most popular option in the wake of post-communist disintegration and social chaos, notably in the former Yugoslavia (Conversi 2000a).

7 Louis Kriesberg's (1998) book on 'creative' conflict resolution may provide an antidote to Safran's chapter.

8 On this see the chapter on 'Adopting conflict strategies' in Kriesberg (1998).

9 One can obviously dispute whether is there such a thing as 'culture'. What we can tangibly identify are only cultural artifacts whose reproduction is depending on inter-generational transmission – although we tend to interpret and classify them according to our notions of the moment.

10 Many nowadays 'religious' wars can paradoxically be described as 'atheist' wars (Conversi 1999).

11 Among the earliest critics, see Ajami (1993: 2ff). Ajami rebuts, more convincingly, that 'civilizations do not control states, states control civilizations'. See also the dedicated issue of *The New Republic*, whose front cover is devoted to 'Europe's long, vicious war against Islam in the Balkans' (Ajami 1994: 29–37). See also Edward W. Said, 'The Clash of Ignorance', *The Nation*, 22 October 2001.

12 A 1932 quote by the official Belgrade 'propagandist', Dr Radovanovitch, director of the Press Bureau of Belgrade's Presidency of the Council, can clarify this point:

> [Thessaloniki] has never been Greek; it has a Serb city peopled with Southern Serbs. Its affiliation to Greece has been its death sentence! It will not revive, it will not find again its lost prosperity, until it becomes again the great commercial port of the Balkans towards the Mediterranean and the Orient. And it cannot become this great port unless it returns to Yugoslavia, of which it is a natural and historical dependency. It is the same with Drama, Seres, Janina, Kastoria, which have been of no importance since they were delivered to the degenerate Greek nation.
>
> (Radovanovitch, cited in Pozzi, 1935: 101)

At that time, Serbian expansionism identified the entire Macedonian region up to Thessaloniki as 'Southern Serbia' (Michas 2002).

13 Henry A. Kissinger, 'Doing Injury to History' *Newsweek International*, 5 April 1999. See also the milestone investigative work by Hitchins (2001).

14 In particular, by underpinning governments and politicians opposing intervention in Bosnia, cultural determinism initially served the interests of non-interventionists, but was used consequently to champion Western military intervention in 1999.

15 There is hence a gulf between the 1914–16 mass extermination campaigns and the massacres of 1894–96. But, even by 1894, nationalism was already an influential force in Turkey as it came entirely from the West (Melson 1996). From an Anatolian perspective, the Balkans are indeed 'the West'. And the Young Turks' nationalist movement

was inspired by, if not mimicking, its modern post-1789 Western archetypes. Young Turks army officials fought against victorious nationalist uprisings in the Balkans and ended up imitating them while forging links with German nationalism (Dadrian 1996).

16 One exception may be Spain, further to Léon Poliakov's *The Aryan Myth* and as shown by Douglass' chapter, which deals precisely with the '*conversos*', for whom mere conversion was no longer sufficient to avoid persecution and had to demonstrate their purity of blood in order to get a fair trial. In more than one sense, Spain was prototypically modern, but it was so ahead of the time, that is, before mass industrialization.

17 For a detailed critique of this view, see Conversi (1998a, 2000b) which traces its genesis and trajectories from Slobodan Milosevic to Lord Carrington, then on to US Secretary of State Warren Christopher and down to Anglo-Saxon academia and public opinion. See also Conversi (1998a), Cordell (2000), Deckers (2000), and Jeffery and Paterson (2000). In general, there is a propensity to stress conflict between European countries and regions, rather than cooperation. More recently the US administration has tried to sabotage the International Court of Justice (ICC) in The Hague.

18 Incidentally, an essentialist approach informs several anti-European trends in the Bush administration, devoted to break apart any further move towards European unification. This notably involves an emphasis on all sorts of ethnic 'hatred', notably in the Balkans. For instance, Macedonian and Greek media and scholars have denounced the US administration connivance with Greater Albanian aspirations in Macedonia, while the flow of weapons and cash between the USA and the major guerrilla group in Macedonia has been well documented (see Joanna Coles 'I will fight for my people', *The Times*, Wednesday, 28 March 2001; and Chris Hedges, 'Albanian War Cry Rises Half a World Away, in Staten Island', *The New York Times*, 19 March 2001). Macedonian public opinion is convinced that the USA are behind homegrown terrorism. In general, there is a US propensity to stress conflict between European countries and regions, rather than cooperation.

19 For France's historical ties with Serbia, see Birke (1960).

20 On Britain's pro-Serbian role, see Conversi (1998b, 2000b) and Simms (2001).

21 As for pro-Russian sentiments in Serbia, Stephen Clissold defined it as *ignorant admiration*. He recalls that during World War II 'Moscow did not . . . lift a finger to help her new ally [Serbia] during the latter's ensuing ordeal [the German invasion], and withdrew recognition from the government of the dismembered state with cynical promptness. Yet when, on 22 June 1941, the Soviet Union was invaded, these things were forgotten in Serbia in an upsurge of popular emotion' (Clissold 1966: 212). On Russian-Serbian relationships, see Mendeloff (1999).

22 Anzulovic's (1999) approach also moves within the parameters of cultural determinism: accordingly, myths of war and revenge (especially the Kosovo myth) have shaped perceptions of interethnic encounters to the extent of influencing political developments and determining the very rise of Milosevic. In other words, Milosevic did not make the myths, rather the myths made Milosevic.

23 On the influence of language maintenance on political choices, see Conversi (1997), Cormack (2000) and Wright (1999). On the relationship between cultural nationalism and political tolerance, see Guerin and Pelletier (2000).

24 This author has followed simultaneously an institutionalist and a culturalist approach, although with a more considerable focus on cultural factors (Conversi 1997). A prominent attempt to emphasize the mutual relationship between institutions and culture in a balanced way, although with no emphasis on ethnicity, is Robert Putnam's work on civic traditions in Italy (see Putnam 1993, particularly Chapter 2 on 'Changing the rules' and Chapter 5 on 'Tracing the roots of the civic community').

25 The term 'bloc' should be intended here in its fully-fledged totalitarian significance, as an Orwellian steam-rolling machine devoted to homegenize culture, freezing it for posterity.

26 Allen Buchanan (1991: 51) points out that German unification can only succeed if

West Germans perceive the enormous transfer of wealth to the Eastern part as redistribution among one people, rather than redistribution to another people: 'The greater the identification of the benefactors with the recipients, the less likely the benefactors are to see themselves as suffering the injustice of discriminatory redistribution.'

27 See *The Guardian*, 22 July 1996: 7.
28 On the rise of neo-racism in unified Germany, see Ramet (1994).
29 On the candlelight demonstrations against xenophobic violence which gradually changed the public mood, see Kinzer (1994).
30 For a synthesis, see Barber (1995: 90ff.).
31 This has been attempted only in totalitarian regimes such as Iraq, North Korea and China. See Bobson Wong 'China closes 17,000 internet cafes', *Digital Freedom Network*. 21 November 2001. [http://dfn.org/focus/china/internetcafes-closed.htm].
32 On the political use of the anti-terrorism 'industry', see the landmark study by Zulaika and Douglass (1996).
33 A fresh example is Silvio Berlusconi's far-right regime in Italy, supported by US President Bush, which in July 2001 referred to the suppressed anti-globalization demonstrations as backward-looking, acting outside the bonds of rationality, and adverse to the inevitable advance of globalization which would lead the nation to progress – and simultaneously hinted at a 'red' conspiracy to subvert social order and the country's government.

References

Ajami, Fouad 1993. 'The summoning'. *Foreign Affairs*. 1 September. 72(4).

—— 1993. 'In Europe's shadows'. *The New Republic*. 21 November. 211(21): 29–37.

Almond, Mark 1994. *Europe's Backyard War: The War in the Balkans*. London: Heinemann.

Anderson, Benedict 1992. *Long-Distance Nationalism: World Capitalism and the Rise of Identity Politics*. Berkeley, CA: Center for German and European Studies, University of California.

Anzulovic, Branimir 1999. *Heavenly Serbia: From Myth to Genocide*. London: Hurst/New York: New York University Press.

Barber, Benjamin R. 1996. *Jihad vs. McWorld*. New York: Ballantine Books.

Bauman, Zygmunt 1989. *Modernity and the Holocaust*. Ithaca, NY: Cornell University Press/Polity Press.

Behrend, Hanna 1995. 'Inglorious German unification'. In Hanna Behrend (ed.) *German Unification. The Destruction of an Economy*. London: Pluto Press.

Behrend, Manfred 1995. 'Right-wing extremism in East Germany before and after the *Anschluss* to the Federal Republic'. In Hanna Behrend (ed.) *German Unification: The Destruction of an Economy*. London: Pluto Press.

Bennett, Christopher 1994. *Yugoslavia's Bloody Collapse: Causes, Course and Consequences*. New York: New York University Press/London: Hurst.

Birke, Ernst 1960. *Frankreich und Ostmitteleuropa im 19. Jahrhundert*. Cologne: Bohlau.

Blankenburg, Erhard 1995. 'The colonisation of East Germany: imposition of law and cultural identity'. In Keebet von Benda-Beckman and Maykel Verkuyten (eds) *Nationalism, Ethnicity and Cultural Identity in Europe*. Utrecht: University of Utrecht/European Research Centre on Migration and Ethnic Relations (ERCOMER), Comparative Studies in Migration and Ethnic Relations, no. 1.

Brown, David 2000. *Contemporary Nationalism: Civic, Ethnocultural, and Multicultural Politics*. London: Routledge.

Buchanan, Allen 1991. *Secession: The Morality of Political Divorce from Fort Sumter to Lithuania and Quebec*. Boulder, CO: Westview Press.

Bunce, Valerie 1999. *Subversive Institutions*. Cambridge: Cambridge University Press.

Clissold, Stephen 1966. 'Occupation and resistance'. In Stephen Clissold (ed.) *A Short History of Yugoslavia: From Early Times to 1966*. Cambridge: Cambridge University Press.

Coakley, John 1992. 'The resolution of ethnic conflict: towards a typology'. *International Political Science Review*. 13(4): 343–358.

—— 1994. 'Approaches to the resolution of ethnic conflict: the strategy of non-territorial autonomy'. *International Political Science Review*. 15(3): 297–314.

Connor, Walker 1984. 'Eco- or ethnonationalism'. *Ethnic and Racial Studies*. 7 (October): 342–359.

—— 1993. 'Beyond reason: the nature of the ethnonational bond'. *Ethnic and Racial Studies*. XVI (July 1993): 373–389.

—— 2001. 'From a theory of relative economic deprivation towards a theory of relative political deprivation'. In Michael Keating and John McGarry (eds) *Minority Nationalism in a Changing World Order*. Oxford: Oxford University Press.

Conversi, Daniele 1995. 'Reassessing theories of nationalism: nationalism as boundary maintenance and creation'. *Nationalism and Ethnic Politics*. 1(1): 73–85.

—— 1997. *The Basques, the Catalans, and Spain: Alternative Routes to Nationalist Mobilization*. London: Hurst/Reno: University of Nevada Press.

—— 1998a. *German-Bashing and the Breakup of Yugoslavia*. Seattle: University of Washington Press/Henry M. Jackson School of International Studies (The Donald W. Treadgold Papers in Russian, East European and Central Asian Studies. 16 (May)).

—— 1998b. 'Les relacions anglosèrbies entre les dues guerres mundials'. *L'Avenç*. 226 (July): 6–12.

—— 1999. 'Nationalism, boundaries and violence'. *Millennium. Journal of International Studies*. 28(3): 553–584.

—— 2000a. 'Central secession: towards a new analytical concept? The case of former Yugoslavia'. *Journal of Ethnic and Migration Studies*. April, 26(2): 333–356.

—— 2000b. *La desintegració de Iugoslàvia*. Barcelona/Catarroja: Editorial Afers-El Contemporani.

—— 2001. 'Post-communist societies between ethnicity and globalization'. *Journal of Southern Europe and the Balkans*. 3(2): 193–196.

—— 2002. 'The dissolution of Yugoslavia: secession by the centre?' In John Coakley (ed.) *The Territorial Management of Ethnic Conflicts*. London: Frank Cass.

Cordell, Karl 2000. 'Germany's European policy challenges'. *Regional and Federal Studies*. 10(2): 141–145 .

Cormack, Mike 2000. 'Minority languages, nationalism and broadcasting: the British and Irish examples'. *Nations and Nationalism*. 6(3): 383–398.

Dadrian, Vahakn N. 1996. *German Responsibility in the Armenian Genocide: A Review of the Historical Evidence of German Complicity*. Watertown, MA: Blue Crane Books.

Deckers, Wolfgang 2000. 'Two souls, twin realities: German foreign policy from Slovenia to Kosovo'. *Central Europe Review*. 3 July, 2(26).

Donia, Robert J. and Fine, John V.A. 1994. *Bosnia and Hercegovina: A Tradition Betrayed*. New York: Columbia University Press/London: Hurst.

Eller, Jack David and Coughlan, Reed M. 1993. 'The poverty of primordialism: the demystification of ethnic attachments'. *Ethnic and Racial Studies*. 16(2): 183–202.

Gellner, Ernest 1981. *Muslim Society*. Cambridge: Cambridge University Press.

—— 1983. *Nations and Nationalism*. Oxford: Basil Blackwell/Ithaca: Cornell University Press.

—— 1994. *Conditions of Liberty: Civil Society and Its Rivals*. New York: Allen Lane/Penguin Press.

Gray, John 1998. 'Anarcho-capitalism in post-communist Russia'. In *False Dawn: The Delusions of Global Capitalism*. London: Granta Books: 132–165 .

Grosby, Steven 1994. 'The verdict of history: the inexpungeable tie of primordiality'. *Ethnic and Racial Studies*. 17(1): 164–171.

Guerin, Daniel and Pelletier, Rejean 2000. 'Cultural nationalism and political tolerance in advanced industrial societies: the Basque Country and Catalonia'. *Nationalism and Ethnic Politics*. 6(4): 1–22.

Guibernau, Montserrat 1999. *Nations Without States: Political Communities in a Global Age*. Oxford: Blackwell Publishers.

Henders, Susan J. 1997. 'Cantonisation: historical paths to territorial autonomy for regional cultural communities'. *Nations and Nationalism*. December, 3(4): 521–540.

Herman, Edward S. and Chomsky, Noam 1988. *Manufacturing Consent: The Political Economy of the Mass Media*. New York: Pantheon Books.

Hertz, Noreena 2001. *The Silent Takeover: Global Capitalism and the Death of Democracy*. London: Heinemann.

Hinkle, Lawrence E. and Wolff, Harold G. 1956. 'Communist interrogation and indoctrination of "enemies of the state"'. *AMA Archives of Neurology and Psychiatry*. 76: 115–174.

Hitchins, Christopher 2001. *The Trial of Henry Kissinger*. London: Verso .

Hobsbawm, Eric J. and Ranger, Terence (eds) 1983. *The Invention of Tradition*. Cambridge: Cambridge University Press.

Hodge, Carole 1999. *The Serb Lobby in the United Kingdom*. Seattle: University of Washington Press/Henry M. Jackson School of International Studies (The Donald W. Treadgold Papers in Russian, East European and Central Asian Studies. 22).

Huntington, Samuel P. 1997. *The Clash of Civilizations and the Remaking of the World Order*. New York: Simon and Schuster.

Jeffery, Charlie and Paterson, William E. 2000. 'Germany's power in Europe'. In Helen Wallace (ed.) *Interlocking Dimensions of Integration*. London: Macmillan.

Keating, Michael 1999. 'Asymmetrical government: multinational states in an integrating Europe'. *Publius*. 29(1): 71–86.

Kinzer, Stephen 1994. 'Demonstrations for tolerance'. In K.H. Jarausch and V. Gransow (eds) *Uniting Germany: Documents and Debates, 1944–1993*. Oxford: Berghahn Books: 267–269.

Klein, Naomi 2000. *No Logo: Taking Aim at the Brand Bullies*. New York: Picador.

Kriesberg, Louis 1998. *Constructive Conflicts: From Escalation to Resolution*. Lanham, MD: Rowman and Littlefield Publishers.

Kroeber, A.L. and Kluckhohn, Clyde 1952. *Culture: A Critical Review of Concepts and Definitions*. Cambridge, MA: The Museum.

Lecours, André 2000. 'Theorizing cultural identities: historical institutionalism as a challenge to the culturalists'. *Canadian Journal of Political Science*. 33(3): 499–522.

Lijphart, Arend 1977. *Democracy in Plural Societies: A Comparative Exploration*. New Haven and London: Yale University Press.

—— 1996. 'The puzzle of Indian democracy: a consociational interpretation'. *American Political Science Review*. 90: 258–68.

Loughlin, John 2000. 'The transformation of the state and the new territorial politics'. *L'intégration européenne entre émergence institutionnelle et recomposition de l'état*. Paris: CEVIPOF–CERI.

Lustick, Ian 1979. 'Stability in deeply divided societies: consociationalism versus control'. *World Politics*. 31: 325–44.

Malcolm, Noel 1994a. *Bosnia: A Short History*. New York: New York University Press.

—— 1994. *Kosovo: A Short History*. New York: New York University Press.

Melson, Robert 1996. 'The Armenian genocide as precursor and prototype of twentieth century genocide'. In Alan S. Rosenbaum (ed.) *Is the Holocaust Unique?* Boulder, CO: Westview Press: 87–100.

Mendeloff, David 1999. 'Sympathy for the devil: historical beliefs, mass education, and the Russian reaction to the Kosovo War'. Paper prepared for delivery at the 1999 Annual Meeting of the American Political Science Association, Atlanta. 2–5 September, 1999 (http: //pro.harvard.edu/papers/007/007020MendeloffD.pdf).

Michas, Takis 2002. *Unholy Alliance: Greece and Milosevic's Serbia in the Nineties*. College Station: Texas A&M University Press (Eastern European Studies. 15).

Monbiot, George 2000. *Captive State: The Corporate Takeover of Britain*. London: Macmillan.

Norris, H.T. 1994. *Islam in the Balkans: Religion and Society Between Europe and the Arab World*. London: Hurst.

Panzig, Christel 1995. 'Changing the East German countryside'. In Hanna Behrend (ed.), *German Unification: The Destruction of an Economy*. London: Pluto Press.

Poliakov, Léon 1974. *The Aryan Myth: A History of Racist and Nationalist Ideas in Europe*. Trans. Edmund Howard. New York: Basic Books.

Pozzi, Henri 1935. *Black Hand over Europe*. London: The Francis Mott Company: 101.

Putnam, Robert D. 1993. *Making Democracy Work: Civic Traditions in Modern Italy*. Princeton, NJ: Princeton University Press.

Ramet, Sabrina P. 1994. 'The radical Right in Germany'. *In Depth*. 4(1) Winter: 43–68.

—— 1999. *Balkan Babel: The Disintegration of Yugoslavia from the Death of Tito to the Insurrection in Kosovo*. (3rd edn 2002). Boulder, CO: Westview Press.

—— and Coffin, Letty 2001. 'German foreign policy toward the Yugoslav successor states, 1991–1999'. *Problems of Post-Communism*. 40(1): 48–64.

Rieff, David 1995. *Slaughterhouse: Bosnia and the Failure of the West*. New York: Simon and Schuster.

Rugman, Jonathan and Hutchings, Roger 1996. *Ataturk's Children: Turkey and the Kurds*. London: Cassell.

Simms, Brendan 2001. *Unfinest Hour: How Britain Helped to Destroy Bosnia*. London: Allen Lane/Penguin Press.

Smith, Anthony D. 1996. *Nationalism in a Global Era*. Cambridge: Polity Press.

—— 1998. *Nationalism and Modernism: A Critical Survey of Recent Theories of Nations and Nationalism*. London: Routledge.

Takei, Milton 1998. 'Collective memory as the key to national and ethnic identity: The case of Cambodia'. *Nationalism and Ethnic Politics*. 4(3): 59–78.

Williams, Robin 1994. 'The sociology of ethnic conflict: comparative international perspectives'. *Annual Review of Sociology*. 20: 49–79 .

Wright, Sue (ed.) 1999. *Language, Democracy, and Devolution in Catalonia*. Clevedon and Philadelphia, PA: Multilingual Matters.

Zulaika, Joseba and Douglass, William A. 1996. *Terror and Taboo: The Follies, Fables, and Faces of Terrorism*. London: Routledge.

15 Walker Connor

A bibliography, 1967–2001

Articles

'Self-Determination: The New Phase'. *World Politics*. xx (October 1967): 30–53.

Ibid. Translated into Japanese and published in *Nichibei Forum*. xiv (April 1968): 39–60.

Ibid. Translated into Italian and published under the title 'Nationalism and Self-Determination'. In *Lo Spettatore Internazionale*. iii (July–October 1968): 521–545.

Ibid. Republished in Robert Pfaltzgraff, Jr. (ed.) *Politics and the International System*. (2nd edn). New York: J.B. Lippincott Co. 1972: 161–180.

Ibid. Republished in George Lanyi and Wilson McWilliams (eds) *Crisis and Continuity in World Politics*. (2nd edn). New York: Random House, 1973: 66–78.

'The Ethnic Dilemma in Marxist-Leninist Doctrine'. *World Affairs*. cxxxii (June 1969): 5–12.

'Ethnology and the Peace of South Asia'. *World Politics*. xxii (October 1969): 51–86.

Ibid. Translated into Japanese and published in *Nichibei Forum*. xvi (1970): 1–18 in March issue and 22–38 in April issue.

'Myths of Hemispheric, Continental, Regional, and State Unity'. *Political Science Quarterly*. lxxiv (December 1969): 555–582.

Ibid. Republished in W.A. Douglas Jackson (ed.) *Politics and Geographic Relations*. (rev. edn). Englewood Cliffs, NJ: Prentice-Hall, Inc., 1971: 361–379.

'Ethnic Nationalism as a Political Force'. *World Affairs*. cxxxiii (September 1970): 91–97.

'Nation-Building or Nation-Destroying?' *World Politics*. xxiv (April 1972): 319–355.

Ibid. Translated into Ukrainian and published in *Suchanist (Contemporary Times)*. 146 (February 1973): 89–99.

Ibid. Republished in David McClellan, William Olson, and Fred Sondermann (eds) *The Theory and Practice of International Relations*. (4th and 5th edns). Englewood Cliffs, NJ: Prentice-Hall, 1974 and 1979

Ibid. Republished in John Stone (ed.) *Race, Ethnicity and Social Change*. North Scituate, MA: Duxbury Press, 1977: 238–269.

'The Politics of Ethnonationalism'. *Journal of International Affairs*. 27(1) 1973: 1–21.

'The Unwithering National Question'. *Problems of Communism*. xxiv (March–April 1975): 80–86.

'An Overview of the Ethnic Composition and Problems of Non-Arab Asia'. *Journal of Asian Affairs*. 1 (Spring 1976): 9–25.

Ibid. Republished in Tai Kang (ed.) *Nationalism and the Crises of Ethnic Minorities in Asia*. Westport, CT: Greenwood Press, 1979: 11–27.

'Political Fusion and Ethnic Fission'. *Concilium*. xiii (No. 1, 1977): 13–24. Translated into Croatian, Dutch, French, German, Italian, Japanese, Polish, Portuguese and Spanish.

Ibid. Republished as the introductory chapter in Andrew Greeley and Gregory Baum (eds) *Ethnicity*. New York: Seabury Press, 1977: 1–8.

'A Nation is a Nation, is a State, is an Ethnic Group, is a . . .'. *Ethnic and Racial Studies*. 1 (October 1978): 377–400.

Ibid. Republished in Nic Rhoodie (ed.) *Intergroup Accommodation in Plural Societies*. London: Macmillan and New York: St Martin's Press, 1979, under the title 'Ethnonational Versus Other Forms of Group Identity: The Problem of Language': 53–83.

Ibid. Translated into Hungarian and published in *Vilagosag* (1988/89) under the title 'Nemzet, Allam, Nemsetallam' ('Nation, State, Nation-state'): 645 *et seq.*

Ibid. Republished in Anthony Smith and John Hutchinson (eds) *Nationalism*. Oxford: Oxford University Press, 1995.

Ibid. Republished in C.J. Napier, *Modern African Politics*. Pretoria: University of South Africa Press, 1997.

'Ethnicity, Race and Class in the United States'. *Ethnic and Racial Studies*. iii (July 1980): 355–359.

'Nationalism and Political Illegitimacy'. *Canadian Review of Studies in Nationalism*. vii (Fall 1980): 201–228.

'Nationalism and its Ideological Competitors'. *Canadian Review of Studies in Nationalism*. x (Fall 1983): 277–282.

'Eco- or Ethno-nationalism'. *Ethnic and Racial Studies*. vii (October 1984): 342–359.

Ibid. Translated into Slovenian and published in Rudi Rizman (ed.) *Studije o Etnonacionalizmu* (*Studies of ethnonationalism*). Ljubljana: Zbornik, 1991: 297–317.

'Leninist National Policy: Solution to the National Question?', *Hungarian Studies Review*. xvi (Spring–Fall 1989): 23–46.

'When Is a Nation?' *Ethnic and Racial Studies*. 13 (January 1990): 92–103.

Ibid. Republished in Anthony Smith and John Hutchinson (eds) *Nationalism*. Oxford: Oxford University Press, 1995.

'The Leninist Legacy'. Hearings before the Committee on Foreign Relations, United States Senate. *The Future of U.S.-Soviet Relations*. Washington, DC: US Government Printing Office, 1990: 131–141.

'From Tribe to Nation?' *The History of European Ideas*. 13 (Number 1/2, 1991): 5–18.

'The Spectre of Ethnonationalist Movements Today'. *Perspectives on Teaching Peace and World Security Studies*. (April 1991): 1–7.

'The Nation and its Myth'. *International Journal of Comparative Sociology*. 33 (January–April 1992): 48–57.

Ibid. Simultaneously published in Anthony Smith (ed.) *Ethnicity and Nationalism, International Studies in Sociology and Social Anthropology*. lx (1992).

'Beyond Reason: The Nature of the Ethnonational Bond'. *Ethnic and Racial Studies.* xvi (July 1993): 373–389.

Ibid. Republished in Anthony Smith and John Hutchinson (eds) *The Oxford Reader on Ethnicity.* Oxford: Oxford University Press, 1996: 69–75.

Ibid. Republished in Michael Hughey (ed.) *New Tribalisms: The Resurgence of Race and Ethnicity.* New York: New York University Press, 1997.

'Introduction'. *Ethnic Studies.* 10 (1994): 3–8.

'Maîtres Chez Nous'. *International Journal of the Sociology of Languages.* 110 (1994): 137–143.

'Europeos y Nacionalistas' ('Europeans and Nationalists'). *Revista de Occidente.* (Madrid), 161 (October 1994): 81–96.

Chapters in books

'Nationalism Reconsidered'. In Thomas Schlesinger (ed.) *The State.* Syracuse, NY: International Studies Association, 1973: B1–B45.

'The Political Significance of Ethnonationalism Within Western Europe'. In Abdul Said and Luiz Simmons (eds) *Ethnicity in an International Context.* Edison, NJ: Transaction Books, Inc., 1976: 110–133.

'Ethnonationalism in the First World: The Present in Historical Perspective'. In Milton Esman (ed.) *Ethnic Pluralism and Conflict in the Western World.* Ithaca, NY: Cornell University Press, 1979: 19–45.

'America's Melting Pot: Myth or Reality?' *Societies in Transition.* Hamburg, Germany: University of Hamburg Press, 1979.

'United States and Self-determination'. In Natalie Hevener (ed.) *The Dynamics of Human Rights in United States Foreign Policy.* Edison, NJ: Transaction Books, Inc., 1982: 101–121.

'The Impact of Homelands Upon Diasporas'. In Gabriel Sheffer (ed.) *Modern Diasporas in International Politics.* London: Croom Helm, 1985: 16–46.

'Ethnonationalism'. In Samuel Huntington and Myron Weiner (eds) *Understanding Political Development.* Boston: Little, Brown, 1987: 196–220.

Ibid. Translated into Japanese and reprinted in *Shiso.* April 1995: 26–45.

'Prospects for Stability in Southeast Asia: The Ethnic Barrier'. In Kusuma Snitwongse and Sukhumbhand Paribatra (eds) *Durable Stability in Southeast Asia.* Singapore: Institute of Southeast Asian Studies, 1987: 32–59.

'Democracy, Ethnocracy, and the Modern National State: Paradoxes and Tensions'. *II World Basque Congress.* Vitoria-Gasteiz: N.P., 1987.

Ibid. Translated into Spanish and reprinted in Alfonso Perez-Agote (ed.) *Sociologia del Nacionalismo.* Vitoria, Spain: Gobierno Vasco, 1989: 111–130.

'The Interrelated Histories of Shi'i Islam and Persian Nationalism'. In Milla Riggio (ed.) *Ta'ziyeh: Ritual and Popular Beliefs in Iran.* Hartford, CT: Trinity College Press, 1988.

'Ethnonationalism and Political Instability: An Overview'. In Hermann Giliomee (ed.) *The Elusive Search for Peace.* Oxford: Oxford University Press, 1990: 9–32.

'Nationalism and Patriotism: The Clash of Allegiances'. In Donald Horowitz (ed.)

Research on Ethnicity. Washington, DC: Woodrow Wilson International Center for Scholars, 1991: 23–34.

'The Soviet Prototype'. Originally published as Chapter 3 in the *National Question in Marxist-Leninist Theory and Strategy*) republished as Chapter 1 in Rachel Denber (ed.) *The Soviet Nationality Reader: The Disintegration in Context*. Boulder, CO: Westview Press, 1992: 15–33.

'Soviet Policies Toward the Non-Russian Peoples in Theoretic and Historic Perspective: What Gorbachev Inherited'. In Alexander J. Motyl (ed.) *The Post-Soviet Nations: Perspectives on The Demise of The USSR*. New York: Columbia University Press, 1992: 30–49.

'Diasporas and Foreign Policy'. In D. Constas (ed.) *Modern Diasporas in World Politics: The Greeks in Comparative Perspective*. London: Macmillan, 1993: 167–179.

'Elites and Ethnonationalism: The Case of Western Europe'. In Justo Beramendi, Ramón Máiz and Xosé M. Núñez (eds) *Nationalism in Europe Past and Present*. Santiago de Compostela, Spain: Universidade de Santiago de Compostela, 1994: 349–361.

Preface to Joshua Fishman, *In Praise of the Beloved Language: The Content of Positive Ethnolinguistic Consciousness*. The Hague: Mouton, 1997.

'Probing the Nature of the Ethnonational Bond'. In Alfonso Pérez-Agote (ed.) *Collective Identities in the Contemporary World*. Bilbao: Universidad del Pais Vasco, 1997.

'Ethnic Identity: Primordial or Modern?'. In Trude Andresson, Beate Bull and Kjetil Duvold (eds) *Separatism*. Bergen: University of Bergen Press, 1997: 7–40.

'Some Factors Influencing the Longevity of Peaceful Interludes to Ethnic Violence'. *Proceedings of the International Peace Studies Symposium*. Okinawa: Okinawa International University, 1997: 49–65.

'Discussion of Transstate Security'. In Richard Schultz, Roy Godson and George Quester (eds) *Security Studies for the 21st Century*. Washington, DC: Brassey's, 1997: 119–123.

Foreword to Thomas Spira, *Encyclopedia of Nationalism*. Gulf Breeze, FL: Academic International Press, 1999: vi–vii.

'National Self-Determination and Tomorrow's Political Map'. In John Courtney *et al.* (eds) *Citizenship, Diversity and Pluralism*. Montreal: McGill-Queens University Press, 1999: 163–176.

'From a Theory of Relative Economic Deprivation Towards a Theory of Relative Political Deprivation'. In Michael Keating and John McGarry (eds) *Minority Nationalism and the Changing World Order*. Oxford: Oxford University Press, 2002: 114–133.

'Homelands in a World of States'. In Montserrat Guibernau and John Hutchison (eds) *Understanding Nationalism*. Oxford and Malden, MA: Blackwell Publishers, 2001: 53–73.

'A Primer for Analyzing Ethnonational Conflict'. In Symeon Giannokos (ed.) *Ethnic and Religious Conflict: Religion, Identity, and Politics*. Columbus, OH: University of Ohio Press, 2002: 21–42.

'Probing the Nature of the Ethnonational Bond'. In John Stone and Dennis Rutledge (eds) *Race and Ethnicity for a New Millennium*, London: Blackwell, 2002.

Books and occasional papers

The Study of Nationalism: A Bibliographic Essay Concerning the Literature in the English Language. Washington, DC: US. Department of State, 1975.

The Uniqueness of the American Ethnic Experience. Occasional paper commissioned by the United States Information Agency, Washington, DC: United States Information Agency, 1975.

The National Question in Marxist-Leninist Theory and Strategy. Princeton, NJ: Princeton University Press, 1984.

Mexican Americans in Comparative Perspective. Washington, DC: Urban Institute Press, 1985.

'Democracy and the Survival of Multinational States'. *Freedom Papers*. Washington, DC: United States Information Agency, 1994.

Ethnonationalism: The Quest for Understanding. Princeton, NJ: Princeton University Press, 1994. 2nd printing, 1996.

Etnonazionalizmo: Quando e perché emergano le nazioni. Rome and Bari: Edizoni Dedalo, 1995. Italian edition of *Ethnonationalism*, translated by Daniele Petrosino.

Etnonacionalismo. Madrid, Spain: Trama Editorial, 1998. Spanish edition of *Ethnonationalism*, with a new preface, translated by María Corniero.

Ethnonationalism Today and Tomorrow. Keynote address at the Conference on Ethnic Dimensions in International Politics, Amritsar: Guru Nanek Dev University Press, 2001.

Ethnonationalism. Under contract to Krieger Publishing Company.

Index